PUBLIC HISTORY:

Essays from the Field

Revised Edition

PUBLIC HISTORY:
Essays from the Field

Edited by
James B. Gardner
and
Peter S. LaPaglia

KRIEGER PUBLISHING COMPANY
MALABAR, FLORIDA

Original Edition 1999
Revised Edition 2004
Reprint Edition 2006 with corrections

Printed and Published by
KRIEGER PUBLISHING COMPANY
KRIEGER DRIVE
MALABAR, FLORIDA 32950

Library of Congress Cataloging-in-Publication Data

Public history : essays from the field / edited by James B. Gardner and Peter
   S. LaPaglia.–Rev. ed.
       p. cm. – (Public history series)
   Includes bibliographical references and index.
   ISBN 1–57524–244–3 (pbk. : alk. paper)
       1. Public history.   2. Public historians. I. Gardner, James B., 1950– .
II. LaPaglia, Peter S., 1943–   .   III. Series.
D16.163.P84 2004
909–dc22

                                                                        2003065672

10 9 8 7 6 5

CONTENTS

ACKNOWLEDGMENTS

While we happily take credit for conceptualizing and organizing this volume, the truth is that what follows is not our work but that of the twenty-seven authors, who eagerly accepted our invitations to write chapters, wrote thoughtful and reflective essays on their work as public historians, and responded amiably to what surely seemed like trivial queries and meddlesome suggestions from us. While neither we nor they met every deadline, we all moved forward with consistent good will and determination. That we pulled this all together is testimony to the commitment those twenty-seven have to their work and the enterprise of history. All have earned our thanks for their contributions.

We would also like to thank several other people who were instrumental in this project: Barbara J. Howe, not only one of the editors of the preceding volume, *Public History: An Introduction*, but also the editor of the series in which this volume first appeared and the individual responsible for recruiting us and giving us our marching orders; Mary Roberts, our editor at Krieger, who never failed to provide the encouragement and support we needed to keep moving with what at times seemed an overwhelming task; Jane LaPaglia, who helped us pull together revisions and updates for the new edition; and five colleagues who provided much needed advice and direction in the recruitment of authors—Jane Alkin, David Allison, Jacqueline Goggin, Beth Luey, and Page Putnam Miller.

THE EDITORS

James B. Gardner is associate director for curatorial affairs at the National Museum of American History, Smithsonian Institution. He holds a B.A. with honors in history from Rhodes College and an M.A. and a Ph.D. in history from Vanderbilt University. He previously served as a consultant with History Associates Incorporated and LaPaglia & Associates, as deputy executive director of the American Historical Association, and as director of education and special programs for the American Association for State and Local History. He has served as president of the National Council on Public History and of the Society for History in the Federal Government, on the board of editors of *The Public Historian,* as chair of the nominating board of the Organization of American Historians, as chair of the membership committees for both NCPH and SHFG and on advisory committees for the James Madison Memorial Fellowship Foundation, Syracuse University, and numerous other institutions and projects in history, the humanities, and higher education. As a lecturer and conference speaker, he has appeared on the programs of such diverse national organizations as the American Association of Museums, the American Council of Learned Societies, and the American Association of Colleges and Universities as well as at meetings, conferences, and seminars sponsored by local, state, and regional organizations. Dr. Gardner's publications include *Ordinary People and Everyday Life: Perspectives on the New Social History* (1983), *A Historical Guide to the United States* (1986), and contributions to *The Public Historian, Museum News,* and other periodicals and anthologies.

Peter S. LaPaglia is president of LaPaglia & Associates, a museum consulting firm. He holds a B.A. and an M.A. in history from Middle Tennessee State University and was a Kellogg Foundation Fellow at the Smithsonian Institution. He has worked in various capacities in the museum field, including director of the Wichita Falls Museum and Art Center, director of seminars and workshops for the American Association for State and Local History and chief curator at the Tennessee State Museum. His professional activities include service as president of the Mountain-Plains Museums Association, on the governing council of the American Association of Museums (AAM) and on the accreditation visiting committee for AAM. His client list comprises numerous national recognized institutions such as the Smithsonian Institution, Louisville Slugger Museum, International Bluegrass Music Museum, and National Cowboy Museum and Western Heritage Center.

INTRODUCTION TO THE REVISED EDITION

Revising this volume for publication involved both updating information and broadening the coverage to include an important new area of work for public historians. The former encompassed updating both the appendix (you'd be surprised how many organizations have changed location over the past four years) and the authors' biographical information. A number of the authors have changed jobs since 1999, which means their essays now draw on previous rather than current work, but they have all confirmed that their perspectives and approaches to public history remain the same. While there have been a few other revisions to update material in the essays, what really distinguishes this edition is the addition of a new essay, "On the Web: The September 11 Digital Archive," by James T. Sparrow. It expands the coverage of Part III, "The Practice of Public History," to encompass the virtual world of the Internet and the web, challenging public historians to think differently about how we do our work and who "the public" is. We know you'll find this addition provocative and informative.

INTRODUCTION

Those of you familiar with the literature of public history will know well this volume's illustrious predecessor, *Public History: An Introduction,* edited by Barbara J. Howe and Emory L. Kemp and first published by Robert E. Krieger Publishing Company in 1986. Over the past decade, that volume has become a key resource for the field and an indispensable asset in public history education. Thus, when we were approached in 1996 by Professor Howe, now the editor of the Public History Series at Krieger, and Mary Roberts, editor at Krieger, about compiling a new edition, we were understandably daunted by the prospect. But Howe and Kemp had concluded that their volume needed updating—that much has happened in the field over the past decade that needs to be addressed—and they did not want to take on the task themselves. With a bit of reluctance, we agreed to try our hand at it and were essentially given carte blanche to work with the existing volume, individual essays, and/or the basic concept. We quickly concluded that choosing among and tinkering with the individual essays would probably just create a muddle, neither as strong as the original nor as up-to-date as possible. We decided instead to produce a new volume, which builds on the original conceptualization but provides entirely new essays from a new set of authors.

In recruiting authors, we sought a variety of perspectives, including not only self-declared public historians but others who identify themselves in different ways but whose work is clearly within the realm of public history. As you will see from the roster of contributors and their biographies, we have indeed managed to put together a group that reflects the diversity of the practice of public history today. The most obvious differences among them are the varieties of work in which the authors are engaged, the different job titles they hold, and the varied institutions and agencies in which they work. As diverse personally as they are professionally, our authors come from varied socioeconomic and educational backgrounds, have followed very different career paths, and come from all parts of the country. While this group may not be definitive, they do represent an interesting cross section of the current field.

Given the diverse backgrounds and experiences of our authors, it was inevitable that they would approach their assignments in a variety of ways. While the authors in each section received the same charge, each had a different perspective and different concerns and thus responded differently. Rather than try to force the authors into a regimented format and organization, we encouraged them to approach their topics in diverse ways, to choose those issues and concerns that they feel are most critical to understanding their work, and to engage in personal reflection. Thus the volume's subtitle—*Essays from the Field*. The point is not just to differentiate our volume from that of our predecessors but to emphasize the varied perspectives of the authors. The result, we feel, is an engaging set of essays on what it is like today to work as a public historian.

We have followed the same basic three-part organization used by Howe and Kemp but with our own definitions and topics. The first section provides "An Overview of Public History," with two essays that provide the context for the subsequent two sections. Patricia Mooney-Melvin's essay on "Professional Historians and the Challenge of Redefinition" addresses the relationship of public history to the larger history profession and the importance of the "public" role of the public historian. In the second essay, "Becoming a Public Historian," Constance B. Schulz focuses on the education of public historians, suggesting how that education has changed over time and delineating common purposes, themes, and elements.

Part II, "Varieties of Public Historians," is organized according to kinds of positions in which public historians work—the basic ways in which we define ourselves and our work. We asked each author to draw directly upon his or her experience, providing an overview of basic roles and responsibilities, the historical context of the work and how it has changed over time, the process and the products of work, professional issues and concerns, professional networks, specialized education and continuing education opportunities, and future directions. The point is to give readers a feel for the work, not instruct them on how to do it. Rather than try to group them in awkward or misleading ways or suggest some priority or ranking, we have titled the thirteen essays with basic position names (with occasional subtitles added by the authors) and simply arranged them in alphabetical order.

In Part III, "The Practice of Public History," the focus shifts from the position to the work context, focusing on the extent to which *where* you work shapes what you do as much as your official title or job description. Each author was asked to address what it is like to work in a specific kind of institution, agency, or organization—the basic functions of the workplace under discussion and differences within (such as between publicly and privately funded), the historical context of the workplace and how it has changed over time, the role of the public and other constituencies, special issues and concerns, and future directions. Each author was asked to address how the specific work context affects an individual's work as a public historian, considering, for example, the extent to which responsibilities within an institution require versatility and flexibility on the part of the individual, a willingness to work outside traditional job descriptions. As with the previous section, the point is to give readers a feel for the work, not instruct them on how to do it. The eleven essays in this section are titled with basic workplace descriptions (and occasional subtitles added by authors) and are grouped—the first three focus on kinds of properties managed, the next five deal with institutions defined by the geographic/political areas they serve, and the next two look at public history and business from two different perspectives. The final essay looks at how the practice of public history changes on the web.

While some of the essays may parallel those in the earlier volume, others are very different. Some topics, such as media and film, were not included at all in the previous volume, and others, such as historic houses, were dealt with only tangentially. While doubtless there are holes in our taxonomy as well, we have tried to come up with a more inclusive view of what public historians do and where they are today. That goal has made it impossible for us to include case studies of particular programs or institutions, as the previous volume did, although our authors frequently draw upon their own experiences to illustrate larger issues or points. And, the reader will find less focus than in the previous volume on the use of traditional research, writing, and analytic skills and more on the development of both broader perspectives and more specialized skills and techniques as public historians redefine what it means to be a historian. Together, these essays convey the healthy complexity of the public history field today.

While readers may pick up this volume to read a few essays on areas of particular interest, we encourage you to read more widely. You will be surprised at what you can learn from others—we certainly were.

PART I

AN OVERVIEW
OF PUBLIC HISTORY

INTRODUCTION

As a quick look at the table of contents for Parts II and III of this volume will demonstrate, the field of public history encompasses a broad range of work and wide variety of institutions. Is that evidence of complexity or of fragmentation? What is this thing called "public history" and do its parts add up to a coherent whole? The authors of the two essays that follow address this issue of definition from two different perspectives: Patricia Mooney-Melvin looks at what it means to be a professional historian and whether or how public historians fit that definition, while Constance Schulz focuses on what makes public history education distinctive.

In "Professional Historians and the Challenge of Redefinition," Mooney-Melvin traces the professionalization of history in the United States in the twentieth century, focusing on the self-segregation of historians in academic employment and the narrowing of audiences to academic colleagues. The consequence, she concludes, has been the marginalization of professional historians from American society. In calling for a reconceptualization of the profession to embrace the work and perspectives of public history, her goal is not so much to enhance the status of public historians within the profession as to reconnect historians generally with the larger civic community in which they live and work. In her redefinition, public history ceases to be just a worthy alternative field and assumes a central role in fulfilling the profession's responsibility to engage society in understanding its past.

While Schulz similarly emphasizes that public historians are historians first and foremost, she also argues that their education makes them distinctive, not only from other colleagues in the discipline but from those in museology, library science, and other related fields. Unlike the latter, students in public history programs learn the knowledge and methods of history, and their professional identities are as historians. But in contrast to historians in traditional programs, public history students learn to address a public rather than academic audience, work with a more inclusive range of primary sources, and give more priority to cross-disciplinary and collaborative work.

The two essays lead in somewhat different directions—Mooney-Melvin calls for a redefinition of history to *integrate* public history into the larger profession, while Schulz emphasizes how public historians' training makes them *distinct* from other historians. But there is no real difference of opinion here, just two sides of the same coin. Together they help us better understand the common professional ground that we share—a commitment to fostering public understanding of and appreciation for the past.

*PATRICIA MOONEY-MELVIN is associate professor and gradu-
ate program director at Loyola University Chicago. She earned her
B.A., M.A., and Ph.D. in history at the University of Cincinnati.
Prior to her appointment at Loyola, she taught at the University of
Arkansas at Little Rock, the College of Wooster, and the University
of Cincinnati. Dr. Mooney-Melvin is a past president of the National Council on Public History and has served on the editorial
board of* The Public Historian *and on the boards of the Illinois
State Historical Society, the Arkansas Women's History Institute,
and the Rogers Park/West Ridge Historical Society. Dr. Mooney-
Melvin's professional activities include serving as a guest curator
or exhibit consultant for a number of museums and making numerous presentations at meetings of the American Association for
State and Local History, the National Council on Public History,
the Organization of American Historians, and other organizations. Her publications include* Making Sense of the City: Local Government, Civic Culture, and Community Life in Urban America *(2001),* The Organic City: Urban Definition
and Neighborhood Organization, 1880 1920 *(1987),* The
Urbanization of Modern America *(1987),* American Community Organizations: A Historical Dictionary *(1986), and*
Reading Your Neighborhood: A History of East Rogers
Park *(1994), as well as numerous articles and reviews in such
publications as* History News, The Public Historian, *and the*
American Quarterly.

PROFESSIONAL HISTORIANS AND
THE CHALLENGE OF REDEFINITION[1]

Patricia Mooney-Melvin

From the time I entered graduate school, I have been intrigued with the
ways in which historians have thought about their profession and their notion of audience as well as the relationship between the history historians
make and the history the public receives. My frustration, as I reflect on my
years as a historian, is that the profession as a whole, despite the efforts of
numerous individuals and a few organizations, has proved remarkably re-
sistant to altering a definition of historian and audience that has grown

static, an artifact of a different time and place. The profession's resistance
to change in this area, I believe, has laid the groundwork for its own marginality within American society and has contributed to the general breakdown of the larger civic community.

Michael Kammen, in his introduction to *The Past Before Us: Contemporary Historical Writing in the United States,* has suggested that ever since the
formation of the American Historical Association (AHA) in 1884, the
"guild has had a penchant for introspection." As evidence he cites a range
of reports sponsored by such groups as the American Historical Association, the Social Science Research Council, and the American Academy of
Arts and Sciences that focus on the "state of the discipline" at various
points during the twentieth century.[2] Not all of this contemplation
has been the result of reports produced by interested organizations. In-
dividual historians have added to this literature as well. Arthur M.
Schlesinger's *In Retrospect: The History of a Historian* (1963), Timothy
Donovan's *Historical Thought in America: Postwar Patterns* (1973), Oscar
Handlin's *Truth in History* (1979), Peter Novick's *That Noble Dream: The
"Objectivity Question" and the American Historical Profession* (1988), and
Joyce Appleby, Lynn Hunt, and Margaret Jacob's *Telling the Truth About
History* (1994), for example, provide windows into more particularistic re-
flections on the nature of historical study in the United States.[3]

What is striking about virtually all of this introspection is the lack of attention paid to whether or not the prevailing definition of the professional historian should be reexamined in light of changes in both the context and content of the practice of history. Some exceptions, of course,
exist. Joan Hoff, in a 1980 article entitled "Is the Historical Profession an
'Endangered Species'?" acknowledged that the way in which contemporary historians thought about their profession left out constituencies, such
as that of the independent scholar, important during the early years of the
profession's development. Hoff exhorts the professional community to return to the "good old days" when the profession was not dominated by academic historians,[4] unfortunately missing the point completely that the
presence of amateur or independent historians was merely an accommodation on the part of the professionalizers. Gerda Lerner, in her 1982
presidential address delivered to the Organization of American Historians (OAH), pointed to the necessity to broaden the understanding of
"professional roles."[5] Despite her own experience with marginalization,
Lerner fails to portray this broadening as little more than pragmatic,
band-aid reform. Her vision is the world of add-ons, rather than of reex-
amination and overhaul.

Even in studies such as Theodore S. Hamerow's *Reflections on History and
Historians,* with its focus on "what it is like to be a professional historian"

as opposed to an examination of the nature of historical scholarship,[6] the definition of historian is treated as a fixed category, unrelated to time and place. The only time and place of importance in the defining process, at least as far as the professional historical community is concerned, is that of the period when the professionalizers' construct of historian emerged and took root. Given the way in which we subject everything else to reinterpretation and contextualization, I find it curious that we are so loathe to examine—even at the most superficial level—the appropriateness of this definition in light of other aspects of the profession's past and present experiences.

What characterizes a profession? The literature on professions suggests that very few professions actually conform to any particular model. At the same time, however, it is clear that most analysts agree that professions generally possess certain attributes. In addition, those studying the professions point out that very few professions are able to monopolize completely the market for their services. Balancing the desire of any group to exercise control is the level of public acceptance of the arguments put forward by professional marketing campaigns. Often a tension exists between the desire for monopolistic control, the demand for specialized services, the vision of the professionalizers, and the public's willingness to accept professional claims for status. The result of that tension provides the limits in which any professional activity takes place.[7]

The literature on professionalism identifies four basic attributes. First, professionals receive formal training in a setting—usually academic—to ensure quality and competence. Second, professionals possess knowledge and skills that are demonstrable in some applied fashion. Third, the professional ethos includes some commitment of service to society beyond a desire for personal profit. And fourth, professional organizations have the power to define standards and regulate their own affairs as well as the obligation to ensure that professional knowledge and skill will be used in a "socially responsible" fashion.[8]

Where does the historical profession fit into all of this? Although the basic outlines of the history of the historical profession are generally recognized, the tendency of historians to focus on the nature of historical scholarship and its role as a professionalizing force has left relatively unexamined the relationship between professionalization in history and the changing nature of the social, economic, cultural, and political context in which professional development over time has taken place. We know a lot about the context in which the profession emerged and the goals of the professionalizers. We know much less about the history of the profession in the twentieth century, its relationship to American society, and why historians have clung so tightly to a definition that has lost its utility.

The professionalization of history was part of a larger redefinition and institutionalization of knowledge that took place throughout American society during the late nineteenth century. The organization of the American Historical Association in 1884 was symptomatic of efforts to exert control over particular branches of knowledge. By the beginning of the twentieth century, professional historians—for whom history became a corporate task and a specialized career—were on the ascendancy.[9] As Hoff has suggested, the historical profession was not populated exclusively by academic historians during the early decades of professional development. However, what she sees as an integrated unity of different types was, in fact, a period of staged decline for those for whom history was an avocation. Peter Novick more accurately describes what was happening: the membership of amateurs and their selection as presidents of the AHA during the early years of association growth was not acceptance of equals but rather "was a matter of legitimatization, and accommodation with a still important constituency." After 1907 academic historians became more likely to hold the presidency of the AHA, and after 1928 virtually all presidents were academically trained and employed historians.[10]

The definition of the historian that emerged from the formative years of professional growth was one which stressed objectivity, research, the increase of knowledge, and employment within an academic setting. Historians' allegiance was twofold: to "objective historical truth" and to colleagues committed to the pursuit of that truth. Professional status demanded formal graduate training in history that emphasized technique and the use of primary sources. Supporters of professionalism increasingly stressed the importance of academic employment, which, of course, added teaching to the duties of a professional historian. And finally, professionalism precipitated the redefinition of the historian's audience from the general reading public to academic colleagues as peer review became the central vehicle for monitoring the quality of historical scholarship. As described by J. H. Hexter, "the life of the professional historian [was] the life of teaching, silent study, work, and writing, interspersed with brief orgies of gossip" (meaning, in this context, another form of judgment by peers).[11] Any other pattern—while tolerated as in the case of Charles Beard, for example—was suspect, and those involved usually were rendered invisible as far as members of the profession were concerned.

By the end of World War II, professional historians possessed all four attributes associated with professionalism. They received their training in a university setting and, when worthy, were admitted to Novick's "community of the historically competent."[12] They demonstrated their knowledge and skills in the college or university classroom, while training graduate students, and by publishing the results of their research in increasingly specialized publications. Historians had professional organizations to set standards and monitor quality. And finally, there was a commitment, although very lukewarm and expendable, to service. The professional historian, as a 1963 publication of the American Historical Association suggested, possessed two obligations. One was to increase knowledge, through research and writing, by adding new facts about the past or developing new interpretations. The other was to transmit, "by teaching and writing, the existing body of knowledge."[13] Historians carried out these obligations within the confines of a college or university campus.

Professional historians rarely have enjoyed the sort of monopolistic control associated with the professions of medicine or law. For better or worse, as John Higham has noted, the "fluidity and openness" of history kept it from becoming "an arcane discipline. Although its critical operations [were] exacting, its fundamental tasks of organizing data into a design and thereby recreating the life of the past [did] not depend on any systematic methodology. Nor [had] history a special language of its own. Consequently professional historians [were] unable to immure themselves completely within a specialized sphere."[14] But the explosion of academic positions after World War II and the insularity that came with the restricted professional audience gave historians the false luxury to ignore the historical interest and "history-making" that took place outside of academe.[15]

The public's need for "history-making," or the "process by which people preserve and interpret the past and then reinterpret it in the light of new questions,"[16] ensured that an engagement with the past on the part of the public continued regardless of the disinterest expressed by the professional historical community. In short, the apparent accessibility of history as well as a need for the understanding that knowledge of the past can provide on the part of the general public exerted limits on the level of control exercised by professional historians over the research, writing, and presentation of history—despite the determined efforts of the professionalizers.

Who was ignored by the "community of the historically competent"[17] during the profession's halcyon days between 1884 and 1970? As the profession matured, its members paid increasingly less attention to two specific categories of people. The first group was composed of those individuals who possessed the appropriate educational credentials but who for one reason or another worked in historical organizations and archives, for the federal government, or as independent historians. The second category included groups, most particularly precollegiate educators, the general reading public, and visitors to historic sites.

Although the lion's share of historians resided comfortably in academic departments before 1970, others found themselves using their historical training and applying their knowledge of the past under circumstances quite different from those of the university or college campus. State and local historical societies, archival institutions, and the National Park Service all had academically trained historians as directors or staff members. At institutions such as Colonial Williamsburg, the New York State Historical Association, and the National Archives, as well as within the bureaucracy of the Park Service, historians served as administrators; developed educational materials; researched and wrote exhibitions; engaged in interpretation; and appraised and processed collections. Some of their activities involved skills acquired in addition to their training in history. Other aspects of their employment drew directly upon their ability to undertake research, subject their findings to analysis, and construct a narrative.[18] What made these historians different from those laboring in the academy was their audience, their presentation format, a more regulated work environment, and their limited reliance on peer review. As far as the profession was concerned, they were outside the pale.

The federal government employed historians in a variety of positions in addition to those in the National Park Service and the National Archives. During the 1930s, historians worked in a number of New Deal initiatives. The Department of Agriculture had an active historical program. A number of historians entered government service during World War II, many serving as intelligence analysts for the Office of Strategic Services under the direction of Harvard historian William Langer. Still others were under contract with the State Department and branches of the military. The end of the war sent many of these historians scurrying back to college and university campuses. Others, however, remained in government service and over the next two decades the number of federal historians grew. Useful as their service to the government may have been, most academically based historians questioned the objectivity of their work. In the eyes of the professional historical community, their scholarship was less rigorous, their audiences less discerning, and their work environment less protected from the intrusion of other agendas. With only a few exceptions, the major historical organizations paid scant attention to the needs and accomplishments of these individuals.[19]

The other category ignored by the academically based historical community included groups not necessarily with professionally trained historians in their ranks but for whom history had some importance. During the early years of the profession, historians had hoped to exercise some control over the type of history available in the nation's elementary and secondary schools. As late as the 1930s, for example, the American Historical Association controlled the editorial board and the financial resources for the magazines produced for high school teachers by the National Council for the Social Studies. The professional historical community contributed articles as well as provided oversight. But such direction was increasingly challenged by educators interested in exerting their own control over what was taught in the schools. As it turned out, the historical profession essentially caved in rather than vigorously contest this challenge.

By the 1950s historians could not agree on whether history should even be a required subject. Some historians were unsure if there existed a convincing rationale to include history in the curricula of primary and secondary schools. Other historians warned that history was used more for indoctrination than understanding. Most historians seemed to care very little if history grew less important in elementary and secondary education. Charles G. Sellers, one of the few historians who appeared to care about this issue, found that his colleagues were indifferent to anything other than the importance of their own courses. Poorly taught history in the precollegiate school system, in their eyes, resulted from inadequately trained teachers, not lack of direction or input from the professional historical community.

Social scientists, Sellers found, showed an interest in working with teachers to develop new learning strategies to facilitate their ability to expose students to the insights garnered through the study of the social sciences. Historians, on the other hand, were unwilling to spend any time on an endeavor that would involve thinking more about teaching, training teachers, or curricular reform. To do so would impinge on their own research.[20] It was easier to do nothing.

Oscar Handlin went so far as to suggest in 1961, for example, that little would be lost if history were removed from the high school curriculum altogether. According to Handlin, it is only possible to teach "facts" in high school. However, observing the level of knowledge of his college students, Handlin concluded that students fail to learn the facts presented to them in high school because the facts possess no meaning for them. Young people, he found, only learn things that appear relevant to them. In his opinion, it would be better to slot instruction in history at the college level. At this point, he argued, students who are bright enough to be admitted to college would be able to see the relevance of facts, and by implication history, to the world around them.[21]

As the 1960s drew to a close, educators and social studies replaced historians and history in providing what concern with the past remained in the curriculum after the expansion of math and science offerings in the "post-Sputnik" world of precollegiate education. Sellers asked if historians even cared that history was "on its way out of the schools." He wondered if society would have to rest its hopes on the American Legion to save the teaching of history in the schools.[22]

Professional historians also seemed uninterested in the loss of the general reading public. Despite a campaign by Allan Nevins in the late 1930s for a popular history magazine, funding difficulties and the outbreak of World War II essentially rendered the project stillborn. In the meantime, the American Association for State and Local History inaugurated a popular, and ultimately successful, history magazine of its own, *American Heritage*. When taken over by Time-Life in 1954, *American Heritage* blossomed into a glossy, highly visual, popular magazine that brought history to the public. Few academic historians rushed to be included in the pages of *American Heritage*. Instead, journalists, military personnel, and history aficionados narrated tidy stories about the American past. While their articles explored a variety of topics, they were often devoid of context and usually lay outside of the historiographical trends that characterized the scholarly interests of the historical profession. However, read over the years by millions of Americans, *American Heritage*'s approach to the study and interpretation of the past—not that of the professional historical community—has influenced a sizeable number of the history-reading public's view of what constitutes history and historical writing. In addition, the expansion of the paperback market, which brought historians' monographs into the classroom during the 1950s, further rendered this segment of the book-buying public less important for academics.[23] They did not need to depend on the general public to swell the market for their books.

And finally, the professional historical community abdicated any responsibility it may have felt for the millions of Americans who received their education in history at the nation's historic sites. After World War II, all the ingredients were in place for a public interested in combining education and entertainment: "good roads, millions of motor cars, a working class that had won two-week vacations, a better educated citizenry, a national preoccupation with historical origins, and a growing number of historical exhibition areas offering a variety of experiences to put twentieth-century families in direct touch with their past."[24] Americans took to the road and visited historic sites, shrines, monuments, and museums as well as fished, swam, hiked, and shopped. Their sense of history was often inaccurate, but their adventures provided them with a sense of the past and an opportunity to "experience a way of life" no longer contemporary.[25] As in the case of the readership of *American Heritage*, the history portrayed to these visitors often did not reflect an understanding of the dynamic interpretive construct of the past discussed within the confines of the professional historical community.

Abandonment of these groups represents a reflection, in part, of professional historians' declining commitment to the larger society of which they were a part. Unlike some professions, the historical profession's adoption of the service component associated with professional status had been problematic at best, and service was not "widely accepted as a part of the profession's corporate responsibility."[26] Charles Beard and Carl Becker, unlike many of their colleagues, believed that history possessed a social purpose. History existed for society; it was not just the property of individual historians.[27] But such views represented a minority position within the profession. The majority of the members of the guild concurred with Thomas Cochran's position as expressed in a letter to Richard Hofstadter: "'the public be damned.'"[28] It was much more liberating to write for a small circle of friends.

And then came the period of crisis in the 1970s. Some historians agreed with Oscar Handlin that the crisis was one of scholarship and internal control within the profession. According to Handlin, the discipline had fragmented. No longer did the historical community possess a sense of common purpose. Instead, historians chased fads and relied too much on social science methodology. They wrote monographs with little concern for their place within the "canon." How could anyone possibly assess such work? The profession had accepted affirmative action. It had compromised the search for "truth."[29]

For many other historians the 1970s brought an employment crisis. All of a sudden there seemed to be too many historians for too few jobs in academe. The historical profession's lesson in "humility," wrote Hamerow in the mid-1980s, meant that a whole "generation of young scholars" was "decimated. Anyone training graduate students knows what a tragic experience it is to see dedicated and talented men and women go through . . . years of advanced study only to find, after they get their doctorates, that there is no need for them."[30] Should this have been such a surprise when the profession had worked very hard to keep the definition of what it meant to be a professional historian so narrow as to almost ensure its senescence?[31]

Richard Kirkendall, then executive secretary of the Organization of American Historians, wrote in a report prepared for the OAH in 1976 on the status of history in the schools that "history is in crisis and history's crisis is not merely a part of the larger difficulties of academic life at the present time. History's crisis has proportions of its own."[32] And the central element that made history's crisis "its own" was the issue of definition. The job crisis in history existed not because historians were not needed nor because there were too many of them. More to the point was the fact that most historians believed that historians could only reside in the world of academe.[33] They had left themselves only one choice. "If the current employment crisis provokes an identity crisis in the historical profession," wrote Arnita Jones in 1978, "it may be to the lasting benefit of both historians and the public."[34]

Unfortunately, I believe, it did not provide enough of a jolt to force an insular profession into productive introspection about its identity. However, because the dimensions of the crisis seemed so great, the major historical associations felt they had to do something, and the result was the formation of the National Coordinating Committee for the Promotion of History (NCC) in 1977. The NCC argued that "public perceptions about the value of historical knowledge and skills were inseparable from the problem of the employment of historians." In this context, the goal was not just to find places for historians to combat the short-run crisis. Instead, attention needed to be focused on "building bridges" between the university and the world outside of the academy on the one hand and on forging "closer ties" between academic and nonacademic historians on the other.[35]

This was certainly progress, but it sidestepped the issue of definition rather than confronting it directly. This approach allowed the profession to focus on employment as opposed to identity. The discussion that ensued framed the issue as Lerner later did—as an add-on issue rather than a reconceptualization. Established professional organizations and history departments talked not of a new vision of the professional historian but of "alternative" careers.

By the late 1970s public history entered the professional vocabulary. Advocates of public history argued that professional historians were individuals who possessed certain qualifications and who could put their knowledge and skills to use in the world. Place of employment was not the defining issue; training was. Public history became an organizing principle for those who were already employed as historians in nonacademic settings, historians who believed in the importance of communication with a broader public, as well as those individuals interested in pursuing history as a career but not inside the academy. By the early 1980s a variety of history departments introduced public history into their curricula, and by the mid-1980s the first graduates of these programs emerged.[36]

Reaction of the historical profession to public history was mixed. Some historians were hostile and unwilling to accept the proposition that "real" historians worked outside of academe. A number of individuals with professional credentials already working outside of the academy bristled at the notion that public history was "new," for they had been using their training in a wide range of institutional settings for years. Concerns were raised about ethical issues relating to the practice of history outside of the university.[37] Yet other historians welcomed public history, with its emphasis on a dynamic combination of historical training, expansion of traditional notions of locale and audience, and service to society.

In her 1992 "Viewpoint" in *The Public Historian*, "Reflections on the Public History Movement," Page Putnam Miller argued that public history had accomplished a great deal since 1982. And, of course, there is a lot of truth in what Miller said. The American Historical Association's current "Statement on Standards of Professional Conduct" clearly states that "the historical profession is diverse, composed of people who work in a variety of institutional settings and also as independent professionals."[38] It further defines the range of scholarship and teaching more inclusively than in the past, although I question the depth of the membership's knowledge of or commitment to this position.

Miller pointed to four other accomplishments as well. First, new professional associations, such as the National Council on Public History and the Society for History in the Federal Government, were formed and have provided arenas for public historians to share information, discuss their research, and focus on issues of mutual concern. Second, the establishment of new journals, such as *The Public Historian*, have offered new venues for sharing methodological approaches and showcasing public history–related research and analysis. Third, editorial policy changes in established journals like the *Journal of American History* have allowed for the inclusion of new features that reflect the legitimatization of different approaches to communicating information about the past. And finally, Miller applauded the "pioneering research initiatives undertaken by public historians," such as the development of a "methodology for the historical investigation of land use at toxic waste sites."[39]

Perhaps I am too demanding. Perhaps I should be happier that some change for the better has occurred within the profession. And perhaps I am unreasonable. Nonetheless, I am not satisfied. I continue to find my colleagues in the academy more than willing to let me know that public history is not "real" history and that my students must be less talented because they opted for public history rather than "traditional" history. I see graduate students being trained in ways that replicate the narrow vision of history that the profession has so lovingly crafted over the years, a vision that may be tattered around the edges but incredibly resilient despite the "job crisis" of the relatively recent past. Change has come to the two major historical associations although only barely so to the AHA if the 1995 annual convention was any indication of its vision of the history profession.

If we revisit the two categories of people ignored by the profession before the crisis period of the 1970s, it is clear that some improvement has occurred since I entered the profession as a graduate student in 1971. There is greater acceptance of those folks who inhabit the world of the first category, i.e. those individuals who possess the appropriate educational credentials but who for one reason or another work in historical organizations, archives, the National Park Service, for the federal government, or as independent historians. These historians are more integrated into the academically oriented profession than they were twenty years ago. There are positive signs that our understanding of what constitutes scholarly research and publication has become more inclusive, thus enhancing the profession's ability to increase and disseminate information about the past.[40] And while the redefining may appear on the surface to have more of an impact on the academy, it also serves to focus attention on the fact that the increase of knowledge can occur under a variety of different conditions.

It is with the fate of the second category that I find myself concerned, for it is in the profession's relationship to the larger world that the unwillingness of the profession to confront the vision of what it means to be a professional historian directly relates to marginality, abdication of civic responsibility, and, in the end, professional angst. When I listen to all the verbiage surrounding the National Standards for History, or the controversy over the Smithsonian's exhibition of the *Enola Gay,* or the agitation over the proposed Disney's America theme park, I see a profession that has made little progress in confronting the fact that it possesses so little understanding of the audiences it so blithely cast aside before the 1970s. I see, as well, a profession that has forgotten that history matters.

What will our legacy to future generations of historians be? Will we leave them a past that provides them with a very narrow vision of what it means to be a historian? Will we trap them with a mindset that continues to suggest that the boundaries of their professional status represent the world of the academic community? Or, will we bequeath them a world in which they, as professional historians, practice their craft in a range of different contexts?

Historians must do more than bemoan the desire of the public for a past that bears precious little relationship to the past of historians. If the professional historical community cared about what the public learned about the past, it would participate more directly and visibly in the efforts to present responsible interpretation to visitors at historic sites, museums, historical societies, and monuments. Doing so would allow the public to better see historians as integral players in the definition, preservation, and interpretation of America's historical experience. Jamil Zainaldin, president of the Federation of State Humanities Councils, summed up the situation nicely in a recent discussion of service and scholarship. According to Zainaldin, "the more that our publics know about us, the more they will come to share our values for our craft and help support the practitioners, the higher education institutions, museums, historical societies, and similar institutions that share our mission."[41]

We need to be concerned as well about the world of precollegiate education. In one sense Oscar Handlin was right. Relevance or relationship to one's life is important in stimulating a desire to broaden one's understanding of history. His solution, however, to leave the introduction to history to a more intellectually prepared population is not the best approach. History can and should be introduced in primary and secondary school classrooms. It should be done, however, in such a way as to lay the foundation for learning how to learn, ask questions, and seek answers. In the process students not only will gather the "facts" but also will begin to understand them and remember them.[42]

Students' lack of historical knowledge about the past results in an inability to see themselves, their families, and their communities as part of the larger process of American history. If students fail to see their own histories as important, they do not believe that they can have an impact on their environments. One of the ways in which people "learn to be members of society" is to feel engaged in it. History is central to identifying, analyzing, and interpreting the values upon which civil society depends.[43] All historians should remember that they are citizens as well as scholars and that they possess some responsibility to the larger civic community.

None of this can happen, however, unless the profession as a whole confronts the issue of professional definition. We need to use the same scrutiny we employ when we examine other aspects of the past when we look at the way in which the professionalizers defined *historian* during the early years of professional growth. The prevailing "official" definition is a social construct not a truth. If we approach the study of our profession with the understanding that the only constants should be evolving characteristics and changing contexts instead of fixed categories,[44] then it might be easier for the profession to embrace the idea that the definition of the professional historian we inherited need not be static, that the natural order of things suggests redefinition. If this were to happen, the conditions responsible for the angst and dissatisfaction felt by the historians replying to the *Journal of American History*'s survey[45] on the practice of American history would largely evaporate. History and historians would emerge as more important components of our civic culture and, as a result, possess more opportunity to participate in the various conversations about our past and its meaning today.

NOTES

1. This article appeared in a slightly different form as "Professional Historians and 'Destiny's Gate,' " *The Public Historian* 17 (Summer 1995): 9–24. See this version for a fuller discussion of sources, especially on background material on the various arenas where historians work outside of university settings.

2. Michael Kammen, ed., *The Past Before Us: Contemporary Historical Writing in the United States* (Ithaca: Cornell University Press, 1980), 19–20. Material in this volume represents the AHA's assessment of the state of the discipline of history in America during the 1970s.

3. Arthur M. Schlesinger, *In Retrospect: The History of a Historian* (New York: Harcourt, Brace & World, Inc., 1963); Timothy Paul Donovan, *Historical Thought in America: Postwar Patterns* (Norman: University of Oklahoma Press, 1973); Oscar Handlin, *Truth in History* (Cambridge: Belknap Press, 1979); Peter Novick, *That Noble Dream: The "Objectivity Question" and the American Historical Profession* (New York: Cambridge University Press, 1988); and Joyce Appleby, Lynn Hunt, and Margaret Jacob, *Telling the Truth About History* (New York: W. W. Norton & Co., 1994).

4. Joan Hoff Wilson, "Is the Historical Profession an 'Endangered Species?' " *The Public Historian* 2 (Winter 1980): 5,19.

5. Gerda Lerner, "The Necessity of History and the Professional Historian," *Journal of American History* 69 (June 1982): 9,17.

6. Theodore S. Hamerow, *Reflections on History and Historians* (Madison: University of Wisconsin Press, 1987), xi.

7. Talcott Parsons, "Professions," in *International Encyclopedia of the Social Sciences,* ed. David L. Sills, Vol. 12 (New York: Macmillan, 1968), 536–47; Gerald L. Geison, ed., *Professions and Professional Ideologies in America* (Chapel Hill: University of North Carolina Press, 1983), 3–7; and Nathan O. Hatch, ed., *The Professions in American History* (South Bend: University of Notre Dame Press, 1988), 1–12. See also Mary O. Furner, *Advocacy and Objectivity: A Crisis in the Professionalization of American Social Science 1865–1905* (Lexington: University Press of Kentucky, 1975); Magali Sarfatti Larson, *The Rise of Professionalism: A Sociological Study* (Berkeley: University of California Press, 1977); and Robert Dingwall and Philip Lewis, eds., *The Sociology of the Professions: Lawyers, Doctors, and Others* (New York: St. Martin's Press, 1983).

8. Hatch, *Professions,* 1–5; Geison, *Professions,* 3–5; and Parsons, "Professions," 536.

9. See Furner, *Advocacy and Objectivity;* John Higham, *History: Professional Scholarship in America* (New York: Harper Torchbooks, 1965), 6–17; Thomas Bender, *Intellect and Public Life: Essays on the Social History of Academic Intellectuals in the United States* (Baltimore: Johns Hopkins University Press, 1993); and Samuel Haber, *The Quest for Authority and Honor in the American Professions, 1750–1900* (Chicago: University of Chicago Press, 1991).

10. Wilson, "Historical Profession," 5–7; and Novick, *Noble Dream,* 49.

11. Novick, *Noble Dream,* 47–52; Higham, *History,* 6–7; and J. H. Hexter, *Doing History* (Bloomington: Indiana University Press, 1971), 82–85. See Bender, *Intel-*

lect, 3–15,30–46, for an insightful discussion of what he calls "disciplinary professionalism" and its divorce from the larger civic culture.

12. Novick, *Noble Dream,* 52.
13. W. Stull Holt, *The Historical Profession in the United States.* AHA Publication No. 52 (New York: Macmillan Co., 1963), 1.
14. Higham, *History,* 68–69.
15. Lerner, "Necessity," 10; and Wilson, "Historical Profession," 4.
16. Lerner, "Necessity," 10.
17. Novick, *Noble Dream,* 52.
18. See, for example, Edwin C. Bearss, "The National Park Service and Its History Program: 1864–1986—An Overview," *The Public Historian* 9 (Spring 1987): 10–14; Gary Kulik, "Designing the Past: History Museum Exhibitions from Peale to the Present," in Warren Leon and Roy Rosenzweig, eds., *History Museums in the United States: A Critical Assessment* (Urbana: University of Illinois Press, 1989), 3–37; and William F. Birdsall, "The Two Sides of the Desk: The Archivist and the Historian, 1909–1935," *American Archivist* 38 (April 1975): 159–73.
19. See Martin Reuss, "Public History in the Federal Government," in Barbara J. Howe and Emory Kemp, eds., *Public History: An Introduction* (Malabar, FL: Robert E. Krieger Publishing Co., 1986), 293–309; and Novick, *Noble Dream,* 303–6.
20. Charles G. Sellers, "Is History on the Way Out of the Schools and Do Historians Care?" *Social Education* 33 (May 1969): 509–16
21. Oscar Handlin, "Live Students and Dead Education: Why High School Must Be Revived," *Atlantic Monthly,* September 1961, 29–34.
22. Novick, *Noble Dream,* 368–72; Sellers, "History," 514; and David Pratt, "The Functions of Teaching History," *The History Teacher* 7 (May 1974): 410–25.
23. Roy Rosenzweig, "Marketing the Past: *American Heritage* and Popular History in the United States," in Susan Porter Benson, Stephen Brier, and Roy Rosenzweig, eds., *Presenting the Past: Essays on History and the Public* (Philadelphia: Temple University Press, 1986), 21–49; and Novick, *Noble Dream,* 372–73.
24. Charles B. Hosmer, Jr. "Historical Preservation, Tourism and Leisure," *Monumentum* 13 (1976): 81.
25. John Jakle, *The Tourist: Travel in Twentieth-Century North America* (Lincoln: University of Nebraska Press, 1985), 286,288; and Patricia Mooney-Melvin, "Harnessing the Romance of the Past: Preservation, Tourism, and History," *The Public Historian* 13 (Spring 1991): 35–48.
26. Theodore J. Karamanski, "Introduction: Ethics and the Use of History," in Theodore J. Karamanski, ed., *Ethics and Public History: An Anthology* (Malabar, FL: Robert E. Krieger Publishing Co., 1990), 6–11.
27. See Carl Becker, "Everyman His Own Historian," *American Historical Review* 37 (January 1932): 221–36; Novick, *Noble Dream,* 255; and Bender, *Intellect,* 91–105.
28. Thomas Cochran to Richard Hofstadter, 13 April 1948, Cochran Papers, Box 1 as quoted in Novick, *Noble Dream,* 374.

29. Handlin, *Truth,* 1–24; Hamerow, *Reflections,* 24–27; and Novick, *Noble Dream,* 607–9.

30. Hamerow, *Reflections,* 6–7.

31. See Theodore Levitt, "Marketing Myopia," *Harvard Business Review* 38 (July/ August 1960): 45–56 for a discussion of a process that can render industries obsolete through definitional rigidity. See also Noel J. Stowe, "The Promises and Challenges for Public History," *The Public Historian* 9 (Winter 1987): 47–56.

32. As quoted in Arnita Jones, "The National Coordinating Committee: Programs and Possibilities," *The Public Historian* 1 (Fall 1978): 49–50.

33. See, for example, David Clary, "Trouble Is My Business: A Private View of 'Public' History," *The American Archivist* (Spring 1981):105–12; and David Clary, "Write When You Find Work: Advice for Graduate Faculty on Training Employable Historians," *The History Teacher* 12 (November 1978): 65–85.

34. Jones, "National," 52.

35. Ibid., 53.

36. For information about the origins of public history see Robert Kelley, "Public History: Its Origins, Nature, and Prospects," *The Public Historian* 1 (Fall 1978): 16–28; Howe and Kemp, *Public History;* Benson, Brier, and Rosenzweig, *Presenting the Past;* Barbara J. Howe, "Reflections on an Idea: NCPH's First Decade," *The Public Historian* 11 (Summer 1989): 69–85; and Philip V. Scarpino, "Common Ground: Reflections on the Past, Present, and Future of Public History and the NCPH," *The Public Historian* 16 (Summer 1994): 11–21.

37. Terrence O'Donnell, "Pitfalls Along the Path of Public History," *The Public Historian* 4 (Winter 1982): 65–72; Howard Green, "A Critique of the Professional Public History Movement," *Radical History Review* 25 (1981): 164–71; Novick, *Noble Dream,* 510–21; and Karamanski, *Ethics and Public History: An Anthology.*

38. American Historical Association, "Statement on Standards of Professional Conduct" (1993), 1–3.

39. Page Putnam Miller, "Reflections on the Public History Movement," *The Public Historian* 14 (Spring 1992), 67–70.

40. See, for example, Report of the American Historical Association Ad Hoc Committee on Redefining Scholarly Work, "Redefining Historical Scholarship," *Perspectives,* March 1994, 19–23; and Ernest L. Boyer, *Scholarship Reconsidered: Priorities of the Professoriate* (Princeton: The Carnegie Foundation for the Advancement of Teaching, 1990). Not everyone is comfortable with the notion of redefining scholarship. See Lynn Hudson Parsons, Joan Shelley Rubin, and Owen S. Ireland, "Redefining Scholarship: Some Problems," *OAH Newsletter,* February 1995, 6–7.

41. Jamil S. Zainaldin, "Service and Scholarship," *OAH Newsletter,* February 1995, 6.

42. Sellers, "History," 514–16; and Richard H. Brown, "Richard H. Brown Replies," *Social Education* 31 (November 1967): 584–87.

43. For a useful discussion of civil society see Ivan Karp, Christine Mullen Kreamer, Steven D. Lavine, eds., *Museums and Communities: The Politics of Public Culture* (Washington, DC: Smithsonian Institution Press, 1992).

44. For a useful way to approach the historical study of professional activity see Donald M. Scott, "The Profession that Vanished: Public Lecturing in Mid-Nineteenth-Century America," in Gerald L. Geison, ed., *Professions and Professional Ideologies in America* (Chapel Hill: University of North Carolina Press, 1983), 13–14, 27–28.
46. "The Practice of American History: A Special Issue," *Journal of American History* 81 (December 1994). For all the agitation expressed about practicing history today, only one commentator, Pablo Pozzi, mentioned that it might be time "to rethink the profession itself" (1111).

CONSTANCE B. SCHULZ is professor of history, co-director of the Public History Program, and managing editor of The Papers of Henry Laurens *at the University of South Carolina. She earned her B.A. at the College of Wooster and her M.A. and Ph.D. in history at the University of Cincinnati. Prior to joining the faculty at South Carolina, Dr. Schulz taught at Georgetown University, the University of Maryland Baltimore County, the College of Wooster, American University, and the University of Maryland University College and worked with the Documentary History of the First Federal Congress at George Washington University as a National Historical Publications and Records Commission Fellow in Documentary Editing. Dr. Schulz's many professional activities include service on the board of directors and the nominating committee of the National Council on Public History, the National Historical Publications and Records Commission, the nominating committee and the public history committee of the Organization of American Historians, and the editorial boards of the* Journal of the Early Republic *and the* American Archivist. *Her publications include* Witness to the Fifties: The Pittsburgh Photographic Library, 1950–1953 *(1999),* Bust to Boom: Kansas Photographs from the Farm Security Administration, Office of War Information, and Standard Oil of New Jersey Documentary Projects, 1936–1949 *(1996), and* Kiplin Hall and its Families: A History *(1994).*

BECOMING A PUBLIC HISTORIAN

Constance B. Schulz

How do you become a public historian? Some may think it more than a little ironic that in order to become a public historian at the end of the twentieth century one of the most effective means is to seek training within the academy. Moreover, for a field which in its earliest years as an identified speciality was (mistakenly) too often simply defined by what it was not—i.e., not academic history—many of its most effective advocates and practitioners today make their livings in college and university history departments teaching graduate (and some undergraduate) students how to become public historians.

In addition, many individuals doing work in institutions that employ public historians—work that on its surface may seem indistinguishable from that done by public historians—do not consider themselves to be historians at all, much less "public" ones, and the training by which they entered their professional positions may have either much or nothing at all in common with that of their historian colleagues. Librarians and archivists whose academic degrees are in library or information science programs; documentary (and other) editors and publishers whose training may have been conducted in English departments or schools of journalism; museum curators and administrators who studied art history, biology, or anthropology; directors of state or local historical societies whose academic credentials were earned in a college of business or public administration—all may share with public historians their professional identities as archivists, editors, museum curators, and cultural agency managers, but not necessarily their identity as historians. This is, by and large, a good thing. The goals and practices of public history are often interdisciplinary in their scope and require cooperation in collegial enterprise for their implementation. Yet while the best public history education includes elements of the content and approaches of these collateral fields, it also has a focus that is uniquely its own.

The route by which many of today's new practitioners come to be public historians is quite different from how one became a public historian in the past. Indeed, many professional public historians currently in leadership roles in the profession became historians through traditional academic B.A., M.A., or Ph.D. history programs and went "public" through on-the-job training as site interpreters at National Parks, as processing archivists at state archives or historical societies, as curators or registrars at local museums, as self-taught experts in historic preservation law who volunteered to save local landmark buildings or neighborhoods. Still others began working in the field as "amateurs" in the best sense of that word: as men and women who loved and admired the past and the artifacts and places associated with it and were determined to preserve them for the enjoyment of others in their communities. Understanding that good will was often not a sufficient resource for the tasks they faced, these members of the "public" became historians through industry and necessity, founding or joining community historical societies, seeking out and contributing to historical literature, taking history courses at local colleges and universities, or attending national historical professional meetings.

THE CONTEXT: PROFESSIONAL ASSOCIATIONS AND MUSEUM AND ARCHIVAL TRAINING

Even before the creation of the National Council on Public History (NCPH), key professional organizations associated with the practices of public history played a major role in transforming both academically trained traditional historians and community-based amateur historians into public historians. The American Association for State and Local History (AASLH), the Society of American Archivists (SAA), the American Association of Museums (AAM), the National Trust for Historic Preservation (NTHP), the Association for Documentary Editing (ADE), the Society for History in the Federal Government, and other cultural studies professional organizations have all seen education of their members, both practical and theoretical, to be a major part of their purpose and function. They have published basic instructional literature in their respective fields, established professional journals that offer analysis of important theoretical issues and case studies of good working practices, instituted newsletters to link members and their concerns, and sponsored introductory seminars on professional practices as well as more advanced workshops on technical innovations. They have had an important impact on the professionalization of public history workplaces by developing and promoting national professional standards for ethical behavior and practical problem solving. In some geographical areas, and for some small local institutions with limited financial bases, the training these organizations provide through workshops and publications is still the primary means by which staff can become public historians.

Professional associations have been equally important in the development of academic professional training in their respective fields. Examples from the museum and archival fields illustrate how early that interest began and how central the issue of professional education was to the purposes of professional associations.[1] From its founding in 1906, the American Association of Museums called for a university-based training program for museum professionals comparable to that for other professions. One of the earliest formal museum training programs was a course taught by Paul Sachs in 1921 at a museum—the Fogg Art Museum—but within the larger academic setting of Harvard University. Yet by the mid–twentieth century, of thirteen such formal training programs within a museum, only one was in history; the remaining dozen were in art and natural history museums, and only a few were associated with a university at all. Not until the establishment in the early 1950s of the Winterthur Museum and Hagley Foundation programs in the University of Delaware

American Studies and history departments did museum studies programs with a historical focus find a secure academic base.

Other cultural institutions took a slightly different approach to linking
academic credentials with museum training. Prompted by concerns expressed by the National Trust for Historic Preservation and the AASLH
about the need for professionally trained administrators at museums and
historic sites, Colonial Williamsburg established in 1958 a short-term
"Seminar for Historical Administrators." Designed originally for "high
caliber scholars . . . from the top universities who had the talent, credentials, and energy to revitalize museum interpretation," the Seminar still
exists as a widely respected intensive three-week immersion in museum
theory and practice that provides a nonacademic credential for museum
administrators and would-be administrators.[2]

By the late 1970s, academically based programs specifically designed
for museum training were in place at the State University of New York
College at Oneonta (the Cooperstown program), George Washington
University, John F. Kennedy University in California, and New York University. To encourage these and other academic programs, the AAM created an ad hoc "Museum Studies Curriculum Committee" in 1972 and
charged it with the task of preparing a "Museum Studies Curriculum
Guide," which the committee published in 1973. The committee, revi-
talized in 1976 as the "Museum Studies Committee," recommended establishment of museum training standards though publication in the
November-December 1978 issue of *Museum News* of a list of minimum
training standards for museum professionals, a statement on preparation
for museum careers, and a review of museum hiring practices. This early
guidance was superseded in January 1983 by the AAM Council's adoption
of a more extensively articulated "Criteria for Examining Professional
Museum Studies Programs," published in the June 1983 issue of *Museum
News*. Since its creation in May 1990, the AAM's standing Committee on
Museum Professional Training (COMPT) has continued to study and
make recommendations on the content and purpose of undergraduate
and graduate courses of museum education and has recently begun discussions of the need for a revised series of "criteria" for professional museum studies.[3]

Graduate programs in museum studies, or associated disciplinary graduate programs that offer specific courses in museum theory and practice,
are increasingly the preferred entry to the museum profession. Nevertheless, AAM, the six regional museum associations, and most state museum associations also support a "continuing education" approach to
specialized training for museum professionals. In addition, many museum staff, who were hired without such training in history museums or

historic sites, have turned to workshops and other specialized training opportunities offered by the American Association for State and Local History.[4]

In contrast to museum professional training, which originated in the needs of art, science, and a few history museums for trained curatorial staff, in the archival profession the earliest interest in the need for professional training was articulated by professional historians, while the first formal academic training program began in a library school. At about the time when a handful of states were beginning to establish archives departments to preserve state records, long before the establishment of the National Archives in 1934, custodians responsible for the care and administration of manuscript and archival materials met within the American Historical Association in 1909 to discuss standards for common practice and an appropriate means of education and training for conveying those standardized practices to historians wishing to enter the archival and manuscript curator field.

One of the earliest concerns of the Society of American Archivists, founded in 1936, was the establishment of sound archival training, for which a Committee on Education and Training was created in 1937, chaired by historian Samuel Flagg Bemis. Bemis's report, completed in July 1937 and published by the SAA in its journal *American Archivist* in 1939, initiated a discussion that has continued within the profession ever since: should professional training be in history departments, library schools, or some independent academic unit? Bemis proposed a two-tiered system—"archivists" for major institutions who would be educated within history departments with a Ph.D., and "technicians" for smaller collections of historical documents who might hold an M.A. in history but also receive training in library cataloging techniques.

While Bemis saw the study of history as central to the training of archivists, others, including Margaret Cross Norton, director of the Illinois State Library, and Solon J. Buck, then director of publications at the National Archives, proposed that library schools might best be able to provide effective training in archival practices. In 1938 and 1940, Buck and then Norton taught such a course within the library school at Columbia University. But the library school model was not universal. In 1939, Buck persuaded the history department at American University in Washington, D.C., to begin teaching courses in archival administration, complemented by internships provided at the National Archives, to educate those responsible for the administration of large masses of business and government records.[5]

Nor did the earliest formal archival training occur only in a university setting. When it proved difficult to replicate the American University semester-long program in other regions, prompted in part by the urgings of a joint committee of the SAA and the AASLH on the need for practical training in archives nationwide, American University, the Maryland Hall of Records, and the National Archives cooperated to establish a summer institute in 1945 at the National Archives to instruct archivists in basic principles and practical techniques. That two-week program still flourishes, offered twice a year in Washington.[6] Although in archives, as in museums, the preferred entry level training for the profession is a graduate degree, many currently practicing archivists received their only formal training at the National Archives Summer Institute or in comparable regional programs such as that sponsored by the Georgia Department of Archives and History and the Society of Georgia Archivists.

The SAA established a Committee on Professional Standards and Training in 1953–54, a committee which has essentially continued in operation, although renamed the Committee on Education and Professional Development (CEPD). In 1977, the committee published the first SAA "Guidelines for a Graduate Minor or Concentration in Archival Education," replaced in 1988 by the SAA "Guidelines for Graduate Archival Education Programs." Both the 1977 and the 1988 "Guidelines," recognizing the likelihood that archival graduate education would continue to take place in history departments and library schools, placed a high priority on the teaching of theory and practice particular to the emerging needs of the archival profession, and argued that while "workshops, institutes, and single courses . . . still have a place in archival education" that these alternatives "are not sufficient in themselves for equipping individuals to function as archivists." The 1988 Guidelines spelled out in detail the "Curriculum Elements" essential for the content as well as the structure necessary for a university program in graduate archival education.[7]

To reinforce the importance of broadly based university training as an entry into the profession, SAA established an "Education Officer" within its own professional staff, and began publishing an "Education Directory," listing those universities which provided training and specifying what courses each offered. SAA members played a crucial role in creating a system of postemployment "certification" of individual archivists through examination, administered by the independent Academy of Certified Archivists (ACA, established in 1989); CEPD successfully urged the ACA to allow graduates of university archival degree programs to sit for the exam immediately, rather than requiring them to wait until the end of a two-year period of archival employment. In 1994 the SAA Council adopted a rigorously defined set of "Guidelines for Development of a Curriculum for a Master of Archival Studies Degree," the full text of which is included in the SAA *Directory of Archival Education*. Like AAM, the

SAA continues to offer postemployment training for working professionals through sponsorship of workshops, and has discussed standards for evaluating continuing education programs. But it is clear within both of these disciplines that university-based graduate education is increasingly the preferred preparation for entry into the profession.

THE PUBLIC HISTORY MOVEMENT AND THE ESTABLISHMENT OF PUBLIC HISTORY EDUCATION PROGRAMS

Begun in the 1950s, university-based, graduate-level education was well established by the 1970s as the preferred basis for becoming a professional in museum, archival, and other cultural agency institutions. However, a divergence began to emerge between programs located in history departments and primarily oriented toward historical analysis, and those more closely linked to other academic departments or programs, preparing students in the professional skills of other disciplines. Before the 1970s, graduates of traditional academic history programs working in public historical agencies sometimes experienced a sense of alienation from or found little welcome in the academically oriented professional historical associations. Some found a more welcoming professional association home during the 1950s and 1960s within the American Association for State and Local History, with its emphasis on the historical study of individuals and communities and on the identification, preservation, and use of local historical resources.

AASLH was founded in 1940 when the Confederation of State and Local Historical Societies, a constituent organization established within the American Historical Association in 1904, withdrew from the AHA in part because of the reluctance of the parent academic scholarly organization to value community-based history on a level with the journal- and monograph-based scholarship produced by academic historians.[8] AASLH's orientation, however, was towards the practice of history in its myriad forms outside the academy, rather than in defining academic preparation for such practice, although it did publish the first set of "Standards for Historical Agency Training Programs" as a four-page detachable brochure in the July 1981 issue of *History News*.

By the time of that publication, a significant movement, labelled "the public history movement," had emerged in the mid 1970s from two sources: the first was the creation of graduate "applied" or "public" history programs within academic history departments, consciously designed to train historians for "alternative careers" to that of the professorate.[9] The second was the increasing identification of trained historians working in government agencies and the private sector with their common general ties in history, rather than with the specific professional orientations associated with their employment.[10]

The academic component of the "public history movement" grew out of the tradition of graduate academic training to prepare students for public professional careers described above for museums and archives, but its approach was different: the new programs did teach specific skills in archival, museum, cultural agency administration, and public policy analysis, but their focus was on celebration of and nurturing within students an overarching professional identity as historians. Although some of these early programs concentrated primarily on preparation for careers in one kind of public agency—such as Auburn University, whose program founded in 1972 offered only archival training, or Middle Tennessee State University, whose historic preservation program was founded in 1973—many were more broadly based, aimed at developing public history generalists with at least introductory training in archives, museums, cultural agency administration, local history, historic preservation, oral history, public policy analysis, or other skills. In January of 1979, the National Coordinating Committee for the Promotion of History (NCC), created by the major historical associations in 1977 to support expanded professional opportunities for historians, released the results of a survey of forty-eight new courses or programs of study for training of public historians within history departments. The survey's findings divided the programs into three broad categories of studies offered: archives and information management, cultural resources management (within which were included both historic preservation studies and museum administration), and "applied research," which the survey defined as "application of historical training to work in institutions whose purpose is not basically related to history." Many of the programs surveyed in 1978 have survived and flourished. Of the fifty-seven listed programs in NCPH's 1996 *Guide to Graduate Programs in Public History,* fourteen trace their origins to the 1970s.[11]

Some critics of the public history movement accused its academic promoters of being more concerned with the "job crisis" in the academy and the need to find career opportunities for history Ph.D.s who seemed otherwise unemployable in the mid-1970s than with the need for trained historians in the public sector. Yet the 1978 NCC survey suggested that the forty-eight new public history programs it had studied were often in non-elite university history departments, many of which did not offer the Ph.D. Arnita Jones, then NCC Executive Director, explained that these public history graduate programs "seem to have developed from local concerns, or at the impetus of a single person who dabbled in the field, liked it, and saw the opportunities for others." Indeed, she noted that at a number of academic institutions which had begun public history programs, "all the elements of the new training have existed, and the new programs have been recognized only after the fact."[12]

The creation of a new public history professional identity and organization grew in part out of the establishment of academic programs. Robert Kelley, who initiated the program at the University of California at Santa Barbara, claimed to have invented the term "Public History" in 1975.[13] In 1978, Kelley's Santa Barbara colleague G. Wesley Johnson used part of a Rockefeller Foundation grant to publish the first issue of *The Public Historian*, which was modelled on academic historical journals in its study of practices in the emerging field. A series of sponsored "public history" conferences between 1978 and 1980, involving a wide range of historians employed in public agencies and many of the faculty from newly created academic programs, led to the incorporation in May 1980 of the National Council on Public History (NCPH). Impressed by the quality of the initial independently produced issues of *The Public Historian* and seeing a need for an established professional journal for the field, the original NCPH steering committee adopted it in 1980 as the organization's journal, cosponsored by the University of California at Santa Barbara. Through this journal, its newsletter, and its annual meeting, the NCPH has increasingly taken the lead in defining the field as a whole.

From its earliest years NCPH has played a role in defining for history departments the training and education necessary to transform history graduate students into public historians. Among the first programs it launched were a nationwide network for public and applied history students to exchange ideas and questions, and a second network for their teachers to exchange course descriptions and curricula. Between 1981 and 1985, NCPH offered a quarterly newsletter, *Teaching Public History,* to further encourage the development and professionalization of public history education within university history departments.[14] In 1986, NCPH published the first comprehensive listing of graduate programs, *Public History Education in America: A Guide;* a second version listing fifty-four U.S. and three Canadian public history programs was published in 1990, and a third appeared in 1996.

The information provided by the *Guide,* volunteered by the history department faculty whose programs were listed, raised in the minds of some members the question of whether NCPH ought also to establish accreditation standards to help distinguish among the widely varying content and quality of programs claiming to offer graduate public history education. In 1988, the NCPH board of directors created a Committee on Accreditation, later renamed the Committee for Professional Standards, which in

1990 sent questionnaires to more than 150 institutions that claimed to offer instruction in public history. The preliminary results of that survey, published in March 1992 as "Analysis of the 1990–1991 Survey of Academic Programs in Public History," were inconclusive, and NCPH did not at that point pursue further the issue of accreditation. Despite its decision not to get involved in this issue, however, like its counterpart organizations the National Trust for Historic Preservation, the American Association of Museums, and the Society of American Archivists, NCPH continues to monitor public history education closely, has a standing Committee on Education, regularly provides opportunities for public history faculty to meet and exchange ideas at its annual meetings, distributes course and curriculum information to help those establishing new programs,[15] and continues to publish guides to existing programs.

PUBLIC HISTORY ACADEMIC EDUCATION TODAY: AN ANALYTICAL OVERVIEW

Public history academic education, with its roots in academic preparation for careers in particular fields, such as museums and archives, emerged within history departments in the 1970s and enjoys the support and scrutiny of a national professional association. But a glance at this volume's table of contents with its long list of the widely varying kinds of work in which public historians are involved may well lead the reader to wonder whether or if professional training can have any unifying elements or common themes. While it is true that "public history" training can and does specialize and that those seeking to enter the field need to look carefully at the particular kinds of professional positions for which a specific educational program they are considering provides preparation, public history education today rests on a number of common *purposes, themes,* and *elements.*

The common *purposes* of public history education are to prepare historians trained in the traditional historical skills of research, interpretation, and writing to apply those skills in a broad variety of public settings in order to bring an understanding of the past to bear on the issues, problems, and enjoyment of the present, and to preserve the sources that make that understanding possible. The common *themes* in public history education are these: the insistence that the primary sources for understanding the past are not limited to the written word but encompass buildings, sites, landscapes, artifacts, orally transmitted memories, visual materials, and most recently, electronic records; the insight that it is the broader contexts of local, regional, national, cultural, or thematic histories that provide meaning to the specific details of the historical problems which public historians are charged with solving; and the understanding that historical work is often teamwork in which individual efforts or expertise must be linked in cooperation with contributions of others. The common *elements* in most public history training are these: development of a professional level of proficiency in the historical methods of research and writing and in the content of some specific area of historical study; immersion in or intense study of the basic theoretical principles and technical skills of a historical arena within the public domain (a museum, an archives, a business, a historic site); and opportunity to practice the combination of historical methodology and technical skills within a professional setting under the guidance of a working profession practitioner. It has reached a level of maturity in the late 1990s that is reflected both by the diversity of its offerings and by the strengths of its core. Let us turn now to an examination of how those commonalties are combined to prepare public historians for careers in the broad range of occupational activities whose descriptions comprise the remainder of this volume.[16]

The first element that public history programs provide—what public or applied history degree programs almost universally have in common—are curriculum designs that ground students firmly in the knowledge and methodology of history. Of the fifty-seven programs listed in the 1996 NCPH *Guide*, only four do not specify a history department as their sole institutional home. Forty-seven state unequivocally that it is a history degree which they offer and make clear that, in addition to whatever else they study, students must master at a graduate level a knowledge and understanding of the history of a nation, region, or people. While not all of these list as part of the curriculum described in the *Guide* the particular courses that form the general graduate history program, sixteen specify that they require courses in historical or research methodology, and six list as part of their public history requirements a course in historiography. More striking still is that twenty-six require students to complete a thesis or thesis project, while another eighteen make a thesis optional—many with the caveat that it is strongly recommended. Only six pointedly do NOT require a thesis.

What this suggests is that the unique component that public history programs provide for those whom they train for careers in a broad range of private and public cultural agencies or in American businesses is their historical perspective. The traditional historical reading and writing seminars, the conscious focus on the importance of understanding for a particular place or people the content of historical experience and of change over time, the exposure to the historiographical discussions of changing interpretation of the past—all prepare public historians to place museum exhibits, manuscript collections or archival records, public policy issues, and historic landscapes and neighborhoods within broader regional, national, or even world contexts. Moreover, students in these programs are given specific training in historical research methods and are expected to undertake a sustained investigation of a topic or a problem using primary original source materials, to arrive at independent conclusions based on their research, and to organize their findings systematically into a lengthy report or well-written thesis.

Where this training differs from that of more traditional M.A. or Ph.D. candidates, however, is in three specific approaches to the study of the past.[17] Implicit in all public history programs is an assumption that the audiences for whom their students will be conducting research, arriving at independent conclusions shared through the written word or some other form of public presentation, are public rather than academic audiences. Thirty-four of the programs which listed their course offerings for the 1996 *Guide* made this explicit in their requirement that all students take an overview or introductory course in public history, its practices, its audiences, and its particular methodologies.

Public historians can and do contribute to the monographic literature and the professional historical journals of their chronological, regional, or thematic historical specializations. But they also have a carefully nurtured understanding that a broad range of public communities have an interest and a stake in the past. These communities learn about and participate in history through visiting museums, watching historical documentaries, conducting genealogical research, supporting local historical societies and house museums, and enjoying state and national park historic sites. Public history audiences are also made up of government agency administrators needing systematic descriptions of the impact of past policy decisions, of CEOs demanding documentation from company archives of corporate compliance with legal requirements, of corporate clients requesting accurate data about past land use and industrial technologies. Public historians must learn to respond to the interests and work toward the goals of their audiences, rather than simply to please themselves in the topics they chose to study and the timetables and deadlines under which they conduct their work.

A second difference from traditional historical studies is that the primary sources to which pubic historians turn are broadly inclusive, rather than almost exclusively found as written documents. This conclusion is confirmed by study of a sampling of course overviews offered in NCPH's *Collection of Public History Course Syllabi* (1996). In one course description after another, instructors point students to the historical analysis of photographs, of film, of artifacts, of oral interviews, of the built environment of structures and buildings, or of the manipulated environment of landscapes. Public history students also receive more advanced training in the identification and location, analysis, and incorporation of these sources into their work through the specific public history field courses offered in historic preservation, archives and editing, museum studies, oral history, and media.

A third area of difference between public history programs and the more general graduate history curriculum, complementing this emphasis on a variety of historical sources, is a broadened awareness of the varieties of disciplinary perspectives through which those sources can be perceived and interpreted. Most public history programs include in their curriculum interdisciplinary courses in anthropology and archaeology, art and art history, historical geography, folklore, business administration, policy studies, library and information science, and others. Although recently traditional historical studies have begun to draw on interdisciplinary methodologies for historical analysis, it is public history programs that have taken the lead and pointed the way to the advantages of cross-disciplinary studies.

The second major element of public history graduate education is that which prepares students for entry into a specific public workplace where history is practiced. But where the first element—the common historical professional core—unites public history programs in common goals, the second differentiates programs from each other. The list of concentrations in which particular programs provide such training is extensive: archives and records management, editing and publishing, historic preservation and cultural resources management, museum studies, oral history, business, media, public policy, and historical administration. If knowledge of historical research methods, study of broad historiographical trends, and the ability to conceptualize and carry out sustained historical studies make public historians generalists, it is their mastery of the specialized needs of the workplaces they plan to enter that makes most public historians also particularists. Individual programs may legitimately offer students specialization in more than one area: the most commonly combined studies are those in archives, museums, and historic preservation or cultural resources management training. Others may combine one or more of these with intensive training in administration, with the history and corporate needs of business, with study of government policy-making processes, or with the specialized techniques of filmmaking or other public media. Prospective students seeking to identify an academic program appropriate to their own interests and career goals are well advised to analyze what each program offers and the support system it has in place to make good on its promises.

Public history programs seek to provide for whatever specializations they offer both an understanding of the theoretical framework and a thorough grounding in the practical skills and technical demands of a particular field. Whether it be in archival courses articulating fundamental principles for appraisal and arrangement, in historical agency administration studies of theories of management style, or in museum courses that examine the nature and use of objects made by humans, broad intellectual mastery of issues and concerns central to each area of study is an essential part of the difference between university-based preparation for a discipline and on-the-job training in it.

In addition to a holistic view of their discipline, students also need practical solutions to everyday problems they will face and a range of technical skills particular to the varied forms of historical materials with which they will work, whether that be objects, documents, films, oral histories, buildings, landscapes, or the more intangible realities of policy and decision making or of agency administration. Here the second and the third common elements of public history education overlap: techniques and skills can be described and analyzed initially in the classroom, but for students to master them successfully they must also be practiced. Hands-on instruction, sometimes described generically as a "practicum," is often built into the classroom study of a subject, but most public history programs demand a more rigorous practical application of newly learned skills in the formal mechanism of an internship.

Internships are a universal component of the public history programs described in the 1996 NCPH *Guide:* forty-four of the fifty-seven require them, an additional five recommend them highly, and the remainder make them available. While internships vary considerably in their duration and definition of requirements, almost all immerse students full time for a substantial period in an institution representative of that in which they seek professional careers, under the careful supervision of an academic advisor and an experienced professional in the field. Some public history programs take pride in—indeed may require of an internship experience—placing their students in paying positions for this component of their training. Most allow and give academic credit for internships without pay; all require that the student be treated as the equivalent of a professional staff member.

The second and third elements in public history education—intensive training in a particular field's theory and practice, and an extended opportunity to apply that training in a real-world setting—provide the basis for another common theme for public history education: historical work as a corporate rather than an individual enterprise. While the requirement for completion of a thesis implies the ability to carry out historical study on one's own, most other public history curriculum requirements focus on cooperative and interdisciplinary approaches. Course curricula illuminate the processes by which students in public history programs learn to work together: class members form teams to prepare national register nominations in historic preservation courses, they divide up tasks to write grant applications in archival administration courses, they pool their skills to design and construct an exhibition in museum administration courses. In doing so, they learn the necessity of allocating tasks efficiently, the importance of dependability, and the ability to work toward deadlines.

Because of the need for a broad intellectual perspective on the discipline and the importance of the availability of local professionals who can be invited to give guest lectures in classes or to supervise in-class and internship practica, public history programs most frequently provide specialization in those fields in which there is a professionally staffed independent institution accessible nearby. A well-established working relationship with a local history museum, the state archives or the manuscript collections of a university library or historical society, nearby businesses, or the State Historic Preservation Office is often the hallmark of a successful public history academic program.

How can a prospective public historian learn about the academic programs available and evaluate whether a particular program is the appropriate choice for becoming the kind of public historian one wishes to be? The most complete and accurate information about existing public history training programs is provided by guides to such programs published by the major professional organizations in public history's various fields. The National Council on Public History, established in 1980, published its first *Public History Education in America: A Guide,* in 1986, updated it in 1990, and again in 1996. The Society of American Archivists publishes an annually updated *Directory of Archival Education,* which includes a copy of the endorsed SAA "Guidelines for the Development of a Curriculum for a Master of Archival Studies Degree." The American Association of Museums took over this task from earlier efforts of the Office of Museum Programs of the Smithsonian Institution. The series *Museum Studies International,* whose sixth edition was issued in 1993, combines brief descriptions of undergraduate, graduate, and internship training opportunities in the United States and abroad. In its place AAM published *A Guide to Museum Studies and Training in the United States.*[18] The National Park Service prepares on a regular basis an issue of its periodical, *CRM,* focused on training in cultural resources management; the "Short Term" version of the "Cultural Resource Training Directory," published annually since 1989, describes training opportunities (usually nondegree) of less than six weeks duration. The National Park Service also issues less frequently, in conjunction with the National Council for Preservation Education (NCPE), a "Directory of College, University, Craft and Trade Programs in Cultural Resource Management (Long Term)" which not only describes graduate programs in historic preservation but also provides a comprehensive bibliography listing other directories for related programs.

Public history education faces a number of important challenges. Perhaps the most important of these reflects the impact of the computer age and the information revolution on history and historical study. Whether locating, authenticating, or using the primary sources on which all historians depend, public historians will increasingly turn to electronic information networks. Such networks have great potential for providing historians with new audiences, new technical mechanisms for applying historical skills, new venues for promoting the importance of the past. They have equal potential to diminish the influence of professionally trained historians upon public understanding of the past, as uncritically evaluated "historical" source material can be created for or transformed into electronic formats and instantly made available to vast and unsophisticated audiences. Public historians, already committed to reaching out to a broad variety of publics, stand in a unique position to lead the profession into active involvement in these issues. How public historians and the academic programs in which they are educated respond to this challenge, learning to use the new technologies creatively, will have far-reaching consequences.

With this exciting prospect before the historical profession, becoming a public historian can be both an absorbing pursuit, and the doorway to a lifetime involvement in the study and practice of history where it matters profoundly: in neighborhoods and communities, in board rooms and on Main Streets, in the midst of the public marketplaces of ideas and actions.

NOTES

1. Museums and archives are two of the major fields in which public history academic programs most frequently focus. A third, historic preservation, has somewhat different academic roots. A useful overview of that movement's legacy can be found in Michael Wallace, "Reflections on the History of Historic Preservation," in Susan Porter Benson, Stephen Brier, and Roy Rosenzweig, eds., *Presenting the Past; Essays on History and the Public* (Philadelphia: Temple University Press, 1986), 165–99.

2. Laurence Vail Coleman, *The Museum in America* (Washington, DC: American Association of Museums, 1939) 2: 419–23; and Philip D. Spiess, "Museum

Studies: Are They Doing Their Job?" *Museum News* (November/December 1996): 32–35.

3. COMPT Membership leaflet; see also the most recent issue of the COMPT newsletter, *COMPT Time,* December 1996.

4. The most complete description of museum training alternatives available, along with a detailed "Directory" to programs offered, can be found in Victor J. Danilov, *Museum Careers and Training, A Professional Guide* (Westport, CT: Greenwood Press, 1994).

5. Jacqueline Goggin, "That We Shall Truly Deserve the Title of 'Profession': The Training and Education of Archivists, 1930–1960," *American Archivist* 47 (Summer 1984): 244–49. See also the discussion of early archival education and training in Terry Eastwood, "Nurturing Archival Education in the University," *American Archivist* 51 (Summer 1988): 228–38; and Ernst Posner, "Archival Training in the United States," in Kenneth Munden, ed., *Archives and the Public Interest; Selected Essays of Ernst Posner* (Washington, DC: Public Affairs Press, 1967).

6. During the 1990s the Institute was offered briefly in regional archives centers, as well as in Washington, but at the writing of this chapter, the practice of regional programs had been discontinued.

7. The guidelines were published in annually in the *SAA Directory of Archival Education;* see for instance *Directory, 1991–1992* (Chicago: Society of American Archivists, 1992), 11–16.

8. Gerald George, "The American Association for State and Local History: The Public Historian's Home?" in Barbara J. Howe and Emory L. Kemp, eds., *Public History: An Introduction* (Malabar, FL: Robert E. Krieger Publishing Company, 1986), 251 ff. See also Michael C. Scardaville, "Looking Backward Toward the Future: An Assessment of the Public History Movement," *Public Historian* 9 (Fall 1987): 35–43. An excellent overview of the early history of the AASLH can be found in George Rollie Adams, "Planning for the Future, AASLH Takes a Look at Its Past," *History News* 37 (September 1982): 12–18.

9. Barbara Howe noted in her National Council on Public History presidential address that those in "alternative careers" were "getting tired of the label" as early as 1978. Howe, "Reflections on an Idea: NCPH's First Decade," *The Public Historian* 11 (Summer 1989): 71.

10. Dianne Martin, "History Goes Public," *History News* 34 (May 1979): 121–24. The AASLH designated this issue of *History News* as a "theme issue" on the topic of public history.

11. Ibid, 125–27; and Howe, "Reflections on an Idea," 70–71. Parker Hubbard Cohen, comp. and ed., *A Guide to Graduate Programs in Public History* (Indianapolis, IN: National Council on Public History, 1996).

12. Martin, "History Goes Public," 126.

13. George, "The AASLH: The Public Historian's Home?" 256. Though the field at large has come to be known as "public history," within the academic community the term was not universally adopted, some history departments choosing to label their graduate degree programs "applied history" instead.

14. Howe, "Reflections on an Idea," 71–75.
15. The most recent of these was compiled and edited by Parker Hubbard Cohen and Robert Vane, *A Collection of Public History Course Syllabi* (Indianapolis, IN: NCPH, 1996).
16. Unless otherwise specified, the analysis that follows is based on information compiled in Cohen, *Guide to Graduate Programs;* on the material in the NCPH's Committee on Professional Standards preliminary summary, *Analysis of the 1990–1991 Survey of Academic Programs in Public History* (Murfreesboro, TN: Center for Historic Preservation, 1992); and responses to a 1994 questionnaire completed by thirty of the fifty-seven programs listed in the 1990 NCPH guide at the request of the author of this chapter as part of an evaluation of the "Applied History Program" at the University of South Carolina.
17. Several sources for the comparison between academic and public history training are available. The brief study by Phyllis K. Leffler and Joseph Brent, *Public and Academic History: A Philosophy and Paradigm* (Malabar, FL: Robert E. Krieger Publishing Company, 1990) puts the issues involved into a thoughtful framework. Walter Rundell, Jr., *In Pursuit of American History: Research and Training in the United States* (Norman, OK: University of Oklahoma Press, 1970) examined and critiqued traditional historical training at about the time that the public history movement began; and Ann D. Gordon, *Using the Nation's Documentary Heritage: The Report of the Historical Documents Study* (Washington: National Historical Publications and Records Commission, in cooperation with the American Council of Learned Societies, 1992) more recently examined one aspect of that training.
18. Robert Paul Davis, comp. and ed., *A Guide to Museum Studies and Training in the United States* (Washington, DC: American Association of Museums, 1997).

PART II
VARIETIES OF PUBLIC HISTORIANS

INTRODUCTION

Readers may be puzzled by the decision to organize the essays in the section that follows alphabetically. Why not pair or group them to reflect similarities or connections? Otherwise, how is the reader to make sense of thirteen different "varieties" of public historians? First of all, we alphabetized the essays in order to avoid suggesting any hierarchy or career progression—all public history positions are created equal, and all are essential to the larger enterprise in which we are engaged. But that is not all. We also want to challenge readers to look at the field in different ways, to explore different connections, to think about the many and complex ways in which we connect across job descriptions. By avoiding easy categorizations, we can begin to address more fully the interconnections among public historians.

Consider, for example, manuscript curators and specialists. What other positions would you pair them with? One possibility might be archivists and records managers, whose responsibilities similarly focus on preserving and providing access to mainly two-dimensional or paper collections. Or perhaps working with manuscripts is more like working as a librarian or bibliographer, since the latter similarly focus on building collections and providing research services, albeit for published rather than unpublished materials. But what if, instead of focusing on the type of collection, we look at the processes of work. As the essays that follow will demonstrate, manuscript curators and specialists may have more in common with museum curators, who similarly develop collections with specific foci or concentrations through donations and purchase.

Or consider, for example, with whom to pair museum curators. As suggested above, the most similar might be manuscript curators and specialists, if you focus on the processes of work. But what if you shift to another side of the museum curator's work—exhibition development? In that case, the most similar occupation group might be interpreters and museum educators, who share the curator's commitment to using objects and collections to help the public better understand the past. That commitment in turn links both of those occupations to film and media producers and editors and publishers, whose principal orientation is to the public rather than to colleagues within the profession.

Rather than provide more examples, we urge you to read the essays yourself and look beyond the usual associations and connections to explore the complexity of the field. Look for commonalities and differences in collections or sources, skills, functions or processes of work, and end products or goals. Only then will all the pieces begin to fit together into the whole of public history.

MICHAEL J. DEVINE is director of the Harry S. Truman Presidential Library. He received his B.A. in history from Loras College and earned an M.A. and a Ph.D. in history from Ohio State University. Prior to his appointment to his current position, he served as director of the American Heritage Center at the University of Wyoming. He previously held positions with the Illinois State Historical Society and Illinois Historic Preservation Agency, Historic St. Mary's City, the Greater Cincinnati Consortium of Colleges and Universities, the Ohio Historical Society, and the Ohio American Revolution Bicentennial Advisory Commission. He has taught at Ohio University and several other institutions and has been a Fulbright lecturer in Argentina and Korea. Dr. Devine's professional activities include serving as president of the National Council on Public History and on the Wyoming Council for the Humanities and the Wyoming Parks and Cultural Resources Commission. The author of John W. Foster, Politics and Diplomacy in the Imperial Era, 1873–1917 *(1981), Dr Devine has also published numerous articles in such publications as the* American National Biography, History News, Ohio History, *and the* Pacific Historical Review.

ADMINISTRATORS: STUDENTS OF HISTORY AND PRACTITIONERS OF THE ART OF MANAGEMENT

Michael J. Devine

Historical agency or organization administrators of my generation often came into the profession by accident. Until the 1970s, there were no public history programs, and virtually all history graduate programs trained historians exclusively for careers as classroom teachers. The story of my entry into the field of public history administration is probably not too different from that of others.

In 1974, I was completing my doctoral dissertation and searching desperately, with no success whatsoever, for a teaching position in a university or small college. A colleague of mine at Ohio University, where I was teaching on a part-time and temporary appointment, asked if I would be interested in a job with the Ohio Historical Society as director of the Ohio American Revolution Bicentennial Advisory Commission. I told my well-intentioned friend that I was really interested in a teaching career, but I did thank him politely for the offer to be of assistance. He then told me what the job paid, and my level of interest picked up considerably—even though the only requirements for the administrator's position were a bachelor's degree in any field and a valid Ohio driver's license.

Looking back now, more than 20 years since I discovered administrative work almost accidentally, I find it difficult to think of how I could have had a more rewarding career. I found challenging employment in a variety of institutions in various parts of the country. I have enjoyed consulting on management issues in twenty different states for all sorts of museums and historical organizations, large and small, public and private. I have had the opportunity to put together teams of skilled professionals to work on fascinating projects and learned to scrape together financial resources from foundations, corporations, individuals, and government agencies for important endeavors. I have been involved in coordinating the development of more than $50 million worth of capital projects, worked on the initial efforts to advance National History Day from a local Cleveland, Ohio, history fair to a nationwide event, and initiated a multimillion dollar, fifteen-year project to document the legal career of Abraham Lincoln. Best of all, I have had numerous opportunities to work with extraordinarily talented and dedicated staff, caring volunteers and trustees, civic-minded public officials, and conscientious legislators. Of course, I have also encountered a few "turkeys" along the way.

Administrators (or directors) in historical agencies and organizations work at many different levels, and program size and complexity can vary widely. A program head or department manager of a large institution may have a much larger budget and staff than the executive director of a small museum. When I began my career with the American Revolution Bicentennial programs in Ohio, my staff consisted of one secretary. As director of the Illinois Historic Preservation Agency, I had a staff of more than 250 full-time equivalent positions with a budget in fiscal year 1991 exceeding $13 million. Yet the administrative tasks and challenges were very similar in both jobs.

HISTORIANS AS ADMINISTRATORS

What makes a good administrator or director? No foolproof formula exists, as far as I can tell. My observations and experiences lead me to believe that there are basically three essential elements for successful administration. First, directors must know the nuts and bolts of their agencies and possess basic skills in interpersonal communication, management, and budgeting. Second, directors must have a sense of vision, and it is, therefore, essential that administrators of history programs know history and know it well. Chief administrators create their institutions' overall programmatic courses because only directors communicate regularly with the board, staff, support groups, and various publics on a direct basis. Only directors are in the position to pull together the information needed to design their institutions' visions. Third, directors must serve as tireless, resourceful, effective principal spokespersons or advocates for that vision. In other words, they must be able and willing to lead.

A career in management is not for everyone. Some excellent historians make poor managers, just as many individuals who may be outstanding salesmen, engineers, or accountants become failures when placed in administrative positions in the corporate world. Those who love history and are trained as professional historians need to assess carefully their own personalities, skills, and career goals before accepting a career track that will lead to a life as an administrator. A great deal of time and energy must be expended to succeed in administrative work, and all good administrators find themselves on the road many nights. There are endless committee meetings, speaking engagements, and presentations to all types of audiences at all hours of the day and night (my least favorite are the "Sunshine Rotary" groups that have coffee and doughnuts at 6:30 A.M.). Schedules frequently are filled with after-hours receptions. Disputes among staff and embarrassing fiascoes always occur at the most inopportune moments—such as right before a legislative budget hearing, or just as the board is about to consider an extension of the chief administrator's contract. An extraordinarily successful university president, who was also a fine historian, once told me that a good administrator had to have the memory of an elephant, the cleverness of a fox, the strength of a lion, and the stomach of a goat.

Administrators of history institutions should be professional historians with advanced degrees, a master's degree or Ph.D. in history. Individuals with backgrounds in business, public relations, or fund raising lack the knowledge of history necessary to be persuasive and authoritative enough to advance the programs they are responsible for directing. Stephen F. Weil of the Smithsonian Institution has studied the problems of museum management as closely as anyone, and he argues that, in selecting a director, subject specialists with administrative ability will be more effective than the management generalist. Weil writes, "The director, after all, does more than simply direct staff and formulate the museum's various points of view. . . . He also acts as its principal spokesman. . . . He must speak in terms that can command the respect of its board, its patrons, its visitors, its community, its commentators and even its critics."[1] What Weil has written about the museum director applies to the administrators of any public history program.

While historians who serve as administrators need to understand history and know what makes good history, they must realize that they cannot do all the research, writing, or curating that they would like to do. Much has to be delegated to others. At the same time, however, it is easy for historians to get so caught up in administrative details that they forget they are historians. Good managers of historical agencies must maintain the balance between their management efforts and their professional interests. Historians in administrative positions must remain current on the literature. They must pursue writing opportunities and remain involved in professional associations. Only a good historian can recognize, appreciate, and reward outstanding staff work in an historical agency.

Those who direct historical programs quickly discover that management is an art rather than a science, and the art must be practiced with relentless effort. There exists a vast literature on all sorts of methods, from management by objectives (MBO) to total quality management (TQM), and some administrators find this useful. However, the real work of administrators is assembling the best people possible, motivating and directing them, securing the resources, building a productive work environment, evaluating results, rewarding accomplishments, and correcting problem areas. While effective administrators seek to build consensus, it is unrealistic to expect everyone to agree on everything all the time. Therefore, administrators must be capable of making sound decisions and taking decisive actions. This is where a knowledge of history, historical practices, and professional standards is essential. Administrators cannot make good choices and act in an affirmative manner if they do not understand what history programs are all about, are too far removed from the day-to-day operations, are unconcerned or uninformed about the details, complexities, and nature of programs, or are unable to discern good staff advice from bad. I have seen institutions where the chief administrator was enthusiastic about seminars in management science but failed to understand that listening, understanding, communicating, caring, and leading are actually arts that require constant practice. Some individuals have a talent for and interest in the arts; some do not. No management seminar can compensate for administrators' lack of knowledge, interest, and concern for the programs they are administering. No seminar on fund-raising techniques can assist administrators who cannot articulate in explicit detail the plans and aspirations of their programs with a sense of commitment and passion. No motivational programs, complete with 500-watt, high-powered speakers, can make up for administrators' failures to reward outstanding staff work, provide sound judgments concerning allocation of resources, or attend to staff problem areas in a manner that is both timely and appropriate. In other words, I have never seen a healthy, well-run history program where the chief administrator was not an energetic student of history and a faithful practitioner of the art of management.

FUNDING AND GOVERNANCE

Historians in administrative positions face a number of problems unique to the historical profession. Budgets always seem to be particularly bare boned, and historical agency administrators must devote a great deal of time and effort generating the financial resources necessary to keep their institutions moving in a positive direction. Governance presents another set of problems. Historical administrators are often governed by individuals or boards of individuals with little interest, sympathy, or understanding of the mission of an historical institution.

To deal with funding issues, history administrators must be capable of building solid partnerships, usually with support from both public and private sources. And the competition can be fierce. Fund raising may require appearances before legislative hearings, the governor's budget chief, county commissioners, city council, foundation officers, corporate executives, and individual philanthropists. It is not easy for one individual to make credible presentations to the myriad of individuals that historical agency administrators must address. Moreover, those holding the purse strings are often unsympathetic, or even downright hostile, and the drastic reductions in funding for the National Endowment for the Humanities have made matters even worse. Increasingly in the 1990s, corporate relations officers and foundation executives have focused their attention on social welfare issues such as homelessness, AIDS prevention and awareness, antipoverty programs, and crime prevention. They tend to see withholding support for history programs as not dangerous or at least not immediately threatening to the public well-being.

Meanwhile, some of those responsible for public funds tend to see support for historical programs as far less essential than finding jobs for their friends or filling potholes. When placed under a secretary of state, lieutenant governor, director of the Department of Economic Development, or the Commissioner for Tourism, the historical agency is viewed as less a priority than glitzy, high-profile, big-dollar programs housed in the same government department. When history's value is measured by the creation of jobs or the generation of tourism, disasters result. One extraordinarily difficult state budget director, with whom I did battle for six years, sincerely believed that the state's historic sites should be sold off, perhaps to the Disney Corporation. He was not in the least impressed that one of these magnificent sites, Cahokia Mounds, had been designated by the United Nations as one of only two World Heritage Sites in the United States (the other being the Grand Canyon). Meanwhile, he could see absolutely no justification for spending any public money whatsoever on the state's archives or the state's historical library. Fortunately, neither the governor nor the majority of the state legislators shared the state budget director's lack of vision. Still, for me it was a tough, uphill fight every year, requiring the well-orchestrated efforts of agency trustees, board members from various support groups, volunteers, and politically influential allies.

Boards of directors and trustees of historical agencies present a set of complex problems as well as fascinating opportunities for administrators. There are many conscientious, hard-working trustees of historical agencies, and they take their roles very seriously. They provide hundreds and hundreds of hours of volunteer time, help raise needed funds, frequently make sizable personal contributions, and serve as indispensable advocates for public history programs. Good board members also provide linkages with key external groups, buffer the institution from outside pressures, and serve as an important balance between staff enthusiasm and political and financial realities. Poor board members, on the other hand, interfere with management, avoid financial responsibilities, lack interest, fail to take their responsibilities seriously, or confuse their personal agendas with their duties as trustees.

Most chief administrative officers report to a council, board of trustees, or commission. Since, among other things, these governing bodies hire, evaluate, and compensate the chief administrator, working effectively with a governing board is absolutely essential. The trustees or board members hold the responsibility for the overall well-being of the institution, and the administrator (director, president, or CEO) serves as the individual employed by the governing body to implement its policies for advancing the institution's mission. The director or administrator does not establish policy, although it is the job of the administrator to set an agenda and guide the governing body with sound advice and solid information. In addition, the director manages operations (including all personnel issues and budgetary transactions) and implements the policies as established by the board.

Governing boards come in all imaginable sizes and formations. Most often, public historical agencies have boards appointed by an elected official (governor, mayor, secretary of state, or chairman of a county commission). Private institutions tend to have governing boards that are self-selecting or elected by the membership of the historical society. Frequently, one finds hybrid bodies where some of the members are appointed by an elected official and some are elected by the membership of a private historical society. It is not at all uncommon for boards to have *ex-officio* members, such as state legislators, school superintendents, or county commissioners. There are as many variations of boards as there are history programs, and all boards require the thoughtful attention of the administrator. Any administrator quickly learns that a conscientious, public-spirited, and knowledgeable board is worth its weight in gold, and a great chair is worth about ten times that in platinum.

Why do many historical agencies have less than stellar governing boards? Perhaps this is because many people mistakenly think history is like baseball—an interesting but not overly important subject about which nearly anyone can consider himself an expert. Everyone has seen a baseball game, maybe played in Little League, or even at a more advanced level. Likewise, nearly everyone has seen a historical documentary on television, read a history book, or taken a history class somewhere in the past. Unfortunately, many individuals with just the most superficial knowledge of history consider themselves experts, and the consequences are similar to the situations where owners of major league baseball teams try to make decisions that should be left up to the managers in the dugouts. Just like unwise owners of baseball teams, governors, legislators, city councils, and mayors who fail to see history as a serious enterprise often appoint less than qualified board members. A historical agency is seen as a "safe" institution where any political appointee with marginal competence, or no competence at all, can serve on the governing board without doing too much damage. Situations abound where weak, incompetent, or politically ambitious individuals do serious damage. This is perhaps the most difficult and perplexing problem with which historical agency administrators have to deal.

Here are a few horror stories that will have an all too familiar ring to most experienced historical agency administrators. Once, I consulted for a southern transportation museum where the board was extremely upset with its director because she had offended some volunteers who were old cronies of several board members. What offense had she committed? I discovered that she had insisted that the volunteers working on the model train layout put their empty beer cans away when they finished their evening's efforts. In another case where I served as a consultant, the trustees of a small Midwestern museum were prepared to fire their new director because she had the locks changed on the museum building. She did this, I discovered, because all thirty of the board members had keys, and several of them were in the habit of letting themselves in at all hours and rearranging items in the storage areas and on display. I observed a trustee of a major state historical society who, for more than two years, never attended a complete trustee meeting. He had a very personal agenda (and one that was in direct conflict with the institution's policies) for a site in his hometown, and he only sat in on those parts of the meetings dealing with his petty interests. Another trustee I had to deal with used to call me at all hours once or twice a month insisting that I fire one staff member or another. He frequently forgot after a week or so just who it was he wanted me to fire. By then, however, he had identified someone else he wanted canned.

Membership on governing boards is constantly changing because individual members usually are appointed or elected to serve for a specified term; and the coming and going of chairs, vice chairs, and members present challenges and opportunities to which the wise administrator must be always alert. Frequently, the administrator can discreetly influence the elevation of particularly strong, enlightened, and effective individuals to positions of authority. However, often an administrator is powerless in the changing of the guard and watches with chagrin as quality leadership is replaced through the process of normal rotation, election, or political appointment. Even worse are those situations where weak and ineffective leadership becomes entrenched and remains in place year after year. Institutional memories can be short, and some boards tend to focus on the problem of the day rather than the long term—despite the administrator's best efforts to emphasize the big picture. Perhaps this is why top administrators seldom rise through the ranks at one institution, and most chief executives of historical programs have significant experience in at least two or three organizations. Those entering careers in public history administration should be prepared to move geographically if they plan to advance their careers. This situation is by no means unique to the public history profession, and in contemporary American culture it is reflected in the hiring of school superintendents, college presidents, and corporate executives.

In situations where the chief administrator of a historical institution reports directly to an individual (mayor, lieutenant governor, director of commerce, university provost, or president), there is usually an advisory board of some kind to assist the administrator in setting policies and to aid in generating public and/or private support. Although these advisory boards do not have the statutory power or fiscal responsibilities of the governing boards of state agencies or government entities, they can and often do play extremely important roles. They can serve as buffers against the whims of insensitive or uncaring bureaucrats, they can be effective advocates with a wide range of constituents, and they can provide invaluable contacts in the foundation and corporate community. Usually, the administrator can have considerable influence, or even complete authority, in placing individuals with interest, commitment, and clout on advisory boards. The social, economic, and political leverage generated by such groups can often far surpass those which have statutory governing authority. In such cases, the advice of the advisory board can be considered as good as policy. No wise administrator would ever ignore the advice of a well-connected, highly motivated, and sincerely interested advisory body.

ADMINISTRATORS AND THE HISTORY PROFESSION

Sadly, our major professional associations, in particular the American Historical Association (AHA) and the Organization of American Historians (OAH), have taken virtually no interest in the management of our nation's museums, historical societies, state historic preservation offices, and state and federal historical offices and agencies. For decades, they have failed to advocate, in any forceful manner, for professionalism in the management of historical institutions and agencies. To a large extent, this is because organizations such as the AHA and OAH have been controlled by academics who, secure in their tenured positions, see themselves as the trainers of others who will serve as academics like themselves. They have viewed employment outside academe as tantamount to no employment at all. A friend of mine told me a story of an associate who worked for the Smithsonian Institution for many years. He was proud of the experience he had enjoyed in developing texts for blockbuster exhibits that were viewed by hundreds of thousands of people. At one point, this individual was asked to return to the institution where he had received his doctorate degree to talk to graduate students. After telling the graduate students enthusiastically about his life's work, one of his graduate professors came up to him following the presentation and said, "It's too bad you never found a job in the history profession. You would have been an outstanding historian."

In spite of the fact that we have had public history programs at graduate institutions for over two decades, many in the teaching profession still hold the view that historical agency administrators have somehow found employment *outside* of the profession. Incredible as it may seem, not a single history department in any Ivy League school or Big Ten university listed any faculty member with a specialization in public history as of 1996. Nor did public history appear in the listings for Johns Hopkins, the University of Chicago, North Carolina at Chapel Hill, or the University of California at Berkeley.[2] Clearly, major doctorate-generating graduate programs are still convinced that their precious graduates will find university teaching positions, despite the fact that nearly 35 percent of those receiving Ph.D.s in history as of 1993 found employment outside of academe (up from just 10 percent in 1977).[3] Preoccupied with desperately grasping on to the perks of the tenure system, historians in academe have been silent about issues involving professionalism in museums, government agencies, and state historic preservation offices. To my astonishment, I have discovered that even many university faculty who teach public history courses to graduate and undergraduate students have little or no interest in advocating for professionalism. Perhaps this is because many who instruct students in our university public history programs have no administrative experience outside of the university.[4] They have few contacts with administrators and are simply unfamiliar with the dynamics of administration. Therefore, they feel it is best to avoid any unpleasantness associated with a lack of professionalism in historical agency management, such as when an individual with only a bachelor's degree in journalism or agronomy is named to direct a major historical institution. Meanwhile, even the tiniest county library board insists on an M.L.S. degree when hiring someone to direct its program. I find it difficult to believe that law school faculty would sit on its hands if a Ph.D. in history with no formal training in a law school were named to a state supreme court. Would the medical profession accept a historian as Surgeon General of the United States?

Recently, a few hesitant and timid steps indicate that some change on the part of professional organizations may be underway. The National Coordinating Committee for the Promotion of History (NCC), housed in the AHA offices in Washington, D.C., monitors political developments in the nation's capital. The NCC has advocated, with some success, for continued federal funding for the National Archives and the National Endowment for the Humanities, has pushed for more professionalism within the National Park Service, and, in cooperation with other professional organizations, raised concerns over the appointment of a nonhistorian as Archivist of the United States. But NCC is only a one-person office. While both the National Council on Public History (NCPH) and the American Association for State and Local History (AASLH), an organization founded in the early 1940s by historians who felt the academe-based AHA did not serve their needs, provide forums for those employed in various public history endeavors, neither has practiced historical advocacy in a consistent or vigorous manner, and both organizations have avoided issues related to professional standards. In the late 1960s Congress envisioned accreditation of all cultural institutions as a requirement for receiving federal support; however, after three decades, only the American Association of Museums (AAM) has established professional standards and an accrediting process.

TRAINING AND QUALIFICATIONS

Public history programs at the graduate and undergraduate levels serve a useful purpose, although I question the obvious lack of administrative credentials of the many junior faculty who direct public history programs. Course work offering an introduction to the field of public history can provide an important component of any graduate program. Even those graduates who do go on to careers in university teaching would be well served by the exposure to museums, archives, historical libraries, historic site administration, private contracting, and historic preservation. In particular, internships appear to present an extraordinarily useful introduction to the wide world of history beyond the classroom, and graduate programs should seek to provide greater flexibility in their course and dissertation requirements to allow for internship experiences. However, the rigor of research and writing should never be sacrificed for an overload of course work in public history, because, time and time again, the public history administrator will rely on his or her background and training in history and historical methods to solve administrative problems.[5]

What are the best qualifications for those historians seeking careers in the administration of a historical program or agency? From my observation of dozens of historians who have been successful administrators, I believe there are several characteristics that all the best administrators of historical agencies have in common. Good administrators enjoy working with people; they are willing to listen to various points of view and work hard to resolve conflict. They are successful in building consensus among staff, governing boards, and funding entities, but they are also capable of making tough decisions and taking decisive action when necessary. The best administrators gain satisfaction from forming a work environment that enables others (researchers, curators, exhibit designers, preservation officers) to succeed in their work. They are willing to put in a great deal of time and effort; they are resilient, streetwise, patient, and persistent. Above all, they know history; they love history; and they want to share their enthusiasm for learning about the past with wide audiences.

CONCLUSION

Many years ago, when I was in graduate school, I happened to watch an interview on television in which one of the world's leading historians was asked for his definition of history. The venerable old historian responded, "History is stories about the past." At first, I was disappointed with this seemingly simplistic definition. However, the more I thought about it, the more I realized this is a precise definition of history. And, after many years, I have come to understand that administrators in the public history profession are really, at the very core of what they do, telling stories about the past.

NOTES

1. Stephen F. Weil, "The More Effective Director: Specialist or Generalist?" in Kevin Moore, ed., *Museum Management* (London and New York: Routledge, 1994), 278.
2. *Guide to History Departments in the United States and Canada, 1995–1996,* 21st Ed. (Washington, DC: American Historical Association, 1995).
3. Numbers supplied by Robert B. Townsend for a series of articles which appeared in the American Historical Association's *Perspectives* during 1997.
4. For more on this issue see Michael J. Devine, "Public History Beyond the Classroom," *OAH Council of Chairs Newsletter* 45 (June 1995): 2–4.
5. For an interesting report by two traditionally trained historians who found satisfying careers in private contracting, see Lee Anderson and Kathy Pennington, "Is There Life After Graduate School? Maybe in Public History," *Perspectives* 35 (January 1997): 9–10.

ROY H. TRYON is state archivist and records administrator, South Carolina Department of Archives and History. Both a certified archivist (CA) and a certified records manager (CRM), he earned his B.A. in history at Sacred Heart University, his M.A. in history at Fordham University, and his M.A. in library science at the University of Michigan. He previously served as Delaware state archivist and records administrator and on the staffs of the Balch Institute for Ethnic Studies, the State Historical Society of Wisconsin, and the Bentley Historical Library at the University of Michigan. His professional activities include service as the State Historical Records Advisory Board coordinator for both South Carolina and Delaware, as the president of the National Association of Government Archives and Records Administrators, as chair of the Council of State Historical Records Coordinators, and in various capacities for the Association of Records Managers and Administrators, the Society of American Archivists, and other organizations. Mr. Tryon's publications include Program Reporting Guidelines for Government Records Programs *(1987),* "The South Carolina Archives: A Decade of Change and Program Development," *The American* Archivist *(Spring 1997), and* Into the 21st Century: A Plan for South Carolina's Historical Records, 2000–2005 *(2000).*

ARCHIVISTS AND RECORDS MANAGERS

Roy H. Tryon

Archivists and records managers present a special challenge for anyone attempting to describe them together. Though both are concerned with the records of organizations and institutions rather than the papers of individuals, there are distinct differences in the practices and the ultimate goals of archivists and records managers. Generally speaking, archivists are concerned with noncurrent records and records managers with current ones. In both cases, the emphasis is on service, not historical scholarship, though of the two professions archivists have the closest affinity to history. Archivists and records managers often find themselves working together; indeed, in a growing number of situations, they are part of the same department within a parent institution or organization. Archivists and records managers work in all levels of government, businesses, colleges and universities, churches and other religious organizations, social and professional associations, and hospitals and social service and cultural organizations. As an archivist for an historical society and two special libraries, I have dealt with the records of a variety of institutions and organizations. My main experience, however, has been in government, coordinating statewide archives and records management programs.

DIFFERENT ROLES AND RESPONSIBILITIES

The goals of archivists and records managers are quite distinct from each other. For archivists, the goals are to ensure that the appropriate records (amounting usually to only 1 to 2 percent of the records created) are retained to document the history of the institution or organization, that those records are properly cared for and preserved, and that they are made available for research. Archivists cite their role in preserving the "institutional memory" as a justification of their importance to their parent agency.[1] Moreover, they serve a wide variety of researchers. Their clients may be a corporation's own policy makers researching past management decisions in evaluating a new course of action or individual citizens researching their family history among the records of a state or local government. A very small percentage of most archives' researchers are scholars.[2]

In contrast to archivists, records managers work to ensure that records are managed efficiently and effectively and that those records which are no longer needed are disposed of as soon as possible. Records managers cite their contribution to the organization's efficiency as justification for their importance to an organization or institution. They see themselves as part of a larger resource management effort that includes the organization's personnel, information systems, financial, and management support departments. Records managers develop programs that ensure that the right records are available when needed, that critical or vital records are identified and protected, that useless records are destroyed in a timely fashion to minimize the cost of storage and/or to protect the organization from litigation, and that proper practices and/or technologies are employed to store and retrieve needed records.

It might appear from these descriptions that archivists and records managers have very little in common and that, given the dissimilarity of their orientation and goals, they might even want to avoid each other's company. This sometimes happens. It is not uncommon to hear archivists lament that records managers are too concerned with destroying records; records managers often refer to the archivist's penchant for keeping too much and making demands on the records manager's time and resources.[3] In many situations, however, the two work together quite well.

In managing institutional and organizational records, archivists and records managers complement one another in their activities. Records managers ensure that records are well organized and accessible, that they have assigned retention periods, and that those retentions are adhered to. Archivists' role at the most basic level is to contribute to the development of appropriate retention periods, identifying the small percentage of records that may have continuing or enduring value. Archivists may also contribute to decision making on technology and storage options as they may affect still active but historically valuable records.

Archivists have a longer term perspective about record keeping and record use than do records managers. Archivists are more familiar with an organization's history and changes in operations and structure over time and also have a knowledge of the type of records that may interest researchers. Researchers use an organization's records in a much different fashion than do the office personnel that created and used them in their daily operations. It is this secondary value about which archivists are most concerned. Records managers' work is more rooted in the present and their concerns are the needs and requirements of the bureaucracy and its clients or customers.

Archivists working in conjunction with records managers reap many benefits that they would not have if working alone. Records managers' efforts to systematize the management of and access to records provide archivists with a comprehensive overview of an organization's holdings. That systematization also allows informed selection of those few records deemed of archival value, provides an opportunity to influence decisions about current records which may also be archival, and almost guarantees that records transferred to the archives will be in good order and accessible to researchers with a minimum of preparation. Working in cooperation with records management programs, archivists try to ensure that historical considerations are taken into account in the day-to-day management of records. Without the benefit of records management programs, archivists often fight uphill battles to select and preserve records of archival value.

Records managers reap benefits from working with archivists as well. Committed to providing service to an organization engaged in the hustle and bustle of meeting customer demands or serving clients or patrons, records managers necessarily focus their attention on the immediate needs of an organization rather than those of a future researcher or posterity. It is not that records managers do not care about the future, it is that the demands of their work require a focus on immediate records problems. Records managers are most often hired to make sure records in daily use are managed in the most economical and efficient fashion. The involvement of archivists with records managers in records retention decisions relieves records managers of the burden of making life and death decisions about records based solely on short-term operational requirements. Many institutions that have records management programs do not have archives staff or facilities. In cases such as these, it falls on the shoulders of records managers to act as the archives advocates. If unable or unwilling to do so, it is not uncommon for a records manager to call upon the services of an archivist from the outside to provide input into records retention decisions. In some cases, notably with businesses and professional or social service organizations, arrangements are made with an archives repository (e.g., a historical society or a special collections department of a university library) to accept their archival records.

THE HISTORY OF ARCHIVES AND RECORDS MANAGEMENT

Archivists and records managers have existed since the beginning of record keeping. In the ancient world, the word *archives* was used to designate any collection of written records, not just those of historical or enduring value. It derived from the Greek *archeion* and the Latin *archivum*, both meaning government office and its records.[4] In the United States, distinct professional identities for archivists and records managers are relatively recent. For archivists, it was an evolutionary process facilitated by successive studies and commissions of the American Historical Association (AHA) in the late nineteenth and early twentieth centuries. Many states established archival programs as a direct result of this activity. It was not until 1934, however, that Congress established the National Archives. By that time, the professional interests of archivists and historians had begun to diverge. Archivists' concerns with the management and accessibility of holdings, as distinct from the historian's concern with use and interpretation, led to the archivists breaking away from the AHA. They created their own professional organization, the Society of American Archivists (SAA), in 1936.[5]

Archivists in the federal and state governments charted new territory during the 1930s and 1940s, playing a pioneer role in dealing with the increasingly voluminous records created by modern government bureaucracies. Archivists also became increasingly conscious and articulate about the administrative importance of their work. The government programs and activities of the New Deal era and World War II created an explosion of records that demanded new approaches to management. At the federal level, National Archives staff developed the concepts of the record life cycle (from record creation through use, maintenance, and final disposition) and the key archival structural concepts of the record group and the record series. These core concepts have since been successfully applied to the records of a wide variety of institutions and organizations, not just to those of government. By the late 1940s the National Archives had consolidated and elaborated practices that continue to shape and inform the work of archivists and records managers today.[6]

As the National Archives developed these core archival concepts and practices in the 1930s and 1940s, concern for the better management of current records led to the birth of records management in its modern form. Because archivists were turning their attention to organizing records for research, producing inventories and indexes and guides for their use, and coping with massive storage and preservation problems associated with historically valuable records, they had less time to deal with the day-to-day responsibility for records early in the records' life cycle. A subspecialty developed within the archives field which concentrated at first on separating the "wheat from the chaff" of records through conducting inventories and development of retention schedules. Eventually, just as archivists had split from the historical profession over a divergence in primary concerns and interests, records managers split from the archivists. They left the SAA in 1956 to form the American Records Management Association (ARMA). Today this acronym stands for the Association of Records Managers and Administrators International, with chapters throughout the United States and around the world.[7]

Records managers in the 1940s ventured well beyond conducting inventories and drafting retention schedules. Their primary goal was the improvement of records use, maintenance, and disposition. Over time they, too, elaborated a number of practices to support their primary goals. These include files and forms management; records centers for the intermediate storage of semiactive and inactive records; vital records identification and protection; and micrographics. Beginning in the 1950s, records managers found a very receptive audience in businesses across the country. Much of this interest was cultivated by the National Records Management Council, established in 1947, which promoted records management in the private sector. Companies and corporations which were not susceptible to arguments about preserving history were interested in becoming more efficient. As American society became more litigious, companies were also concerned that they not keep records any longer than absolutely necessary. Records managers, while not abandoning government, definitely had a wide audience to play to, and with this wide audience came many employment opportunities and tremendous growth in and development of the profession.[8]

During this explosion of growth in the records management field, archivists were not left behind. The 1950s through the 1980s witnessed tremendous growth in the number and type of archival repositories. Some corporations even started archives programs! Perhaps the most dramatic growth in archival programs has occurred in colleges and universities. This is reflected in the transformation of SAA from an organization greatly influenced and directed by members from federal and state archives programs to one in which the interests and concerns of college and university, religious, business, and other types of archives are well represented and reflected in association activities. In the meantime government archives programs at all levels, while not completely abandoning SAA, have the National Association of Government Archives and Records Administrators (NAGARA) in which to pursue interests and concerns peculiar to government settings.

For both archivists and records managers, the changes over the past three decades in the number and complexity of organizations and institutions and in the nature of record keeping, have required a great deal of adaptation on the part of the members of both professions. The support and assistance of national-level organizations such as SAA, ARMA, and NAGARA have certainly been a critical factor in the development of new programs in a wide variety of settings.

WORKING AS AN ARCHIVIST OR RECORDS MANAGER

Many factors influence the work of archivists and records managers. The work setting is of primary importance. Is it a combined, separated, or stand-alone program? Is the program a large one, with significant numbers of staff, or one in which most of the work is performed by one or a few individuals? What are the nature and extent of the records to be managed? One matter that both archivists and records managers have in common is that there are many routine duties involved in their work, requiring the employment of clerical and other technical support staff. Most archivists and records managers therefore find themselves in the additional role of supervisor and planner.

Businesses and even most government agencies focus on records management instead of archives. In such situations, the records management program might be a well-developed one that deals with all of the organization's records from creation to ultimate disposition, or it may focus only on certain aspects of records management, e.g., developing retention schedules or providing training in files maintenance. If there is any concern for the historically valuable records, the organization might either delegate that responsibility to the records manager, employ an archives consultant, or seek outside assistance or support (e.g., a state government agency and a local government would look to the state archives and a business might seek assistance from a historical society) to properly identify and secure those records. As an archivist for a state historical society and for a special library, for example, I would sometimes advise institutions about how to identify and care for archival records destined for eventual transfer to my repository. I found that the most useful instruction I could give was on basic records management practices, such as how to file and store records. This help not only enhanced current operations, but also ensured complete and well-organized future archival transfers. Situations like these point up the advantage to archivists in becoming familiar with at least the basics of records management.

Colleges and universities, religious groups, social service and cultural organizations, and governments are most likely to have the greatest concern for the archival aspect of their operations. Within these organizations the actual placement of archivists and records managers ultimately affects their work. For instance, in a university, the archival and records management functions could be combined within a single department or the functions could be divided, with the archives as part of the special collections department of the library and the records management operation a part of the university's support operations or information systems office. Most states combine archives and records management within the same agency, though several do split responsibility, with archives often residing in state historical societies and records management in departments of general services or administration. At the federal level, responsibilities are divided between the National Archives and Records Administration and the General Services Administration. In businesses, the functions are often separate, with the archives function, for example, in the public relations or corporate library area and records management in an administrative support area or in the finance or legal departments. Regardless of their placement and relationship to each other, however, archivists and records managers each have some core activities and expected products of their work.

Though archivists can perform their work without the help of records managers, they can never be as effective as when there are well-functioning records management programs in place. From the perspective of archivists, the role records managers play in facilitating the transfer of historically valuable records to archives is most important. Records managers, however, see the transfer of archival records as only an incidental byproduct of their more wide-ranging activities.

In records management, the most basic and traditional activities are the conducting of records inventories and the subsequent development of records retention schedules. These form the basis for virtually everything else. As with archivists, the basic unit of attention for records managers is the records series (a group of identical or related records that are normally used and filed as a unit). A records inventory of offices often involves inspecting files and working with office staff in completing inventory forms to capture such information as the name of the series; its purpose and how it is used; relationship to other organizational records; the time span, quantity, physical description, and projected growth of the series; and whether the records are vital to resuming operations in the event of a disaster. Based on this information, records retention schedules can be drafted to describe the record series and to assign an appropriate period for its retention. It is at this point, referred to as "appraisal," that records managers need the input of others, not only from those who use the records on a regular basis but also from other potentially interested parties, including management, legal and fiscal officers, and archivists. This consultation may be an informal one-on-one contact or a more elaborate committee meeting held on a regular basis.[9]

The resulting records retention schedule serves as the basis for all other records management services. A comprehensive inventory and records scheduling effort will result in the identification of all of an organization's information assets, regardless of whether their format is paper, microfilm, or electronic media. Based on this information, records managers will know what and when records can be destroyed; when records are inactive or semiactive and if they should be transferred to a records center for interim storage; what records need to be microfilmed or scanned for more efficient storage and/or retrieval; what records need special protection (including duplication) because they are vital to resuming operations in the event of a disaster; what records should be modified or eliminated in various offices because they overlap or duplicate each other; and, finally, what records have archival value and at what point they should be transferred to the archives.[10]

As important as inventories and retention schedules are for records managers, they are only the beginning of their work. It is in ensuring that the retention schedules are properly implemented that much of their labor is directed. This could include educating management about the importance of records management, training office staff to carry out retention instructions and set up and manage filing systems, reviewing and

Records created by organizations and institutions are sometimes stored improperly and under poor conditions. Archivists and records managers rely on records inventory and retention scheduling to determine which records to keep and which to destroy. The records selected for retention are then stored under proper environmental conditions in suitable containers on metal shelving, ensuring their availability for future reference. *Courtesy of the South Carolina Department of Archives and History.*

approving filing equipment and information technology purchases, operating a records center (to store and provide occasional access to
records), dealing with contractors and vendors of microfilming and scan-
ning services (or overseeing such in-house operations), managing internal forms development and distribution (since many records are forms),
and participating in decision making about automation (not only of the
records management function, but also as it relates to the organization's
other functions).

Successful records managers have a good understanding of the technical side of records management and keep up with the latest innovations
in practices and technology. Even more important, however, is their ability to work well with people and to persuade others of the usefulness of
the records management program and its objectives. This skill is crucial
at every level: the records analysts must enlist the support of office staff
in completing inventories; records center staff provide daily services to
individual offices; records managers work closely with information systems staff in deciding on technology applications; and records managers
must coordinate high-level review and executive approval of records retention decisions. A good example from my own experience of this combination of the technical and the personal aspects of the job is the role I
played in planning and implementing a computer-assisted microfilm retrieval system for a state motor vehicle department. Not only did I have
to deal with retention decisions and personnel issues, but I also had to
work with the director of the motor vehicle department regularly on system selection and project workflow issues and problems to ensure a successful ongoing project. Of the two abilities, technical or personal, the
latter is at least as important as the former. The best of technical skills will
be of no use if the records manager cannot convince others of the importance of his or her services.[11]

While records managers are concerned with all of an institution's or
organization's records and their efficient management and use, archivists focus on that small percentage of records that has archival value. To
get at those records, however, they must be active participants in records
managers' inventorying and scheduling work. This does not mean that
archivists actually do the work, but they must be prepared to contribute
to decision making on such issues as the concentration of the inventory
effort and providing useful, timely, and well-justified input on archival retention decisions. (If there is no records management program, however, an archivist will have to conduct his or her own inventory or "survey" of records.) It is here at the schedule development phase that
archivists play perhaps their most important role. Here they identify
records of archival value and allow all others to be destroyed after a spec-

ified retention period. This archival "appraisal" process is much different than the one employed for records management purposes.

There is no formula to guide archivists in appraising records for archival value. The process is considered as much of an art as a science and relies a good deal on archivists' understanding of an organization's origins, development, and mission, as well as their understanding of research use and trends. Ideally, archivists have opportunities to review all retention decisions and to divide the "wheat from the chaff." In some cases, archivists will make decisions about a series of records that are old and are no longer being created. Most of the time, however, they are asked to render decisions on record series that are still in active use and will continue to be created into the indefinite future. Archivists will often make decisions about vast quantities of records, some of which might be comprised of formats other than traditional paper files, including photographs, maps, drawings, audio and video tapes, and computer tapes and diskettes. In the process of identifying such records for the archives, they may also provide input into records management plans to increase operational efficiency by reformatting certain records series onto microfilm or electronic media that might affect its suitability for long-term retention in the archives.

Archivists make appraisal decisions to document significant policy decisions and activities of the organization. A particular record series that no longer has any immediate value to the office that created it may nevertheless have considerable importance later on in proving that an action was performed or a decision made. (This might be necessary in defense against a legal action or to chart the impact of certain practices over time to make informed changes in policy.) Other considerations also come into play in the appraisal process. These include the long-term public relations value of certain series of records; the broader research potential that some series may possess beyond the reason for which they were originally created (e.g., county government probate files created to facilitate the settling of estates are also an extremely important source of information for genealogists, and company product files created in the developmental phase may later be useful to study the effectiveness of sales techniques); legal issues regarding restrictions and public access; the continuing or enduring value of records for the organization; and, in the case of government, ensuring accountability to its citizens (e.g., in the minutes of policy-making meetings, in the files of agency heads, and in the records of functions and activities that significantly impact citizens). In this process archivists may consult others before making a decision. They might work through records managers or go directly to the office of origin to actually inspect the records. They might consult with other archivists on staff or at other institutions, or with historians and other researchers. It should be understood here that appraisal of a particular records series takes into account its place not only within the institution but also its importance within the larger universe of records created and, possibly, in relation to others of its type. In the final analysis, archivists' selection of records constitutes a corporate "memory."[12]

The decisions made at the time of appraisal affect virtually all of the succeeding archival activities. It is often impossible to keep all of the records that might have archival value. Oftentimes, a series of records may be too extensive or difficult to use to justify employing the archives' limited resources for storage and access relative to other records series. Here archivists engage in a form of triage in deciding the fate of records.[13] Once the decision is made through the retention scheduling process to transfer records to the archives, preparations must be made to accession them (i.e., transfer physical and legal custody), arrange and describe them for accessibility, perform any necessary conservation treatment or reformatting to microfilm, store in appropriate containers on shelving in an environmentally controlled and secure facility, provide reference service on them, and conduct outreach and exhibit activities.[14]

Though all of these postappraisal activities are important, two of them require some elaboration. Arrangement and description lie at the heart of what archivists do. Records are useless to anyone unless they are in good order and access is facilitated by a finding aid. While organizational records often do not require much physical sorting to make them useful for researchers, there are times when the order of office records is not adequate or apparent and archivists must impose some order on the series. This is usually a hierarchical arrangement of records series and files under an appropriate record group or subgroup. It is most important to archivists that records of the same office be maintained together (referred to as provenance) and kept in as close to their original order as possible. In most cases much of archivists' work is to ensure that the material in the files is in good condition (e.g., staples and paper clips pulled, fading documents copied) and placed in labeled, acid-free folders and boxes. Related to this activity, much of which can be performed by clerical assistants, archivists are concerned with learning enough about the records to draft finding aids for researchers. There are many kinds of finding aids, from simple box and content listings to more elaborate descriptions of entire record groups which include name and subject indexes.[15]

Just as records managers are concerned with automating many of their functions, archivists are making great strides in automating access to and management of their holdings. Facilitating this work is the Machine-Readable Catalog for Archives and Manuscripts Control (MARC-AMC) format, the employment of which ensures consistency in description for automated access and for information-sharing over national computer networks. The work in most archives today presumes at least a familiarity with, if not a working knowledge of, the MARC-AMC format and its related standards.[16]

Regardless of what kind of finding aid is produced, the primary goal of archivists is to make their holdings available to researchers. Whether in hard copy (typed lists or a full-length published guide to all the holdings) or available over an in-house computer system and/or a national database, the provision of finding aids is only the first step in providing access. Even the most comprehensive finding aid system will not replace archivists who have actually worked with the records, as they have in-depth knowledge of their scope, contents, and relationship to other records in the archives. Like records managers who deal with office personnel and managers, archivists must have good interpersonal skills in order to provide successful reference service. Unlike records managers, however, who will have little difficulty moving from one organization to another even after a brief period of time, archivists' value to their institutions often lies in the knowledge they have acquired about the archives' holdings. This can be developed only over an extended period of years.

PROFESSIONAL ISSUES AND CONCERNS

The issue of most concern to archivists and records managers is the impact of information technology on record keeping. The dramatic increase in the use of computers in the workplace over the past two decades has resulted in more paper files (despite claims that the computer would herald the paperless office) and in significant changes in record formats and systems. These developments directly challenge the ingenuity and resourcefulness of practitioners in both professions. For records managers, the focus is on how to manage the records on magnetic media as well as those ever-expanding paper files. For archivists, the focus is on how to cope with increasing amounts of historically valuable records which are being produced on media with limited life expectancy and hardware and software that are subject to rapid obsolescence. The proliferation of information technology in the modern office affects not only how archivists and records managers perform their duties but their professional identities as well. The development of the electronic office is blurring the distinctions between information professionals.

At the same time that archivists and records managers are grappling with the challenges and opportunities posed by information technology, their institutions and organizations are undergoing other fundamental

Electronic records pose a major challenge to archivists. New approaches and skills are required to ensure that historically valuable information generated by the new information technology is available for research in the future. *Courtesy of the South Carolina Department of Archives and History.*

changes. Many changes in operations and practices and in downsizing of staff and programs directly affect archivists and records managers. In such an environment it is more important than ever for both archivists and records managers to demonstrate their value and importance to their organization. This demonstration can take many forms. Records managers may make regular reports to top management on the impact of their activities on overall institutional effectiveness, institute regular training sessions for managers and office staff, publish newsletters on records management services, and seek membership on teams developing new information management systems or databases. Archivists are also frequently engaged in similar activities, including providing local and national network access to holdings information; developing publications, exhibits, and other promotional activities; and ensuring that staff and management are aware of public relations, legal, and operational usefulness of the archives to the institution or organization. Archivists in state and local governments and other nonprofit organizations are increasingly engaged in fundraising to obtain grants for special projects or to supplement their regular monies. Indeed, a significant amount of my time as an archivist has been spent in applying for grant funds, primarily from the National Historical Publications and Records Commission and the National Endowment for the Humanities, and in administering these funded projects.

PROFESSIONAL NETWORKS

There are some significant differences between archivists and records managers regarding the other information professionals with whom they are in regular contact. Records managers have a strong interest in management and technology issues which is reflected in their often close working relationships with managers, other information management staff (e.g., data-processors and office systems staff), and vendors of records and information management software, equipment, and services. Regular contact with all three types is important for the continued effectiveness of most records managers. On the other hand, the close professional relationships enjoyed by archivists have traditionally been with librarians and historians. The connection with librarians, in particular, is often quite close in many organizations where there is a library function as well as an archives one. The pervasive use of the MARC-AMC format in archival description requires adherence to standards that have their origin, development, and sanction in the library community.

SPECIALIZED EDUCATION/CONTINUING EDUCATION OPPORTUNITIES

Archival and records management education requirements are very different from one another. There are master's level programs for archivists in a number of schools of library and information science and departments of history, or sometimes as part of a joint program in public history. Most provide courses and require a practicum or internship. Such degree programs have become a major route for entry into the pro-

fession in recent years. Many still enter the field with knowledge acquired through other avenues, however, such as attendance at the National Archives' Modern Archives Institute, or workshops, sessions, and
publications sponsored by SAA, NAGARA, regional, and other archival
associations. Though changes are apparent as a result of the challenges
posed by information technology, most successful applicants for archival
positions now have master's degrees in history or in library science as the
minimum educational requirement.[17] As an indication of how important the education issue has become, in 1994 SAA approved guidelines
for the development of a curriculum for a master of archival studies
 degree and is now working on guidelines for post-appointment and continuing education.

In contrast, records managers have fewer well-developed educational
requirements and opportunities. While many individuals with history degrees, such as myself, have moved into records management from an
archives background, there is no required educational credential to become a records manager.[18] In recent years, more schools of library and
information science and some business departments have been offering
graduate level courses in information and records management, but
these are usually isolated course offerings and are not part of a larger
records management degree program. In addition to these opportunities, there are other avenues for initial and continuing education for
records managers. These include an ARMA-sponsored correspondence
course and the sessions at the annual meetings of ARMA and other related professional associations, such as the Association for Image and Information Management.

Affecting the nature and content of educational opportunities for
both archivists and records managers are programs for certifying individuals in both professions. Though not required for entry-level positions, certification requirements do indicate the base of knowledge and
experience necessary in both professions. They also indicate the acceptable education level for archivists and records managers. For
archivists, though individuals with a bachelor's degree are eligible for
certification through 1999, the Academy of Certified Archivists requires
applicants thereafter to have master's degrees. The Institute for Certified Records Managers currently cites the bachelor's degree as the minimum educational prerequisite for certification but allows substitution
of two years of qualifying experience for each year of undergraduate education that an applicant may lack. Both certification programs have experience and examination requirements as well ongoing certification
maintenance processes.

FUTURE DIRECTIONS

The balance of this decade and beyond will be filled with a great number of challenges and opportunities related to the ever-increasing rate of technological change. A decade ago, the Internet and the World Wide Web were not even available for public use. Today, archivists and records managers are working to exploit their potential for wider dissemination of information and publications, for public exchange of professional knowledge and opinions, and for display and public use of archival holdings online. What might the next decade bring?

While it is impossible to predict what the specific situations will be like ten years from now, it is possible to indicate the general direction archivists and records managers will take in the foreseeable future. Increasingly, they are working more closely with each other (and with other information professionals) to ensure that records of vital and continuing value are properly identified and managed. The major impact of information technology on record-keeping practices has begun to blur the traditional relationship between archivists and records managers.

Archivists, in order to be effective, can no longer simply wait until records in electronic formats are transferred to the archives according to a records schedule. Archivists are already becoming involved much earlier in the record's life cycle to ensure that archival concerns are addressed as near as possible to the point of creation. Otherwise, by the time such records are ready for transfer to the archives, it will be too late to address such concerns as incompatible format, hardware/software dependence or obsolescence, and lack of documentation. Archivists are also making major strides in the use of the Internet and the World Wide Web. This will surely continue, with significant portions of archives holdings available online and with electronic mail facilitating reference services at many institutions.

Records managers will also have to conduct a difficult balancing act for some time to come between records in paper and those in electronic formats. It is important that no one, whether archivist or records manager, cut himself or herself off from the new technologies. Indeed, it will be difficult to find anywhere to hide. The next decade should be full of significant changes in both professions, including a questioning of some fundamental concepts and basic practices, a reorientation of traditional duties and responsibilities, and, possibly, a redefinition of what is required for entry-level archivists and records managers. The most interesting times are yet to come.

NOTES

1. Richard Cox, *Managing Institutional Archives: Foundational Principles and Practices* (Westport, CT: Greenwood Publishing Co., 1992), 4–7.
2. James O'Toole, *Understanding Archives and Manuscripts* (Chicago: Society of
   American Archivists, 1990), 46.
3. Robert L. Sanders, "Archivists and Records Managers: Another Marriage in
   Trouble?" *Records Management Quarterly* 23 (April 1989): 12–14, 16.
4. Cox, *Managing Institutional Archives,* 18.
5. O'Toole, *Understanding Archives and Manuscripts,* 33–35.
6. Ibid., 36–37.
7. Ibid., 37–38.
8. J. Michael Pemberton, "U.S. Federal Commissions and Committees and the
   Emergence of Records Management," *Records Management Quarterly* 30 (April
   1996): 66–68; Mary F. Robek, Gerald F. Brown, and David O. Stephens, *Information and Records Management: Document-Based Information Systems* (New
   York, NY: Glencoe Publishing Co. [McGraw-Hill], 1995), 21.
9. Robek, et al., *Information and Records Management,* 56–61.
10. For an introduction to the full range of records management activities, see
    Robek, et al., *Information and Records Management.*
11. Carl Wiese, "Selling Records Management—Do You Know Your Product?"
    Records Management Quarterly 20 (July 1987): 18–20, 22–23.
12. Cox, *Managing Institutional Archives,* 49–82; F. Gerald Ham, *Selecting and Ap-
    praising Archives and Manuscripts* (Chicago: Society of American Archivists,
    1993), 34–36, 51ff.
13. Ham, *Selecting and Appraising,* 58–60.
14. For an introduction to the range of postappraisal archival activities, see Bruce
    W. Dearstyne, *The Archival Enterprise: Modern Archival Principles, Practices, and
    Management Techniques* (Chicago: American Library Association, 1993), 127ff.
15. For a detailed treatment of archival arrangement and description, see Fred-
    eric M. Miller, *Arranging and Describing Archives and Manuscripts* (Chicago: So-
    ciety of American Archivists, 1990).
16. Dearstyne, *Archival Enterprise,* 138–42, 148–49.
17. O'Toole, *Understanding Archives and Manuscripts,* 44.
18. J. Michael Pemberton, "Education for Records Managers: Rigor Mortis or
    New Directions?" *Records Management Quarterly* 25 (July 1991): 52–53, and
    "Records Management Education: In Pursuit of Standards," *Records Manage-
    ment Quarterly* 28 (July 1994): 58, 60–62.

JANNELLE WARREN-FINDLEY is associate professor of history and codirector of the Graduate Program in Public History at Arizona State University. She earned her B.A. in English and French from Texas Women's University and her M.Phil. and Ph.D. in American studies at George Washington University. Dr. Warren-Findley began her career at the National Archives before establishing private practice as a public historian in Washington, D.C. Prior to joining the faculty at Arizona State, she worked on the Department of Defense's Legacy Resource Management Program. She continues to work as a historical consultant for projects in cultural resources management and historic preservation. She has held Fulbright fellowships at the University of Goteborg, Sweden, and at Victoria University, Wellington, New Zealand. She has served as president of the National Council on Public History, on the NCPH board of directors and the council of the Organization of American Historians, and as chair of the board of editors of The Public Historian *and of the public history committee of the OAH. Dr. Warren-Findley's publications include* Human Heritage Management in New Zealand in the Year 2000 and Beyond *(for which she won the first Michael Robinson Award from NCPH);* Training Cold Warriors *(1997); and contributions to* From Engineering Science to Big Technology: Collier Trophy Winners at the NACA and the NASA *(1997),* Exploring the Unknown: Selected Documents in the History of the U.S. Civil Space Program, *and other volumes.*

CONTRACT HISTORIANS AND CONSULTANTS

Jannelle Warren-Findley

A parody of a popular country-western song, "Mamas, don't let your babies become consultants," hung for years on my home-office wall. Seated in my basement office, surrounded by high-tech equipment, good coffee, and classical music, as the Virginia suburbs filled up with ice, snow, and frustrated commuters, I knew the song was wrong. Being in private practice as a historian had both financial and workplace rewards, and I would recommend it to anyone.

On the other hand, it is obvious that I now have a job, and my consulting activities are restricted to a few hours a week. While the rewards of consulting are very real, the drawbacks are also, and it is important to be attuned to changes in one's life or situation or one's own particular psychology which may make working as a consultant less desirable than it is for others. I will try to make clear below both the advantages of historical consulting for individual historians and some of the symptoms of bailout time, while proposing strategies for dealing with them.

My focus will be on the considerations and techniques particular to historians who want to go into private practice rather than to propose a how-to-set-up-a-business essay here. The literature, both in book form and on the World Wide Web and the Internet, that is available to help with the business, marketing, and administrative parts of the effort is voluminous. Classes that address all the aspects of running a small business or a home-based business abound at junior and community colleges and in specialized training programs. Take them, read them, and heed them for the business aspects of this are complex and crucial to your success. But there are particular considerations for those trained to do historical work that will shape the consulting you do.

As the twentieth century draws to a close, the employment situation in which professional historians find themselves appears to be unprecedented. Graduate students trained for work in the academy find that it is undergoing profound change, especially in state university systems. Participants at major historical conventions hear over and over, "the professorate is dead." As higher education leaders debate abolishing the tenure system, instituting workload requirements, and redefining the roles of university faculty, university teachers face the prospect of dramatic changes in their work. Short-term contracts, more part-time faculty without benefits, and revised criteria for employment loom in the future. If professional training is to survive at all, as that job market shrinks and loses much of its allure, the training of graduate students must change to include working outside the academy.

At the same time, businesses are downsizing, and governments at all levels, including the federal government, are reinventing themselves. The Department of Agriculture regrettably closed its history office; the National Park Service recently abolished 25,000 positions; and the Bureau of Land Management has consolidated cultural resources management (CRM), recreational activities, wilderness management, and Native American issues in the office of the historian who was originally chief of cultural resources. But there are still various activities needed by businesses and mandated to government agencies by law that must be done. Consultants, for many administrators, are the perfect answer: they're far cheaper than full-time employees with benefits; they can be task- or project-specific; and they have contracts limited in time and cost. Professional historians will be needed in many of these operations.

Thus there are potential opportunities everywhere for historians who want to work on their own and make a living at doing research, writing, and, often, teaching outside of the traditional classroom. There are a number of steps that you must take before you bid on your first big Corps of Engineers contract, however, because once you bid, it is extremely difficult to back out of the process.

A major step in preparing to become a historian in private practice is to inventory your personal assets. These fall into two categories: your professional skills and your psychological makeup. Each is important enough to discuss separately.

ASSESSING YOUR PROFESSIONAL SKILLS

To assess your professional skills, you should make lists under several categories and think hard and very broadly about what might fit into each. The first category is the subjects in which you specialized as a student and scholar. You should break the categories down, so that you can say, for example, that you specialized in the American West but, within that subject area, you focused on twentieth-century power generation issues, Native American cultural issues in the Southwest, and urban history. Go back through the papers that you did for graduate classes and see whether any of them might help support your argument for a basic level of expertise in various areas. Anything you have presented at a meeting or published is worth looking at closely, since some measure of peer review is often required before your work can be included. Major work, such as a thesis or Ph.D. dissertation, will indicate particular expertise that you may be able to mine for this inventory. You need to remember, however, that such expertise can be described in a number of different ways, depending on how you want to shape your consulting career. A good exercise is to write down as many different ways of describing the same body of work as you can think of: American West, twentieth century, urban, Southwest development, coal, water, nuclear energy, and so forth. Keep that list in your computer to build project-specific resumes and project proposals.

The second category for your professional skills cuts the training process somewhat differently. Think about the kinds of research that you did in your graduate work. Where did you do that research—in a federal archives, for example? Then you should note that you have expertise in researching federal records. You may have worked with laws or legislation in the research process and that may qualify you to research laws or legislation for pay. Perhaps you used historic photographs to help explain something about your research topic. You should note that you know how to handle and interpret historic photographs. Expertise in the analysis and interpretation of local records of various kinds may be just the sort of experience that an administrator at a local agency or historical society needs. Did you interview people for your thesis? Skills in oral history or interviewing techniques can be listed. The process of doing research is a large part of what contract administrators want to pay you to do, and it is really critical to be as clear as possible about the ways that you can help them complete the projects for which they are seeking help. You should never claim to do something that you really cannot do, but a creative look at all the work you have done so far will probably reveal that you can quite legitimately claim a range of research and writing skills.

The third category of professional training includes work experiences. If you have taught at any level, you can argue that you have skills related to public outreach and communication in addition to teaching experience. Computer and other media skills translate easily from the teaching workplace to the consulting one. Administrative skills in one area show the ability to administer contracts in another. Editing projects show the ability to edit contract work. Summer jobs, internships, and part-time work while you go to graduate school may help you create a talents list that potentially matches what a contract administrator is hoping to find.

The fourth category includes any specialized workshops or undertakings. In our public history program, for example, we sponsor specialized workshops in a range of topics, from archival issues to publishing programs in museums to Section 106 (of the National Historic Preservation Act) compliance, among others. None of these makes one an instant expert, but such efforts do show that one's level of familiarity with some of the issues to be addressed by contract work is higher than the more traditionally trained graduate historian. If you have taken such workshops or other kinds of specialized training, make sure you count it as you tot up your skills and resources.

Finally, look carefully over the lists of marketable skills and see if there are areas of interest in which you lack training or experience but in which you might want to work. For instance, you have noticed that historians who do research related to Native American land and water cases get paid very well and you would like to work in that area. You are a western Americanist but have specialized in the urban West and paid little attention to the specifics of tribal history. Figure out how to shore up those areas of weakness—concentrated readings, night courses at your local university, or law courses at your local law school, if they permit nondegree students to enroll. Or you know that it will be important in the long run for someone interested in cultural resources management to understand how archaeology is practiced, since archaeologists dominate the field of CRM in the United States. Find a summer field school to attend or sign up for a federal agency's on-site volunteer programs. Or you realize that you need to know something about architecture if you are a historian who wants to practice historic preservation. Call your local chapter of the American Institute of Architects, for example, and ask about training or internship opportunities. Filling out your practice with this kind of additional training will often pay for itself very quickly and gives you confidence in your proposals and your bids.

Sometimes, however, the unpredictable knowledge or abilities are what get you started—that's how I got started. I landed my first consulting job because I was born and grew up in Arizona. The Salt River Project in Phoenix needed a researcher in Washington, D.C., who was familiar with researching federal records but who also knew enough about Arizona place names not to stray far afield geographically in the Bureau of Reclamation records. I lived in the Washington, D.C., area; had been on the staff of the National Archives and Records Service (now Administration) for a brief period before I entered graduate school; and had learned how to do research in those records efficiently—how to think like a government agency rather than like a library browser. Moreover, as a staff member at NARS, I had worked in the records of the Department of the Interior, of which the Bureau of Reclamation is an agency.

But the clincher for that first assignment was that I knew, because of social studies classes in both elementary school and high school, when I was looking at a place name in the vicinity of Phoenix as opposed to one outside of Flagstaff or Tucson or Yuma. When asked if I could do the job, I answered "yes" with little doubt that this combination of skills and knowledge would enable me to find the materials needed.

That first experience of paid research in federal records led to my establishing the particular expertise that I would build on over the fifteen years I worked as a historian in private practice. I started out as a researcher of federal records. I discovered that I enjoyed searching out materials in the National Archives and its branches, and that my archival experience could bring me work. Through the Salt River Project assignment, I became familiar with the Bureau of Reclamation and other water-related records. That familiarity led to a good deal of legal research concentrated on water rights and land issues in the arid West for the next three years. One set of lawyers would pass my name on to another set, so that I worked with large projects such as the Navajo-Hopi land case and smaller efforts such as investigations of the decisions surrounding the early treaties between the Yakima and the federal government. I became familiar with records groups that held materials related to those I had re-searched initially, as well as holdings outside of the federal records system, such as those in the files of the various courts concerned with land and water issues.

In a totally unexpected way, these first projects led to microfilmed records projects that I would not have thought initially to claim to be able to manage. The Salt River Project assignment had also involved ordering large quantities of materials microfilmed for use in the Phoenix facility. I had worked with microfilming projects while I was on the NARS staff, so the effort was not entirely new. But having had the experience of coordinating one such project, I found that other institutions outside of Washington whose holdings included or might include federal records on microfilm were willing to hire me to locate, mark, order, and then check microfilm produced by the National Archives unit. Such projects led me into subcontracting work and forced me to learn very quickly the legal complications of hiring others to help with large projects for short periods of time. While microfilm may no longer be the medium of choice for many institutions, the lesson is the same: one's ability to recognize unexpected opportunities nonetheless can serve to build one's business, as it did mine.

Eventually I decided that large microfilm and photocopy projects involved more administration that I was interested in doing and that research in land and water records was not closely enough tied to my training in twentieth-century cultural history. There was a level of records investigation beyond which it was not practical for me to think about going because there are simply too many other historians with more specialized training in Native American or American West or environmental history methods and issues.

The question became: how could I take the skills which I had already demonstrated and use them in subject areas where I had demonstrated expertise? I wrote my dissertation on the Federal Music Project of the Works Projects Administration during the New Deal period, but symphony research contracts appeared to be nonexistent. However, I knew a great deal about other arts and cultural activities in the nineteenth and twentieth centuries because I had done so much context work on the dissertation and on later publications arising from it. Upon investigation, I realized that historic preservation and cultural resources management were areas in which my Ph.D. in American studies, extensive work on cultural institutions of the United States, and knowledge of federal records might provide a better fit.

While I pondered how to break into a research field for which my training fit but was not obvious, one day in 1984 I was offered a subcontract to work on part of a large Army cultural resources management project. I had been listed in the National Coordinating Committee's *Guide to Historical Consultants* (1981), and the project director used that publication to find me. (The National Council on Public History now maintains a consultants' list on its Web page that serves a similar purpose.) My assignment was to search the records of the Army Corps of Engineers for information about and drawings and maps of World War II munitions factories. Work on that Army project convinced me that I could combine my research skills and cultural interests in new ways. I next bid on a National Park Service contract and researched fifty-four statues and monuments in the core of Washington, D.C. With two add-ons for the Lincoln Memorial and Jefferson Memorial, I was sure that such research was what I wanted to do.

ASSESSING YOUR PSYCHOLOGICAL MAKEUP

The work described above grew out of my original assessment of my historical skills and ongoing reassessments of experience and opportunities, but it developed as one opportunity after another presented itself. Therein lies the second area in which you should do serious self-study: in addition to your listable skills and training, do you have the interest in and psychological profile to do what is basically very rewarding but very high-risk, unpredictable, constantly challenging work? The how-to-do-it books give you excellent charts through which to analyze your entrepreneurial interests, and you should definitely pay attention to them. But for historians, another kind of assessment is necessary to fill out this part of your profile, and it is wise to do this one before you commit yourself to the idea of consulting.

I would begin this section of self-study with the lists recommended above and would label each of the entries "like" or "don't like." Once you determine what you "like," you need to ask yourself why and what that means about the kind of work you will be best at. For example, you noted that you "like" research. Now pursue that further. Do you like to do research on someone else's topic? If you were a research assistant in graduate school, you know something about this process. Do you like to do research in libraries where you can find things under topics, or in archives where you find things by organization? Do you like to research for hours at a time, or in short spurts of effort? Do you get up in the morning to go out and do research, or do you procrastinate and put it off as long as possible? The way you feel about and perform the work that you are offering to sell to other people will tell you a great deal about what parts of the historical research and writing process you will be able to tolerate as a daily job.

I discovered, for example, that I am much happier finding information—doing the primary and secondary research—for applied use than I am writing it up for a scholarly audience. To me, the search is exciting detective work, but, once I know the answer to the research problem, I am primarily interested in explaining it to people who might use it to solve problems or implement policy. Having my work used in that way gives me a real feeling of accomplishment which theoretical analysis never stirred. Others, however, may come to realize that they basically do not like to do research or prefer to write directly for a scholarly audience, and will conclude that their work as professional historians had better take some other form.

Second, you should think about the work environment in which you feel comfortable and productive. Do you like to work by yourself? While there is a tremendous amount of networking activity to attend to as a historian in private practice, much of your work life is spent in isolation. Yours may be the only voice you hear for much of the day. And while that isolation means no supervisor or administrator is looking over your shoulder, it also means that nobody tracks your production schedule but you. Are you a self-starter? Remember that nobody will remind you that the contract deadline is fast approaching. Do you wash your hair or play video games when you are unsupervised? No professor or graduate advisor will hover, making sure that you are getting your research results organized and written up. Most clients don't want to know how you did it, but simply wish to have the results in as compact and accessible a form as possible on time.

On the other hand, in certain situations, the contract historian is hired specifically to be part of a team of researchers working on a project. Cultural resources management is one area, for example, where historians find themselves working with historical architects, archaeologists, biologists, and geologists, among others. Teamwork requires particular skills, especially the ability to work as a team member rather than as the sole expert. Teamwork also requires that the historian understand the work of those other disciplines and where his or her effort fits in. Because traditional professional training in history on the whole prepares the student to work as an isolated scholar in a very clearly defined discipline, the shock of having to perform in a team and in a multidisciplinary context is often quite overwhelming. For those historians who cannot share the expert spotlight, a contract that requires teamwork is not likely to be comfortable. It might be worth it to take a team-training workshop to examine your reaction to such activity before you commit yourself to working in a structure that you cannot abide.

Another source of stress in historical consulting is the frequent lack of a predictable time structure. This is another issue that you must consider as you profile yourself psychologically. Compared to the tightly structured calendar of a job or even of university life, where classes start on a certain day and meet for a certain number of times and then end, research projects often do not start when you expect them to; often, for legitimate reasons, take more or less time from what you initially expected; and sometimes run longer than you had planned. Any historian who cannot live comfortably with some degree of ambiguity should not consider going into historical consulting. I know one former historical consultant who could not tolerate the period of decision making before a contract was awarded. By the time the start date occurred, every client was frazzled by the increasingly frustrated consultant calling repeatedly to try to obtain information that was not yet available. Needless to say, the former consultant has gone on to other work, much to the relief of clients everywhere.

This unpredictability of work assignments has another effect that you need to factor in as part of your analysis. Unpredictability forces the consultant to pursue many projects at once and sometimes results in too much work to do when the work arrives. Obviously, a level of unpredictability also makes one's financial arrangements unstable so that, particularly in the beginning stages of consulting work, backup funds or a second income are essential to get you through your first several assignments.

In addition to analyzing what you like to do and what you can tolerate in relation to specific stress points, there is one final area of consulting work that you must consider carefully—the way you feel about doing work that you may not be able to control. The client frames the question that you will work on and uses your work for the project. Being a historian-for-hire is just that, and clients buy your work and your expertise. They do not necessarily use it in ways that you find rewarding or, indeed, ethical.

There are two sets of questions to consider as you think about the issues posed by this piece of the consulting pie. First, can you as a professional stand up against whatever pressures may be brought by the client to undermine your ability to do the best and most responsible job that you can for that client? For example, the client makes it perfectly clear that he does not want you to find anything significant in the historical context study you are doing of a particular area. Will that expectation force you to skip over information that potentially is significant? It is important to make sure that your confidence in your historical skills and historical judgment is such that you can bring an honest and comprehensive report back to the client, regardless of what the client hopes to find.

The second question relates to your choice of employers. Do you respect the sort of work that the agency or individual does? Do you have confidence that the person for whom you are doing work will use it in a manner consistent with your own values? This is not to say that the client will use it in the way that you would have chosen. Rather you should consider the possible uses and make certain that you feel confident that your work will not be distorted or manipulated by those for whom you choose to work. Historians sometimes blunder into situations of great personal and professional discomfort because they have not understood the ways in which their work can be used. For example, law cases rarely have room for the kind of "on-the-one-hand, on-the-other-hand" argument that historians use to indicate the complexity of historical information, and lawyers will look for your answer, "yes" or "no," to whatever question they are researching. The historians' autonomy takes second place—or sometimes, last place—in contract work to the clients' needs or expectations.

You have now evaluated your skills and your ability to negotiate the particular stresses of contracting work. The last characteristic that you need to seek in yourself is the ability to enjoy the elements that make the job stressful. In consulting, you learn new things constantly: you learn the vocabulary of other disciplines; you discover that your research skills can be applied in areas that you have not considered working in before; you learn how to work in teams, or to network, or to keep up professional and personal contacts even though you are working alone. The final attraction for me in historical consulting is that I never do the same thing twice and am always stretched to learn something that I have not known before or to analyze familiar issues in new ways. Working as a consultant is very different from teaching, with a captive audience that does not know very much. While I often have clients who do not know much about history, they are all adults who have clear points of view, and I find it challenging and interesting to explain what historians do and why to that audience. The exhilaration and stimulation are much of the reason that I do consulting work.

GETTING STARTED

How do you start? I fell into my first couple of jobs, and it was not long before my bank book showed that there was something wildly wrong with the way I was doing business. I had never taken a business or accounting course, and the idea that my hourly rate had to cover expenses if my contract did not provide for them separately had not occurred to me. I was paying for transportation to the research site, long-distance telephone calls, and other expenses out of my hourly rate and that left me with virtually no income. I had no idea that a Schedule C form produced by the Internal Revenue Service is a great boon to the self-employed. Finally, I tended to charge what I was offered until a lawyer in Washington told me that I charged too little to be taken seriously.

In other words, do not try this at home. If you want to start a consulting service, do your homework first. Inventory your assets, as noted above. Then make a business plan. Nowhere in my graduate education did anyone ever suggest to me that, in order to be a practicing historian, I would need to learn to be a business manager and be intimately familiar with tax law, accounting procedures, proposal writing, budgeting, and similar techniques. I learned where I needed expert help, such as an accountant who would, at minimum, do my taxes every year, and where I could teach myself, such as monthly billing and accounting. It is important to be very honest with yourself about this part of the process: if you really hate bookkeeping and holding on to little slips of paper for a year, then consulting may not be for you.

There are resources to help you begin the process. Join the National Council on Public History and their Consultants Group. Check the Web for sites that will help you plan. You may want to check out the self-help books in the business section of your local bookstore or library (remembering to keep the receipts, if you buy them.) One of my colleagues at the university discovered the "secret" of small business courses at the local community college. Get as much information as you can to help you organize the initial steps to establish your business. You will need to select a name for yourself or your company, estimate your start-up costs, and make a business plan.

A business plan, specific instructions for which can be found in most how to do-it small business and consulting texts, charts the way you expect your consulting service to develop. It should lay out, in as much detail as you can muster, the ways in which you plan to reach your goals as a working professional. It should lay out what your start-up costs will be and how you plan to cover those—your savings, a second job, a bank loan? It should talk about your target clients (lawyers or federal agencies or corporations) and the services you can provide for them. You should identify a break-even point for your business, so that you know when the business has actually begun to turn a profit or, if not, when to terminate your consulting services. Be as conservative and realistic in your planning as you possibly can, and update the plan frequently. It will help chart your course.

CONCLUSION

But to quote another country music song, you also have to know when to fold 'em, when consulting is no longer what you want to do. As exciting and stimulating as my full-time consulting work was, my life changed in such a way that living on the edge was no longer either attractive or possible. I found that talking to my four-year-old on the phone from across time zones in Point Barrow, Alaska, or Tokyo or Berlin was, finally, no longer what I wanted to do. "My mom went to work yesterday, and she didn't come home," he told his preschool teacher and then burst into tears as I flew off for a three-week business trip to Japan, Okinawa, and Korea. At that point, I decided that a more predictable schedule and fewer uncertainties in my work situation were needed. That's an important recognition, because consulting is intense and demanding enough that you have to be able to produce enough energy to keep the business going, ever out there finding work and then doing it. I needed to use my energies in other ways.

However, if you have done your inventory of skills and psychological traits and want to be a historical consultant, I would encourage you. Being a historian in private practice calls on your training and creativity in many different ways and allows you to keep on learning for as long as you practice. Few other jobs allow historians to work to their fullest capacities as professionals, and let them practice history full-time.

CANDACE FALK is editor and director of the Emma Goldman Papers at the University of California, Berkeley. After receiving an A.B. and an A.M. at the University of Chicago, she earned a Ph.D. in political theory and history in the History of Consciousness Program at the University of California, Santa Cruz. Honors include a fellowship from the John Simon Guggenheim Foundation. Prior to establishing the Goldman Papers project, Dr. Falk served as journal editor and research associate at the Southeast Asia Resource Center in Berkeley and the Center for Social Research and Education at Oakland. She has also taught at UC Berkeley, UC Santa Cruz, and the Stockton State College of New Jersey. She has served on the American Historical Association's Joan Kelly Prize Committee for Women's History and Feminist Theory, the boards of the Catticus Corporation and Cultural Research and Communications, the advisory board for the Beatrice M. Bain Research Group on Women and Gender, and the Joint American Historical Association–Organization of American Historians–Society of American Archivists Committee on Historians and Archivists. Her publications include Emma Goldman: A Documentary History of the American Years, 1890-1919 *(2003; vols. 2–4, in preparation),* Emma Goldman: A Guide to Her Life and Documentary Sources *(1995),* The Life and Times of Emma Goldman: A Curriculum for Middle and High School Students *(1992),* Love, Anarchy, and Emma Goldman, A Biography *(1984, rev. 1999), and a sixty-nine-reel microfilm edition of the* Papers of Emma Goldman. *She has also contributed essays to such works as* Jewish Women in America: An Historical Encyclopedia. *Dr. Falk has appeared on the programs of the Association for Documentary Editing, the Berkshire Conference on the History of Women, the National Council on Public History, and the Organization of American Historians and has given papers at numerous special conferences and programs.*

DOCUMENTARY EDITORS: NOT AS BORING AS IT SOUNDS

Candace Falk

Documentary editors carry quite an impressive array of historical actors into posterity. Each editor is surrounded by a virtual army of the dead—an invisible, active, influential world long past. The documentary editor, like other historians, acts as a kind of ad hoc guardian of agitated spirits laid to rest only when their words are etched into the historical record. While other historians select and interpret the past, the documentary editor preserves history by presenting the full texts, allowing the reader to experience the immediacy of the authentic voice.

The satisfaction of hands-on historical research and writing is unusually high in these projects. In the case of the Emma Goldman Papers, the project on which I have worked, this satisfaction grew out of locating, gathering, and publishing in microfilm over 20,000 letters, writings, newspaper clippings, and other documents; publishing an analytic guide; and annotating a multivolume selected book edition. Most editors take immense pleasure in the collaborative effort to bring the pearls of the past to the present in authentic form, unmediated by layers of written interpretation but informed by a profound understanding and analysis of the period and the people that constitute the subject of their work. This total immersion creates great scholarly resources but requires singular dedication to one's subject—and enough humility to remain in the wings for many years while bowing to the task of giving the actors of the past their fullest possible voice.

The danger lurking beneath such a long-term relationship is captured well in a joke circulating about the perils of "codependency"—a term that can sometimes describe the editor's relationship to the subject: Question—What happens to a codependent before they die? Answer—The life of somebody *else* flashes before them! Although this particular psychosis also can easily be applied to biographers who are awestruck by the years of research required to track a life story, the documentary editor's pursuit of an amazing and minute array of details about the events and people that surround the life of his or her subject often requires several decades of work. Not alone in this state of mind and being, the documentary editor works collaboratively with others equally possessed—or as we call them at our project, "Goldmaniacs." Steeped in the particulars of the subject's life, an entire editorial staff often lives with precarious boundaries between the past and the present. Years of reading personal letters inevitably lead the editors into relationships of their own to the correspondents—affection and respect for some, antipathy and disdain for others. Such intense engagement with the material extends, but also seeps into, one's own experience. I have observed many documentary editors whose intimate knowledge of their subject has bolstered their own strength and insight, and oddly enough some who have come to resemble their subject in their manner of self-presentation, in somewhat the same fashion as dog owners might take on the look of their pets.

THE EMMA GOLDMAN PAPERS

My own venture into the world of documentary editing did in fact begin with my dog, "Red Emma," when I was in my twenties. I had named
her after Emma Goldman, the "Queen of the Anarchists" who lived from
1869 to 1940. Almost everyone in the new women's movement of the
1970s was naming things after her—health collectives, dogs, even babies.
T-shirts bore her name and face and paraphrased her: "If I can't dance,
it's not my revolution." Goldman stood for freedom, women's independence, and free expression against all odds and became a symbol of
courage and passion; her example evoked feelings of hope and expectation in people taking their first steps into political activism.

My energetic hound bounded with me into a Chicago guitar shop that
happened by chance to house in its storeroom weathered letters between
Emma Goldman and her lover Ben Reitman—correspondence which
might have remained undiscovered to this day had I not been asked the
name of my beloved retriever. In an era when feminists declared that "the
personal is political," it was eye-opening to see in those yellowed love let-

Portrait of Emma Goldman writing at her desk, ca. 1910 [Brown Brothers]. From
*Trial and Speeches of Alexander Berkman and Emma Goldman in United State District
Court, in the City of New York, July, 1917* (New York: Mother Earth Publishing As-
sociation, [1917]). *Courtesy of The Hoover Institution on War, Revolution and Peace.*

ters the jealous inner torment of a spokeswoman for free love, a fore-mother of women's independence. Fascinated, but almost embarrassed by the intrusiveness of my serendipitous find, my first response was to keep her secret, thus protecting Goldman from any hint of mockery that might be elicited should her letters become public. When the owner of the shop safeguarding these epistles of love called me a year later asking whether I might be interested in buying the letters, loyalty to my staunch sister-of-the-past prompted a mad search for funds to purchase, with the intention of sequestering, the revealing evidence of Goldman's vulnera-bility. Only upon being persuaded by the pleading of an archivist of the value of preserving in a public repository even the most private material of a public woman did I begin to understand the importance of safe-guarding the verities of documentary history.

With the letters in a public archive, I felt a personal responsibility to assure that the illicit correspondence was presented with the respect that a great foremother of women's freedom deserves. I began to write *Love, Anarchy, and Emma Goldman,* a biography that linked Goldman's public vision with her private reality. To situate the Goldman-Reitman letters in the context of her entire life, I embarked on countless research trips to archives and private collections throughout the United States and Canada and even across the Atlantic to Amsterdam's International Insti-tute for Social History, where Goldman herself deposited many of her papers.

Several years into this historical detective work, I was contacted by a representative of the National Historical Publications and Records Com-mission (NHPRC) in Washington, D.C., and urged to apply for the edi-torship of the Emma Goldman Papers. The NHPRC had been established by Congress in 1934 with a mandate to support the preservation of the nation's rich documentary history. The NHPRC's scholarly editions were intended to be the building blocks from which the country's history and heritage would be reconstructed and taught for generations. Grants for the publication of the papers of the Founding Fathers began in the 1950s, and by the 1970s the NHPRC had expanded its vision to include suffrag-ists, labor organizers, African-American leaders, and other representa-tives of a broader spectrum of the American experience. It was in this win-dow of liberalism that Emma Goldman was added to the wish list of documentary editions. I was excited to be part of this historical moment of openness and eager to make the written artifacts of Emma Goldman's remarkable life an indelible part of the country's official documentary record. I looked forward to the prospect of being paid for research that I was already doing, sharing archival finds beyond the scope of my own book, and presenting a comprehensive, balanced accounting of Goldman's life in collaboration with a staff of editors. With a new baby in my arms, I was lured also by the flexibility of the work.

WORKING AS A DOCUMENTARY EDITOR

The first task for all documentary editions is gathering copies of all the original material relating to the person who is the subject of the edition, no matter how seemingly insignificant. Those materials may be as few as 500 documents or as many as 100,000 papers and may be housed in one or two main archives or, like the Goldman Papers, spread across the globe in over 1,000 archives and private collections. While some projects like the Woodrow Wilson Papers publish the full range of papers in print volumes, most projects now combine a comprehensive microfilm collection with selected book editions. The size and scope of the 20,000 document microfilm edition of the Goldman Papers is large but not unusual; atypical for the American collections was the extent of the international search for Goldman materials.

Archives, at least before the digital age, were geared to the scholar who chooses to reproduce documents selectively rather than to the documentary editor who essentially needs photocopies of the full collection. This more elaborate transaction necessitates negotiation and the ability to reassure the archive that the documentary collection will not supersede the original one, and a guarantee that the permission usually required of scholars before publishing from the rare material will be referred back to the repository. A documentary editor democratizes access to rare documents, minimizing the privilege of money and time that are otherwise necessary for visiting unique manuscript collections scattered throughout the world. Thus, the editor performs the role of both an archivist and a historian in the process of publishing a comprehensive microfilm and selected papers book edition.

The realization of what supporting a documentary editing project entails comes gradually. Securing a place in a university with a research library is a prerequisite. Ideally a papers project should be directed by a tenured faculty member. A director who is not part of the formal teaching faculty must find a sufficiently interested and committed faculty member willing to be a conduit and advocate for the editing project. In our case, Pulitzer-Prize-winning historian Leon Litwack's commitment to the principles of freedom, his assertion of the fragile right of dissent, and his generosity of spirit created the ideal collegial relationship; he agreed to serve as the chair of the faculty advisory board for the Goldman Papers.

And although the documentary editor bears the responsibility to see the project through, even a research institution has an uneasy relationship to those who are not part of the formal teaching faculty. Unless you are assuming a position in an already established project, creating a supportive structure in which to proceed with the edition is critical. Our first faculty liaison was a cutting-edge feminist sociologist who was sympathetic to the idea of the work but unfamiliar with, and wary of, the time commitment and attention to detail that historical editions require. Still, she was the catalyst for the Emma Goldman Papers' first home in a three-foot by five-foot alcove of a sociology research institute on the University of California at Berkeley campus. Within a year, we built walls around the alcove, and in the next year we overflowed into the hall and the conference room and finally lobbied for our own space. By this time, as editor/director I employed a research associate, an archival consultant, a computer programmer, and several student assistants. (It would be ten years before the university directly supported my salary—an act of generosity by a research provost, who would eventually find himself pressured to withdraw long-term support in favor of projects more integral to the university faculty mission.)

Because historical editing is so collaborative in nature, even a compassionate and loose hierarchy has its awkward moments. Especially as director and editor of the Emma Goldman Papers, I had to develop the capacity to live with the contradiction of being the leader (and administrative boss!) of a project devoted to an anarchist who stood for resistance to all forms of control—though, as an aside, please note that she herself had no problem commanding others to work with her in her challenge against authority. Exaggerated forms of this intermittent and genuine confusion about the issue of control and shared responsibility weave through the life of the project, complicated by periodic suspicion and disapproval expressed in some American anarchist publications for the fact that the Goldman Papers' baseline support has come from a government that only seventy years before succeeded in casting her out as part of a dramatic wave of deportation.

To add a layer of confusion, the institute that housed the project viewed us with a great deal of curiosity, in part because our concerns were more historical than contemporary but also because the nature of our collaboration required office hours more similar to an administrative staff than an academic one. Most documentary editors work in a loose hierarchy as "blue-collar academics" spending long hours in an office together. The satisfying camaraderie of working toward a shared goal is sometimes offset by the sinking realization that after years of graduate work in preparation for the flexibility and individual freedom inherent in teaching one's own courses and managing one's own time, the documentary editor is bound to the structure of an office. Thus the documentary editor must weigh the advantages of a stable group of colleagues and the drawbacks of the isolating elements inherent in the work.

The director of the project takes responsibility not only for the scholarly integrity of the project but for administrative and staff concerns. Because the director must devote more time to administrative and fundraising tasks while the other editors concentrate more on research and editing, there is a structural tension in the way the work is perceived within and outside of the project. Although documentary editions are the product of the joint efforts of every person engaged in the work over the life of the project, often this collaboration is not appropriately recognized. The editor/director whose perseverance and vision see the edition through completion receives accolades from the public and yet feels the discomfort of knowing that his or her colleagues do not receive acknowledgment commensurate to their scholarly contribution. The incongruence between the actual work and the way it is perceived and received is often personalized within the project, resulting in an awkward tension that is part of the structural underside of documentary editing. This internal dynamic coupled with the fiscal insecurities and the immensity of a task that always takes longer than projected periodically generates feelings of personal inadequacy. A documentary editor must have the personal and professional stamina to withstand the contradiction between the level of dedication and skill required for the work and the constant unpredictability of its material and professional rewards.

On the other hand, those who use the work of a scholarly edition are generally amazed by the intellectual detail that an editor can impart about the subject of study. When the papers project assembles an exhibition or an editor gives a lecture to a university or community group, the positive response is a reminder that the work has meaning beyond the scholarly editions and is very rewarding—though the full staff often only experiences such tributes secondhand. The real reward to the group is the publication of the volumes, the coherent intelligence of the collective effort that will have a life of its own, beyond the project.

BOOK AND MICROFILM EDITIONS

A documentary editing project produces primary and analytic resources that become the source material for scholars in a wide spectrum of fields of historical research. In the course of gathering the documents and annotating their contents for a comprehensive microfilm and selected book edition, as well as for a guide to the life and documentary sources of the subject and the subject's host of associates, scholars from very diverse fields become critical colleagues. For example, the first series of the Emma Goldman Papers covers, among other milestones, Goldman's immigration from Russia to the United States in the 1880s; her involvement with immigrant labor groups in the 1890s; her false implication in President McKinley's assassination in 1901 and the concurrent anti-anarchist laws that took effect (culminating in her 1919 deportation with a boatload of other immigrant anarchists); her involvement in bringing European and Russian theater to New York; the 1906 inception of her influential anarchist literary and political magazine, *Mother Earth,* both domestic and international in its scope; and her various involvements with social movements of this period including birth control, free speech, the Modern School movement,[1] and anticonscription. Because the history of the contribution of anarchism, especially to the establishment of the right of free expression, has been largely neglected, the sources for such a volume are rare and scattered, requiring not only knowledge of a variety of social movements but of people otherwise forgotten. To do justice to Goldman and to this era between the 1880s and 1919, the editors had to collaborate with specialists in a wide array of historical studies and to master the details of the legal, social, cultural, and political history of the time themselves.

The second series, 1920–1940, includes Goldman's two years in Bolshevik Russia and her subsequent exile in Sweden, Germany, England, France, and Canada. The volume documents her early prescient critique of Soviet repression of free expression, the isolation within the left that Goldman weathered for articulating her controversial views, as well as some striking examples of the receptivity she experienced internationally, especially from young Chinese revolutionaries. A short lecture tour of the United States that Goldman was permitted to make during the Roosevelt administration offers a point of comparative reflection of attitudes and politics considered threatening in 1919 and more mainstream by 1934. Goldman's lectures during that visit document a growing apprehension of the rise of fascism, Naziism, and Stalinism. The volume also showcases newly uncovered communiqués written to and from Goldman from 1936 to 1938, when she acted as the official English language propagandist for the Spanish anarchists during the Spanish civil war. The documentary context of the period preceding her death in Canada in 1940 includes her work for Spanish women and children displaced by the war and the public attention she rallied to the impending threat to free expression by the Canadian War Measures Act.[2] Thus, the second volume requires a grasp of Goldman-related specifics of European, Canadian, Russian, and Chinese history and a familiarity with material in various languages, including Russian, Catalan, and Chinese.

The level of detail and breadth of knowledge required for the annota-

tion of the volumes is massive. The editors of the Emma Goldman Papers
share with other documentary editors of papers projects (no matter what
their subject or the size of the collection being edited) the equally im-
posing challenge of wide-ranging historical research that marks the integrity, creativity, and contribution of a great documentary edition. From
the outside, editing projects appear to be an exercise in repetition—doing the same kind of work, on the same person or era, day after day, year
after year; yet the experience of viewing the past through the eyes of the
person for whom or the subject for which the edition is created is a fascinating exercise in the organization and analysis of historical material.
Although there are moments when the plethora of detail makes the documentary editor especially vulnerable to the time-worn cliché of not seeing the forest for the trees, stepping back for perspective, the layers upon
layers of historical knowledge and insight encountered over the years are
breathtaking and are their own reward.

Although the book editions are the most visible and perhaps most gratifying part of the documentary editing field, the years of searching for, organizing, and identifying documents and what seemed like the endless details of preparing a 20,000 document collection for microfilming not only
prepared the ground for the volumes but was an accomplishment of historical research and perseverance in itself. To fill an immediate historical
gap more quickly than could be accomplished through printed volumes,
all the women's papers projects (Elizabeth Cady Stanton-Susan B. An-
thony, Jane Addams, Margaret Sanger, and Emma Goldman papers) were
assigned first the task of amassing material for microfilm editions.

These "Cinderella" projects create a standard of order and thorough-
ness, yet those long years in the background of a book-based historical
profession render such microfilm treasure troves of documentary sources
almost invisible—and by extension created an underclass within the documentary editing profession. Professional meetings rarely address issues
pertaining to microfilm editions (other than discussing the technicalities
of how to transfer the material from microfilm to CD-ROM or online format); funding agencies minimize the time and skill it takes to create a
comprehensive collection; and the editors themselves feel isolated from
the profession as a whole. Even the scholar who benefits from the project's
years of concentrated searching and organization usually neglects to cite
the microfilm as the source for historical documents and instead cites only
the archive of origin. The research assistance aspect of the work of a documentary editing project is often perceived as being more closely related
to that of a librarian bringing information off the shelves of a library than
as a collaboration among research scholars sharing the fruits of their own
long-term labor. While the use of the annotated material is a goal of the

field of documentary editing, there is an inherent awkwardness about giving everything away to the scholars or the filmmakers who then incorporate the project's work into their own undertakings without revealing how much of their research was purely derivative. And sometimes the same historians who judge the collection of archival material that is integral to the creation of a comprehensive microfilm edition as "journeyman" research work ironically spend a lifetime writing about a very small cache of original documents they may have come across in the course of their own research. A comprehensive collection of documentary material can become the basis of a myriad of scholarly work, and often the lightning rod for future historical writing. The documentary editor inevitably confronts the cognitive dissonance between personal experience and professional perception of the field of work, and needs to venture out of the temporal university system of rewards—and take solace in the knowledge that the microfilm and book editions will be lasting and positive contributions to public history.

The Emma Goldman Papers went the extra mile to make the microfilm accessible—with standard AACR2 headers[3] for future single-item online listings, introductory historical essays for each reel, name indexes for all correspondents, and subject indexes for its government document collection. Rather than define Goldman narrowly by her correspondence and writings alone, the collection includes documents that reflect how the media and the government perceived her—with an extensive newspaper clippings file as well as government documents and surveillance records. In the spirit of honoring Goldman's historical legacy as a public figure, the editors realized that the construction of her life from the documents amassed and published in the microfilm collection actually had many significant gaps and thus didn't accurately reflect the phenomenal pace and breadth of her public lectures—the impressive number of towns, languages, and topics she commanded. We decided to add to our other work on the edition almost an additional year and a half ferreting out the dates and places of her talks; this chronology proved to be among the most useful and sought after of all the documentary resources of the Goldman Papers. The chronology was published in the guide to the microfilm, *Emma Goldman: A Guide to Her Life and Documentary Sources*. Although I received the Kanner Award on behalf of the project for the Best Bibliographical Work in Women or Gender History from the Western Association of Women Historians, it is safe to say that none of our supporters, federal or university, were pleased with the publication delay, and there was quite a bit of tension within the project about the efficacy of taking such a risk when the more visible and sought after book edition was in turn delayed as well.

This vignette illustrates the tension between a commitment to a thorough and accurate historical record and the external pressures for material results, and underscores the intense responsibility to "History" that a documentary editor begins to assume—a sense that this is *the* critical time for creating a meticulous documentary record. Without the precision of the Goldman chronology, for example, the entire microfilm edition would not appropriately reflect Goldman's historical legacy as a public woman, even though the scope and content of the correspondence, writings, government documents, and newspaper clippings presuppose such a life. Thus the documentary editor is really working with posterity in mind, regardless of whether such dedication makes sense in the short run. Possessed not only by the subject of the papers project, but also by the long view of history, the documentary editor takes a personal sense of history into the future.

PUBLIC OUTREACH

With the amazing breakthroughs in the accessibility of information in the computer age, broader public dissemination of the scholarly work in documentary editions is now possible. Among the most exciting developments for the Emma Goldman Papers has been its inclusion in the Berkeley Digital Library SunSITE,[4] which offers a taste of what is to come in the future of documentary editing. The Goldman site includes the guide, facsimile documents, newsreel footage, and a sampling of ancillary projects and products of the Goldman Papers. Each month, thousands of people check the Web site from all over the world and write to the project about their interests in individuals or events related to Goldman or her associates—descendants of her circle offer memories and photographs, students access information for their history papers, theater and cinema groups find sources of inspiration as well as authentic material for their work. Thus, the international interest in Goldman, her work, and her legacy is confirmed. The years of scholarly work combined with advancing tools for the dissemination of knowledge will shape the future of the field of documentary history—a perfect complement to a book edition, but not its displacement.

The Goldman Papers has expanded its reach in other ways over the years. Recognizing how long it will take for high school teachers to access and incorporate material from a massive scholarly edition, the editors solicited a grant to hire specialists and jointly write a Goldman curriculum, now in circulation at middle and high schools across the country and reconfigured for the National Center for History in the Schools' unit on free speech.

To add a visual component to our work, we created a traveling exhibition on the themes of Goldman's advocacy of reproductive rights and freedom of expression. The exhibition has toured universities across the country, accompanied by a lecture and slide show that always gives me the pleasure of seeing the immediate positive impact of Goldman's history to current concerns. The exhibition can now be viewed online, along with reproductions of documents from the collection and even a film image of her speaking to the press in 1934.

The varieties of outreach will no doubt become more interesting with time and the advancement of information technology. Established figures in American history, like past presidents or founding fathers, have a public component to their historical memory outside of the documentary editions; but an individual like Emma Goldman, for whom being written in or out of the historical record is itself a political act, mandates that the documentary editor take on an added responsibility to create public awareness of its subject. Our collective commitment to the critical importance of protecting the history of freedom fighters like Goldman served the function of keeping the project from breaking down in despair at all the odds against finishing it, always outweighing the waves of adversity we faced. At the Emma Goldman Papers, public outreach seems imperative and integral to the larger scholarly mission of documentary editing. Yet there is a very mixed message sent from federal funders about what aspect of the work is of value. While they encourage the idea of bringing scholarship to the schools and support interest in computer access to scholarly material—creating the aura of national responsibility for these projects of the National Archives—there is little compensation or reward for the time it takes to bring scholarship to the public in a thoughtful and accessible format. The editing project develops a split identity and often hides its public face from the funders of the scholarly editions.

REWARDS AND TRIALS

Over the years, the variety of work under the heading of documentary editing attracts an amazing and eclectic array of colleagues. The Goldman collection was created from the contributions and international cooperation of scholars, archivists, librarians, relatives and associates of Goldman, translators, activists, filmmakers, playwrights, collectors, other documentary editors, publishers, funders (especially those who helped the project get its start), and administrative staffs far and near. Living within but somehow very much outside the university, survival as a documentary editor—in intellect and spirit—forges deeper bonds to those who share in the work at different levels of engagement. The sweet experience of corresponding with revered Chinese anarchists in their nineties who have stretched their strength to write their recollections of Goldman and her influence is almost unmatched in other fields. The joy of meeting researchers and curators of anarchist archives in Italy, Spain, France, and England, after years of corresponding and exchanging pictures and gifts is amazing. Working with the daughter of Emma Goldman's manager and lover to promote the work of the Emma Goldman Papers feels like a gift of continuity from the past. Meeting and interviewing such pillars of history and free speech as Roger Baldwin, the co-founder of the American Civil Liberties Union, whose career was inspired by Emma Goldman, change one's own life and in a small way integrate the documentary editor into the life of the subject. Every trip I've taken since my work on Goldman began has included something of her life and associates—my honeymoon was no exception. In Cuernavaca, in the mid-1970s, Goldman's exiled anarchist comrades, Mollie Steimer and Senya Fleshine, scolded my new husband and me for allowing the state any authority over love—reminding us that a "companion" needs no legal bond. They wished us riches in life "in the best sense," which is also ultimately what my connection to Emma Goldman as the editor and director of her documentary collection has given me.

But for the documentary editor, along with the riches come the trials. Although a comprehensive edition is at best a select representation of the complexity of a life, such a task takes an inordinate amount of time, the kind of time that most academics would not consider investing because the professional returns are so surprisingly low. Collaborative work generally is not rewarded, nor is the final product—annotated letters and papers—viewed as original, even though such volumes require sustained, intellectually demanding, and creative work. While prizes for monographs and books multiply, there is no formal recognition for a well-edited documentary edition in either of the two major historical organizations—the Organization of American Historians and the American Historical Association. And, it is a rare history department that trains its students in the art of documentary editing.

This peripheral standing is in part driven by economics, politics, a shift in the style and priorities of historical practice away from original texts, away from "great" individuals and towards social history (although the papers projects always amass the papers of thousands of associates along the way), and the general lack of knowledge about the skills and creativity intrinsic to the field. Thus, the financial support for the work is often quite precarious—unlike European archives that house and pay salaries to editors to publish material from their collections, archive libraries in the

United States do not support documentary editions, and history departments with rare exception do not carry the salaries or provide the office
space required by an editing project. There is no tenure in the field, unless you are also on the teaching faculty, and in fact, the longer one works
on an edition the more precarious is the base of support—a kind of "reverse tenure." Dependent in large part on grants from the National Historical Publications and Records Commission, the National Endowment
for the Humanities, and private foundations, the political climate as well
as current intellectual and technological trends often dictates the course
of funding. Documentary editors are not the sheltered academics that
are often the brunt of conservative attack; in fact, over time the editors
develop a kind of market savvy—an ability to write grant proposals, create commemorative items ("Emmorabilia" at our project), and build rap-
port with the public that is driven by a survival instinct as well as historical principle. In the long run this "outward bound" approach forces the
documentary editor to develop some very useful skills in an age when the
mode of academic work is constantly changing.

The high quality scholarly work of an annotated collection is the necessary, irreplaceable base from which the new computer age can offer unprecedented distribution and access to historical material. Yet labor- and
cost-intensive historical scholarly book editions are rapidly being shelved
by federal granting agencies as the electronic preservation of contemporary archival records becomes the priority. After over a decade of being
tossed about by economic insecurity, I offer an important caveat to the
historian who becomes a documentary editor—a field that requires years
of scholarly commitment to an edition—beware of the land mine of
sparse resources that constantly threatens to sabotage the work. The time
line for the work will be mediated by fiscal conditions, by scholarly concerns, and by new technologies. When I signed on as the editor and director of the Emma Goldman Papers in 1980, I had no idea it would take
two decades to complete, nor that I would have to raise over a million dollars in funds in the process, nor that as the completion draws near, the
solid support of the NHPRC and the University of California would become more tenuous.

CLOSING WORDS OF ADVICE

A documentary editing project is a long-term relationship, requiring
constancy and devotion, the ability to weather hard times and to honor
and respect one's subject. In the work of an edition, one comes to know
many people—sometimes blurring the edges between those who are living and those who are alive only in their vibrant correspondence to Gold-

man. The caveat for all those who enter this profession is to remember to honor the particulars of your own life and time, not to devalue your own desires, actions, friends, and associates as less important than your seemingly larger-than-life subject. As a counterpoint to the perils of intense engagement with the details of the past, and of the life of a person long gone—the prerequisite for the work of documentary editing—affirm the singularity of your own spirit more vividly, more adamantly, and in this way you will honor the person who over time will become your historical companion "in the best sense."

NOTES

1. Fueled by outrage at the brutal execution in Spain in 1909 of anarchist Francisco Ferrer, who had established schools that fostered free thinking independent of the Church, anarchists, including Emma Goldman, helped organize "free schools" throughout America, paced to the individual child and fostering creativity.
2. Prohibiting possession of "antifascist" subversive literature loosely defining threats to Canadian national security, this law was used in 1939 to imprison several Italian anarchists living in Canada who were part of Goldman's circle of friends.
3. AACR2 is the acronym for Anglo-American Cataloguing Rules, 2nd edition, which provides a standard format for document control and retrieval. Widely used by nearly all major research libraries, AACR2 headings will prove invaluable for future single-item online listings.
4. See http://sunsite.berkeley.edu/Goldman.

.

DANIEL GREER is an associate editor for Healthwise, Inc., a publisher of consumer health information in Boise, Idaho. He earned a B.A. in history at Boise State University and did graduate work in the Public History Program at Arizona State University, where he received a certificate in historical editing and publishing. He has held editorial positions at Arizona State and Boise State and for the National Council on Public History and served eight years as a book editor at Mountain Press Publishing Company in Missoula, Montana.

EDITORS AND PUBLISHERS: MAKING BOOKS FOR READERS

Daniel Greer

Working as an editor for a small press entails doing a lot of things beyond strictly editing copy. Upon being hired as a book editor, I anticipated marking copy on a daily basis as my primary responsibility. There was something comfortable about the notion of going to work each day and methodically editing a chunk of manuscript—correcting its punctuation and grammar and writing little queries to the author in the margins. But at the end of each day, while I prepared lists of the most urgent things to do tomorrow and in the days to come, I found I had less and less time to edit as the broader tasks associated with project management came into focus. Soon I began to understand that book editing is not a cut-and-dried job, and that copyediting is not its chief function; it is an intricate process of ushering the author's product, a raw manuscript, through an incredibly involved series of steps that result in the publisher's product, a polished book.

My first job out of school landed me in Montana as history editor for an independent trade publisher. The press's hundred or so books in print focused on the history of the American West, geology and natural history, a few horse titles, and assorted others that more or less stood alone. The diverse list exhibited a willingness on the part of the publisher and founder of the press to take on almost any project that he thought might sell enough copies to turn a profit. It was largely a seat-of-the-pants operation, in spite of its forty-year history—about twenty as a printing business and twenty more as a book publisher. When I arrived, I had the distinction of being its first bona-fide editor. The press and I educated each other in many positive ways: I contributed mostly theory and principles, plus a little experience, while the press taught me much about practical applications and the necessity of compromise.

My duties included evaluating proposals, developing and acquiring new projects, serving as the primary liaison between authors and the press, editing and preparing projects for production, coordinating any necessary freelance assistance, communicating my activities with others at the press through meetings and editorial reports, writing advertising copy and developing marketing strategies, and even taking orders over the phone and sometimes packaging them for shipment. Everyone at a small press does a little of everything. You may concentrate on your particular specialty, but you end up doing whatever needs to be done.

My graduate training in scholarly publishing at Arizona State University prepared me surprisingly well to handle the odd array of tasks. It supplied me with a solid enough framework and understanding of the field that I could grasp the necessity for all parts of the whole to come together, even though I had never actually performed most of the individual chores on my lists of things to do. And my training in history also provided me with some valuable tools that helped me judge the scholarly standards of various book projects. The theories we studied in historical methodology suddenly had practical applications. Little did I know in school how useful the principles of historiography would be in my job. There have been many instances, in the midst of some task or another, when I have found myself recalling bits and pieces of what I learned in school.

STAGING A STRATEGY

If you've ever seen or read a book that was self-published—a practice more common than ever in this day of desktop publishing—then you probably can appreciate the value of professionalism and teamwork. The effort that goes into publishing any book, especially one of high quality, is enormous. The job is too big for any single person to pull off. Every writer needs an editor. When editors write, they need an editor! And few editors have the talent of a skilled designer (formerly called a typesetter until computers forced a shift in emphasis). And the cooperative marketing effort should never be undervalued or underrated.

Writer, editor, designer, marketer—all must pool their resources, imaginations, and energy to get a book off the ground. And those four roles barely scratch the surface of the networking necessary to propel each book from a publisher's list securely into the hands of individual readers. This essay fortunately need not delve into every far-flung aspect of the book business. Most publishers, however—and certainly most editors—deal with these four primary aspects. The editor's scope of responsibility, in fact, is pivotal. The following paragraphs offer more detail about how the editor navigates a book project from the author's keyboard, through the stages of production, and into the marketer's lap.

MEASURING THE MARKET

One of the foremost realities editors, publishers, and writers must understand and think about every day is that our books must sell if we are to remain in business. There's no future in publishing books people won't read. In times past, university presses and other nonprofit publishers could rely at least somewhat on subsidies to finance esoteric treatises on obscure topics. Commercial presses never enjoyed that luxury. In today's economy, however, the price of paper, printing, and binding alone—never mind the elusive but significant costs of overhead and marketing—does not permit any publisher to produce books that languish in the warehouse. And, in any case, isn't the main purpose of books not simply to store information but to disseminate it? In the realm of commercial publishing, for sure, and even among nonprofit publishers, books must be not only available but inviting and accessible to readers.

So the first task for an editor or publisher to consider is which projects will yield a return on the quantifiable publishing investment, which is sizable (about the price of a new car for each book). Lacking a crystal ball or other supernatural medium, we have to think pragmatically. What sorts of books does the press have on its backlist? Which books on the backlist have been reprinted most often (or at all)? The longer a book remains in print and the more copies of it sell, especially beyond its initial printing, the more capital it brings to the press.

Generally, publishers prefer to match any new book with a proven companion; an existing book that has sold well and remains popular with readers can help pave the way for a new treatment on the same subject. The conventional wisdom is that if readers enjoyed the earlier book (shown by their willingness to buy enough copies for the publisher to recoup its expenses and make even a modest profit), they will also enjoy a new book that delivers more of what they liked before.

But no self-respecting publisher is in business solely for the money. Although financial reality must receive its due, most publishers operate within the parameters of a mission. The mission outlines a few select topics—the publisher's niche—aimed at an audience the publisher knows and understands, or at least tries to. The more a press understands about its perceived audience, the better its editors are able to determine which proposals have a chance of succeeding as books.

The tricky thing about a book "audience" is that it is not some tightly defined group confined in an auditorium. Rather, it's a loose conglomeration of individuals that shifts and swells according to the popularity of the topic at hand, the quality of an author's insight into the topic, and the press's effectiveness in packaging the product and capturing that particular audience's attention. It's a slippery business, and in the end marketing plays a key role in how well any book sells. However insightful and eloquent an author may be, and however diligent and meticulous are the editor's hand and eye, it is most often the creativity and cunning of the marketing effort that determines the success of a book.

PROCESSING PROJECTS

Ground zero for any book is the author's domain. Although we still refer to the author's product as a "manuscript," virtually no one these days writes a book in longhand. "Typescript" might be a more accurate label, but it has never taken hold in popular parlance. And now typewriters are passé as well. Most publishers request, if not demand, that authors submit their final manuscripts on computer disk. What's the point of taking the time to retype 50,000 to 100,000 words (computers tell us exactly how many) and risk introducing countless typos? Editors have so much more to do than proofreading.

How is a project selected for publication? Proposals, letters of inquiry, and even entire manuscripts—some solicited, most not—land on an editor's desk with regularity. The editor must spend as little time as possible determining which of these have potential to evolve into a book suited to the press and which must be dispatched without delay. After you've done this for a while, you develop an instinct for it. You look over the proposal, letter, or manuscript and take an internal inventory— check your gut instinct. Then you quickly ponder the elements that sway you one way or the other. The image that invariably comes to my mind when considering whether I am willing to spend months, perhaps even years, working with an author to turn a project into a book is the constantly bobbing column of mercury Stephen Cox, director of the University of Arizona Press, wrote about:

> You glance at the title page. (Is there a title page? Up.) Has the author presumed to type the name of your publishing house on the title page? Down. You glance at the table of contents. Are the chapters about 25 pages of typescript in length? Up. Are there some very short chapters and some very long?

Down. Is the manuscript more than 400 pages in length? Down. More than 600 pages? Far down.

Next you read the first sentence of the first page of text (the preface, no doubt). Does it grab you? Up. Is it apologetic? Down. . . . You read the first paragraph of the preface, and the second, with the column of mercury bobbing up and down in your mental gauge.[1]

The idea is to stay in touch with your perceptions and be honest. Is the project well conceived, well defined, and responsibly written, or did the author send you a first draft of a half-baked idea? Is it double-spaced? Are the pages numbered? Are direct quotations properly documented? Are there any illustrations? What kind? How many? (Contrary to what many people seem to believe, the reproduction and publication costs of a reasonable complement of photographs—enough to break up the text every few pages—are not as expensive as the liability of leaving them out.) Does the author have all necessary permissions or violate any copyright? Does the author realize that writing the manuscript is only half the job and that making it into a book will require more time and a lot more work?

If a project does not in some fashion look promising, the editor must not encourage the author. Certain realities dictate certain responses. Some presses use a standard brush-off line: our schedule is full. That's usually true, in a way. There's never enough room to take on a lousy project, yet there's always room to squeeze in a good one. Some presses send form-letter rejections. I hate that, and so do authors. Surely their effort deserves some semblance of a personal response, perhaps even a pointer in the right direction.

It's good policy to be kind to potential authors, even when you are telling them to take a hike. You can reject their work for one reason or another—it's good to let them know—but be careful not to reject the person. Well-reasoned criticism helps authors refine their work; crass, thoughtless comments discourage them not only from trying your press again but also from recommending it to their writer associates. Within a publisher's niche, author-editor relationships exist in a complex network of far-reaching tentacles. At some point, if a particular editor remains behind the desk long enough and a particular author continues to write the sorts of books that the press publishes, their paths are going to cross; most likely, their reputations will precede their meeting. Just as books take anywhere from about nine months to three years or so in the publishing incubator, so editors need to keep their sights focused far down the line. Publishing is a long-haul type of business.

If an author's submission appears up to par and fits within the mission and goals of the press, the editor needs to do several things. First and foremost is to get the manuscript into the hands of a subject specialist (or two) to confirm that the work is solid, that the author has used sources and references appropriately, and that the work offers well-reasoned interpretations. The sort of person best suited to this task is usually someone who has written at least one respectable book on the subject, someone who can distinguish between a contribution to the field and a rehash of the same old stuff. The press offers to pay a token honorarium of $100 or $200 for this service and guarantees the reader's anonymity (from the author) as a means of garnering an undiluted evaluation. If the reader recommends publication, the editor may ask for a prepublication endorsement to use in the catalog and other promotional materials. It's never too early to begin thinking about marketing.

Usually the editor and the author discuss marketing during their first conversation. "What audience did you have in mind when you wrote the manuscript?" "What makes your book stand out from others on this subject?" The editor should ensure that the author is willing to play an active role in selling the book by giving talks, granting interviews, signing books at bookstores, and so on. The editor may want to know if the author has any cover ideas in mind.

Authors often inquire about contracts and royalties before the editor develops any concern about them. Most contracts are heavily slanted toward the publisher, granting the press all the rights to everything and inconspicuously mentioning that the author will receive a royalty based on book sales, which means the author gets no money until after the book is published, perhaps a couple of years down the road. This may be harsh news for authors, especially new ones. In the interest of forging good relations, the editor should empathize and explain that the press also invests handsomely in each project before recovering any expenses. Most authors have a day job or other source of income, and few who write scholarly books could ever earn a living from book sales. Writers, like publishers, usually are not in this business solely for the money.

Some of the New York publishing houses apparently can afford to pay handsome advances on an author's royalties. They tend to have extravagant marketing budgets and put a lot into selling books all at once—a flash in the pan. Within a few months, the marketing campaign is all over and any leftover books are remaindered. In the realm of small independent presses or university presses, advances range from nonexistent to very modest. Sometimes a press can cough up a good-faith token for the insistent author of a promising project, perhaps a few hundred to a couple thousand dollars. It's rarely enough to keep bread on the table, but it can soothe the sting of research expenses, photograph fees, or other material costs such as computer needs.

If the reader(s) returns a favorable report, the press will offer a contract to the author. At that point, others at the press may begin to factor the new project into the ever-evolving forecast of new books, some of which might still be a couple of years from publication. A launch meeting outlines marketing strategies, budget allowances, design ideas, and editorial needs. The project is penciled into a schedule for copyediting (often by a freelance), announcement in an upcoming catalog, and a preliminary forecast for production. Although new books may be released in any month except (usually) December, they are announced as either fall or spring titles. It's time to start making lists of all the loose ends and figuring a way to braid them neatly together. Many elements are common to all projects, but each book has its own special circumstances and considerations, and it is the editor's responsibility to see that nothing slips through the cracks.

INSTANT INFORMATION

One of the crucial aspects of editing and publishing books is keeping track of everything. There is no substitute for an effective filing system and a reasonably functional memory. Having several dozen projects going at once, in various stages ranging from born yesterday to recently published, is all the more reason to write down everything and remember the rest. Phone notes, correspondence, decisions made during meetings, and scores of ticklers need to be organized, available, and decipherable. When an author calls and wants an update or has a new patch to add to the quilt, the editor needs ready access to reliable information.

After the work is copyedited, the author must review it and, inevitably, there will be another round (or two or three) of editorial changes. One of the great benefits of word processing is the potential for electronic editing—making changes directly on the screen instead of marking up manuscript pages with lines, arrows, and carets that sometimes leave authors seeing only red. Of course, every author is entitled to know exactly what changes an editor makes, and that's as it should be. The goal of electronic editing is not to slip an editor's will past the author. Instead, it allows both author and editor to view the revised copy uncluttered by its previous incarnation. Marks on paper, especially when they contrast as red and black do, bring out a natural urge on the part of the reader not to flow with the revision but to second-guess each change. (Little wonder that traditional author-editor relationships can become adversarial when they are built less on what is right than on what is wrong.)

Most authors I have worked with have been surprisingly willing to permit unmarked changes to their manuscripts. If they encounter wording that does not ring true to their intent, they simply refer back to their original version and reconsider. Reading a clean, revised copy of the manuscript places the focus where it should be—on how the material reads now. This practice also eliminates the need for editors to go back and enter each change approved by an author, leaving more time to reconcile each other's concerns on matters not yet resolved or, better yet, move on to the next step.

Whether the old-fashioned way or electronically, the editor works through editorial changes with the author and gathers any lingering elements, such as late photographs or permissions or maps. The files containing notes, reminders, and lists become vitally important as the project reaches its crescendo.

Suddenly it seems everyone is getting anxious. The intense back and forth of editing has the author and editor tuned in to each other like never before. Advance orders for the book have marketing wanting assurance that the project is on schedule. Production is poised to merge the project in with its flow. Everything seems to be happening at once. At this point, the author gets a break while the editor shifts the focus to coordinating with production.

PRODUCTION AND PROOFING

By the time the final changes to the manuscript are made, the editor will have prepared production to receive the project in all its various elements—manuscript (title page, copyright information, dedication, contents, preface, foreword, chapters, notes, and bibliography), disk, photographs and other graphics (maps, charts, drawings, etc.), cover art, cover copy, and flap copy. Sometimes the production staff may contribute toward preparing maps or other graphics; usually, if it is part of the book's contents, it is the author's responsibility. The editor may contract with a freelance artist for such things and charge it against the author's royalty.

The designer works up several options for various elements and the overall treatment of each book, then discusses them with the editor. Together they make appropriate decisions for the book. The last thing a good designer needs is an editor overriding his or her sense of good taste and balance. Usually the designer knows best, and a good working relationship with the production staff is always in the editor's and the project's best interest. This is one of the areas where cooperative teamwork yields the best results.

After the book is laid out, with photographs placed according to the author's and editor's specification, the page proofs are ready for proof-reading and indexing. The editor arranges both steps, which are usually done concurrently, often by freelancers. A copy goes to the author as well. The corrected pages from the proofreader and author are checked by the editor and then submitted to production for entering the changes. At this point, the only acceptable changes are corrected typos or errors of fact (which are the author's responsibility to catch). While those changes are being entered, the editor checks and edits the index.

When the editor determines the page proofs are letter perfect and the index has been laid out, the project is ready for the printer. Usually the printer also prepares half-tones (dot-image reproductions) of the photographs as well; this allows the printer to harmonize the relative shades and clarity of text and images as they appear in the final product. Before running the entire job of perhaps 3,000 to 10,000 books, the printer prepares a "blue-line" from the printing plates and sends it back to the publisher for a final going-over, checking each page for broken type, skewed alignment, general print quality, and for anything that might have been missed earlier. Editorial corrections at this stage will cost dearly, but the printer will correct its own errors free of charge.

MARKETING MECHANICS

It is impossible to overemphasize the importance of marketing. All the effort that goes into writing a book, the attention to detail in editing it, and the incorporation of high-quality production values can result in an enormous waste of resources if the book never reaches a significant share of its intended readers. And the sheer number of books being published these days makes it easy for some great ones to become lost in the fray.

Marketing begins when a press accepts a book for publication. (It could be argued that marketing begins with the author's concept and approach in writing the book and pitching it for publication, but it becomes a team effort at the press.) During the initial launch meeting, the press starts to develop a strategy and a schedule for a book, starting the marketing wheels turning.

New books are announced in the publisher's trade catalog, which is aimed at the publisher's sales representatives, distributors, wholesalers, and individual booksellers. The editor, with input from the author and press marketer, composes a description of the book geared to generate interest among those who will be selling it. If possible, a representation of the cover art or cover concept accompanies the announcement, and perhaps a sample of the book's interior as well. Just like ordinary readers, sales people are moved by images that complement the text.

The publisher's sales representatives, who generally carve up the potential market (all or part of the United States and often some portion of the international scene) into a handful of regions, are the first to hear about the book, usually at a major annual meeting such as the American Booksellers Association. The sales reps are the ones who will pitch the book to various large and small booksellers in their region. What they want to know is: "How are we going to move this product through the system?" If the book has shortcomings that could affect sales, they let the publisher know. Some of their concerns might be: the book is not consistent with the publisher's list, making it an awkward fit with booksellers that usually sell a particular press's titles (for instance, a publisher of children's fiction suddenly trying to sell reference books, or a publisher of animal books deciding to produce how-to books on home repair, or perhaps a publisher of Civil War history inexplicably coming out with a book on ancient Egypt); the cover or text is not appropriate for the intended audience (for instance, having juvenile illustrations in a book aimed at mature readers); or perhaps that similar topics or treatments have previously been tried and failed in the marketplace. Often the criticisms are not so broad. Perhaps their comments will lead the publisher to make minor adjustments to the book, such as coming up with a more engaging title or more descriptive subtitle. Often no changes are recommended, and the sales reps are merely eager to receive the new title and move it through the system.

The press marketer, the project editor, and the author work together to identify all of the possible readers for each title. They list which publications, such as professional journals or popular periodicals, might bear fruit from advertising. They obtain mailing lists for direct-mail flyers. They arrange for the author to conduct talks, presentations, book signings, and perhaps radio or other media interviews. They try to think of any angle to inform a book's audience that it is available, and they exhibit books at various meetings and gatherings where readers congregate.

By the time a new book arrives at the publisher's warehouse, the editor or marketer will have drafted a press release. It is mailed, usually with a complimentary copy of the book and a press catalog, to newspapers, magazines, and journals that might choose to review the book. Each time a review appears, especially if it is a good one, it becomes a form of advertisement. The more prestigious the publication that runs a review and the more positive its appraisal, the better is the potential for a book to enjoy a long and successful life.

For writers, editors, and publishers alike, professional networks are essential. By associating with various groups and attending events appropriate to the types of books with which they are involved—such as historical society conferences for history books, booksellers meetings for all types of books, and selective gatherings of authors according to the agenda at hand—they come into contact with each other and with readers in search of their products. Such meetings often spawn serendipitous events—someone who knows someone else who has a project or an idea that bears fruit. You never know when or exactly how a publisher and an author may discover each other.

EDITING IS NOT FOR EVERYONE

Editing is a loose term that gets applied to a variety of jobs in the publishing field. Clearly, not all editors edit copy, and many of those who do lack the skills and temperament necessary to excel at it. Copyediting is both a skill and an art. Although its principles can be taught, most people acquire the ability to edit through experience. Appreciating its finer points may be one of the best ways to distinguish those who can excel at editing from those who cannot.

The best copy editors have an eye for details, none of which are too small to notice and most of which are not too small to care about. People who lack such qualities call those who have them "anal retentive" and "nitpicky." If you cannot get used to such labels and move beyond them, editing probably is not for you. But if you revel in trying to determine correct from incorrect or, better yet, more correct from less correct, the field of editing may be a safe harbor for your idiosyncrasies. The caveat, however, is that you cannot become so lost in detail that you lose sight of the big picture. And the intrigue of focusing on details cannot be at the expense of resolving them in different ways for different occasions and moving on when you might rather linger or revisit them.

Some people simply are not cut out for copyediting. Perhaps they would rather write, and they see editing as something they can do while pursuing their true goal; after all, both jobs use language. It is possible for a writer to edit, just as it is possible for an editor to write, but each requires its own frame of mind and calls upon very different sets of skills and priorities. Generally, writers focus on broadcasting information and are legitimately concerned with incorporating as many bits of it as possible to achieve accuracy. Expressing valid ideas does not require intimate knowledge of a language's rules. An editor focuses on how the information is received. The editor runs interference between the writer and the reader, cutting out excess verbiage, cleaning up technical aspects such as grammar and punctuation, and clearing a path so the reader can understand the writer's point.

On the broader end of the spectrum, an editor's educational background is an essential part of doing the job well. It is important to have historians editing history. They understand the processes of research and the need to write and interpret history. There is not only truth but also job security in the adage that each generation must reinterpret history for itself. As our society's values change, so do our questions and concerns. Reinterpreting history lends insight to our condition. Who better than a historian, equipped with the skills of analysis and critical reasoning combined with a knowledge of the existing literature, might question an author's points or argue angles that could well be lost on the editor who lacks such training?

If editing appeals to you, get some experience. Internships and graduate programs often present opportunities for students to test their talents and develop their skills. You might start by proofreading newsletters or assisting an editor (or professor) in charge of some publication. Another way to break into the field is by contacting publishers and offering your services as a freelance; you will probably be given an editing test for starters and may not receive copyediting assignments until you have proven yourself with proofreading jobs.

The bible for book publishers in the humanities is *The Chicago Manual of Style*. Some graduate programs use it to augment editing instruction. The University of Chicago also offers short courses in various aspects of editing, including how to use the *Chicago Manual*. Just about any style guide can be useful to students, but be aware of the purpose or audience for each. Journalists, for instance, follow the *Associated Press Stylebook*. It is good for news writing but inadequate for book publishing.[2]

Editing and publishing can lead to richly rewarding careers for public historians. Making books for readers is really a lot of fun, and educational, too. Because I have been fortunate enough to edit a number of books on western history, which is also my area of special interest in history, I have had the pleasure of getting to know many of the people who have made important contributions to this field. I have personally worked on several books that present unique perspectives, and most of them were by authors who had not previously published. The challenge and privilege of being intimately involved with emerging voices are exciting and gratifying.

Public historians understand the need to celebrate the practice of history beyond the academic setting. Our choice to emphasize this aspect of our education both qualifies and obligates us to bring the best qualities history can offer to the largest possible audience. Certainly the field of publishing seeks to do this. As historians ourselves, we demand high standards of authors who write history for public consumption. Our duty to the responsible study of history and our desire to make it accessible to the public are desperately needed in books. Editing is one way of making a difference in how history is digested by society.

NOTES

1. Stephen Cox, "An Editor's Chrestomathy," *Scholarly Publishing* 15 (October 1983): 22.
2. *The Chicago Manual of Style,* 14th ed. (Chicago: University of Chicago Press, 1993); Norm Goldstein, ed., *The Associated Press Stylebook and Libel Manual,* 6th ed. (Reading, MA: Addison-Wesley, 1996).

NINA GILDEN SEAVEY is the founder and director of the Documentary Center (formerly known as the Center for History in the Media) at George Washington University. She earned her B.A. at Washington University and her M.A. in history at George Washington University. A filmmaker for over twenty years, her most recent film, The Ballad of Bering Strait, *was the winner of the Audience Award at the Washington International Film Festival and was an official selection of the International Documentary Association's theatrical showcase, "Doctober." Seavey's previous work includes* A Paralyzing Fear: The Story of Polio in America, *which was nationally broadcast on PBS in October 1998 and won an Emmy Award for Best Research in a News or Documentary Program and the Erik Barnouw Prize for the Best Historical Film of the Year. Her publications include the companion book to* A Paralyzing Fear. *In addition to filmmaking and teaching in her annual Institute for Documentary Filmmaking, Seavey launched in 2003 "SILVERDOCS: The AFI/Discovery Channel Documentary Festival" and serves as chair of the festival. She also serves as a consultant to the media program at the Duke Ellington School for the Arts in Washington, D.C.*

FILM AND MEDIA PRODUCERS: TAKING HISTORY OFF THE PAGE AND PUTTING IT ON THE SCREEN

Nina Gilden Seavey

Historical documentary has come to play an ever more important role in how the American public and students of history learn about the past. The proliferation of long-form documentary programs and series produced for broadcast and cable networks such as PBS, the Discovery Channel, Turner Broadcasting, HBO, the History Channel, among others, has made historical documentary a part of the standard fare for viewing audiences. In addition, museums and other educational venues have incorporated short-form video and film histories as components in their exhibitions and public programs. Finally, new technologies such as CD-ROM and the World Wide Web have made historical photographic and motion picture images a graphics feature of all of our communications landscape. Indeed, for much of the American public, the viewing of these visual history pieces is frequently the only exposure to historical content that many will ever experience; the majority of Americans just do not read history books any more.

Many historians have not yet embraced this new visual mode of communication. By ignoring it, however, historians have become more isolated within the ivory tower than ever and may well cease to be the arbiters of current historical debate. Moreover, when historians do enter the visual realm, they act more frequently as critics of already produced programming rather than as participants in the active process of making a film. Therefore, the separation of the historian from the body of visually produced material has given rise to a new breed of historian: the filmmaker/historian, usually a film director who has no historical training but who has a great enthusiasm for historical subjects. Consequently, much of the American consciousness about history is now being conveyed by this new breed of self-taught filmmaker/historians. This is all the more reason for historians to retrain their thinking and consider taking their text off the page and bringing it to the screen.

THE HISTORIAN AND THE FILMMAKER

In the past, the relationship between the historian and the visual media has been a tense one. For the historian, there is a mistrust of filmmakers as if one were encountering an alien being. On the part of the filmmaker, there is frequently an impatience with the amount of dialogue and inconclusiveness inherent in the academic historic debate. Put simply, historians love the complexity of the historical task, and filmmakers find complexity a problem in an already visually, narratively, and auditorially complex medium.

These tensions are compounded by the fact that history and filmmaking do, in actuality, have diametrically opposed goals. The task for the historian is to arrive at some kind of truth. The historian takes the available evidence, evaluates its significance, and provides some contextual meaning and broader historiographic insight. The goal for the filmmaker, on the other hand, is to first and foremost engage the audience in the principle of the "suspension of disbelief," i.e. to create a filmic reality that allows the audience to believe a story as if it were true—whether or not the story is factually correct in whole or in part.

As history, documentary tries to approach truth in the most responsible way. It is an ethical responsibility for filmmakers to stay as close to the facts as possible, and most documentarians undertake this task seriously. But the film must work on its own terms; that is to say, it must have a dramatic structure that allows the audience to enter into a story line that evolves from beginning to middle to end, with all of the dramatic development and climax that makes film a compelling story-telling medium. The use of historical evidence, then, is measured in the broader context of achieving important filmic goals.

Therefore, historical documentary is not simply "history on film." It is a film that has a historical story line and that uses historical evidence to tell its story. And herein lies the tension between the two disciplines. Historians use historical materials to explicate and explore historical truths and their meaning. Filmmakers use historical materials to create a window into past places, times, events, and characters that may or may not illuminate a broader historical construct. Although coming from two very different perspectives, historians and filmmakers must collaborate to ensure that history is represented in as honest and compelling a way as possible in the filmic form.

There are opportunities for historians to participate more directly in the process of documentary making, but the basic methodological issues need to be resolved before historians will view work in the visual media as something other than an errant stepchild of the monograph. Therefore, my goal in the pages that follow is to take historians out of the role of detached critic and place them in the context of appreciating the actual task of producing scripts and choosing images that make historical films work.

FILM AS HISTORICAL INTERPRETATION

In approaching the visual medium, the first problem historians have to overcome is one of professional self-identification. There is still a perception that those historians who are engaged in the documentary process are not "doing history." Instead, they are moving outside of the natural confines of academic dialogue into the realm of "popular culture." Production in the visual media has not yet assumed the relative importance of a good scholarly monograph or journal article. Filmed accounts of the past are seen by the historical profession as somehow contrived, as bowing to "action" over "analysis" and relying too heavily on the descriptive, narrative form. Further, critiques focus on the dramatic requirements of film over historical text as a constructed (some would say, "contrived") form of communication, rather than analysis.

What the academic historian may forget, however, is that the practice of even the highest form of written scholarship about the past is as equally highly constructed as a carefully crafted film. As Hayden White notes: "Every written history is a product of processes of condensation, displacement, symbolization, and qualification exactly like those used in the production of a filmed representation. It is only the medium that differs, not the way in which messages are produced. . . . the historical monograph is no less 'shaped' or constructed than the historical film or historical novel. It may be shaped by different principles, but there is no reason why a filmed representation of historical events should not be as analytical and realistic as any written account."[1] Both the language of the academic historian and the film of the documentarist are then, in some senses, equally constructed. In both forms, we are "creating history" whether through language or images. But it is still insecurity over the "principles" that govern the production of documentary that makes it difficult for the profession to accept the inherent connection between the academic written account and the filmed version.

Audience is a key issue for historians engaged in making documentaries. For millions of people, television and film documentary is the only introduction to history that they will have, except for the history they recall from elementary or secondary schools. This poses both enormous opportunities for the scholarly historian as well as several problems. For the historian who is accustomed to writing for fairly small audiences, the possibility of expressing oneself to a broader group may seem appealing. On the other hand, most historians write for an intelligent, educated group of peers; they, by and large, do not write for the average eighth grader. The need to address adequately the issue of making oneself understandable to a highly heterogeneous and less well-informed audience, while still holding fast to historical principles, can be problematic. Inevitably, the responsibility faced by the historian in articulating the ambiguities of a given historical incident is great. Most viewers are not privy to the intricacies of the historical debate; they find the arguments over the meaning of facts and the broader interpretations of events and historical themes confusing, or even irrelevant. However, in order to maintain the regard of their peers, historians cannot shy away from these standard historical exercises by making history seem concrete and settled. Therefore, the historian/filmmaker must negotiate between the broad educational range of the average viewer and the exigencies of the true historical task.

Moreover, the filmmaker must address the historian's concern for historiographical context or framework as the structure of the film begins to emerge. Thus far, many filmmakers have failed to show the fluidity of the historical enterprise. Documentaries present historical analysis as static; the view of the period in which the documentary is produced, then, is the definitive one. This, of course, misrepresents the complexity of the historical work. The ever-changing current-day ideologies which govern historical thought and the impact of the discovery of new forms of evidence must be incorporated into the understanding of an historical subject depicted on the screen. Revisionist history must be related clearly as a juxtaposition against conventional theories. And questions about future interpretations must be raised. Otherwise, the audience is tricked into thinking that the documentary that they have watched is the definitive, final analysis.

It is in this question of historical complexity that the central tension between the documentary producer and the historian must be addressed. Whereas the historian is wholly concerned with the notion of "truth" as best defined by the evidence, the television or film producer is necessarily preoccupied with such truths as they can be translated into a dramatic story line, high ratings, and informed entertainment. Therefore, producers frequently tend to ignore historical advice which they perceive will lead down a convoluted path.

Many producers see film and television as a wholly "sequential medium, so to say, in which episode follows on episode, without respite. This clearly means that the medium is ideally suited to telling stories and anecdotes, creating atmosphere and mood, giving diffuse impressions. It does not lend itself easily to the detailed analysis of complex events; it is difficult to use it to relate coherently complicated narrative histories, and it is quite hopeless at portraying abstract ideas."[2] In other words, many filmmakers do not see film as a framework for historical dialogue. Such an attitude trivializes historical work, and it is the basis of historians' derision of those who work on film and television projects.

While many film documentarians reject the notion that historical and intellectual complexity can be introduced into the documentary process, it is still incumbent upon them to engage in historical interpretation. Together, the filmmaker/historian team can convey these complex questions and issues in language that is not too convoluted. To avoid complexity is to do a disservice to the richest and most intriguing aspects of the human experience. This complexity, however, need not and should not render the documentary unintelligible or unapproachable to the general public. If handled deftly, by those who understand both the historical task and the exigencies of the visual medium, interpretation can play an important part in the documentary process.

More importantly, because of the cost of producing documentaries in today's marketplace, once a program has been produced, the chance that the subject will be redone within the foreseeable future is doubtful. Therefore, one is ever more obligated to convey the sense that the debate over the historical period has not ended. In spite of the filmmaker's desire to make history seem easy, both the presentation of a historiographic context and a sense of the range of analysis are necessary for an honest portrayal of the past.

ORAL AND VISUAL EVIDENCE IN FILM

The presentation of historical complexity plays only part of the historian/filmmaker's task. The larger question of evidence is equally challenging. As in the case of the article or monograph, film documentarians must look at notebooks, diaries, secondary texts, manuscripts, government documents, and the whole array of other evidence to evaluate one's historical palette. As in any historical enterprise, each piece of evidence must be weighed alongside other pieces of evidence to determine the questions of veracity in the broader historical context. This tenet holds particularly true in the presentation of historic material in the visual medium; but the task is much more complicated.

Filmmakers must address two additional challenges. First, there is the selection of oral historical evidence, i.e., "What one will hear." And second, there is the selection of the visual material, i.e., "What one will see." The central question raised is whether either the audio and visual elements of film are, in fact, evidence at all or whether they are merely illustration. Is oral history on film not really historical evidence at all but merely staged anecdotes? And are the films, photographs, and drawings which comprise the visual elements of historical documentary not really visual evidence but just "pictures" or "illustrations"?

Without question, the use of oral historical evidence in documentary (or what the filmmaker would call "audio") is different from that used for support of a written text. In text, one can interview literally scores of oral historical subjects. The use of these interviews can be abundant, and an archive of rich oral material can be developed. In writing text, these interviews can be interwoven and recollections cross-checked for historical accuracy.

But film is different. The goal of the filmed interview is to get the appropriate story/recollection/commentary on the screen. A filmmaker wants to find exactly the right kind of person, with the right kind of delivery, with the right "qualification" to carry the message. It is, in many senses, a question of casting. When shooting film versus videotape, this phenomena is ever more important as the cost of film and its processing far exceeds the cost of tape and makes the documentarian ever more cautious about "over-interviewing."

The result of this difference of intended purpose between oral material gathered for historical research and those interviews that are conducted for use in documentaries is its ultimate impact on the viewer. The interviewee in the documentary inevitably becomes the authoritative source—not one of a chorus among many, but the definitive purveyor of information. In the limited time allocated to any given subject within the documentary context, the decision to use an oral history interview can, therefore, be a potent one. Therein lies the trap into which a viewer can fall.

The subjects of these interviews, frequently eyewitnesses to a given event or an important person, can give the appearance of providing a special kind of window on the past which can be erroneous or misleading. As historian Michael Frisch notes: "[We can] come to view oral-historical evidence, because of its immediacy and emotional resonance, as something almost beyond interpretation—as a direct window on the feelings and, in some senses, the meaning of past experience. This tendency. . . . produces dramatic editing choices, and makes for vivid documentary, but it is equally problematic: to confer unquestioned authority on direct experience is usually to mystify, rather than bypass the process of interpretation."[3] Simply "having been there" does not necessarily give one the ability to make insightful, authoritative historical judgments on a given set of events. As Robert Rosenstone, who, as a historian, has worked on several film projects, aptly points out, the fallacy here is to equating "memory with history."[4] In fact, one might postulate that participating in a historical event actually limits one's view as opposed to studying a variety of evidence at a later date. "[T]hose who 'were there' tend to be at best prisoners of the frameworks we seek to place in perspective, and at worst self-serving apologists for their own past actions."[5] As such, the use of direct-experience oral histories should be used by filmmakers to suggest, augment, and highlight historical interpretation, not as sole interpretive authority. Unfortunately, too many filmmakers give into the impulse to use interviews to convey the drama of an event without regard to such issues—primarily because it can make for great films, but perhaps not great history.

The use of historians on camera is usually more judiciously implemented than eyewitness accounts. Historical documentary filmmakers are accustomed to working with scholars, using their comments in the scripting process, and ultimately interviewing them on film. Again, however, one should not be fooled into thinking that these interviews are not equally a matter of "casting the right character for the role." Shelby Foote was perfect casting for Ken Burns's *The Civil War* in spite of the fact that there are many other, much more eminent Civil War historians. But Mr. Foote's lyrical southern drawl, his scruffy comportment, and his verbal facility with the intricate detail of Civil War life made him irresistible as an on-camera commentator. Other scholarly comments can be woven into the narration of a film, but the commitment by a filmmaker to shoot an interview with a historian carries with it a broader need to convey the historical subject matter in a dramatic, pleasing, albeit intelligent, manner. There is nothing more disastrous for a filmmaker than a brilliant historian who can't "tell his own story."

Equally challenging is the selection of the visual evidence or, in filmmakers' parlance, "pictures." The objective of the camera angle's eye is not as easy to determine as the validity of a written source. Diaries, we know, are subjective. Demographic material, somewhat less so. But one must also question the objectivity of the camera that creates the illusion of reality for the film or television audience. Photographers or cinematographers are, by definition, diarists of sorts. They tell stories through their own eyes, making many choices about what is important for us to know and what is not. As viewers, however, we tend to accept this illusion of reality as actuality. But the visual image is not evidence in and of itself. It must be weighed against other pieces of primary and secondary sources to determine its import. Visual evidence can, like the oral history interview, only highlight the historical narrative. A picture cannot speak a thousand words; it can only be illustrative of the lessons of the past.

Sometimes the selection of archival images are more suspect than one can imagine. Historians of film have learned that newsreels produced about World War II and Korea, for example, were frequently staged to serve the public relations goals of the creators. Earlier practices of dramatic recreation can often confuse current producers of documentary films about the origins of such footage and its accurate depiction of events.

A certain sophistication in the selection of visual evidence in the production of competent historical documentary is therefore imperative. In the same way that historians question the economic, political, and social context of each piece of evidence, so too must historians/filmmakers learn to ask pertinent questions about the visual materials presented before them. Does it matter whether a scene describing an event occurring in the 1840s uses as an illustration a photograph taken in 1890? Can an image portraying an event that took place in one part of the world be used to describe a similar event which occurred half a world away? Most historians would be shocked by the use of such "evidence" in historical documentary. Most filmmakers would not.

For filmmakers, the construction of the truth is broadly defined; it is not a question of piecing together just the right evidence side by side. In fact, if such rigorous standards were held by filmmakers, many historical subjects would go unexplored on film for lack of appropriate evidence. The "truth" for the historical filmmaker lies in the idea of a "general truth about the subject" not in its specifics. The whole sense of how a historical event occurred and its overriding meaning are more important than whether each component part correlates exactly to the subject matter. It is a question of deriving the "historicity" of a subject as opposed to creating an exact replica of the event. Once a true sense of the historical idea is established, then the specific constructs of it are more open to creative selection.

Clearly, the integrity of the historian/filmmaker is at stake in the creation of this visual concept of "historicity." In the same way, however, that historians always select what they perceive to be relevant pieces of evidence to support their assertions, so too can the historical documentarian make candid determinations about what visual material to shoot and use in the editing room. It is not that a selection process is occurring which is crucial here. Instead, it is the intelligence and mindfulness of such selections that make the process a potent one.

The final issue in the use of visual evidence is the problem of a lack of such evidence. It is important that the pictures match the descriptive narrative and have some correlation to the oral history interviews. The most binding constraint on the historian/producer is when there is no visual evidence at all from which to choose. For those historians and filmmakers who work in the context of twentieth-century economic, political, and intellectual history, absence of evidence is not frequently a pressing problem. Even for those documentarians of the nineteenth century, there are often rich historical resources, both written and visual, for certain periods, such as the Civil War. But for those historical films in which there is no visual evidence, the documentarist's historical skills are truly put to the test.

When confronted with no visualization, documentary can truly enter into the realm of the imaginary. The use of art work, lithographs, etchings, and other renderings help create a sense of the past. And increasingly, the filmmaker turns to dramatic film techniques to recreate a scene or place from the past. Filmmakers frequently direct reenacted scenes with actors/reenactors. Similarly, they use the camera to create the "ambiance" of a place or event. The use of subjective camera techniques or "point-of-view" shots can make viewers feel as if they are actually having a given experience. Moreover, actorless scenes created by moving the camera through constructed "environments" with photos and artifacts placed "in situ" are now commonplace in historical documentary. Such scenes allow viewers to feel as if they have entered into a place once inhabited by historical subjects. Frequently these scenes are quite effective in creating a sense of mood or place, drawing the documentary away from the traditional use of evidence and bringing the viewer into the historical idea in a more dramatic way.

Ultimately, producers of documentaries have to come to grips with their own inherent limitations: that in a mass medium, the public is cap-

Producer and co-director Nina Gilden Seavey and director Paul Wagner setting up a shot in front of the Alamo for their film *The Battle of the Alamo* for the Discovery Channel. *Courtesy of the Center for History in the Media, George Washington University.*

tivated by the pictures. When such visual evidence is not at hand or does not wholly match an event, we cannot abdicate the responsibility to investigate such subjects. Therefore, some other visual mode needs to be constructed to compensate for such lack. These techniques will continue to be developed as documentary makers increasingly draw from innovations in dramatic filmmaking and animation. And the historical profession will inevitably be forced to develop standards and methods that govern the acceptable form and use of these techniques.

THE FILM SCRIPT

The script, or the documentary narrative, poses yet another opportunity and responsibility for the historian/producer. Historians are accustomed to thinking about text and composition as a form of scholarly presentation. This is problematic in television and film where what "sounds good" to the listener is essential to telling one's story in an effective way. In the documentary narrative "the tempo is different, there can be no recall, no flipping back of the page, no elaborate parallel themes by footnotes or parenthesis."[6]

For better or for worse, much of historical training encompasses the mastery of complicated text. Therefore, when approaching a process whereby the entire goal is to simplify, reduce, and speak without ambiguity, historians are often at a loss. Frequently they will attempt to interject complexities which the audience or the visual material cannot abide. But one can speak intelligently without convolution. The basic limitation of the film and television medium is its commitment to making an issue "understood"; it is perhaps this constraint that many historians refuse to accept. It is, however, an inescapable part of the documentarist's landscape that the words which are chosen as descriptors of the visual and oral history evidence be as "journalistic" as possible. Although some scholars may feel differently, the press for making the narration work positively as a storytelling device does not inherently erode the historical value of a documentary project. It is merely a means to allow the visual medium to work within its own context.

A related key issue of documentary narrative is that of length. The academic historian's concept of oral or written exposition does not have the limitations which television or film places upon it. The number of words used in a one-hour lecture is significant; the length of most articles can run anywhere from two to forty pages. The visual media offer no such temporal latitude; there is no allowance for all-encompassing analysis. In order to maintain the interest of the audience, narratives can generally consume approximately one-quarter of the program's length.[7] This narrative, coupled with music, interviews, and discrete periods of silence, will not correspond for the academician to the amount said in a standard lecture or journal article. Failure to adhere to these essential standards, however, will render the program into nothing more than "a kind of illustrated radio programme."[8] Again, if conveying the historical message in the most effective manner is the goal within the constraints of such a mass medium, then the issue of limiting the length of one's message is merely part of the documentary process which the historian must accept. Failure to abide by such constraints merely detracts from and defeats the ultimate purpose of such historical programming, which of course, is to engage in compelling, lively, and informed education.

CONCLUSION

The context for academic discussion about the role of the historian in the documentary production process has radically changed over the past ten years. With the large numbers of programs produced, historians are being dragged, liking it or not, into the age of the visual expression of historical ideas. There has been, however, surprisingly little written that reflects these changes. With the multitude of historical documentaries produced, the doors have been opened for audiences to accept a more complicated and sophisticated approach to history. And, conversely, these documentaries have paved the way for historians to participate in a historical dialogue that exists outside of the historical text, and outside of the academy.

Today, historians and their students can begin to test the rules which govern the historical documentary exercise. Technology has assured that, from the highest funded film to the lowliest budgeted in-classroom exercise, all can participate in the historical documentary arena. New film and television technologies have made experimentation in the visual media accessible not only to those in the communications industry but throughout the academy as well. One can easily write, shoot, and edit one's own documentary or oral history project within the confines of a not-very-well equipped institution.

Therefore, the environment is ripe for historians to use the visual form as a distinct means of scholarly expression, and we have the rare opportunity for an interesting scholarly debate on the ideas that can guide these activities.

History has necessarily been a profession devoted to the written word. Without increased discussion and consensus on the knotty methodological problems that face those who make the jump to the visual media, history for the American public will continue to be produced by those who are well intentioned, but historically naive. The professional historian will be, as now, left standing on the outside looking in.

NOTES

1. Hayden White, "Historiography and Historiophoty," *American Historical Review* 93 (1988): 1194, 1196.
2. Jerry Kuehl, "History on the Public Screen II," in Paul Smith, ed., *The Historian and Film* (Cambridge: Cambridge University Press, 1976), 178.
3. Michael Frisch, "Oral History, Documentary, and the Mystification of Power: A Cast Study Critique of Public Methodology," *International Journal of Oral History* 6 (1985): 119–20.
4. Robert Rosenstone, "History in Images/History in Words: Reflections on the Possibility of Really Putting History onto Film," *American Historical Review* 93 (1988): 1174.
5. Frisch, "Oral History," 123.
6. Donald Watt, "History on the Public Screen I," in Alan Rosenthal, ed., *New Challenges for Documentary* (Berkeley: University of California Press, 1988), 436.
7. Jerry Kuehl, "History on the Public Screen II," 177.
8. Ibid., 177.

ANTOINETTE J. LEE is special projects manager with the National Center for Cultural Resources of the National Park Service. She earned her B.A. in history at the University of Pennsylvania and both an M.Phil. and a Ph.D. in American civilization at George Washington University. Dr. Lee previously served as a historian for the National Register of Historic Places, education services coordinator for the National Trust for Historic Preservation, and as a consultant and freelance historian. She teaches in the M.A. Program in Historic Preservation at Goucher College and has taught previously at George Washington University. Dr. Lee's publications include Architects to the Nation: The Rise and Decline of the Supervising Architect's Office *(2000),* Buildings of the District of Columbia *(1993),* Past Meets Future: Saving America's Historic Environments *(1992),* The American Mosaic: Preserving a Nation's Heritage *(1987), special issues of* CRM, *and reports such as* Held in Trust: Preserving America's Historic Places *(1991).*

HISTORIC PRESERVATIONISTS AND CULTURAL RESOURCES MANAGERS: PRESERVING AMERICA'S HISTORIC PLACES

Antoinette J. Lee

Historic preservation involves often challenging decisions about the value or importance of a building or place, and historians play key roles in that assessment process. Usually, these historians are not college or university professors but are affiliated with a governmental agency; employed by a consulting firm; associated with a private, nonprofit organization; or working as independent historians. Who are these historians and how do they presume to make such key public policy pronouncements?

For many years, historic preservation was a grassroots activity, populated largely by volunteers. Many of them were associated with a single property, such as the Hermitage in Tennessee or Mount Vernon in Virginia. As the U.S. Congress expanded the responsibilities of the federal government in conservation and preservation, evidenced most notably in the establishment in 1916 of the National Park Service, a cadre of historians was employed to assist with decisions about preservation and interpretation. Similar programs in state and local governments and the expanded operations of private, nonprofit preservation organizations further spurred the demand for historians.

But it was not until the mid-1960s that the preservation movement really took off. Redefined as "cultural resources management," the National Historic Preservation Act of 1966 and its subsequent amendments set up a national historic preservation partnership bringing together the National Park Service, other federal agencies, state historic preservation offices, local governments, Indian tribes, and the private sector. It established core programs, such as the National Register of Historic Places, the Historic Preservation Fund, technical assistance and training, the Certified Local Government program, and the system by which federal agencies survey and inventory historic properties and use this information in project planning.

Reinforcing the 1966 act were key pieces of related legislation, including archaeological legislation that directed federal agencies to assume broad responsibilities for evaluating the impacts of their programs on historic resources and for managing historic properties under their jurisdiction. Accompanying tax legislation provided incentives for rehabilitating historic buildings, which have been replicated in many state tax codes. These programs, as well as parallel programs at the state, tribal, and local governments levels, set the stage for a greater number of historians to work in the historic preservation/cultural resources management field over the past three decades.

BASIC ROLES AND RESPONSIBILITIES

Because the National Park Service leads the national historic preservation partnership, its definitions have national applicability. The National Park Service defines "cultural resources management" as "the range of activities aimed at understanding, preserving, and providing for the enjoyment of cultural resources." It includes research, planning for actions, and stewardship of these resources in the context of overall operations. It also includes support for the appreciation and perpetuation of related cultural practices. This definition can apply as well to "historic preservation."

According to the National Park Service, a "cultural resources specialist" is a professional trained in one of the cultural resources fields. Included are anthropologists (applied cultural anthropologists, archaeologists, ethnographers, and ethnohistorians), architectural historians, architectural conservators, archivists, curators, historians, historical architects, historical landscape architects, landscape historians, and object conservators. In other words, historic preservation is not the exclusive preserve of historians—they must work in cooperation with individuals from other disciplines.

Moreover, many governmental agencies are under increased pressure to make the nomination documentation and review process more accessible to the public. To many, increased accessibility means that interested members of the public should be able to participate in this process without resorting to the cost of hiring a professional historian—that the quality of the documentation is more important than the formal qualifications of the person who produces it. Many able amateur historians produce authoritative documentation on historic properties, while some academic historians are not experienced in producing the kind of documentation needed for preservation work.

Producing documentation is a more complicated task than many, whether professional or amateur, realize. When historic preservation was largely an activity of private, nonprofit organizations and individual initiative, historians conducted research on properties for preservation and interpretation without consulting with members of the public. The historian had a single client—the organization or individual who sponsored the project. Today, because much of the work of historic preservation takes place as an outcome of legislation at all levels, historians must consult with affected parties at the same time that research is being conducted and must understand the process by which properties are considered for formal designation or registration. They must comprehend the criteria by which properties are evaluated, comply with standards for documentation, and be adept at justifying the significance and thus eligibility of properties for various levels of formal recognition.

Much of this work is performed under contract by a consulting firm or an independent historian. In government historic preservation offices, few government historians undertake all needed research and documentation work. Instead, they administer contracts for studies, advise consulting historians, and perform editorial work on final documents. Or, the client for such work may be a private organization or a community group interested in preserving a historic place. The work then is submitted to the government officials responsible for evaluating and processing the documentation.

But responsibility does not end with a report. In order to be effective preservationists, historians must work as advocates for the significance of historic properties. They must be prepared to present oral testimony before review boards, planning commissions, and local governing boards or speak before community groups and professional peer groups. They

Preservation historians document types of buildings that often are overlooked by the public. Historians working for the National Park Service's Historic American Buildings Survey/Historic American Engineering Record (HABS/HAER) documented significant late nineteenth/early twentieth-century industrial buildings in Dubuque, Iowa, as part of a larger effort to record outstanding examples of the country's heritage through measured drawings, large-format photography, and written histories. These documents are available to the public through the HABS/HAER collections that are housed, serviced, and maintained by the Library of Congress. *Photograph by Clayton B. Fraser for HABS/HAER.*

should even be prepared to face off in public meetings with historians hired by the "opposition" to argue the nonsignificance of historic places. In any case, they must translate dry, factual information into compelling reasons why a property should receive the formal recognition that will warrant even modest levels of governmental protection and involvement when designated properties are threatened.

This kind of historical work moves research and documentation out of the ivory tower and into the public arena, benefitting members of the public who value historic places as community resources. A historian's work can achieve the relatively modest success of causing a single building to receive official recognition and any financial and protection benefits that may accompany this recognition. But in some instances, a historian's work may serve to transform local and regional planning philosophy because of overriding public interest in the historical values of an area or district.

WORKING AS A PRESERVATION HISTORIAN

The usual first step in any historic preservation effort is research and documentation on the property or properties that private or public clients want studied. Sometimes a development or construction decision is pending, thereby requiring an expedited documentation process in order to address an immediate situation. At other times, the client may request that a survey of an area or of a group of potentially historic properties be undertaken to facilitate decision making at some future date.

The documentation of a historic property often is conducted at facilities familiar to historians, e.g., libraries and archives. However, because much of the documentation work is carried out on properties of local interest, historians also must become familiar with local sources of information, such as institutional records associated with a neighborhood, school system, library system, or church. They must search creatively for sources because often the information on the properties may not be readily available in standard research institutions. And they may need to undertake oral histories to record information that cannot be found in organized collections. Frequently, they must resolve contradictory information provided by these sources. Fieldwork is also necessary, requiring time devoted to walking the area of the historic property—under perhaps less than comfortable conditions—and making notes on the property's attributes and condition.

In documenting properties for historic preservation purposes, historians must be able to provide written descriptions of the physical evidence—buildings, groups of buildings, street systems, archaeological remains, industrial structures, and open spaces—and that requires a vocabulary acceptable to technical experts and yet understandable and meaningful to the general public. Historians must be able to provide incisive narrative statements of significance and justify their evaluation of the historical significance of a property in ways that can move the listener—whether a peer historian or a member of a public board or commission—to support the property's preservation.

The product of the preservation historian's work most often is a report or a nomination for designation or listing. This work may stand on its own or may be incorporated into a larger report on an area. Much of the preservation historian's work remains in the area of unpublished reports because that is what is required to achieve a preservation decision. Publication of the results most often is not in the "scope of work" for a project. There are many places in which to publish preservation documentation, but turning the report into an acceptable publication normally is at the initiative of the individual historian.

After a property has received recognition or designation at one or more levels of government, historians may be involved in preparing historic structures reports on the history and condition of a building or structure. They may complete and process forms needed for building owners to receive tax benefits for rehabilitation of historic buildings or participate in evaluations of impacts of potential development projects on formally recognized historic properties. They also may prepare interpretive materials, such as published walking tours, guides, exhibition catalogs, and books on historic places.

Thus, historians who work in historic preservation are working in applied history in its best sense. The client provides the topic for research and documentation and sets forth the compensation for this work. The client also defines the time period in which the work must be completed and the purposes to which the information will be applied. All of these conditions are negotiable, but, in any case, historians undertake research at the request of and on the terms of others. Although, in some cases, historians may identify a research and documentation need and then seek funds to underwrite their own project, the freedom to define projects is the exception, rather than the rule.

As individuals move beyond the level of survey historian and begin to administer studies and surveys for government agencies or private organizations, they inevitably move into administrative/review roles. This moves them away from the traditional role of historian. While they may carry the title of and identify themselves as historians, they actually will be program managers.

PROFESSIONAL ISSUES AND CONCERNS

The major professional issue facing historians who work in historic preservation/cultural resources management is the comparability of their work with that in the academic world. In preservation, the title "historian" is much more loosely defined than it is in the academic world. Preservation historians cover the range from an individual who has earned a Ph.D. in history or a related field and published widely in the field, to the park ranger who interprets historical themes to the public. Many do not have doctorates but have an M.A. or a B.A. degree in history or a related field. Historians with Ph.D.s are more common in consulting firms or as independent historians, where a doctoral degree is helpful in securing contract work.

The gap between academic historians and preservation historians begins in the graduate and undergraduate programs which train historians to work in the historic preservation, applied history, or public history fields. For the most part, these programs are conceived, administered, and taught by historians who have spent their entire careers in the academic world. Some have served on boards of local historical societies or community organizations or even on state historic preservation review boards, but they are essentially academics. The courses they teach are relevant to the work that historians actually perform in historic preservation, but the connection sometimes can be tenuous. Most of a student's experience in the real world of historic preservation takes places in internships and directed research projects, where the work is overseen by someone who works in the historic preservation field. After graduation, the student's subsequent accomplishments may be only partially understood by academic mentors, who better understand those who have moved into other teaching positions.

The gap between the professional worlds of preservation historians and academic historians persists throughout a career. The products of the preservation historian likely will not receive the same weight in evaluating professional accomplishments as teaching and writing scholarly monographs and academic journal articles. But a small number of historians may bridge the gap by working full-time as preservation historians and then adding on part-time teaching responsibilities and undertaking publications that may attract the attention of academic historians.

On the other hand, many preservation historians wish that academic historians would undertake historical research and publish works that would find a ready audience among preservationists, such as local histories that provide a context for evaluating physical places. While some historians in both sectors are attempting to work on areas of mutual interest, it is likely that this gap will persist.

PROFESSIONAL NETWORKS

Despite the efforts of many traditional historical organizations to reach out to preservation historians to gain their membership and participation, most preservation historians opt to belong to their own organizations. During the 1960s and 1970s, many organizations, such as the National Council on Public History, were founded to represent the interests of the nonacademic historian. Many preservation historians also belong to organizations which welcome general members of the public interested in historic preservation. These organizations include the National Trust for Historic Preservation, the Society for Industrial Archaeology, and the American Association for State and Local History. All of these organizations produce newsletters and even journals, which provide places for essays and research that might not find a receptive audience in traditional academic journals.

Beyond furnishing the benefits of publications, conferences, and networking, these organizations provide information that is crucial for successful work in historic preservation. A preservation historian, for example, may learn of a survey of a group of buildings in one location that will be helpful in a survey of a similar group of buildings in another location. From these organizations, historians may learn of funding sources that may assist with supporting a needed study of potentially historic properties.

Despite the proliferation of historic preservation organizations, many historians will maintain their memberships and participate in special sessions on nonacademic topics at meetings of traditional historical associations. For example, many graduates of American studies programs will maintain their memberships in the American Studies Association, while graduates of history departments may be members of the American Historical Association or the Organization of American Historians. However, their work may never be published in those organizations' journals.

In addition to joining and participating in organizations, many historians belong to informal roundtables, discussion groups, and luncheon organizations for the sake of networking. Many preservationists network through computer listserves and learn about the latest developments in their field through the Internet. Several comprehensive Internet home pages are administered through organizations such as the National Council for Preservation Education, the National Park Service, the National Trust for Historic Preservation, and the Federal Preservation Forum.

SPECIALIZED EDUCATION AND CONTINUING EDUCATION OPPORTUNITIES

Until the early 1970s, much of the training for preservation historians occurred in traditional history departments. Many of these historians "fell" into historic preservation work by accident, while others entered the field after having been dissuaded from an academic career by the academic glut of the 1970s. Still others entered the historic preservation field after obtaining an M.A. degree in history and sought to apply their interest in the field without obtaining a Ph.D. degree.

The earliest master's level programs in historic preservation developed in the late 1960s and early 1970s at Columbia University, Cornell University, the University of Vermont, Boston University, George Washington University, and Middle Tennessee State University. American studies programs expanded as well in the post–World War II era and took on specializations in material culture studies and nonacademic historical work, providing a new venue for training for historic preservation careers. Museum training programs and architectural history departments also turned out graduates who were employed in historic preservation work.

After this initial period, a virtual flood of new graduate programs in historic preservation and cultural resources management, applied history, and public history beckoned to students. Most of them were founded by academic historians with a genuine interest in these topics, and they developed the essential linkages with public agencies and private organizations. Some academic programs were the products of efforts by academics to revitalize otherwise sleepy history departments with infusions of students interested in history, but with no prospects of ever teaching history at the college or university level.

Most degree programs in historic preservation consist of the following elements: a core of courses in history, historic preservation principles and practice, architectural history, preservation documentation, fieldwork, and material culture. Allied courses in building materials studies, urban history, and historical archaeology may fill in the curriculum. The second element is practical experience, whether through internships or part-time employment with a historic preservation organization or agency. The third is hands-on experience with using historical skills to document and advocate a historic property, whether in a paid or volunteer capacity. For many preservationists, a fourth element is enrollment in one or more of a great variety of summer institutes, summer field schools, and summer internships.

Even after assembling this basic foundation of knowledge, gaining employment in historic preservation is not guaranteed. Historic preservation is a small and competitive field. Graduates must ensure that they develop a list of contacts active in the field who are familiar with their work. They must be willing to invest time in publishing their research work. Graduates also must be open to working in locations or positions that may not be their first choices, thereby acquiring valuable experience that may later facilitate moving to more desirable positions in other parts of the country or with other types of organizations.

Once employed in a historic preservation position, historians must invest their own resources in keeping up with their professional as well as academic field. They should attend conferences, accumulate a substantial library of publications, and enroll in continuing education opportunities. There are numerous opportunities for broadening a historian's knowledge of the field and for establishing oneself as an expert in one or more aspects of historic preservation.

FUTURE DIRECTIONS

Because the work of historians in historic preservation resulted from the tremendous increase in preservation legislation at all levels of government, historians should work to strengthen the historic preservation "safety net" that now provides consideration for historic properties in the face of development pressures and offers incentives for private investment in historic preservation. Like the rest of the governmental establishments, preservation programs are subject to downsizing, reinventing, and flattening. Preservation historians should be advocates not only for specific historic places but also for the laws that hold the designation and protection process in place. They also must maintain vigilance over the historic records and sources for the kind of documentation on which many preservation decisions are based.

Another important concern is keeping "history" in historic preservation. Many preservation historians feel that historic preservation has become a business and a tool for developers to achieve the minimum of preservation for the maximum of investment return. The American historic preservation system is notable for its utter pragmatism. Keeping the connection with history is an important goal and one that holds the greatest appeal for the general public. It is the general public, after all, who will support the retention and the increase in the historic preservation organizational infrastructure.

Accordingly, preservation historians must become more attuned to the historic places that are valued by the nation's diverse cultural groups. These may include properties that are not architecturally notable but are important to interpreting the history of a group, often an ethnic group. For example, an abandoned farmstead in Montana may be one of a group of historic farmsteads which represent the influx of Scandinavian settlers in the late nineteenth century. An urban neighborhood may be important in understanding the lifeways of early African American migrants from rural areas to the city. When working with these kinds of properties, historians must consult with the affected groups and understand the historical values from the groups' points-of-view.

Preservation historians will continue to cooperate on joint efforts with academic historians. Both kinds of historians have a great deal to gain from greater cooperation in the areas of contextual studies and interpretation of historic places. Each has much to lose by maintaining separate standards and areas of influence. Most preservation historians want

The work of preservation historians often reveals broader historical trends in a community, state, region, or nation. The Central Young Woman's Christian Association (YWCA) Building in Richmond, Virginia, was constructed in 1913–14 to provide employment services, room and board accommodations, and physical fitness programs to women who worked in the city's tobacco factories, department stores, and offices. It operated a similar program for African American women at another building. The Central YWCA building remained a whites-only facility until the mid-1960s, when the YWCA integrated all of its programs and centers and promoted the elimination of racism in other areas of Richmond life. The Virginia State Historic Preservation Office documented the building and nominated it to the National Register of Historic Places for its significance in social history and architecture. *Photograph by H. Christopher Slusher. Courtesy of the National Park Service.*

to be accorded the same respectability as academic historians. Most academic historians want to have the kind of public impact on society that preservation historians take for granted.

Regardless of the employer, preservation historians can take pride in their essential role in representing the public's interest in protecting America's historic places. Their work serves the public in the thousands of communities nationwide that benefit from the national historic preservation program. While academic historians may leave books to posterity, preservation historians leave preserved historic places for the public benefit.

MARK HOWELL is principal in the firm Howell Consulting. He holds a B.A. and an M.A. in American studies from the College of William and Mary and a certificate from the Seminar for Historical Administration. Prior to forming his own business, he was the director of Program Development at the Colonial Williamsburg Foundation in Williamsburg, Virginia. During his tenure at the Foundation, Mr. Howell worked his way through the ranks serving, at various times, as a waiter, tradesman, character interpreter, dancer, militiaman, publications editor, presentation skills trainer, content instructor, and program manager. Mr. Howell is a frequent speaker and facilitator at numerous workshops, conferences, and professional meetings and consults in the museum field on such topics as staff training, program planning, and professionalism.

INTERPRETERS AND MUSEUM EDUCATORS: BEYOND THE BLUE HAIRS

Mark Howell

Credibility. It is the soul and validation of any profession. Yet even today the museum professionals responsible for communicating an institution's message to the public still struggle for this recognition. Heck, they struggle for the recognition that they constitute a profession, period, much less one worthy of being recognized as responsible teachers to our society. I still remember when I announced my intentions to be an interpreter to my parents: they smiled, nodded, then tried to think where they had gone wrong. I don't think they perceived museum interpretation as a real job at the time. To them, and to many others, museum interpreters were little old ladies, scions of the local history society, who made their way down to ye olde house museum every Sunday afternoon to awe visitors with their ability to trace local families' roots back to the Mayflower and marvel over how well-made things were back in the good ole' days.

Museum interpretation and education as a field is still emerging and evolving. As history museums continue *their* evolution as scholarship-based institutions of learning, interpreters and educators are becoming increasingly important as staff members who are contributors to the process of education, not merely the mouthpiece of the institution. As such, tomorrow's educators—and this is true of anyone entering the education field—are increasingly obligated to be serious and continuing students of history. Today's interpreters weave historical scholarship, object analysis, and contemporary issues together to create stimulating experiences for the visitor and are downplaying the usual dates, quaint stories (This may not be true, but it's *such* a darlin' story . . .), home decorating tips, and advocacy of how great life was "back then."

History museums that survive into the twenty-first century will be institutions *about* the past, not shrines *to* it. They will continue to be repositories for historical objects, but, more and more, they must be effective at relating the importance of those artifacts to a modern audience. What does it mean if a house museum in North Carolina that interprets the early nineteenth century has the original family's accumulation of furniture from Baltimore and Boston? The fact that they are neoclassic in design and very pretty? Well, that's a start, but the interpreter who surprised her audience by using those objects to show how that family fit into early America's intercostal economy made history relevant, purposeful. History as an accumulation of facts is no history, but history that draws a distinction between past and present creates a valid reason for a family to stop by and see what antiques and famous (and not so famous) dead people can tell us, not only about them but about us.

GETTING TO KNOW YOUR VISITORS

Museum visitors are volunteer learners. The occasional husband or recalcitrant school class on a field trip notwithstanding, people come to history museums looking for more than decorating tips; they come of their own free will, looking for meaning. They also come with preconceptions, some good and some not so good. Their perceptions of history and history museums can be either a blessing or a curse. Other museum visits, grade school history classes, television miniseries (shudder), and gramp's reminiscences condition how visitors relate to the museum experience and their understanding of the past. Each person is different, and each will assimilate information a little differently. But, in the end, either consciously or unconsciously, most adult learners are looking for the answer to one question: "Why is this important?" The interpretive staff who regularly answer this question will be the interpretive staff whose museum will continue to exist in these coming years of financial restraint and decreasing government support.

Museum visitors also come with expectations. Good interpreters learn very quickly that today's audience is very discriminating and increasingly critical of how time is spent. Time is a precious commodity these days, and potential museum visitors have a myriad of other possibilities vying for their attention. Since interpreters are often the only human representatives of the museum the public meets, their skills as communicators have increasingly become as important as their historical knowledge. In the past several years, exhibit design teams have begun to regularly include museum educators as equal partners to ensure a balance between curatorial and scholarly concerns, aesthetic ideals, and the clarity and relevance of the message being delivered.[1] Display and label copy must be more user friendly, enticing, and engaging than ever before or the museum will lose its audience to all the activities out there saying that they represent the best experience for the leisure time the family has available.

What the public wants out of its history may not always be what the interpreter feels is best for them. Many come seeking a reaffirmation of lost ideals; some come wistfully fantasizing for a purer, simpler time, to escape from today's burdens, a few aren't exactly sure why they came. More often than not interpreters find themselves in the dilemma of being between the visitor's romantic notions of the past and the scholarly evidence that is often to the contrary. What to do, what to do? Visitors typically want THE answer; they want it in black and white: "Was the Industrial Revolution a good thing for the country or not? Come on, we have dinner reservations at 6:00!" In this world of shortened attention spans and sound bites, the complex shading of history can often be a frustration for the visitor if not presented appropriately by the interpreter. Too often public history is dumbed down to its lowest common denominator, the result being a pablum of information that overgeneralizes and avoids controversial topics. Public history must be rooted in scholarly inquiry and not be a reiteration of the mythic past inscribed in popular memory.[2] It must then be *adjusted* to the learning styles of a mass audience, not diluted to a superficial presentation, all safe and easy.

DECIDING WHAT TO INTERPRET

One of the challenges facing the museum interpreter and educator is the education of the public not only in a site's history or an exhibit's relevance but in the process of *how* we interpret history. The scholarly interpretation of history is just that: an interpretation. It is not a simple recitation of facts. History becomes relevant when it is analyzed and the slant given to the analysis is often prompted by the current state of society. Our understanding of the past is as much a reflection of the generation doing the research as it is the period being studied. If history were a ball, placed on a pedestal like a globe, each succeeding generation would approach it, turn it a little, study it, and move on. The next generation would turn it a little more, studying the same ball, the same basic facts, but from a different perspective, and so on.

The interpretation of history in museums in the 1950s was as much a reflection of the Cold War as it was of the past, and the virtues of democracy were shown in all their glory. By the 1960s and 1970s, the ball had been turned ever so slightly by the civil rights movement and the Vietnam War. Now the foundations of the country were being questioned. Historian Fawn Brodie questioned whether Thomas Jefferson had slept with slave Sally Hemings; the treatment of Native Americans by Manifest Destiny-minded whites was being reevaluated. Multiculturalism in the 1980s, the impact of technology, and a reassessment of political history in the 1990s . . . The ball will always be turned and studied, and each interpretation will be relevant to that particular generation. So individuals growing up in the 1950s who learned most of their history at that time may not immediately understand, or want to understand, the history that is presented in a current museum exhibit or interpretation.

Curators and educators involved in a recent exhibit at the Smithsonian Air and Space Museum of the *Enola Gay*—the B-52 bomber that delivered the atomic bomb on Hiroshima—found out the hard way that public opinion and history, particularly history that involves people who are still living, can be a very strong mix. The exhibit design team decided to focus on the impact of "The Bomb" on the postwar world instead of using the recently restored fuselage of the plane to celebrate the winning of the war as veteran groups demanded. It's a long story, but the museum ended up recasting the exhibit under a barrage of criticism. The problem? They misunderstood the impact their interpretation would have on the public. Their interpretation wasn't wrong, but they failed to take into account the sensitivity of the issue.

Most of us will probably never have to go through such a torturous experience, but the lesson learned is important. Effective interpreters must understand not only the process of interpreting history but their audience as well. Finding that fine line between what the visitor wants to hear and what *you* think they should hear is as much a part of the job as knowing the information. Scholar Bernard Lewis wrote that "what happened, what we recall, what we recover, what we relate, are often sadly different. The temptation is often overwhelmingly strong to tell it, not as it really was, but as we would wish it had been."[3] It is the responsibility of the institution and the interpreter to honestly weigh, judge, prepare, and present their historical information in as responsible and objective a manner as possible so that the visitors are not told *what* to think but are given the tools to come to their own conclusions. In other words, the interpreter's job is to get the visitors to *think*. Well, this is easier said than done. After all, these folks are on vacation or an afternoon jaunt. Thinking is hard work and getting people whose brains are set on cruise control to think is even harder, but it is what the job hinges on.

CONNECTING IDEAS, OBJECTS, AND PEOPLE

The primary function interpreters and museum educators perform in accomplishing this end result is explaining to the visitor the relationship between information and objects. For interpreters in a historic setting, it is showing the interrelationships between objects, spaces, and the persons who once used them and placing them into a historical context. Take, for example, tea. An effective interpreter, standing in the parlor of a wealthy colonial Philadelphia merchant, might pick up a single teacup and explain its relationship to the variety of specialized items surrounding it that made tea drinking as much a social ceremony as it was a break from the day's activities. The parlor, set aside for such ceremony, could then be brought into the equation and then populated with the sorts of persons who might be (or were) invited to the gathering to show how something as simple as tea was used to reinforce station and gentility. The symbolism tea represented in the years leading up to the Revolution might be explored or America's dependence on and affinity for English goods, particularly Chelsea porcelain, could be broached. Fashion, technology, terminology, social and political values, ceremony, and biography could all be explored by examining something as simple as a teacup. If we can do all this with a colonial teacup, just think what a twenty-third-century interpreter will do with a paper cup from the late 1990s!

Museum educators are assisting in doing the same things with exhibits. In the 1980s the Henry Ford Museum in Dearborn, Michigan, retooled its display of its outstanding automobile collection. Instead of limiting the exhibit to the car and its technological and aesthetic development, the team charged with the presentation chose to show the impact the automobile had in shaping American society throughout the twentieth century. The cars are still displayed in all their beauty but are now shown in relationship to such themes as leisure time, mobility, technology, and industrial design, and visitors to the exhibit walk away understanding how the automobile's evolution has fundamentally shaped the world they now live in. The relationship between curation and education was joined to provide visitors with an experience that is both enjoyable and edifying.

Traditionally, museum interpretation has been presented to the public in the third-person voice. These interpreters are contemporary with their audience in helping them understand the values, actions, and attitudes of the past. Later we will discuss interpretation that presents information in the "first person"—persons who presume to be contemporary to the past—but the former technique is much more prevalent. Third-person interpreters can be found in a variety of situations. They give tours of a site's grounds or a historic house or are stationed at key points. They are also used on bus tours and neighborhood walks, pointing out landmarks, preservation projects, and local history, or leading groups through museum exhibits.

Successful interpreters these days know as much about adult and child education and communication techniques as they do about the history they are presenting. Audience interaction, storytelling, the use of inquiry, biographical narrative, and problem solving are all parts of the arsenal employed by interpreters who are truly effective in engaging the minds of their audiences. Even something as subtle as the use of a single word or name can change the tenor and immediacy of an interpretation in the hands of a skillful interpreter. Consider the difference in these two extracts of an interpretation of a slave cook in the home of a wealthy gentry family:

> The cook's duty to her master was to ensure that dinner was prepared by two o'clock.
> Lydia's duty to Mr. and Mrs. Wythe was to ensure that dinner was in place by two of the clock.

The interpreter's personalization of the characters who once inhabited this scene makes them more real in the visitor's mind; the use of terminology of the period acts as an oral artifact that reinforces the atmosphere of the past as much as the dining table the visitor is standing in front of. The audience no longer thinks of history as a faceless collection of social classes and activities but as flesh and blood. As the eminent historian G. M. Trevelean once wrote:

> The poetry of history lies in the quasi-miraculous fact that once on this earth, on this familiar spot of ground walked other men and women as actual as we are today, thinking their own thoughts, swayed by their own passions but now all gone, vanishing after another, gone as utterly as we ourselves shall be gone like ghosts at cockcrow.[4]

To capture this poetry in an exhibit or tour is to breathe life into the dead once again, if but for a moment.

In the last twenty years the use of "first-person" interpretation has slowly been evolving into a form of presentation that is now being perceived as almost equal in standing and reputation to more traditional techniques. This is a broad title for a variety of techniques. Often called "living history," it encompasses interpreters in period costume going about some activity; dramatic presentations staged in auditoriums, exhibit areas, and neutral spaces (such as a classroom); "fourth-wall" scenes, where interpreters taking on the roles of historical characters recreate scenes in a historic setting without acknowledging the presence of the audience; and "character interpretation," perhaps the most demanding of all in that it requires the interpreter to extemporaneously interact with the audience as a particular historical personage.

There is still much debate on the validity of first-person interpretation. Poorly done, it can misrepresent and trivialize history. Some will argue that we can never know the actual feelings and opinions of persons from the past, and, as a result, we do a disservice to their memory by attempting

Interpreters who take on the role of a person of the past are able to impart information about the age they are representing as well as the values and attitudes that were common at that time. *Photo by Judy Beisler. Courtesy of Mystic Seaport Museum.*

to bring them back to life. These naysayers would suggest that composite characters be utilized to represent the general attitudes of a particular class of people from the era. It's a question that still rages on. Either way, however, character interpretation can evoke the values and attitudes of another era in a way a third-person interpreter can only begin to demonstrate. A modern interpreter might read a quote or evocatively explain, for example, the discrimination felt by a nineteenth-century Chinese immigrant railway laborer, but to see a first-person interpreter *express* those sentiments makes the impression more immediate and real. Everyone knows, of course, that it's just pretend, but in this day and age of Disney and CD-ROM escapism, more and more people are willing to play along. To be able to sit down with a woman portraying a doctor in nineteenth-century Mystic Seaport Museum and discuss everything from childbirth and sexuality to gender discrimination and the effects of industrialization on children is a very powerful thing indeed. Such ability requires an enormous investment of time, research, and preparation, and, as a result, many museums limit their use of first-person interpretation to scripted presentations with limited interaction with the audience in order to preserve the integrity of the historical content. Either way, it is a way to dramatize the past and help paint a visual image in the visitor's mind of what persons of another era believed and did. Often it's as if the visitors had but held a mirror to themselves, so closely do the generations mimic one another. Other times the clash of values is so great that visitors valiantly set out to change the character's mind, only to discover the difference to be too great, causing them to reexamine their own values in relation to those of another person in another time. The character interpreter can then pocket his or her paycheck with a clear conscience and warm feeling of a job well done.

BECOMING AN INTERPRETER OR MUSEUM EDUCATOR

In reality, it is very difficult to make a living as a historical interpreter. Only a few museums are able to hire interpreters year-round; most are able to provide only seasonal work. Many museums rely on docents—volunteers from the community—to communicate their message and rely on staff members, commonly called museum educators, to coordinate, train, supervise, and model the art of interpretation. These are the folks who design and evaluate the usefulness of tours, develop and produce resource packets for schoolteachers, assist in the production and evaluation of exhibits, create and promote the public programs of the institution, *and* help write the grants that fund all of these initiatives.

Above all, they are advocates. They are charged with knowing and help-ing to develop the museum's constituency and in representing that com-munity to the institution's staff. They are the ones who ensure that chil-dren are considered when new programs or exhibits are being designed, making sure, for example, that exhibit designs do not obstruct visibility for little ones. Conversely, they are advocates for the museum, ensuring, for example, that school districts are aware of how indispensable the mu-seum's programs are to their curriculum and that every child in the com-munity *must* come to see them or the children's entire intellectual de-velopment will be forever lacking!

Well, okay, that last sentence is a bit extreme, but it does express the attitude that museum personnel must possess to be successful these days. They must go into the career convinced that a history education is not optional in today's society. Children need to be trained in the critical thinking skills that historical scholarship and understanding employ in order to be able to compete in the world. For adults, history is not merely a nice thing to have in the back of one's mind; it's critical to under-standing where we are as a society and how we got here and making in-formed choices as to where we're going. Museum educators must believe this and put all their strength and effort in convincing the public of this, not necessarily overtly, but through the impressions made by the pro-grams and exhibits they produce.

Perhaps you're beginning to realize that a career in the presentation of public history in museums requires much, much more than merely possessing a history degree or an enthusiasm for some aspect of the past. It requires a passion and respect for what has come before as well as spe-cific character traits, not the least of which is a love of people (and not just dead ones!). Interpreters are preservers of history and advocates for its usefulness and importance. It is all too easy to bend a fact or overem-phasize an anomaly when first you discover that it gets a rise out of the audience. We all want to be loved, to make people laugh, and even the best of us might put our personal self-esteem before the integrity of the historical narrative. Shakespeare, indirectly, had an opinion along these lines. Nothing miffed the great bard more than to have some actor rewrite his lines. In *Hamlet,* he has the Dane instruct the players to

> let those that play your clowns speak no more than is set down for them, for
> there be of them that will themselves laugh to set on some quantity of bar-
> ren spectators to laugh too, though in the mean time some necessary ques-
> tion of the play be then consider'd.[5]

Humor has its place, but not at the expense of the past. That which we speak must come from the historical record, and not some fanciful imagination. In other words, to thine institution's goals and objectives be true. (Sorry, Will.)

The interpreter must be objective. But what does that mean? An interpreter or museum educator cannot possibly present all that is known and must purposefully pick and choose from the available data to form and organize a coherent interpretation. That means that some information will not reach visitors; the interpreter has consciously withheld some information from them. Does this action remove objectivity from the presentation? Only if the interpreter is intentionally skewing or misrepresenting the historical record or using history to support a personal agenda. Twisted and pulled enough, facts can be made to support virtually any conclusion; a good interpreter will rely on credible scholarship, not hearsay or assumptions.

The large-patterned wallpaper installed in George Mason's home, Gunston Hall, may not be aesthetically pleasing to the twentieth-century eye, but it allows the interpreter the opportunity to explore another generation's concept of beauty. *Photo by Charles Baptie. Courtesy of Gunston Hall.*

Along these lines, interpreters need to encourage visitors to accept the past on its own terms and not impose modern sensibilities on it. People of the past can be made to look pretty silly if held to a standard they were not aware of. Take, for example, the aesthetics of a particular period. The passage of colonial Virginian George Mason's home, Gunston Hall, is lined with large-patterned wall paper, and moldings are finished in flat white trim, reflecting the popular neoclassic designs of the period. To our eyes the scale and color seems extreme, and the temptation to chide or mock the past on its sense of beauty is great.

The same can be said for the attitudes women held regarding their roles in society in the various periods of our history. Their opinions regarding their role in public life do not correspond to modern egalitarian ideals, and, again, it becomes easy to measure them against a current standard that they were not even aware of. Better to accept them for what they were and point out the level of influence women seemed to wield in the privacy of the home—that rounds out the picture with both sides of the issue, and women become complete people, not ignorant, superficial caricatures. I shudder to think how disreputable interpreters of the twenty-third century will label us when discussion comes up of our track record on the use of, say, internal combustion machines and our drive to extract petroleum from the earth. Without a balanced regard for how American society was influenced by this development, we will come off looking pretty foolish ourselves.

Interpreters must be willing to take risks. They must be able to read audiences and then decide how far they can stretch them without pushing too far. Simply answering questions or reaffirming preconceptions is not good enough; visitors must be taken to a higher level of understanding or expectation than when they arrived. Effective interpreters will put their reputations on the line and constantly try a variety of techniques, depending on the situation at hand, to challenge visitors, and they will be willing to come up short every so often if it means that, more often than not, the risk results in a higher level of learning than would have been offered by a safe lecture-style presentation that limits visitor involvement, interaction, and, as a result, retention of information.

This includes a willingness to tackle controversial issues. The effective interpreter will not shirk from confronting the issue of slavery or religion, even if it means acknowledging that a popular founding father or local favorite son possessed either enslaved persons or values in contradiction to our own. *How* they present it is the key. A clear understanding of the facts and empathy both for the subject and sentiments of the audience are essential. The subject should not and cannot be ignored with the excuse that the interpreter didn't want to hurt anyone's feelings and make

Effective interpretation involves the audience not only physically—as with this discussion of Africans' passage to America—but mentally and emotionally as well. *Courtesy of the Colonial Williamsburg Foundation.*

persons feel uncomfortable. Certainly the intention is not to depress or anger these volunteer learners, but there are ways to excite an audience, to encourage them to work through a difficult topic and become edified by it and not alienated from it. Visitors are not only learning with their intellect; they are learning with their heart as well, a fact that all too often goes lacking.

If an interpreter is able to do all this, the end result will be visitors with a better understanding of both a past world and their own. Effective interpreters are as aware of current events as they are of the past; such an understanding helps bridge the gap between past and present and makes an interpretation more relevant. Ultimately, the interpreter hopes to get the visitor to see larger issues, to put their exhibit or tour into a larger context. In the cartoon, Calvin is wrong. Despite the exaggeration of his example, historians, interpreters, and museum educators must be generalists to some degree in order to understand the conditions of their specialty, whatever it might be.

French educator Anatole France once said: "Do not try to satisfy your own vanity by teaching a great many things. Awaken people's curiosity. It is enough to open minds; do not overload them. Put there just a spark. If there is some good inflammable stuff, it will catch fire."[6] Effective in-

Calvin and Hobbes   by Bill Watterson

terpreters are aware of their limitations and the visitor's capacity to take information in. If visitors walk away without all the questions answered, or if all the information at their disposal was not used in order to inspire the audience to continue the examination of an issue—either through books (available in the gift shop!), other museums, or return visits—then they will have done their job. As Voltaire once remarked: "The way to be a bore is to say everything."[7]

Many of these skills are innate; many can be learned. The art of interpretation is generally a part of any graduate program that addresses museum education or museum studies. There are also several publications devoted to developing the skills of interpreters. One of the best is an old classic by Freeman Tilden first published in 1957, *Interpreting Our Heritage*. Its precepts are still in vogue today. A more recent book that also addresses such topics as learning styles and teaching techniques is *The Good Guide*, written by Alison Grinder and E. Sue McCoy. Jay Anderson has presented a good overview of first-person interpretation in *Time Machines: The World of Living History*.[8]

There are also several good periodicals that regularly address practical, philosophical, and ethical issues in the field of interpretation. The National Association of Interpreters (NAI) publishes a quarterly magazine called *Legacy* that regularly tackles the variety of concerns in the field today. *The Docent Educator* is a publication that draws heavily on its subscribers for articles that are germane to what is happening in the trenches these days.

The best way to learn, and appreciate, the art and mysteries of the job is to do it. There is no shortage of opportunities for docent positions, internships, or summer positions in museums or at historic sites throughout the country. There are also several nonprofit organizations in the United States and Canada that regularly sponsor conferences and workshops in various aspects of interpretation. Hundreds of interpreters converge on the annual conference of the previously mentioned NAI (which is predominantly geared to nature interpreters, though this is rapidly changing). The largest organization devoted to public history in the museum field is the American Association for State and Local History (AASLH). Through publications, conferences, and workshops, AASLH encourages professionalism and scholarly responsibility at all levels of the field. A more informal and member-run organization with a particular appeal to historic sites is the Association for Living Historical Farms and Agricultural Museums (ALHFAM). Its regional associations and annual conferences offer its constituency several opportunities throughout the year to gather and discuss common issues and concerns. As if this were not enough, there are a wealth of state and regional organizations addressing the entire breadth of museum issues and many of their conferences and workshops focus on interpretive issues as well.

CONCLUSION

Any profession in the various fields of history involves more than knowledge of the past. Because of the central role that museums play in the public's historical understanding, interpreters and museum educators must be particularly vigilant in maintaining and reinforcing the public's perception of the usefulness and value of history both in the scholarly quality of the content and by the professionalism of the way that it is presented. In the end, though, the challenge of interpretation is in getting the visitor to use the experience. We can't mandate what our visitors do with our information, but we can structure the interpretation in such a way that they will find it so compelling that, as they head for the parking lot, they will have touched the past and come to a better understanding of the human condition. Not bad for a bunch of old blue hairs.

NOTES

1. Barbara Franco, "The Communication Conundrum: What Is the Message? Who Is Listening?" *Journal of American History* 81 (June 1994): 156–58.
2. Paul Boyer, "Whose History Is It Anyway?" in Edward T. Linenthal and Tom Engelhardt, eds., *History Wars: The Enola Gay and Other Battles for the American Past* (New York: Metropolitan Books, 1996), 139.

3. Bernard Lewis, *History: Remembered, Recovered, Invented* (Princeton: Princeton University Press, 1975), 71.

4. Quoted in Simon Schama, "Clio Has a Problem," *The New York Times Magazine* (September 8, 1991), 32.

5. G. Blakemore Evans, ed., *The Riverside Shakespeare* (Boston: Houghton Mifflin Co., 1974), 1162.

6. Quoted in Freeman Tilden, *Interpreting Our Heritage* (Chapel Hill: University of North Carolina Press, 1977), xiii.

7. *Oxford Dictionary of Quotations,* 3rd ed., s.v. "Voltaire."

8. Tilden, *Interpreting Our Heritage;* Alison Grinder and E. Sue McCoy, *The Good Guide* (Scottsdale, AZ: Ironwood Press, 1985); and Jay Anderson, *Time Machines: The World of Living History* (Nashville: American Association for State and Local History, 1984).

CHARLES A. D'ANIELLO is associate librarian at the Arts and Sciences Libraries, State University of New York at Buffalo. He holds an A.B. in history from Syracuse University, an M.A. in history from the University of Virginia, and an M.S.L.S. from Syracuse. Prior to joining the University of Buffalo faculty, he served as a librarian at the Richmond Public Library and taught in the Prince William County (Virginia) school system. Mr. D'Aniello is a former president of the Association for the Bibliography of History. His extensive list of publications includes Teaching Bibliographic Skills in History: A Sourcebook for Historians and Librarians *(1993); essays in* The Collection Building Reader *(1992),* Reference and Information Services: A Reader for the Nineties *(1991), and* Conceptual Frameworks for Bibliographic Education: Theory and Practice *(1987); and articles and reviews in* The History Teacher, Reference Services Review, Italian Americana, The Reference Librarian, *and the* Journal of American Ethnic History. *He has also appeared on the programs of the Association for the Bibliography of History and the Organization of American Historians.*

LIBRARIANS AND BIBLIOGRAPHERS
Charles A. D'Aniello

Librarians with history degrees serve in a wide variety of library positions—for example, bibliography, reference, cataloguing, administration, and combinations of these responsibilities—and in a wide variety of settings, from academic, public, and special libraries of all sizes to the libraries of local, regional, state, and national and international historical societies.

In all of these positions the substance and habits of historical training—an appreciation of detail and context, clarity of expression, and a healthy skepticism of facts and assertions—are valuable. These skills are not exclusively possessed by students of history, but historical training contributes to them. Further, a librarian trained in historical research is likely to understand the ways in which historians and students of various levels of sophistication are likely to use libraries and bibliographic and reference sources for historical work. For the historian, library work can

157

be rewarding because it enables one to continue to pursue reading and research interests. This form of engagement can be both fun and intellectually rewarding and enables one to live the life of the mind to the level that talents and desires allow.

Because it is the context which I know best, I will focus on the librarian's role in reference and collection development services in academic and research libraries. In some large libraries bibliographers do not provide reference service at a general reference desk but are available for consultation, but at most institutions librarians have both reference and bibliography or collection development responsibilities. I have worked in both configurations. While much of this essay focuses on the role of the history librarian or history bibliographer, librarians with history degrees are well represented across the spectrum of library positions, from catalogers, to map librarians, to government documents librarians, to administrators. The basic characteristics and skills necessary to enjoy and perform well in all of these positions are the same: a passion for the discipline or area of responsibility, a desire to help others, and excellent communication and analytical skills.

THE WORK CONTEXT

The continually evolving and intensifying use of technology in academic and research libraries in particular, but in many public libraries as well, demands constant learning by librarians. This can be stressful, but it can also be an exciting intellectual challenge. Along with the technology have come sociological changes in the way in which librarians work: teamwork across units of an institution is now common, often driven by the need to design, select, and adjust to electronic systems. Consortial cooperation with other institutions is aided by electronic catalogs and electronic mail, and reference work can often be done away from the reference desk or in response to an e-mail query. Computerization has transformed the way in which library materials are selected, ordered, and cataloged and the way in which bibliographers and acquisitions librarians work and communicate with one another.

Positions in academic and research libraries frequently involve a considerable amount of committee work and some assigned hours, but such positions as reference librarian/bibliographer also offer considerable flexibility both within a day and across a week. The exceptions are librarians working in cataloging and other technical services positions. Here processing is a chain of events and the timely completion of one task (by one individual), is often dependent on the timely completion of another task (by another individual). Thus, while not always the case, production demands and expectations, more tightly defined by days and weeks, are common in these areas. Teamwork is the rule in today's academic libraries and a collegial atmosphere is the norm. While broad directions and goals may be set by higher administration, the realization of goals is generally left to the discretion of the individuals or work groups actually performing tasks.

Academic librarians have many opportunities for on-site training and to attend special seminars, workshops, and institutes, often with at least partial reimbursement. The sharing of computer skills is common at the regular meetings of reference and collection development departments.

REFERENCE WORK[1]

Online catalogs, computerized indexes, and the Internet have dramatically changed the way reference work is done. It is easy today to answer a wide spectrum of questions and explore a broad range of topics. One does not need to understand or recognize as much about the origin of information as in the past, because the flexibility of online search systems enables anyone to find material written on the history of many things. Increasingly, many questions and topics are addressed by resources distributed on computers across the world and accessible through the Internet. In fact, the number of digitized texts and images is now rapidly increasing as are efforts to make them easily searchable through Internet directories, search engines, and special indexing projects. Nonetheless, as in the past, the best reference work is accomplished when a combination of substantive knowledge and reference knowledge and skills is blended, enabling the librarian to interpret a question and translate it into a query of the bibliographic and reference universe. One still must be able to interpret a question, to understand what is asked for—and what might constitute an answer or the beginning of an answer—before the query can be effectively addressed. This requires careful listening as well as knowledge and evaluation. The more connections the librarian can make with personal background knowledge, as well as what can be extracted from interviewing the patron, the greater the chance for a positive and insightful interaction. A seamless blending of substantive knowledge, technical skill, and imagination distinguishes good reference answers, research consultations, and instruction in the use of libraries and reference resources.

Using the traditional card catalog or other bibliographic tools was never without elements of sophistication and subtlety, but using today's ever expanding menu of electronic catalogs and indexes requires even greater mediation. Today's reference librarian can often feel like an instructor in computer applications. Questions on downloading, compression techniques, and the saving of digitized materials are increasingly frequent. In fact, reference librarians are often expected to be skilled searchers of several search systems—databases doing different things or essentially the same thing but often with significantly different search syntax and unique searchable fields. To all involved, this can be exciting, but also often confusing. Nonetheless, in reality, a lot of question negotiation—and question refinement—can occur while the technology is being demystified. In fact, a standard feature of many reference events is now a speedy introduction to database design and the specific protocols and syntax of a specific search engine. How one handles a reference event, as always, depends on the skill, knowledge, and energy of the librarian, as well as the patron's ability to articulate interests and needs. With some patrons the librarian is in a unique position to assist with the clarification of a research question—even to the point of suggesting unappreciated avenues for collateral exploration.

While even searchers for historical information—both primary and secondary—are increasingly well served by electronic resources, it is especially dangerous for the student of history to rely exclusively on this medium. It is always important to remember that the literature indexes itself through the footnotes and bibliographies of its publications—imperfectly, but with a specificity (and idiosyncrasy) only now being approached through the online indexing of a small universe of thoroughly abstracted or full text sources. Also, a host of bibliographic and reference sources remain accessible only in print. And the reference and bibliographic aids of the past, saved in the stacks of our research libraries, are important to historical study. They are important in and of themselves, both for the information they contain, the information they point to, and for what they reveal about the time in which they were compiled or written.

BIBLIOGRAPHIC INSTRUCTION[2]

"Bibliographic instruction," as a concept, is used to describe efforts to teach both the use of libraries and the use of bibliographic and reference sources. Bibliographic instruction can take many forms and occur in many settings. It is a natural companion of reference work in an academic library. In academic libraries instruction is more often than not part of the answering of each reference query or consultation; bibliographic instruction, as a concept, however, describes sessions offered as part of topical courses, special workshops, or stand-alone bibliography courses. Interviews with term paper writers or graduate students as they respectively prepare to write theses or dissertations are also a popular context for instruction.

The focus of bibliographic instruction sessions can vary dramatically, from a response to a specific assignment made by a professor, to the explication of a generally relevant new computer system, to instruction in Internet search techniques, to the presentation of an idealized schematic of a search process designed to suggest the effective sequence and interplay of techniques and resources through a model search. Course-integrated instruction is generally planned in consultation with the course's instructor and may have an assignment attached which practices the skills taught. The immediate goal of bibliographic instruction is to teach students enough to satisfy the needs of the task at hand, sometimes formulaically; but the ultimate goal is to impart sufficient information and skills, acquired through instruction and personal practice, that will enable the student to approach libraries and information sources flexibly and imaginatively. Initially, instruction benefits from a presentation that simulates a reference or research scenario, because the extent of one's imagination—bibliographic and otherwise—is limited by the extent of one's knowledge of sources and their interrelationships. The type of instruction that is offered, its context and its nature, is as much a function of the librarian's personality, knowledge, and available time, as of the proclivities and characteristics of the population to which it is offered— faculty and students.

A concomitant activity with bibliographic instruction is the design of guides or handouts—today much of this activity may be devoted to the development of Web pages. These pages provide the librarian with the opportunity to identify Internet resources especially useful to the clientele served. The design of library aids and guides is an attempt to anticipate reference needs and to respond to them in a carefully thought-out manner. Traditionally, it has been in the designing of these aids that librarians have learned the substantive portions of their jobs. Even librarians with distinguished academic credentials personally benefit from this exercise. In fact, many librarians have commercially published guides, satisfying the formal evaluation publication requirements of their institutions. These internal and external publications can come in infinite sizes and focuses.

An important part of contemporary advanced instruction is the effort to show searchers the ease with which the work of scholars in other disciplines may be accessed. The speed with which the computer can comb a disciplinary universe only vaguely familiar to the searcher can be liberating and very exciting. On this basic level, the librarian is ideally positioned to help researchers enter new territory—exploring and incorporating the concepts and findings of other researchers. While the scholar will still want to consult colleagues in other disciplines, the accessibility of other literatures cannot help but facilitate such consultation and possible collaboration.

Another important task of the history-trained librarian is to alert researchers to the danger that lies in the ease with which much information may be found. Electronic databases have made research so easy that to venture beyond what is included in them is often not done. Information not "canonized" by entry into a database is no less an important part of the historical record than information that is entered. On an even profounder scale, the very nature of historical inquiry is threatened by electronic information and communication. For instance, much communication, in business, industry, and government, is conducted over e-mail and data is sometimes only temporarily saved in electronic form—in short, the very existence, not to mention stability, of such records is uncertain. Already, many paper trails no longer exist to be followed by the historical researcher. Add to these general concerns the continuing need to advise searchers to consider the bias that may color the content and presentation of what they use and, more innocently, its simple scope and breadth. All too often students treat all information with the same respect, assigning disparate electronic and printed sources more or less the same level of reliability.

Finally, librarians are uniquely positioned to encourage and help faculty incorporate Internet and electronic resources into their courses and research. This librarian facilitation can be approached through special workshops and various levels of collaboration and assistance in course design. Simply assisting in identifying Internet links and electronic texts can be a vital and catalytic experience.

COLLECTION DEVELOPMENT[3]

The collection development librarian—whether titled bibliographer, selector, or subject specialist—determines through individual purchases and the implementation and monitoring of approval plans (profiling with a book vendor to either receive books or notification slips automatically in predefined areas) which materials will enter a collection. The long-term research capability of a collection is the product of the day-to-day work of bibliographers. Not only do bibliographers select books and journals, but they must also determine what if audio visual material will be purchased as well as which electronic resources and microform collections to acquire. The bibliographer is also responsible for identifying Internet projects to which to provide links on the library's home page. Some bibliographers even actively solicit gifts, of money or materials, to develop their collections, negotiating with donors and overseeing the processing of donated materials. The breadth of responsibility is now very wide: To function effectively one must learn the quality and focus of publishers; for the strongest parts of the collection, recognize important approaches, concepts, personal names, themes, and topics; know the associations whose projects, conferences, and publications should be monitored; and be aware of the ease or difficulty with which materials may be obtained on interlibrary loan or by visiting a nearby institution. The history librarian must also be familiar with the types of evidence historians use and with the searching approaches likely to be employed by historical researchers. The latter concern may surface in discussions of how materials are cataloged or made accessible through an institution's catalog. In addition, the well-established interdisciplinary thrust of much research requires the bibliographer to often interact with bibliographers of other disciplines and to appreciate the importance of strong collections in other areas.

Deciding the areas in which different levels of collecting intensity will occur, and articulating this plan in a policy, is an important responsibility of the bibliographer. Such policies are the result of assessing the needs of one's clientele: studying the nature and scope of courses taught, reviewing the topics of dissertations completed or in progress, analyzing academic plans, and talking with faculty. Collection evaluation naturally follows the promulgation of a policy. In addition to narrative policies, many libraries use a derivative of the Research Libraries Group's conspectus to record the results of evaluation as well as collecting goals. In the conspectus, possible components of each discipline's collections are described in detail by many standardized lines of descriptive combinations of Library of Congress classification ranges; under these, measures ranging from one to five, complemented by assessments of language characteristics, are given for existing collecting strength, current collecting intensity, and, often, collecting goals. Policies also record consortial arrangements that may have been negotiated by the bibliographer or others. It is through the development of policy and the execution of evaluation that the bibliographer learns the breadth, depth, and scope of the collection(s) for which he or she has stewardship.

Collection development, as well as reference work with a disciplinary focus, requires that one stay familiar with the focus of contemporary learned conversation. This basic and ongoing level of cultural literacy is achieved through a variety of approaches: attending lectures, taking courses, research and writing, watching PBS specials, and, of course, reading books, professional journals, and such publications as the *New York Review of Books, The Times Literary Supplement,* and *The New York Times Book Review.* In fact, in larger research libraries it is customary to acquire titles reviewed in the *NYRB* and the *TLS* and to regularly check the review lists in such publications as the *Journal of American History* and the *American Historical Review*. Clearly, all bibliographers should know the important journals, newsletters, and online discussion lists through which disciplinary practitioners communicate and stay current with scholarship and professional issues. Subscription to the appropriate scholarly listserves, many available through H-Net, is very helpful. Reading what one's clientele reads is a common sense way to acquire the information necessary to make certain its needs are met. On a basic level, it is also an obvious way to "join" in conversation with a broad academic community.

COLLECTION MAINTENANCE

The embrittlement of much of the older material in the nation's libraries has compelled librarians to devote considerable time and money to reformatting, purchasing reprints, or weeding material (either in tacit dependence on or in consortial agreements with other institutions). A knowledge of bibliography, the strength of related institutions, and major electronic projects to preserve material—as well as a sensitivity to actual and potential local needs—all guide librarians when they decide whether to preserve or discard damaged or embrittled items. In addition to preservation concerns, many of the nation's larger institutions are busy weeding duplicated material, no longer relevant to the focus of their institutions, or designating material for remote or on-site storage. The bibliographic universe has, in many instances, already outgrown its store houses; fortunately, digital technologies have evolved to respond to the needs of both preservation and access.

SCHOLARLY CONTRIBUTIONS

The ways in which librarians contribute to scholarly discourse are as varied as the skills, training, and leanings of the individuals holding this title. Some librarians participate in scholarship in a manner indistinguishable from historians teaching in the nation's most prestigious history departments. Others contribute to scholarship by authoring guides to the literatures of the discipline or disciplines for which they are responsible in their libraries. Still others analyze the components of professional librarianship, issues in job performance, service provision, and personnel or financial administration. And, of course, some individuals contribute across this entire range. Most librarians write on topics that have emerged from their job experiences. There is no paucity of library journals in which to attempt to publish one's work—articles and reviews—and they span a range of exclusivity. Association journals draw their editors and editorial boards from their membership. Librarians may also voluntarily contribute to indexing and abstracting services as well as do professional abstracting and indexing for a fee. In addition to publication, like other academic spheres, the library world is served by many annual, biannual, and special conferences. In addition to writing and speaking, the opportunity to do exhibits of varying size and sophistication exists in many libraries.

CAREER DEVELOPMENT

Most librarians in positions requiring subject expertise hold a master's degree in that subject as well as the M.L.S. or M.S.L.S., and Ph.D.s and ABDs are increasingly common. Some schools facilitate the earning of an M.A. in history with an M.L.S. or M.S.L.S. with joint degree programs. Many librarians pursue higher degrees after employment, frequently with some financial support from their employer. Language skills are a definite plus, as is a knowledge of programming and database design.

To varying degrees, librarians make their own jobs. If one possesses sufficient maturity and emotional and physical energy, there is generally enough discretionary time within the work week and beyond to structure a position to meet one's emotional and intellectual needs. For a fulfilling library career, however, time management skills are essential. One must be able to act proactively, establish goals, determine what must be done to achieve them, set priorities, and learn from and work with others as appropriate. To this process must be added the constant learning of new skills. One's ability to meet deadlines, to be dependable to one's colleagues, subordinates, and superiors, to serve regularly and effectively on committees, task forces, and teams, and to do a multiplicity of tasks well buys the freedom to allocate the time necessary to perform these tasks at one's discretion.

The internal career advancement of most librarians is governed and guided by an articulated set of criteria which state the expectations for each rank. In most institutions where librarians are classified as faculty, four ranks are common, modeled after professorial ranks, with progressively advanced levels of accomplishment defining each: assistant librarian, senior assistant librarian, associate librarian, and librarian. For instance, librarians at the State University of New York at Buffalo are expected to demonstrate excellence in the same "basic" areas as other faculty but, in the case of publication, with less quantity. Areas of evaluation, listed in order of importance, are: competence in librarianship, contributions to the libraries and their services, professional contributions, scholarly accomplishment, and effectiveness of University and community service. Librarians at institutions where librarians have been granted faculty status are also eligible for sabbaticals, but this generally occurs only after tenure has been granted. At SUNY institutions, for instance, this benefit is available after six consecutive years of service and after each subsequent period of six consecutive years. One knows if one has been granted tenure after slightly less than six years of service. This tally is comprised either of years of service at one's current institution, or this tenure combined with service at another SUNY institution or elsewhere to the extent stipulated by policy. As one's tenure clock unwinds, periodic reviews occur over the course of which one or two promotions are achieved, resulting in new titles and salary increases. Discretionary increases, when provided by contract, are available and are awarded on merit. Cost of living increases, of course, are also contract driven.

Academic libraries are administratively different from academic departments; far greater interdependence is the rule between individuals, work groups, and departments. Perhaps this is why seminars on team work are regularly offered in the nation's libraries. In fact, the Office of Management Services of the Association of Research Libraries devotes considerable energy to such programs. As libraries undergo a transformation prompted by technology and financial constraints, there are many avenues for new involvement in one's job as well as for administrative advancement both within and beyond one's institution of initial or current employment.

Helpful for making friends, securing advice, and participating in the preparation of publications, events, and services is participation in the American Library Association's History Section and the Library History Round Table, the Association of College and Research Libraries' Western European Subject Specialist Section, and bibliography associations affiliated with historical organizations, such as the Association for the Bibliography of History, which is affiliated with the American Historical Association. These are simply examples; other groups within these organizations and other bodies may also be appropriate.

Many holders of administrative positions in academic libraries have advanced history degrees. Some of this is owed to constricted avenues for advancement in teaching, to the clarity of analysis and expression so valued in historical training, to the high regard in which historians hold the historical record, and to the easy interdisciplinarity, spanning the humanities and social sciences, which comes naturally to the thoughtful possessor of a historical education. As the repositories of our memories, libraries are especially well served with historians as directors, unit heads, and middle managers. The historian holding a library position sometimes finds himself or herself serving as an institutional memory, offering a calm and evolutionary perspective in the constantly changing world of today's research library.

NOTES

1. Charles A. D'Aniello, "Cultural Literacy and Reference Service," *RQ* 28 (Spring 1989): 370–80, reprinted in W. A. Katz, ed., *Reference and Information Services: A Reader for the Nineties* (Metuchen, NJ: Scarecrow Press, 1991), 21–40.
2. Charles A. D'Aniello, ed., *Teaching Bibliographic Skills in History: A Sourcebook for Historians and Librarians* (Westport, CT.: Greenwood Press, 1993).
3. Nancy C. Cridland, "History" in Patricia McClung, ed., *Selection of Library Materials in the Humanities, Social Sciences, and Sciences* (Chicago: American Library Association, 1985), 78–97; for a broader overview of the evolution of historical study and the bibliographic nature of a history collection see Nancy C. Cridland, "History" in Nena Couch and Nancy Allen, eds., *The Humanities and the Library*, 2nd ed. (Chicago: American Library Association, 1993), 45–85; two comments on what new bibliographers should know are Charles A. D'Aniello, "Bibliography and the Beginning Bibliographer," *Collection Building* 6 (Summer 1984): 11–19, reprinted in Betty Carol-Sellen and Arthur Curley, eds., *The Collection Building Reader* (New York: Neal-Schuman Publishers, Inc., 1992), 109–17, and Lynn B. Williams, "Subject Knowledge for Subject Specialists: What the Novice Bibliographer Needs to Know," *Collection Management* 14 (1991): 31–47; of broad utility are the outstanding essays in Peggy Johnson and Sheila S. Intner, eds., *Recruiting, Educating, and Training Librarians for Collection Development* (Westport, CT: Greenwood Press, 1994); useful for understanding the changing work place is Barbara A. Stelmasik and Margaret Maes Axtmann, "Building Bridges Between Acquisitions and Collection Development: Communication Models for the Electronic Environment," *Library Acquisitions Practice & Theory* 20 (Spring 1996): 93–102; for a detailed discussion of the history and future plans of H-Net: Humanities and Social Sciences Online see "H-Net," *OAH Council of Chairs Newsletter* 52 (August 1996) and see especially James P. Niessen, "Librarians and H Net."

DEBRA NEWMAN HAM is professor of history at Morgan State University. She earned her B.A. in history at Howard University, her M.A. in African history at Boston University, and her Ph.D. in African history at Howard University. Prior to joining the faculty at Morgan State, Dr. Ham served as specialist in African American history in the Manuscript Division of the Library of Congress and archivist at the National Archives and taught at Northern Virginia Community College. Her professional activities include service as vice president of the Afro-American Historical and Genealogical Society (of which she was a founding member), on the executive committee and as council secretary of the Association for the Study of Afro-American Life and History, as newsletter editor for the Association of Black Women Historians, on the Leopold Prize Committee of the Organization of American Historians, and on the editorial board of the Society of American Archivists. Her many publications include The African-American Mosaic: A Guide to Black History Resources in the Library of Congress *(1993),* Black History: A Guide to Civilian Records in the National Archives *(1984), and other volumes as well as essays in journals (including the* Journal of Negro History, Minerva: Quarterly Report on Women in the Military, *and* Sage, A Scholarly Journal on Black Women) *and other compilations (including* The Harvard Guide to African-American History, Black Women in America: An Historical Encyclopedia, Global Dimensions of the African Diaspora, *and* Notable Black American Women). *She curated and edited the catalog for the Library of Congress exhibit "The African American Odyssey: Quest for Full Citizenship."*

MANUSCRIPT CURATORS AND SPECIALISTS
Debra Newman Ham

Manuscript curators acquire, organize, and describe the personal papers of individuals or the records of various organizations. Megan Floyd

Desnoyers, in her article "Personal Papers," describes three categories of manuscripts:

1. bodies or groups of personal papers with organic unity—the archives of a person, family, or organization;
2. artificial collections of manuscripts acquired by private collectors from various sources, usually gathered according to a plan but without regard for their origin; and
3. individual manuscripts acquired by an institution because of their special importance to research.[1]

Those hired to be manuscript curators generally are selected because they have an educational or professional background that will enable them to understand the collections for which they are responsible. At the National Archives and Records Administration (NARA) and the Library of Congress (LC), manuscript curators and specialists traditionally have advanced degrees in history, although literary specialists at LC are selected because of their training in poetry and literature.

The work of manuscript curators varies from repository to repository. While most curators solicit and acquire new collections, some also process them, doing the hands-on job of arrangement, description, and servicing to researchers. However, in large repositories like NARA and the LC, manuscript specialists do not do the archival processing themselves but may be called upon to supervise the processing of new collections.

There are several types of manuscript specialists. Some specialize in a particular subject area or time period; others in a type of material, such as incunabula. I served as an African American history specialist first at NARA and then at the LC. Some specialists earn their positions through work with a group of manuscripts with such frequency that they know them better than their fellow staffers and the researchers. These specialists then become extremely helpful to the people who use the collections about which they are so knowledgeable. Others are chosen to be specialists because of their educational or employment background in a particular field of interest. Some actually become specialists because they develop such a personal interest in their subject that they develop a degree of expertise that leads to their formal selection as curators or specialists.

NARA BLACK HISTORY SPECIALIST

The National Archives houses the permanently valuable, noncurrent records of the federal government. I worked as an intern at NARA in 1970 during the summer after I graduated from Howard University and as a part time oral transcriptionist at the John F. Kennedy Presidential Library in Waltham, Massachusetts, while I was pursuing a master of arts degree in African history at Boston University. Upon graduation in 1972, I transferred back to Washington, D.C., to enter the archives training program and serve as the assistant to the black history specialist, Robert Clark. NARA recruited Clark, a professor from Virginia State University, in response to an ever-increasing research interest in African American history. He was the first official specialist, although other staff members at the Archives, who had a vast knowledge of the black history materials available there, served the public as unofficial specialists for many years before Clark arrived in 1971.

As a matter of fact, from the time that the federal government established the National Archives in 1934, professional archivists were impressed with the vast scope of information available among the federal records relating to African American history. As early as 1937, archivist James Mock presented a paper at the annual meeting of the Association for the Study of Negro Life and History. Entitled "Documenting the History of the Negro," the paper stated that archivists had already identified materials relating to African Americans in the records of every department of the government.[2] Several archivists who became actively involved in the black history committee of the American Council of Learned Societies began to produce aids to help researchers locate important materials relating to the subject.[3]

Black history was not, however, the only field in which NARA employed specialists. By the time I joined the Archives staff in 1972, several archivists specialized in other areas such as African history and the history of science and technology. A few years after my arrival NARA appointed a women's history specialist. There were also, in the various branches, archivists who were not officially called specialists but prepared subject guides to records relating to such subjects as Native Americans, Latin America, and various wars.

The NARA specialist generally does not do the work of an archivist, meaning the arrangement of papers and the preparation of finding aids for individual record groups, but serves rather as a subject expert. Because of the arrangement of collections by record group, gaining subject access to federal records can be a very timely and unrewarding process. The specialist facilitates research on a specific subject by scouring records and developing a written guide or a special list on that subject. Ideally, that finding aid should facilitate work for archivists and researchers alike.

In order to put together such a guide, the specialist must become familiar with materials throughout the repository, and I benefitted from simultaneous training at NARA as an archivist and a specialist. As part of my training, I worked in a variety of NARA branches such as cartography, sound recordings, and still pictures, and in each one I found unexpected African American history holdings. Who would dream, for example, that there would be a rich lode of material relating to African American mining communities in West Virginia among the records of the Solid Fuels Administration for War?

NARA AFRICAN AMERICAN FINDING AIDS

When I started as a specialist, NARA staff members were eagerly participating in preparations for the nation's bicentennial year—1976. As part of that effort, Clark directed me to search the military service records for the Revolutionary War to find materials relating to black soldiers. With the aid of student interns, I searched hundreds of reels of microfilm and textual records from the War Department Collection of Revolutionary War Records and the Papers of the Continental Congress. We also searched for free blacks in the 1790 census because slaves who served in the Continental Army were granted their freedom. I produced two finding aids including a *List of Free Black Heads of Families in the 1790 Census* and *List of Black Servicemen Compiled from the War Department Collection of Revolutionary War Records*.[4] These did not purport to provide *all* the names of free black heads of families or African American Revolutionary War soldiers, but they were both well received and stayed in print for many years. As a result of these works Alex Haley invited me to serve as a consultant for his Kinte Library Project, and I became one of the ten founders of the Afro-American Historical and Genealogical Society.

Although I left Clark's office and worked as a regular archivist from 1974 to 1978, I still remained interested in discovering black history records among the four hundred record groups at the National Archives. In 1976 the Archives published a finding aid I compiled, *Preliminary Inventory of the Records of the Social Security Administration,* and I published an article on "Black Women in Pennsylvania in the Era of the American Revolution"—an outgrowth of my work on the census special list—in the *Journal of Negro History* in the same year.[5] A year later the Archives issued my *Preliminary Inventory of the Records of the Office of Economic Opportunity*.[6] My most ambitious finding aid to date appeared in 1977: entitled *Selected Documents Pertaining to Black Workers among the Records of the Department of Labor and its Component Bureaus, 1902–69,* this finding aid included lists of individual documents and articles from several record groups, arranged chronologically under subject headings.[7] During the years that I was preparing this publication, I had the opportunity to produce some articles for scholarly journals and make oral presentations at a wide variety of conferences. My primary purpose was always to highlight the rich lode of archival Afroamericana. The manuscript curators and specialists at NARA and the LC have been regularly encouraged and supported in their efforts to be ambassadors to the scholarly community.

In 1978 NARA appointed me to prepare the guide to black history materials among civilian record groups while Clark was assigned to do military record groups. By this time I realized that the scope of information was enormous. I had literally watched archivists perish in the stacks under mountains of note cards as they unsuccessfully attempted to put together guides of great magnitude and detail. I attempted to focus on a description process that was both doable in a few years and useful to the general researcher, not only the subject expert. I was clear about several things. One, I could not search through every document box in the archives. Two, I could not hope to describe every document or even every series that included black history materials.

I decided to consume the elephant one bite at a time. Systematically, I went to each civilian division at the Archives, looked through the finding aids for each record group, followed up on any leads I found there, and interviewed staff members. Where indexes existed, I checked under Afro, African, Black, Colored, Haiti, Liberia, Negro, and under the names of famous individuals such as W. E. B. DuBois and Booker T. Washington, as well as names of historically black colleges and universities such as Howard, Bethune-Cookman, Hampton, and Tuskegee.

My supervisors instructed me to describe the materials I located first at the record group and then at the series level. A sample entry included: the record group number and title (e.g., RG 208, Records of the Office of War Information); the series title, dates, volume, and arrangement (e.g., Miscellaneous Records of the Advertising and Intelligence Division of the Office of Facts and Figures, 1941–42, 5 feet, arranged chronologically); and finally a description of the pertinent black history materials in the series. This final part—the description of black history materials— was my most original contribution to the guide. The other parts of the description were generally culled from existing finding aids. This careful procedure was utilized so that both searchers and archival staff could easily locate materials.

Each time I prepared a description—and I prepared them as I went along—I submitted a copy to the archivist in charge for any additions and corrections and then added the approved (or at least unprotested) description to a three-ring binder for use by researchers. I felt that the users' ability to understand what I was doing was crucial. Therefore, if they were regularly using the draft, pertinent questions should arise while the guide was still in process. Archival guides had caused a great deal of trouble when both searchers and archivists found themselves unable to locate described materials. I also decided to arrange the guide in numerical order by record group and include information about still pictures, motion pictures, sound recordings, maps, or other related materials. While the final product would not include everything in the Archives relating to black history, it would provide much research potential in the field.

Nineteen eighty-four was a banner year for me. I completed my doctorate in African history and the National Archives published my book, *Black History, A Guide to Civilian Records in the National Archives.*[8] The guide won finding aid awards from the National Archives, the Mid-Atlantic Regional Archives Conference, and the Society of American Archivists (SAA). The SAA prize, called the C. F. W. Coker Finding Aid Award, was endowed in honor of a deceased LC Manuscript Division staff member.

The receipt of the award was providential because it brought me to the attention of the LC Manuscript Division, and I was selected to succeed the Library's second official specialist in Afro-American history and culture, Tom W. Shick. I joined several other specialists in the Division whose areas of concentration included literature, science and technology, early American history, the national period, the Civil War, and the twentieth century.

LC AFRICAN AMERICAN SPECIALISTS—THE HISTORICAL BACKGROUND

I was only the third person at the Manuscript Division of the Library of Congress to hold the official title "Specialist in Afro-American History and Culture," but there were several unofficial specialists who preceded us, one by more than a century. Daniel Alexander Payne Murray—born a free black in Baltimore, Maryland, in 1852—did not intend to be a collector of black history materials, nor did he expect to become the first specialist in black history at the Library of Congress. He was hired as a personal assistant to Librarian of Congress Ainsworth R. Spofford in 1871. Spofford was an abolitionist who believed that African Americans should have a chance to achieve. Murray proved adept at mastering foreign languages and in locating specific titles of library books piled high in the recesses of the Capitol building. (A separate building for the Library of Congress was not opened until 1898.) In the 1890s the librarian requested that Murray prepare a listing of books written by or about African Americans. This began a new phase of his career as a black studies specialist, and he eventually became not only an important bibliographer and collector of published works by African American writers but also the compiler of an immense unpublished encyclopedia of black history. Murray worked at the Library until 1922.

Murray willed his large book collection, about fifteen hundred items, to the Library when he died in 1925, but his family sold his encyclopedia notes and personal papers to the State Historical Society of Wisconsin. Microfilm copies of these records are available at the Library of Congress Manuscript Division. Unfortunately, Murray's books were interfiled with the general collection, and many have now been microfilmed and the originals discarded. From his original collection, 350 pamphlets were kept together and are now housed in the Library's Rare Book collection.[9] Fortunately, Murray had multiple copies of some books, and the Library gave duplicates to Howard University's Moorland collection. Howard's Afroamericana librarian, Dorothy B. Porter (later Dorothy Porter Wesley), kept Murray's book collection intact and also retrieved some of his papers from his home and added them to Howard's collections.

Almost two decades later, another black studies specialist worked at the Library: E. Franklin Frazier, a Howard University sociology professor and author of the well-known works, *Black Bourgeois* (1957), *The Negro Church in America* (1961), and *The Negro Family in the United States* (1986), served as a "Resident Fellow for Negro Studies" at the Library of Congress from September 1, 1942, to August 31, 1943. During the year that he was in residence at the Library, he submitted a report with a detailed list of his duties, which included answering telephone inquiries and letters about black history and culture, talking with researchers at the Library, surveying Library collections to find information about black Americans, and making acquisitions trips in search of black history materials.

Frazier's most important contribution was the acquisition of the Booker T. Washington papers. He traveled to Tuskegee Institute in Alabama to talk with the school's president, Frederick Douglass Patterson, about the collection. Patterson, concerned about the proper preservation of the valuable files, offered more than 180,000 items to the Library. Frazier was as eager to bring them into the Library as the Library was to acquire them. In the 1943 *Annual Report of the Librarian of Congress,* Archibald MacLeish called the collection a "magnificent scholarly resource."[10] In another report that same year, Frazier deemed the collection "perhaps the richest and most important single source of information on the history of the Negro in the United States."[11] Certainly, it was one of the first major black history collections acquired by the Library. Frazier continued to be affiliated with the Library as a consultant in black studies until 1966.

By the late 1960s, partly because of the anticipated commemoration of the 350th anniversary of the arrival of Africans at Jamestown, Virginia, in 1619, and partly because of the Library's acquisition of the vast archives of the National Association for the Advancement of Colored People (NAACP) in 1964 and the National Urban League (NUL) records in 1966, John McDonough, the LC specialist for the national period, agreed to collect information about the Division's manuscript resources for black history. He presented a paper about the subject before the 1969 annual meeting of the Association for the Study of Negro (later Afro-American) Life and History in Baltimore. He subsequently expanded the paper for an extensive article in *The Quarterly Journal of the Library of Congress* entitled "Manuscript Resources for the Study of Negro Life and History."[12] This excellent and comprehensive essay provided the first collective discussion of Manuscript Division resources on this subject.

The 1969 *Annual Report of the Librarian of Congress* noted "the surge of interest in Negro affairs."[13] One of the ways that the Library met this surge was by contracting with Howard University librarian Dorothy B. Porter, "an eminent authority" in African Americana, to prepare *The Negro in the United States,* a bibliography, which was in press at the end of the fiscal year.[14] The *Annual Report* also commented on repeated research requests in the Manuscript Reading Room for NAACP, NUL, Booker T. Washington, and American Colonization Society records. These four collections, in 8,000 file boxes, accounted for more than 1,400 inquiries during the year. Additionally, researchers for the Booker T. Washington editorial projects regularly used the Library's manuscript collections. The Prints and Photographs Division reported that black history subjects clearly led the list of requests for pictorial materials in 1969, reflecting the need for illustrations for African American studies texts and magazine articles. The *Annual Report* indicated that black history also took first place among users associated with television and documentary film projects.[15]

In response to this outpouring of interest, the Library hired its first official "Specialist in Afro-American History and Culture" in the Manuscript Division. Sylvia Lyons Render, who held a doctorate in literature, came from North Carolina Central University, where she spent much of her earlier career researching the life and works of African American writer Charles Waddell Chesnutt. Her primary duties were acquiring new collections of black history materials and aiding researchers.

Render was a prolific writer who prepared many articles and reports relating to the black history collections in the Manuscript Division. She contacted many donors, brought in excellent papers including the Nannie Helen Burroughs collection, and successfully recommended the purchase of important documents for the Library. In 1979, Render developed the idea of naming a Library organization in honor of Murray. She called a meeting of Library employees interested in African American studies and the group organized the Daniel A. P. Murray Afro-American Culture Club, now known as the Murray African-American Culture Association.

Render stayed at the Library until 1983 when illness forced her to retire. During a leave of absence to return for a brief stint to North Carolina Central University, her temporary replacement was a scholar named Juanita Fletcher. Render was followed by Tom W. Shick in 1984, an Africanist from the University of Wisconsin in Madison who had used the Library's extensive American Colonization Society collection for his dissertation. After twelve months at LC, from 1984 to 1985, Shick decided that he would return to academia.

SAME SUBJECT, DIFFERENT RECORDS

When the Library hired me to succeed Shick, my job description indicated that my primary responsibility was to acquire historically important African American history collections from interested donors. Because federal law mandates that agency records come into NARA, I had no experience at all in persuading public figures to *donate* their papers to a historical repository. NARA does have a records *appraisal* branch, but the role of the appraiser is only to determine which of the federal records are permanently valuable. My other LC responsibilities included overseeing the processing, reference, and preservation of each African American history collection assigned to me, recommending the purchase of historical documents, aiding researchers, making scholarly presentations about the records, and providing support for the exhibit, public affairs, and other Library staff offices.

Developing knowledge about the materials in the Library's collections was a lengthy process. Even if specialists are chosen as I was because of their knowledge in a particular field, that does not guarantee that they will have *any* knowledge of the collections they are hired to oversee. There were ten thousand collections at the LC as opposed to only four hundred record groups at NARA—and, apart from the fact that the vast majority related to United States history, none of them were necessarily related in content. Yet over ninety-five percent of the collections at the Library were minuscule in comparison to the size of NARA record groups.

As a black history specialist both at the National Archives and in the LC Manuscript Division, it took years for me to become familiar with the collections. It is relatively easy to procure a list of collections available in your repository, become acquainted with the finding aids that facilitate their use, and understand the location registers for finding the documents in the stacks. To provide more detailed information, however, takes time.

Because the Library houses so many personal papers, the specialists often read biographies—if they are available—of the individuals represented in our collections. Preparing acquisitions reports, answering reference letters, and selecting documents for exhibits also necessitates reading through materials in the collections. It is impossible, however, for the curator or specialist to read through everything. The archivist who processes a collection often becomes an unofficial specialist and proves to be extremely helpful in working with researchers and staff members. Those processing the papers often are the first to locate special "treasures" among the papers, such as poems by Langston Hughes among the National Urban League (NUL) records, or manuscripts relating to W. E. B. DuBois among the files of African American diplomats Hugh and Mabel Smythe.

In attempting to learn the collections, I read every guide that staffers had prepared in the history of the division. I photocopied every page that had African American historical information, pasted the materials on five-by-eight index cards, and filed them alphabetically by name of collection.

SOLICITATION AND ACQUISITION

No responsibility I faced as a Library of Congress specialist was more challenging than soliciting and acquiring new collections. The Manuscript Division maintains an extensive case file which is arranged alphabetically by the name of individuals or organizations. These files were kept even when individuals showed no interest in donating their papers to the Library, had given them to other institutions, or responded in the negative. The case files generally include letters to and from the potential donor, an obituary or a biographical sketch, requests for permission for researchers to use restricted collections, copies of the instrument (deed) of gift, and sometimes narrative reports about curator visits with the donor.

In order to learn about the process for the solicitation of records, I began to search through the case files. I was interested in the way in which other specialists wrote their letters, followed up with donors, executed site visits, and prepared instruments of gift. I wanted to review case files for black history collections solicited by Render and Shick. Many of the individuals they contacted had promised to give their papers or had at least shown a degree of interest but had never actually transferred any documents to the Library. This fact provided me with one of my first tactics for solicitation. I began to write follow-up letters to these potential donors, introducing myself as the new specialist, explaining that I would do what I could to facilitate the transfer of their papers to the Library, and offering to visit them if I could provide help in selecting or packing documents.

Using this process I was able to schedule a few interviews. Just a few weeks after I started at the LC, I went to New York City to visit two African American civil rights activists and one well-known publisher. Although all three were receptive, only two of them actually donated their papers during my tenure at the Library. I soon learned that it could take years of gentle persuasion to get donors to the point of the actual transfer of documents, and the instrument of gift could take many years beyond the receipt of the papers.

In addition to following up on earlier solicitations, I began to make a wish list of the papers of prominent individuals and organizations. After getting the list approved by the head of the Manuscript Division, I began to write to dozens of people trying to interest them in our repository. Since the Library's collection was already very strong in the area of civil rights, I continued to try to bring in papers of activists in that area. I should mention here that donors can be strongly attracted by the stature of related collections in the repository. By this I mean that, for example, political leaders *might* be more likely to place their collections in repositories where other statesmen's papers are held. I also wanted to expand the variety of materials relating to African American women activists and blacks in the fine arts. These were areas in which the LC collection was relatively weak. Sometimes I worked in collaboration with other Manuscript Division specialists. For example, when I was interested in requesting the papers of an African American literary figure, I usually collaborated with the literature specialist. When I expressed interest in a black photographer, I worked along with curators in the Library's Prints and Photographs Division.

Among the important collections acquired during my LC tenure were the personal papers of Robert Russa Moton and Frederick Douglass Patterson, the second and third presidents of Tuskegee Institute; the papers of Tuskegee Airmen commander Noel F. Parish; the beginning of a collection from Judge Robert Carter, a former the NAACP general counsel; huge additions to social psychologist Kenneth B. Clark's papers that had reposed for years in his attic; and numerous transfiles of the NAACP Legal Defense Fund records. I recommended purchase of materials relating to slavery as well—material documenting the mortgaging of human property, records of probate battles over the ownership of slaves, and a Frederick Douglass letter.

Soliciting papers is always a group effort at the Library, and no one

Debra Newman Ham in the Library of Congress Manuscript Division in 1989 holding a photograph of two former presidents of Tuskegee Institute, Robert Russa Moton and Frederick Douglass Patterson. *Courtesy of the Library of Congress.*

person can take sole credit for successful acquisition efforts. This was especially true in the case of the Library's most publicized acquisition, the papers of Supreme Court Justice Thurgood Marshall. James Billington, the Librarian of Congress, David Wigdor, the assistant chief of the Manuscript Division, and I visited Justice Marshall after he announced his retirement in 1991. At that interview in Marshall's chambers at the Supreme Court building, the justice indicated that he intended to give his papers to the Library. He later signed a simple deed of gift indicating that the papers would be open for research use after his death.

When he passed away only fifteen months later in January 1993, his papers, which the LC received in excellent condition, were already processed, on the shelf, and ready for research use. The papers were opened, a public announcement about them appeared in the Library's February 1993 bulletin, and about eight researchers used the materials until May 1993. At that time, one of the researchers, who was a freelance writer working for the *Washington Post,* published a three-part expose, which, based on Marshall's papers, discussed the private deliberations of the nine justices before they made decisions on abortion, civil rights, and other important matters.

The newspapers had a heyday with the expose. The majority of the sitting justices and Marshall's family were livid. They demanded that the papers be closed or opened only to a restricted group of researchers. The Library insisted that it was following the wishes of the late justice and refused to bow to the intense pressure to restrict access. Congressmen, government officials, lawyers, reporters, scholars, and tabloids debated the issue, creating a media blitz of a volume unknown in the Library's entire history. Despite the uproar, the Library won the day, and the papers remained open and available to all Manuscript Reading Room researchers.

Mercifully, most acquisition efforts were not at all controversial. The process of writing letters, telephoning, visiting, and preparing for transfer was usually relatively routine. But critical in every acquisition was the instrument of gift, through which the donor could open the collection to the public and donate literary rights, close the collection for a period of up to twenty-five years, request that each researcher receive permission to use the collection, or restrict or deny reproduction privileges. The donor could also request that any materials not considered suitable for inclusion in the collection be returned. Staff members in LC's Exchange and Gift Division actually executed the formal instrument, which had to be signed by both the donor and the Library's general counsel before it could be considered valid.

After collections arrived, supervisors in the Manuscript Division's processing section scheduled them for processing. As the African American specialist, I approved the processing proposals from the archivists regarding black history collections, answered any questions about the donor and the collection, reviewed the finding aid or register prepared by the archivists, and examined any documents scheduled for disposal.

Sometimes the arrangement and description process necessitated calling donors to ask questions or to get clarification about materials in the collection. Contact with the donor was usually always my responsibility. I also prepared descriptive essays about many of the collections for the Manuscript Division's annual acquisitions report, for Library newsletters, and for exhibits. Besides acquisition efforts and supervision of processing of collections, the specialist also inspects the documents periodically after they are on the shelves to see if they are in need of repair, to recommend microfilming, and to select interesting materials for exhibits. After archivists and technicians processed and shelved a collection, I remained responsible for soliciting and evaluating additions from the donors.

AIDING RESEARCHERS

The specialist also works with researchers. Because the Library had so many African American history requests, especially for the NAACP records, the librarians in the Manuscript Reading Room became familiar with many of the collections and could answer most basic questions with ease. For the majority of the time that I was at the Library, the reading room staff also answered reference letters relating to African American subjects. If, however, the research request or reference letter was too complicated or vague, the reading room staff would refer the researcher to me. At other times I saw researchers because they requested interviews. Possibly the most problematic reference requests were from people who really wanted us to do their research for them. If this was indeed the case, the reading room staff sent the researcher a list of people who lived in the metropolitan area who could be hired to do research for a fee. Occasionally, when celebrities came to do research, we had to find special areas where they could work without interruption.

PREPARING FINDING AIDS

In 1989 the LC publishing office asked me to work with a team of LC employees to prepare a guide to Library holdings relating to African American history and culture. This proposed guide was to be one of a series of four. The subject areas for the other three were the age of Columbus, World War II, and Native Americans. The planned length of each guide was about 150 pages with lots of pictures. Interested Library employees met about the guide, and we came up with a team of seven Library employees and one former employee for the project. The guide's coverage included books, manuscripts, prints and photographs, music, motion pictures, and maps.

Instead of preparing essays about each type of black history record, such as "African Americana in the Music Division," the group decided to prepare a chronological, historiographical essay with materials of various types relating to a single period treated together. Thus, images, music, books, manuscripts, and maps relating to slavery, for example, would be treated together in essay form. My job was to write the descriptions of manuscript materials for the guide, receive essays from all of the other writers, and put all the pieces of the huge mosaic together in a single essay starting at the African slave trade and ending with the civil rights movement.

The slow and sometimes painful process of pulling the guide together resulted in success for the guide team. In late 1993, the Library published

The African-American Mosaic: A Library of Congress Resource Guide for the Study of Black History and Culture, of which I was the editor.[16] Instead of 150 pages, it was 300 pages long, with numerous illustrations. An impressive symposium reviewing the *Mosaic* and African American studies research at the Library took place in February 1994. Panelists included scholars such as Dorothy Porter Wesley, Pulitzer Prize winner David Garrow, Africanist Joseph Harris, and black film expert Thomas Cripps. Both the panelists and the participants expressed their appreciation of any volume that would aid their research and were particularly enthusiastic about the *Mosaic*'s multidisciplinary approach. Wesley, who at ninety had used the Library's resources for seventy years, expressed her delight at learning about resources she had no idea that the library held. The guide later won the Arlene Custer Award from the Mid-Atlantic Regional Archives Conference. In addition to the symposium there was a small exhibit in LC's Madison Building lobby called "Selections from the African-American Mosaic." The exhibit was placed online and has been extremely popular among Internet users.[17]

THE END OF THE MATTER

The specialist position was an interesting, multifaceted job. It took me at least eighteen months to fully understand everything I was expected to do. Achieving a good grasp of the information in the collections took even longer. Routine days were often interrupted by good news from donors, interesting or famous researchers, acquisitions trips, and public programs. With such a wide variety of responsibilities, a specialist needs the savvy and wit of Portia, the wisdom of Solomon, and the patience of Job. I fell a bit short of these paragons of virtue, but I enjoyed myself hugely at the job for eight years.

Between the National Archives and the Library of Congress I spent a total of twenty-four years as a black history specialist. I was lured away in 1995 by the genial air of academia with the prospect of finally doing something in my field of training—African history—and the heady thought of long summer vacations. In addition to African and African American history, I now teach archival theory and public history. For several summers I have continued to work on contract for the LC in the preparation of a major African American history exhibit, "The African American Odyssey: Quest for Full Citizenship," which opened in February 1998. Exhibited in galleries in all three LC buildings, the over 250 items are also available on the Library's Web site, and I have been invited by the LC to identify thousands of other African American history documents to augment them. In the near future I trust that a small fraction of the materials I learned about during my twenty-four years as an African American history specialist will be available electronically in my classroom, thus providing a satisfying consummation of the marriage between my careers.

NOTES

1. Megan Floyd Desnoyers, "Personal Papers,"in James Gregory Bradsher, ed., *Managing Archives and Archival Institutions* (Chicago: University of Chicago Press, 1991), 78.
2. Walter B. Hill, Jr., "Institutions of Memory and the Documentation of African Americans in Federal Records, in *Prologue: Quarterly of the National Archives and Records Administration* 29 (Summer 1997): 87.
3. Ibid.
4. Debra L. Newman, comp., *List of Free Black Heads of Families in the 1790 Census* (Washington, DC: National Archives and Records Service, 1973), and Debra L. Newman, comp., *List of Black Servicemen Compiled from the War Department Collection of Revolutionary War Records* (Washington, DC: National Archives and Records Service, 1974).
5. Debra L. Newman, comp., *Preliminary Inventory of the Records of the Social Security Administration* (Washington, DC: National Archives and Records Service, 1976), and Debra L. Newman, "Black Women in Pennsylvania in the Era of the American Revolution," *Journal of Negro History* 61 (1976): 176–89.
6. Debra L. Newman, comp., *Preliminary Inventory of the Records of the Office of Economic Opportunity* (Washington, DC: National Archives and Records Service, 1977).
7. Debra L. Ham, comp., *Selected Documents Pertaining to Black Workers among the Records of the Department of Labor and its Component Bureaus, 1902–69* (Washington, DC: National Archives and Records Service, 1977).
8. Debra L. Ham, comp., *Black History, A Guide to Civilian Records in the National Archives* (Washington, DC: National Archives Trust Fund Board, 1984).
9. For a more complete treatment of Murray's work, see Debra Newman Ham, ed., *The African-American Mosaic: A Library of Congress Resource Guide for the Study of Black History and Culture* (Washington, DC: Library of Congress, 1993), especially pages 140–45. This section of the guide was largely compiled by Rosemary Plakas, American specialist in the Library's Rare Book and Special Collections Division. Plakas was also the curator of a Library of Congress exhibit about Murray. Murray's pamphlets have been reproduced for the Internet at the following address: lcweb.lcweb.loc.gov/ammem/app/aaphome.hmtl
10. *Annual Report of the Librarian of Congress for the Fiscal Year Ended June 30, 1943* (Washington, DC: Library of Congress, 1944), 85.
11. Report, August 1943, Records of the Library of Congress, Manuscript Division, Library of Congress.
12. John McDonough, "Manuscript Resources for the Study of Negro Life and History," *The Quarterly Journal of the Library of Congress* 26 (July 1969): 126–48.

13. *Annual Report of the Librarian of Congress for the Fiscal Year Ending June 30, 1969* (Washington, DC: Library of Congress, 1970), 54.
14. Ibid.
15. Ibid.
16. Debra Newman Ham, ed., *The African-American Mosaic: A Library of Congress Resource Guide for the Study of Black History and Culture* (Washington, DC: Library of Congress, 1993).
17. The Internet address is lcweb.loc.gov/exhibits/african/intro.html

ANNE WOODHOUSE is the Shoenberg Curator at the Missouri Historical Society, Library and Collections Center. She earned a B.A. in history at Lawrence University, and an M.A. in history and a Ph.D. in cultural history and humanities at Stanford, and an M.A. from the University of Delaware-Winterthur Museum Program in Early American Culture and Museum Studies. She previously served as curator of domestic life at the State Historical Society of Wisconsin, where she curated such exhibits as "Styled to Sell: The Industrial Designs of Brooks Stevens," a pioneer of industrial design. Dr. Woodhouse has participated in numerous teams planning new museums and regional history exhibits and has served as cochair of the Midwest region Curators Committee, councilor-at-large on the Curators Committee of the American Association of Museums, and cochair and judge for the Curators' Exhibit Competition. She has appeared on the programs of such organizations as the American Association for State and Local History, the American Association of Museums, the Organization of American Historians, the Society of Architectural Historians, and the Winterthur Conference.

MUSEUM CURATORS
Anne Woodhouse

Two decades ago, to address the surplus of newly minted Ph.D.s, an annual meeting of the American Historical Association included a session on "alternative" careers for historians. Museum careers were mentioned as a possibility. However, there was only grudging acceptance of that option, and students interested in the history of things as well as ideas or political events were considered antiquarians. Nevertheless, in the intervening years, it has become more respectable for historians to work in museums, and a fair number of history Ph.D.s are now employed by museums as curators or historians. But the situation has now almost reversed itself: a recent letter from the director of a museum studies program cautions that graduates can no longer expect to find curatorial positions and that they must cast their nets more widely. Indeed, compared to other positions, few new curatorial positions are being created. What is it like to be a museum curator in this context? What might a potential museum curator expect?

ROLES AND RESPONSIBILITIES OF A CURATOR

Histories of museums trace their beginnings to private collections. Something in the human psyche seems to motivate people to preserve objects which are meaningful to them, to preserve memory. Many people go to great lengths to form personal collections of many kinds of objects both familiar and unusual. In the medieval period in Europe, holy relics of saints were avidly collected by those with means, and the possession of those relics was believed to convey status and spiritual benefits. The seventeenth and eighteenth centuries in Europe saw the formation of collections of all kinds, from books and manuscripts to freaks of nature, from minerals and shells to works of art and belongings of famous people. But although collecting began as a private passion, it did not always remain so, for some individuals chose to share their enthusiasm, to allow others to visit and study their collections. Today's museums came from that impulse to open collections.

Responsible for a museum's collections is the curator. A defining characteristic of the job of museum curator arises from the title itself: the word *curator* derives from the Latin word for *care*, as one cares for a collection of objects. Care involves building a collection through donations (usually!) and purchase; overseeing its housing and storage conditions; processing new material; maintaining records of information known about each object; conducting research; and determining ways of interpreting the objects to the public. But depending on the size and staffing of the museum, a museum curator may also take on other roles—from director to educator to public relations officer to registrar to custodian.

Unfortunately, the willingness of amateur collectors to take on curatorial positions at low salaries, the abundance of volunteers, and an inability to agree on professional standards have kept much of museum work as a high prestige–low compensation occupation. Nevertheless, the field has professionalized with the proliferation of museum training programs since the 1950s, and job listings now often require a master's degree in museum studies or a related subject specialization. Yet while support organizations such as the Curators Committee of the American Association of Museums exist, their membership remains low in contrast to the soaring number of members of other committees, particularly registrars, educators, and exhibit staff. Many curators evidently are more committed to their original subject specialties than to their roles as curators, are pulled in different directions by their multiple responsibilities, or are by nature less gregarious than their noncuratorial colleagues.

A curator's specific roles and responsibilities depend on the nature of the museum and its collection. History museums cover a vast range from historic houses to outdoor agricultural museums to county historical societies, from city public museums (which may also incorporate science and art) to state museums to national specialized museums. The great majority are small with perhaps one paid professional and much volunteer assistance, but some have sizable staffs with specialized areas of work. A curator in an art museum often can focus on a period and/or geographic area; for a history curator the usual focus is the history of the area where the museum is located. In larger museums, more specialization is possible—art, household furnishings, agricultural equipment, and so forth. However, in contrast to academic historians, most curators are of neces-

Museum curators, like academic historians, have the opportunity to do research. In many cases, this research is focused on objects. The author has been involved in researching many aspects of this chair, including history of ownership and manufacture. In preparation for conservation, the upholstery has been removed from one arm to reveal evidence of construction and original upholstery. *Courtesy of the Missouri Historical Society.*

sity generalists. Although it is sometimes possible to pursue a specialty, it is usually necessary to double in many other areas, doing the equivalent of teaching the survey course in several different fields.

While the basic scope of the collections is determined by the museum's mission, the curator is responsible for assessing the current collections within that context and setting parameters for collecting goals. As the mission changes or evolves, so should the scope of collections—in the past, history collections focused on the unusual, fine, or emotionally meaningful object, but history museums today are also usually charged with collecting and preserving the ordinary, everyday objects of daily life, sometimes a daunting task to locate. The collections may not, however, always correspond to the museum's stated mission—the collections may include objects inappropriate for the institution or may not fully reflect its mission. Many local history collections, for example, focus on the material culture of a particular county, town, city, or state, but typically there is not comprehensive coverage of the recent past. History did not end after World War II, but many historical collections do. Deciding what collections will be important in the future is not always easy but is always challenging, and a museum curator has a unique opportunity to define what artifacts from contemporary society will survive into the future.

Whatever the specific kind of museum, a large portion of a curator's time and attention is devoted to public presentations of the collection. Unlike private collectors, the curator is responsible for fulfilling the museum's function of serving the public. Opportunities to shape the public's historical understanding include developing tours and exhibits, both permanent and temporary; functioning as a public resource to answer questions about both the museum collections and items owned by members of the public; and public speaking, formal teaching, and writing about the museum and its collections.

CARING FOR AND MANAGING COLLECTIONS

In a history museum, the process of curatorial work focuses on dealing with objects and with information about them. Those objects are the foundation for the museum—its reason for existing and the basis for its interpretation of the past—and the curator bears responsibility for assessing and building strong and appropriate collections. But that is only the beginning—the curator also maintains physical custody of the museum's collections, and that entails substantial ongoing responsibilities.

Once acquired, an object is not simply put on the shelf. Preparing an

object to enter museum collections involves completing necessary procedures for gift or purchase and recording physical information regarding
size, description, markings, and so forth. Many history museums use standard terminology and have adopted the system of nomenclature developed by Robert Chenhall at the Strong Museum. This system classifies
things by function and follows a structure of categories and classification
terms. The consistent terminology allows future researchers to retrieve information more easily. When computerized, data retrieval becomes both
quicker and more nearly comprehensive. Keyword searches and sorting
queries make answering many questions quick work, but inaccurately or
inconsistently entered data may be lost in such a search. Some museums
are switching completely from their old card file systems; others maintain
cards for older collections and record new information on the computer.
The Internet offers the potential for connecting these databases and vastly
simplifying searching for both information and artifacts.

Each artifact must also be evaluated for condition and stability, cleaned
only with great care if dirty, conserved if necessary and possible, measured, tagged or numbered, and usually photographed. This involves
handling the object, and the curator must take great care to minimize the
chance of breakage or deterioration. For example, white cotton gloves
prevent finger oils from tarnishing metals, which are particularly sensitive.
Gloves are also occasionally used with other materials, especially porous
ones, if the use of gloves does not result in clumsy handling of fragile objects. Proper care also means that all cleaning, conservation, and num-
bering actions must be reversible, without permanently changing the artifact. There is a growing appreciation of the importance of maintaining
an object's original unrestored condition, which preserves evidence of
both manufacture and usage. (One book on antiques collecting states the
principle inelegantly but succinctly as "buy it ratty and leave it alone.")

Proper collections storage and display conditions are also important,
but most history museums must deal with less than ideal circumstances.
Stable temperature and humidity levels and protection from dust and
light are basic, but museum staff must also be aware of potential hazards
such as fire, water damage from flooding or burst pipes, and disasters like
tornadoes and earthquakes. Vandalism and theft are also possibilities,
and collections must be kept secure not only from external threats but
also internal—staff theft is more common in museums than is generally
realized. Collections with great monetary value must be particularly safe-
guarded. Regular inventories, though time-consuming, are an important
part of museum security.

Collections must be protected off-site as well. Objects loaned for exhibits require careful record keeping; they may also be fragile and

require special handling. If the museum has no registrar, this work may fall on the curator. Couriering artifacts is an occasional duty which may be a pleasant opportunity: I once traveled to Berlin to pick up two paintings from my museum's collection, fill out reports on their condition, and travel home with them.

The curator's specialized knowledge of objects carries with it special responsibilities. Public curiosity about the past and its objects is encouraged by books and television programs about collecting, publicity about escalating prices for antiques, and natural curiosity about family possessions. Museum curators often receive questions about the age, function, manufacturing techniques, possible origins, and usage of objects, and should be willing to share their expertise. They should not, however, provide information about monetary value of either museum collections or personal holdings. Members of the public seeking an insurance value should be encouraged to get a professional appraisal, do their own research in price guides, or query magazine and newspaper columns which identify objects and give guidelines as to value.

Museum curators also should not collect privately material which they curate professionally. This may be more of a concern for art curators than for history curators, though it would be problematic for the latter, for instance, to seriously collect locally made furniture or art for the area covered by their museums. The Curators Committee of the AAM has published guidelines for curatorial ethics.[1]

MAKING COLLECTIONS ACCESSIBLE

Curators not only take care of collections but also make them accessible to the public. The most familiar vehicle for access is the museum exhibit, which can take the form of a furnished historic house, a gallery display of similar items, or an interpretive exhibit organized by theme and carrying heavy educational baggage. Exhibits may be permanent or temporary, making it possible for the museum to treat different topics and bring collections into public view in a changing sequence. This is the aspect of the museum that most people see; it is the tip of the history museum iceberg and the most well known. It may well be the best-funded function of the museum, dwarfing budgets for object acquisition and maintenance.

Exhibits may be object-based (looking at the collections to get ideas) or theme-based (beginning with an idea or concept from history). The development process—moving from concept to a new exhibit—may take only a few weeks for a small display or years for a major one, with time built in for periodic evaluation. Depending on the size of the staff, the curator may be responsible for all aspects of the exhibit—planning, scripting, artifact selection, and installation, as well as educational outreach and any written materials. In a larger institution, however, the curator may be part of a team, which may include some combination of designer, educator, researcher, registrar, conservator, even exhibit developer. The curator's specific role then is to select appropriate objects, contribute to the content of the script, and ensure that collections are displayed with respect for the meaning they convey and their physical preservation.

But funding for new exhibits is no longer as plentiful as it once was, and some museums are focusing on refurbishing and reinterpreting their existing exhibits. Museums which have had static displays for years, like the clocks at the Henry Ford Museum or the ceramics at the Wallace Decorative Arts Gallery at Colonial Williamsburg, have reinstalled these collections to make them more accessible to the general public, to explain the technology by which these products were designed and made, and to talk about usage, history, and taste.

Sometimes the curator's responsibility will extend to the publication of an exhibit catalog, a printed commentary meant to supplement an exhibit and to stand alone after the exhibit has come down. Escalating printing and photography costs have raised catalog prices; perhaps computer technology will replace the printed catalog. Curators may also be called on to authorize reproductions of museum objects, either in three-dimensional or photographic form, for various uses. Research, study, or sale in the museum shop are all possible reasons for reproduction.

Because visiting museums is primarily a leisure activity for many people, exhibitions and other public presentations cannot be pedantic—they must engage the visitor. But can the museum with its limited resources compete with the sophisticated entertainment to which the public is accustomed? Just remember that the public remains fascinated with historical artifacts—theme parks may entertain, but they don't have the "real thing," actual historical objects.

RESEARCH AND TEACHING IN MUSEUMS

Many of the research and teaching skills which historians learn can be put to good use in museum work. Historians are trained to ask questions, sift available evidence, synthesize answers to those questions, and present their conclusions in written or oral form—and all are as important in museums as in any other setting in which historians and public historians work.

In a museum setting, research usually focuses on artifacts or exhibit development rather than the more traditional sources and topics of graduate school, but the process is much the same. Before new acquisitions can be processed into the collections, as much information as possible should be compiled. The donor or seller may furnish a history of the object's manufacture and ownership, but library research is often necessary to establish the details. For those working in museums of local or regional history, a working knowledge of such essential tools as city directories, business catalogues, and newspapers will be useful in answering questions about artifacts made in your area.

But research may also take the form of material culture inquiry, which involves asking questions of the object itself by close examination to reveal information about materials, workmanship, and history of usage. A growing body of writing on material culture can provide a context for this by providing information about related groups of objects and what they can tell us about the people who used them.[2] Sometimes museum curators can contribute to this scholarship as well by sharing the results of their research, although there is less pressure and encouragement to publish in museums than in academia.

Teaching in the museum may often be informal, taking the form of responses to written or telephoned requests for information. People are very curious about objects they own or have seen in a museum and do not hesitate to write or call. Curators share the museum's responsibility to serve the public and should always respond to this curiosity about history and historical objects. Teaching can also take the form of public speaking about the museum and its collections and of developing special public programs and tours, and there may also be opportunities for more formal lectures using slides and objects. Teaching outside the museum may also be possible—many universities have programs in public history or museum studies and are eager to find instructors with practical experience.

PROFESSIONAL ISSUES

Although the historical profession recognizes the employment opportunities of museum work, the pejorative aura of "antiquarianism" has tended to color academic historians' view of museum workers. "I'm not interested in dead things!" was the comment of a graduate school colleague invited to go along on a museum visit during an academic year in Paris. The rise of programs in public history, American studies, and material culture studies has done much, however, to raise the status of museum curators within the historical profession.

Unfortunately, that status does not translate into jobs. Surveys indicate that the number of curatorial jobs created is not keeping pace with those in other museum fields. Growth areas tend to be in fund raising and development, museum shop sales, and exhibits and public programming.

Directors are interested in numbers of visitors and in revenue generated from admissions and sales. Just as colleges tend to regard football teams as bringing money into their coffers, museums focus resources where they most directly lead to increased visitation and revenue—exhibits and public programs—and not in behind-the-scenes care of collections. This leads to an unfortunate rivalry within some museum staffs, and the natural independence of museum curators may hurt their position when other staff members perceive curators as "difficult," as catering only to specialists, and as more interested in the objects than in presenting history to the general public. Curators do not inhabit an ivory tower and may need to make a greater effort to combat this stereotype.

The public has a strong interest in history—just look at the growth of heritage tourism or the success of Ken Burns's documentaries—but that interest does not always extend to history museums. History museums are not perceived as having the glamour of art museums or the excitement and hands-on attraction of science museums. It is therefore vital that museum curators work well with the public in many capacities, encouraging volunteers, convincing donors that the museum is a good home for their treasures, and cultivating public support for museum programs and activities.

Building public support is complicated, however, when the museum presents something controversial. The museum may find itself facing harsh public criticism and the threat of loss of public and private support. In art museums, the controversy may involve the exhibition of works some consider to be obscene or offensive; in history museums, the issue more often involves disagreement over the interpretation of the past, which can be very different for different constituencies. The National Air and Space Museum (NASM) found itself embroiled in such a controversy over its plans to exhibit the *Enola Gay,* the airplane which dropped the atomic bomb on Hiroshima. The exhibit's proposed interpretation stressed the bomb damage and the aftereffects of radiation, which American World War II veterans believed made the Allied forces look like villains. When Congress threatened to intervene on behalf of the veterans, NASM was forced to modify its plans and mount a more celebratory exhibit. For museums which receive significant federal or state funding or which have come to depend on grants from the National Endowments for the Arts and Humanities, the days when a curator could make an independent point of view statement may be numbered.

NETWORKS AND PROFESSIONAL DEVELOPMENT

Especially at small museums, curators may be expected to perform a great many functions with no assistance. It is easy to feel isolated and to miss contact with one's peers. The range of available professional networks can help to fill the need for guidance, information, and support. Curators share the subject-matter professional organizations which academics join as well as museum-related ones. The American Historical Association, the Organization of American Historians, and the American Studies Association are examples of organizations where museum curators mingle with academic historians. In addition, there are the museum-focused groups—the American Association of Museums (AAM) and its international affiliate the International Council of Museums (ICOM), the American Association for State and Local History, and the Association for Living Historical Farms and Agricultural Museums are examples of affiliate groups with strong history components which provide conferences, publications, and other support for history museum staff. There are also specialized organizations, such as the Costume Society and the Decorative Arts chapter of the Society of Architectural Historians, which promote scholarship and provide forums for discussion of their more narrowly focused subjects.

It is not always possible to attend a national meeting, but regional organizations provide accessible activities, conferences, tours, and support. There are six regional museum associations under the American Association of Museums umbrella: New England, Mid-Atlantic, Southeast, Midwest, Mountain-Plains, and Western, which includes Hawaii and Alaska.[3] Often within driving distance, regional conferences include tours and special events at host museums, which provide opportunities to visit facilities with museum colleagues and sometimes even include behind-the-scenes tours with professional staff.

More specifically for curators, AAM sponsors a Standing Professional Committee called the Curators Committee (CurCom), which is an invaluable resource and offers a scholarship to the AAM annual meeting for a new professional curator each year. In the late 1980s, CurCom started an exhibit competition—now also cosponsored by the Committee on Audience Research and Education and the National Association for Museum Exhibition—to reward excellence in exhibit development and presentation, and the recognition this provides is highly regarded in the museum field. Curators of smaller museums should note that the award categories are based on exhibit budget size, so that their efforts are not competing with multimillion dollar shows.

Some regions also have curators' organizations for those who are unable to attend the annual AAM meeting. These groups convene at their regional association meetings. Although the national CurCom is one of the smaller Standing Professional Committees (SPC), participation is often stronger at the regional level—at the 1996 Midwest Museums Conference the Midwest Curators Committee had the largest turnout of any

Entryway to "Recycled, Re-Seen, Folk Art from the Global Scrap Heap," an exhibit at the Museum of International Folk Art, Museum of New Mexico. This exhibit won first prize in the 1996 Exhibit Competition sponsored by the American Association of Museums Curators Committee. The Curators Committee found the exhibit to be an outstanding example of engaging design and sound scholarship on an innovative topic. *Photo by Blair Clark. Courtesy of the Museum of New Mexico.*

SPC organization. This may indicate that curators do congregate with their peers if they can afford to get to a meeting with them.

Finally, there are also state and local museum organizations. Some states such as Wisconsin and Ohio have strong links between the state museum and local or county historical societies. Some cities have groups which are useful to curators, such as the Intermuseum Council of Nashville.

Curators should not overlook collectors' groups. *Maloney's Antiques & Collectibles Resource Directory,* a frequently revised work which is invaluable for answering reference questions, also contains a good listing of clubs and associations which unite collectors and enthusiasts about such disparate areas as coins, buttonhooks, and Charles Lindbergh memorabilia. Collectors often have materials which they are willing to lend for exhibition and can even supply technical information and restoration skills.

All these networks are valuable for support, information, and even mentoring. Some of the larger organizations have actually tried to establish mentoring programs, either in a discussion forum or through matching a new professional with a senior one. The important thing is that help is available for almost every subject and problem, and isolated curators should not feel alone. Perhaps because museums are generally nonprofit and scholarship is shared rather than hoarded, museum workers tend to be an unusually helpful lot.

AAM also provides practical help in analyzing a museum's individual problems with its Museum Assessment Programs (MAP I, II, and III). MAP I and II are particularly helpful for museum curators. MAP I provides an overview of the museum by an experienced museum colleague, pointing out actual and potential problems in the museum's governance structure, policies, record keeping, collections storage, and programs. MAP II, which can be requested only after completion of a MAP I survey, concentrates on collections and is thus of special help to curators. MAP reviewers submit a written report to AAM and the museum being reviewed and can supply information about additional human or material resources. The MAP reports are a very useful way of obtaining an outside expert's opinion and can be very valuable in supporting a curator's recommendation for improving procedures and conditions.

For more formal educational opportunities, there are a number of possibilities. First, museum studies courses are available in specialized undergraduate and graduate programs or as aspects of academic programs in subjects like anthropology, history, art history, and public history. Many of these encourage museum internships, which can be tailored to a particular interest or project and can be arranged for academic credit or not. Occasionally internships offer a stipend either through the academic program or through the museum. A well-planned internship with a completed goal, a tangible product, and a supervisor's recommendation is a valuable way to obtain experience. Volunteer (unpaid) opportunities are more plentiful. Anyone seeking to enter a museum career would do well to get some volunteer experience working with one. However, those seeking careers in museums should realize that volunteer experience is evaluated less seriously than a successful structured internship.

Midcareer opportunities also abound. Research fellowships for pursuing study on a particular topic are available from institutions like the Winterthur Museum, the Getty Trust, and the Missouri Historical Society.[4] Before, during, or after their meetings, museum conferences occasionally offer training sessions on various subjects such as time management, special storage problems, or earthquake preparedness.

Specialized study tours are worth looking into. Though they can be expensive, many offer invaluable access to museums, historic homes, gardens, and so forth; group transportation; and the company of colleagues who may be especially knowledgeable. The Victorian Society and Attingham Park programs offer a combination of lectures by local experts with site visits.[5] Other study courses and tours are offered by auction galleries and museums.

More formal midcareer training also exists. The Campbell Center in Mount Carroll, Illinois, gives short courses in various aspects of conservation and historic preservation. Curators who have management responsibilities or are considering a career move into administration are ideal candidates for the Museum Management Institute, the Seminar for Historical Administration, or other programs designed to hone administrative skills.[6]

FUTURE DIRECTIONS

From the standpoint of managing collections, the computer is changing the nature of museum work. As prices drop, museums can afford laptop computers for entering data directly during the cataloging process, thereby streamlining a cumbersome and repetitive procedure. Information seeking and dissemination generally will be greatly aided by computer networks. Many museums have Web sites, but a large number of them are merely online brochures. Some, however, are truly interactive, and a Museum Computer Network exists to support and encourage further development.[7]

Our understanding of the past and material culture is also changing. Interdisciplinary studies (American studies, material culture studies, regional studies, and so forth) are training potential museum staff in interesting new ways. For example, historical archaeology is bringing new insights to the study and exhibit of artifacts. Archaeology is especially valuable for documenting the material culture of the economically disadvantaged and illiterate, groups which would not have left diaries, letters, or other archival material, and whose possessions were used until they wore out or were destroyed. Of course, archaeological evidence will be weighted towards pieces of breakable items—especially ceramics and glass—and short on precious metals, which could be melted down and recycled, and wood, paper, and textiles, which often do not survive burial.

Indeed, museum collections today encompass new kinds of artifacts and new conservation problems. For the twentieth century, sound recordings and radio and television tapes are being collected as artifacts of behavior, entertainment, and cultural events. And curators and historians are interpreting artifacts in new ways. For example, mass-manufactured items not formerly prized by museums are now being collected and

interpreted as important manifestations of nineteenth- and twentieth-
century culture.

IN CONCLUSION

I was one of the history Ph.D.s of the mid-seventies who retooled via a
museum training program to become a museum curator. It was the right
choice for me. I enjoy museum work and related opportunities much
more than the traditional academic path of teaching and research and
find it exciting to be part of the relatively new field of material culture
and its interpretation. I value the opportunity to teach history through
objects and to use skills and talents not valued in academe. Does it sound
like the career for you? If so, take every opportunity to visit museums and
learn about and from objects, get the best training you can (including
volunteer experiences and internships), and develop your people skills
and your computer knowledge. Be flexible in searching for your first
job—cast your net widely both geographically and in terms of kinds of institutions and organizations. Many of the opportunities may be in small
historical societies, where you'll have broad responsibilities and the
chance to learn which aspects of the work appeal to you more than others. Once on the job, be sure to join museum organizations, network with
your colleagues, and keep up with new developments in the field. Museum curators are a vital part of the historical profession, and we're eager to have you join us. Welcome!

NOTES

1. For a copy of the Curators Committee's ethics guidelines, contact AAM (see
   the "Resources" section of this volume).
2. A good place to begin learning about the field of material culture is *Material
   Culture: A Research Guide,* edited by Thomas J. Schlereth (Lawrence: University of Kansas Press, 1985). This book has chapters on subfields of material
   culture such as cultural geography, history of technology, decorative arts, and
   folklife studies.
3. For information on how to contact a regional museum association, see *The
   Official Museum Directory,* an annual publication of AAM and R. R. Bowker.
4. For information on these fellowship programs, contact the Research Fellowship Program, Office of Advanced Studies, Winterthur Museum, Winterthur,
   DE 19735, 302/888–4649; the Getty Grant Program, 1200 Getty Center Drive,
   Suite 800, Los Angeles, CA 90049-1685, 310/440–7320; and the Research
   Center, Missouri Historical Society, P.O. Box 11940, St. Louis, MO 63112-
   0040, 314/746–4599. For other opportunities, see the newsletters of the

American Association for State and Local History and the American Association of Museums (see the "Resources" section of this volume).

5. To contact the Victorian Society, see the "Resources" section of this volume. For the Attingham Park program, contact the American Friends of Attingham, 285 Central Park West, New York, NY 10024, 212/362–0701.

6. For information on these programs, contact the Campbell Center for Historic Preservation Studies, P.O. Box 66, Mount Carroll, IL 61053, 815/244–1173; Museum Management Institute, c/o Getty Leadership Institute, 1200 Getty Center Drive, Suite 300, Los Angeles, CA 90049-1680, 310/440-6300, email: mmi@getty.edu; and Seminar for Historical Administration, c/o AASLH, 1717 Church Street, Nashville, TN 37203, 615/320-3203.

7. The Museum Computer Network, an AAM affiliate, publishes *Spectra*, a quarterly newsletter. For additional information, contact Leonard Steinbach, Cleveland Museum of Art, 11150 East Blvd., Cleveland, OH 44166-1797, 216/421-7340; email: lsteinbach@clevelandart.org.

ROSE T. DIAZ *is a doctoral student in the History Department at Arizona State University, where she also did her undergraduate work. She is currently a research historian on staff at the University of New Mexico's Center for Southwest Research and previously worked in the Special Collections Department of the University's General Library. Ms. Diaz has served on the board of trustees of the Hispanic Culture Center (NM), on the board of directors of the National Council on Public History (NCPH) as well as its Membership Committee, on the executive council of the Oral History Association (OHA), and as president of the Southwest Oral History Association (SOHA). She has appeared on the programs of the Mexican American Women's National Association, the National Association for Chicano Studies, NCPH, OHA, SOHA, and other organizations and has coordinated or served on the faculty for workshops sponsored by, among others, the Arizona Coordinating Council on History, NCPH, the Northwest Oral History Association, and SOHA.* Her publications include New Mexico Women's Legal History Project Guide *(1994)*, Hispanic Heroes: Portraits of New Mexicans Who Have Made a Difference *(1992), and* Multicultural Resource Guides: A Selected Bibliography *(1990)*.

ANDREW B. RUSSELL *is a doctoral student in the Public History Program at Arizona State University. He earned both his B.A. and his M.A. in history at the University of Nevada, Las Vegas. He has served as the project director for "Japanese American Women of Nevada," an oral history and photo-exhibit project sponsored by the Nevada Humanities Committee and the Las Vegas Chapter of the Japanese American Citizens League. He has presented papers at meetings of the Nevada Historical Society, the Popular Culture Association, and the Western Conference of the Association for Asian Studies. Mr. Russell's publications include articles in* In Focus: Annual Journal of the Churchill County Museum Association, *the* Nevada Historical Society Quarterly, *and* Selected Papers in Asian Studies *(Western Conference of the Association for Asian Studies)*.

ORAL HISTORIANS: COMMUNITY ORAL HISTORY AND THE COOPERATIVE IDEAL

Rose T. Diaz and Andrew B. Russell

In the words of British scholar Paul Thompson, "oral history is as old as history itself." In preliterate societies, "all history was oral history," and in modern times research professionals have rediscovered the value and legitimacy of oral testimony for studying the recent past.[1] At the same time, it is a young field. Oral history only began to emerge as a professional mode of inquiry and documentation toward the middle of the twentieth century. Many authorities count the establishment of the Columbia Oral History Research Office in 1948, under the guidance of Professor Allan Nevins, as the birth of the modern field.[2]

Oral historians from Nevins's time to the present have tried to create new pools of research data by transferring "historically significant" human memories to audio (and video) recordings usually made during one-on-one interviews. With questionnaires and tape recorders in hand, most oral historians are on a mission to capture untold stories and recover information missing in the conventional record. In efforts to recognize that placing one's self "inside the box" can endanger scholastic objectivity, oral historians have tried to identify and improve interview strategies and standardize guidelines to professionalize the craft.

Plying the craft in community settings can be especially challenging and rewarding. While it tests the interpersonal skills and cultural sensitivities of historians, it opens many previously locked doors for interaction and discovery.[3] While people in communities have been sharing oral history among themselves for countless generations, professional interviewers only recently arrived on the local scene. The Columbia project, for example, focused only on "major players in government, business and society." It was not until the 1970s, as historians generally began to study "everyday life" or "people's history," that oral historians began to recognize the value of "non-elite" as well as "elite" stories. Since the 1980s, institutionalized oral history programs and the professional literature have become significantly more inclusive.[4]

At the same time that academic and archival programs were responding to changing political and social realities and shifting research agendas, communities were becoming aggressive in their demands for a greater voice in the documentation process. Change came slowly, however, and many of the early "inclusive" projects continued to collect "elite" or single-sided perspectives on community life and issues. Much of what was called "community oral history" remained deaf to the stories of racial and ethnic groups and to women in general. But this has changed, and oral historians, like historians in general, are now committed to expanding the historical narrative and eager to study groups and individuals at society's "margins," to capture the human drama that will be overlooked, lost, or silenced otherwise.

The trends toward inclusiveness were paralleled by efforts to professionalize the craft. Oral historians have worked hard to establish common goals and guidelines and articulate the basic responsibilities of practitioners. In their various endeavors, they have developed, refined, and occasionally rejected "rules" for gathering verbal testimony. They have sought ways to "test" memory and articulated the difficulties and pitfalls in gathering sound recollections.[5] Recognizing their duty to gather "grassroots" perspectives, they have strived to capture the "voice" of the communities and narrators (sometimes called interviewees, witnesses, subjects, or informants) that they study.

Community oral historians ourselves, we are committed to furthering both inclusiveness and professionalization in the field. In the pages that follow, we will draw from our experiences and the emerging literature to provide a basic overview of the roles and responsibilities, processes, common pitfalls, and varied uses of oral history in community settings. We will emphasize the need for building stronger community partnerships through group projects but will also offer practical advice for individual researchers "turned loose" in community settings.

PARTNERSHIPS

While any given *interview* might be considered a short-term "partnership," most oral history *projects* become long-term collaborative efforts. These larger partnerships will likely involve professional historians, community volunteers and historical consultants, and field oral historians working together in pursuit of the same general collection goal. Frequently, the divisions between participating entities are not as clearly defined as this triangular model suggests. Very often, the roles and functions of these three groups overlap. Nonetheless, it may be easiest to show how community oral history projects function by looking first at the three partnership entities and the roles they typically play.

Like teachers, researchers, museum specialists, and archivists, professional historians frequently interact with the community and employ the basic methods and techniques of oral historians in their daily routines. But many are not trained in the subtleties and nuances of community mapping or oral history methodology, and they and their institutions often act only as advisors, consultants, or sponsors of actual oral history projects. As such, they bring professional skills, oversight, and "quality control" to projects by stressing the need to collect accurate information and verify findings. Public historians, in particular, often merge a unique blend of rigorous academic training, the ability to cooperate productively in team projects, and the capacity to serve as facilitators between agencies and the community. In some cases, they suggest what types of information are most needed by scholars, public collections, and interpretive agencies.[6]

In cooperation with other entities, professional historians help direct the search toward information and topics of historical significance. In line with this goal, they offer expert advice on how to frame, shape, structure, and evaluate research; they might also suggest interview questions that serve competing and parallel interests. At the same time, assisting or directing community-based projects provides professionals with more opportunities to interact and apply their skills in the interest of local communities. This interaction is important, since historians influence the telling of the local, state, and national story. By participating through hands-on involvement, they gain appreciation for individual and community experiences, struggles, and achievements.

Nonprofessional historical consultants and volunteers from the community, the second group in typical partnerships, also bring a great deal of expertise to projects large and small. The importance of encouraging active community participation cannot be overstated. Without active partnerships between research professionals and the community, confusion often arises over agendas and conflicting interpretations of the past. Indeed, communities often question the very necessity of bringing in academic "outsiders" to investigate and validate the community story. An "us and them" mentality left to develop within the "triangle" can quickly cripple a project.

Seeking community involvement is more than a way for historians to gain access into a community. Professionals need to understand that virtually all communities have their own "amateur historians"—community members who collect and preserve group and family memories, ephemera, and memorabilia.[7] These authorities are often overlooked because they may lack professional training and ties to mainstream institutions. But their lack of academic credentials does not diminish their overall effectiveness and dedication. They often maintain specialized libraries and personal collections that save research hours and commonly yield unanticipated documentation treasures. Moreover, these individuals (and community volunteers in general) function as interpreters and cultural brokers—people who define and articulate complex community realities for outsiders. Community consultants and volunteers should be recruited to help with planning, networking, fund raising, collecting, and processing oral history whenever possible. With guidance, they can emerge as "professional" interviewers and increase the likelihood of project longevity.

Oral historians form the third link in this hypothetical partnership triangle. We define oral historians as the individuals coordinating, supervising, or directly involved in the gathering of personal narratives. They are the field practitioners who qualify to direct a project and/or collect interviews by blending good listening techniques and community mapping skills with historical or cultural expertise. (Few qualify as experts in all areas—another reason to expand partnerships.) These field professionals work closely with the community by supervising research, project development, training workshops, fund raising, collection, preservation, and other public programming activities. As the chief (and sometimes sole) administrator, most project responsibilities fall to them.

But that is not all they do. As intermediaries between the other historians and the community, oral historians not only instill and articulate the professional aims of the project but also promote cooperation and function as advocates for the community. As a project evolves and boundaries of knowledge expand, these professionals facilitate the empowerment of diverse voices—they provide the bridge between scholarly research and the community and between individuals and groups within the community by ensuring avenues for mediation of contested information and consolidating issues of competing interest.

THE ORAL HISTORIAN AS PROJECT ADMINISTRATOR

Field oral historians, out of necessity, wear many hats. At the very least, they must mediate and negotiate between the needs and interests of professional historians, the community, and the project. They must also be advocates for professionalism, for maintaining the highest possible standards of research, questionnaire design, interview collection, and preservation. At the same time, they must support the implicit promise of the craft to bring previously undocumented voices, stories, and perspectives into the historical chronicle. All this comes together in their work as projects administrators, in *conceptualizing and planning, budgeting and funding,* and *general administration.*

The conceptualization of an oral history project usually begins with a passionate desire to preserve and interpret local social history and cultural traditions. It proceeds effectively when the passionate individual or individuals immerse themselves in local, regional, and relevant national history and gain a working knowledge of the culture or subculture(s) under study. Too often, it seems, projects have been geared toward *either* history *or* sociocultural topics, generating categorical terms like "episodic," "life-cycle," "folk life," and "ethnic" oral histories. In truth, few oral histories fit into such neat categories.

Project designers should consider exploring historical and thematic topics, like community responses to strikes, wars and homefront activities, local catastrophes, political and social movements, and civil rights struggles. But oral history is also an effective tool for answering questions about home and family life, group associations, spiritual beliefs and practices, work patterns, customs and traditions, and so forth. And, oral history often reveals the uniqueness of individual experiences. Regardless of the interview length and primary focus, project directors should aim for a balance in the types of questions they will ask of their narrators.

Planning community oral history is a dynamic process and projects often grow exponentially. For example, the Center for Southwest Research at the University of New Mexico became interested in an elementary school project featuring African American elders recounting their life experiences. Center staff consulted on the videotaping of some of these presentations, and that later made possible the launching of a larger, jointly constructed oral history project. In another case, the Nevada Humanities Council took an interest in a lone scholar's oral history research examining the Japanese experience in Nevada. The council provided funding for a project that paired the scholar with members of the Japanese American community of Las Vegas in an effort to collect more interviews of Japanese "pioneer" women. A similar preservation interest sparked these two projects to life, but the partnerships formed also influenced the shape, scope, and goals of the research and documentation efforts.[8]

In virtually all cases, budgeting and funding considerations influence greatly the goals and scope of a project. A basic operating budget is crucial. Project planners must become acquainted with the public and private funding sources that operate at local, state, and national levels. They must be mindful that nearly all "investors" operate on yearly funding cycles and set proposal deadlines. Although public funds and tax incentives for research projects are decreasing at an alarming rate, more community industries, philanthropists, and volunteers are taking an interest in the community story. Individuals or projects seeking such funds must be informed, well prepared, and confident as they seek initial and continuing support. And, once funding is secured, the project director must take care to stay within budget. Soliciting and budgeting funds can be a tiring process, but it helps to keep in mind that the "commodity" sought and collected provides the incentive for investment. Human memory is priceless.

Effective administration also means training and tracking the progress of interviewers and support staff. Generally, the project leader recruits volunteers, evaluates their strengths and weaknesses, selects interviewers, and assigns various tasks related to the project. This requires being attentive to human sensitivities but willing to make decisions in the best interests of the project.

The project administrator is responsible as well for the project's relationship to the larger community. Administrators, interviewers, and anyone else who represents the project before the community or the public should constantly reflect on their actions. They need to exercise and improve public relation skills, support community development efforts, and assist with outreach.

In other words, the field oral historian is relied upon from above and below to accomplish manifold short-, medium-, and long-range goals, and that is a mixed blessing. On the one hand, the project leader is often the first to see plans evolve and mature, to see people and ideas come together, and to see results emerge. But he or she also bears most of the responsibility for bringing structure, cohesion, depth of analysis, and accountability to the project. Managing human and fiscal resources to best meet project expectations and deadlines is a constant challenge, but at the end comes the satisfaction of watching professionals and communities cooperate in the gathering of oral history. And in between planning, budget battles, and daily administration, the oral historian directing a project may even find time to practice the craft and conduct some interviews.

PROCESSES FOR GATHERING
COMMUNITY ORAL HISTORY

Oral history is often described as the art of being a good listener. This truism is usually applied to conducting individual interviews, but it might also be applied to the processes of conducting community projects. Field oral historians must listen to the "voices" of previous scholarship, to internal voices within the community, and to their own instincts as they strive to create recorded documents of lasting value. Like roles and responsibilities, the gathering process will vary, but some common patterns prevail in effective community projects.

Oral historians employ a specific research tool, the interview, to add undocumented life experiences, reminiscences, and perspectives to the historical record. Each individual carries a different storehouse of information, shaped by personal perspective, but the narratives of individuals can be framed in relationship to historical events, group experiences, and social changes. Oral interviews can be utilized effectively to recover missing historical data, confirm or refute accepted wisdom, and explore aspects of the past that have been neglected. But none of this will happen without careful planning and training on the front end.

Preliminary and ongoing research should permeate the process of gathering oral history in community projects, and every project should begin with training sessions to improve research skills and teach the processes used in historical analysis. Involving a team of volunteers in research, even inviting them to scan newspaper and census documents, is not as reckless an idea as one might think. We must acknowledge that the powers of perception and the thrill of discovery extend well past the academic sphere. Group project administrators should foster the natural enthusiasm of their volunteers and encourage a sense of maturing team expertise and accomplishment. Team research and directed but open discussions may even reshape a project significantly. And such activities provide opportunities for the administrator or coordinator to identify specific skills, expertise, knowledge, and interest among project staff and volunteers.

All interviewers and other volunteers should also be fully informed about the project goals and issues of particular significance to the community. The short-, medium-, and long-range goals of the project must be clear at the outset *and* remain central as the collection effort evolves, and staff and volunteers alike should be familiar with plans for preservation and access and the potential public uses of the interviews being collected. It is also essential that community sensitivities or conflicting views be discussed early on so that interviewers are not caught unprepared in an interview.

And of course, the training process must include oral interviewing techniques. No actual interviews should begin until an interviewer is "cleared for active duty," since poor interviews at the beginning can destroy a project's credibility. Role-playing and interview practice sessions are important not only in developing skills but in fostering group cohesion and purpose and in helping identify who will be an effective interviewer. The "chosen" may not be the premiere researchers of the group. Nor should they necessarily be the most respected persons from the community. They probably should not be the most outspoken or opinionated members of the group. Interviewers selected and ultimately sent into the field must be good listeners who are well prepared to engage narrators but maintain an adequate distance from the narration process.

Interestingly, some very shy individuals can develop into very capable interviewers as they gain in community awareness and vest themselves in the project. Careful consideration should also be given to the dominant racial, generational, or gender characteristics of the study group when assigning interviewers to narrators, particularly if language is a factor. Group projects allow for creative experimentation in interview dynamics,

At a community oral history workshop in Verde Valley, Arizona, Andrew Russell demonstrates equipment requirements for oral history interviewing.

but remember that effective and well-informed interviewers may be found in any "packaging."

Before beginning the actual interviewing, a basic questionnaire must be developed. Some key considerations need to be addressed in structuring it. For example, what is the purpose and scope of the project? What collection methods will be used (taped and/or videotaped interviews), and what types of documents and photographs are being sought to support or enhance the project? What basic questions or issues are important to scholars and the community? What individuals, issues, and events will demand the most attention in interviews that typically last one to two hours?

The questionnaire should reflect a clear research strategy, but that may require some negotiation. What specific questions will we ask the narrators? What type of memories are most reliable? Which of many "life stories" should be targets for collection? Whose stories have already been recorded? What memories are most important and to whom? Researchers coming to projects from academe, public history institutions, and from the communities will invariably see different possibilities for discovery, preservation, and access, but all should consider the informational needs and desires of future researchers and the importance of anchoring a community's history for its progeny.

Then the interviewing begins. The common-sense rules of the craft dictate that one gathers as many personal memories and perspectives as possible. Keeping time constraints in mind, however, the top priorities should be the best (sometimes the oldest) narrators, and interviewers should direct their subjects toward topics that are of "historical or cultural significance." Judging "significance"—and future significance—is the difficult part, particularly when one is studying the undocumented story of ethnic groups. The best general advice we can offer is to choose core questions that balance historical and cultural topics with individual experiences. Trust your human and scholarly instincts, and listen to the advice of self-identified and respected community experts. Attempt to capture the stories and perspectives that are "asking" to be told. Be prepared to modify your questionnaire, over time or in the course of an interview, and focus on important subjects uniquely familiar to the narrator. Finally, take heart in knowing that any new information collected will increase the historical record measurably.

Another general rule to conducting good oral history is to acknowledge at the outset that every interviewer functions as both an "insider" and an "outsider" concurrently. Whether of Hispanic, Native American, African American, Asian, "New-Immigrant," or "Euro-American" background, whether rich or poor, regardless of race, gender, generational or religious affiliations, interviewers and narrators bring shared and differing perspectives and life experiences to the interview process. In the happy event that a project administrator can match interviewer and narrator by race, age, native language, and gender, it is likely that any number of other countless variables will influence the gathering process. Fostering an understanding of this has both cautionary and liberating affects on those who conduct interviews. It encourages objectivity, sensitivity, and attention to necessary details, and it helps one negotiate around and across boundaries. It can help one anticipate choice openings in the conversation and pre-advise one when it may be best to tread very lightly.

The specifics of arranging, conducting, preserving, transcribing, editing, and interpreting interviews are varied and involved—but not complicated. Every project should locate and follow fairly closely one or more guides to doing oral history. These can be found at many libraries, bookstores, historical societies, and archives. Libraries and archives can often provide unpublished guides, sample release forms, and other materials and advice to aid a project too. These many steps, from arranging interviews to utilizing them, may seem complex to the novice, but they basically involve common-sense rules of practice.[9] On the other hand, the common and uncommon pitfalls of doing community oral history deserve some special consideration.

PITFALLS

However well planned, every community oral history project will encounter pitfalls. Familiar to most oral historians are the horror stories of the interviewer who neglected to obtain a release form or forgot to turn on the tape recorder or microphone. Community-based projects must guard against these common pitfalls and also be aware of problems that frequently undermine group efforts.

As already suggested, administrators and interviewers must be careful not to alienate individuals or groups within a given community. A lack of basic discretion and tactfulness, limited or incomplete disclosure of aims, unprofessional behavior, or a lack of cultural sensitivity can quickly destroy an interview or lead to the breakdown of the entire project. Breaches in confidentiality can be extremely detrimental, as can the appearance that a project is taking a one-sided position in a community controversy. Rebuilding bridges and networks in a community in the wake of unethical or imprudent conduct is more difficult than the original outreach efforts. In any case, mistakes like these strains the limited resources of a project.

Next to gross human error, equipment failure is probably the greatest threat to collecting a good interview. Project planners should obtain the best possible audio or video taping equipment they can find. But they need not spend a small fortune: most of the authors' interviews were conducted on good but inexpensive recorders. The reality is that most community projects rely on individually owned equipment and nonexpert technicians. Try to locate the best and least complicated equipment available. Quality control will be greatly enhanced by using high quality audio or video tape, by immediately duplicating the original recordings, and by using copied "working tapes" for indexing, transcription, and so forth.

The expense involved in transcribing interviews may also impede a project. We feel it best to figure transcription costs into the project design, but indexing interviews is a cheaper alternative that should not be ruled out. (It is sometimes possible to solicit separate grant funds for transcription, after you have interview tapes and indexes in hand.) The point is that projects should not digress into a state of inertia simply because equipment needs, projected goals, and anticipated expenses seem to exceed funding already obtained or pledged. Oral historians need to plan and budget carefully, but they cannot let planning override the actual doing of interviews. They must be responsible but also trust to the future and maintain the momentum of the project, or it will surely flounder.

ETHICAL CONSIDERATIONS

The art of doing oral history has become more sophisticated, demanding, and complex at a time when community groups, composed mainly of "amateurs," have entered into the design and collection process. These trends are not as paradoxical as they might seem. Cooperation and advocacy are essential ingredients of useful and meaningful inquiry through the interview process. At the same time, professionals must remain mindful of their basic roles and responsibilities, follow accepted standards, and take note of the current trends in scholarship.[10] By embodying the inclusiveness ideal and by balancing interests, oral historians can bridge gaps between conventional and applied history and between professionals and communities. This dialectic involving questions of advocacy and neutrality seems to encompass most of the ethical questions confronting contemporary oral historians.

First, we would argue that *advocacy* has a place in community oral history. Even if a scholar sets out to learn more about the Ku Klux Klan (or another hate group), that scholar's mission is to seek relevant information and impressions that characterize the group over a given period of time. The investigator might absolutely deplore the sentiments expressed, but he or she cannot block (indeed must encourage) the free expression of memory. The oral historian advocates in this example not the group's ideals but the creation of an honest record of importance to a much wider group.

In many cases, the interviewer is likely to feel some bond or sense of sympathy, empathy, or compassion with the narrator. It is permissible, even advisable, to let some of these sympathies show through in the interview. Positive advocacy need not be equated with subjectivity. In fact, oral history is one of the few disciplines in which intimacy can actually encourage fuller and richer research results.

Occasionally in an interview one must "side" or "confront" to draw out a comprehensive or more accurate picture or to qualify information that conflicts with what is "known." For example, a narrator might offer information suggesting that "the 'Japs' [Japanese Americans] had a radio transmitter and deluxe maps in the basement during the war." It would be acceptable, in this case, to tactfully confront the witness with conflicting information or ask how he or she came upon this gem. Some interviewers prefer to turn off the recorder to discuss conflicting interpretations. Other interviewers and project directors have made effective use of footnotes or interviewers' comments to qualify erroneous or suspect data. Remember: being neutral sometimes means "neutralizing" information that is known to be false or misleading.

While oral historians have a right and a duty to influence the content of an interview, based on the weight of existing data, the historical framework guiding the project, and with regard to ethical considerations, the primary goal is still to capture undocumented voices and experiences that broaden the resource base. Oral historians must strive for silent opinion and the development of tactful, professional, and neutral guidance skills in the interview setting. When an interview is finished, the views and experiences of the narrator must predominate, and the interviewer's skillful manipulations and corrections should appear only subtly in the record.

CONCLUSION

Oral historians who become involved in community history projects are in a unique position to bridge existing gaps between academe, public history, and the "real world." Functioning as advocates, mediators, and intermediaries, we influence and serve conventional disciplines *and* the community. We work to capture undocumented or disappearing voices that enhance the overall record. Finally, by embracing inclusiveness, partnerships, and the cooperative ideal, we reinvigorate the historical profession and affirm our role as public citizens.

NOTES

1. Paul Thompson, *The Voice of the Past: Oral History* (Oxford: Oxford University Press, 1978; Second Edition, 1988), 22–23, 71. See also: David Kyvig and Myron Marty, *Nearby History: Exploring the Past Around You* (Nashville: American Association for State and Local History, 1982), and Eva M. McMahan and Kim Lacy Rogers, eds., *Interactive Oral History Interviewing* (Hillsdale, NJ: Lawrence Erlbaum Associates, 1994).

2. See Donald A. Ritchie, *Doing Oral History* (New York: Twayne Publishers, 1995), 3–4, for a short history of these changes.

3. See, for instance, Michael Frisch, *A Shared Authority: Essays on the Craft and Meaning in Oral and Public History* (New York: State University of New York Press, 1990); James B. Gardner and George Rollie Adams, eds., *Ordinary People and Everyday Life: Perspectives on the New Social History* (Nashville: American Association for State and Local History, 1983), and E. Tonkin, *Narrating Our Pasts: The Social Construction of Oral History* (Cambridge: Cambridge University Press, 1992).

4. See Ritchie, *Doing Oral History*, 3–4, for discussion of this shift. Also see Laurie R. Serikaku, "Oral History in Ethnic Communities: Widening the Focus," *The Oral History Review* (Spring 1989): 71–87.

5. See the special issue of the *Journal of American History*, "Memory and American History," (March 1989); David Glassberg, "Public History and the Study of Memory," *The Public Historian* (Spring 1996); "Roundtable: Responses to David Glassberg's 'Public History and the Study of Memory,'" *The Public Historian* (Spring 1997).

6. See Stanford J. Rikoon and Judith Austin, eds., *Interpreting Local Culture and History* (Boise: Idaho State Historical Society and University of Idaho Press, 1991), and Ivan Karp and Steven D. Lavine, *Exhibiting Cultures: The Poetics and Politics of Museum Display* (Washington, DC: Smithsonian Institution Press, 1992).

7. We prefer the term *community historian* and use it to describe individuals rooted and/or living in the community who take a special interest in local preservation efforts.

8. Important models for community oral history projects include Laurie Mercier and Madeline Buckendorf, *Using Oral History in Community History Projects,* Oral History Association Pamphlet Series, No. 4 (Waco, TX: Oral History Association, 1992); Stacy Ericson, revised by Linda Morton-Keithley, *A Field Notebook for Oral History* (Boise: Idaho Oral History Center, 1993); Valerie J. Matsumoto, *Farming the Home Place: A Japanese Community in California, 1919–1982* (Ithaca, NY: Cornell University Press, 1993); NMWLHP Board of Directors, *New Mexico Women's Legal History Project: Project Guide* (Albuquerque: University of New Mexico General Library-Development Office, 1994; supplement 1996); Oral History Committee, *Japanese American Oral History Guide* (San Francisco: National Japanese American Historical Society, 1993); and Suva Intermediate School, "Long, Long Ago Oral History Project" (contact Suva Intermediate School, attn: Michael Brooks, 6660 E. Suva Street, Bell Gardens, CA, 90201).

9. Ritchie, *Doing Oral History* is a fine handbook for beginners and advanced practitioners alike. Inexpensive "how-to" pamphlets may be obtained by contacting the Oral History Association (see "Resources" section of this volume).

10. *Oral History Evaluation Guidelines* provides the basic standards for the field. For a copy, contact the Oral History Association (see "Resources" section of this volume).

SYLVIA K. KRAEMER is visiting faculty at Colby College, where she teaches science and technology policy. She received her B.A. from Hollins College and her Ph.D. in intellectual history from Johns Hopkins University. Dr. Kraemer taught at Vassar College, Southern Methodist University, and the University of Maine at Orono prior to her appointment in 1983 as chief historian for the National Aeronautics and Space Administration. Named to the federal government's Senior Executive Service in 1990, she served as executive director of the NASA Advisory Council and director of Policy Development, coordinating U.S. aeronautics and space policy with the White House's Office of Science and Technology Policy. During 2000–2001 she served on the visiting faculty of the School of Public Policy at George Mason University. Her publications include NASA Engineers and the Age of Apollo *(1992) and articles in* Technology and Culture, History and Technology, Social Studies of Science, *and* Science, Technology, & Human Values.

POLICY ADVISORS: HISTORIANS AND MAKING POLICY

Sylvia K. Kraemer[1]

Remarkable as it may seem, over a decade has passed since the publication in 1986 of Richard E. Neustadt's and Ernest R. May's *Thinking in Time: The Uses of History for Decision-Makers*.[2] Here was (and remains) a work which drew much of its significance from the sophistication and detail with which Neustadt and May described what professional historians, striving to survive in the public sector, had considered for many years the important role of historical awareness in the realm of policy making. For Neustadt and May, historical thinking offered not only *content* but a systematic *process* to public officials' deliberation of various policy options. A substantial element in that process was the critical examination of policy makers' own assumptions about the likely causes and most probable outcome of a particular event.

Two years after the appearance of *Thinking in Time*, a small group of historians who had been plying their trade in federal departments and agencies drafted legislation intended to be introduced into the second session of the 100th Congress (1988) by Representative Stephen Solarz of New York.[3] If passed and adopted, the proposed bill would have required each federal department and independent agency to establish an office of historical research. The purpose of such offices would be to "enhance administration and decision making within the Federal government." The documents compiled and research disseminated by these offices would "provide accurate and independent historical accounts of the origins, development, conduct, and effects of the programs and activities of that department or agency," reveal "the evolution of the principal programs, procedures, and activities of that department or agency," "provide historical background information as required for the [department's or agency's] deliberations and activities," and "promote a greater understanding of the activities of such department or agency."[4]

The role of historical knowledge envisioned in this proposed legislation was much less central to the policy-making process envisioned by Neustadt and May (who, after all, were writing more about *history* than about historians) than it was to the roles already being served by countless public information officers, records managers, and librarians throughout the federal government. Moreover, the possibility that existing federal history programs might suffer from the scrutiny involved in the legislative process was reason enough for some historians to withhold their endorsement of the proposal. The bill was never formally introduced into Congress, partly because federal historians themselves could not agree that employing historians should be a statutory requirement of the executive branch.

What was at issue in the 1988 initiative was not whether federal historical programs were valuable, but whether it was good political strategy to *mandate* them. Indeed, the conviction that historical *thinking* and research would produce "better" policy (and the corollary, that *professional historians,* in contrast to librarians and records managers, should staff history offices) was—and remains—a truism. The conviction that "better" policy decisions are those which have been informed by "objective" knowledge generated in scientific, historical, economic, or other academic disciplines, has been axiomatic among progressives for at least a century. It is no mere coincidence that progressivism and the American university both emerged as significant social and political forces during the last decades of the nineteenth century—one thinks immediately of the University of Wisconsin's Richard T. Ely, a leader of the progressives' assault on laissez-faire economics as well as a founder of the American Economic Association.

More pertinent to our own day, the presumption that scientific expertise can improve policy was seminal, for example, in the creation in 1972 of the now defunct congressional Office of Technology Assessment.

Whether one is a historian or a scientist, the temptation to assert the importance of one's discipline to the making of "better" policy is almost irresistible. But, we must ask, "better" for whom, and "better" by what standard? After all, "policy making" is just a more elegant name for *politics,* an activity that is too often dismissed with contempt—which is unfortunate indeed in a society presumably committed to the principle of governance by the governed.

During 1995 and 1996, I had the rare privilege to participate in the development of the Clinton administration's space policy. In the process of performing and managing historical research on aerospace topics and issues as chief historian for the National Aeronautics and Space Administration (1983–1990), I had acquired a fairly comprehensive (and, naturally, historical) view of the aeronautics and space policy issues facing the U.S. government on any given day. This, plus the discovery of a natural affinity for executive responsibilities, led to my appointment in 1990 to the U.S. Senior Executive Service. During one of the innumerable reorganizations that continually agitate the civil service, I found myself relocated in 1995 to the Office of Policy and Plans at NASA headquarters, where my duties included not only policy research but "coordinating" the agency's position in the National Space Policy review that the White House Office of Science and Technology Policy initiated that year, as well as providing executive staff for the policy review. Did my experiences in this policy-making role confirm what I, Neustadt and May, and countless of our colleagues, had argued a decade earlier about the role of history in the policy arena? Before reviewing the substantive issues in the development of the Clinton administration's space policy, however, a few observations on the process are in order.

THE PROCESS

Just as the Congress has its laws and the Supreme Court its decisions, the White House has its "directives" which articulate the president's policy on matters of interest to the executive branch of government. These presidential directives may be decision directives, review directives, or national security directives. Each president is entitled to establish a White House administrative and policy-making structure with its own nomenclature and cast of characters, but all the policy directives that emanate from that structure must, at the end of the day, be consistent with the Constitution and federal statutes to be enforceable.

A senior official of the federal government (including the president) making a policy declaration, however informally or indirectly, is like a magician pulling a rabbit out of a hat. The official may be the one hoisting the rabbit out of the hat, but rarely has been the one who put it there. The process by which the rabbit gets *into* the hat is dominated by immediate staff working with staff from all the federal organizations that may be expected to implement a proposed policy, or are otherwise sensitive to the policy's ramifications. Adequate staff work is an essential, but not sufficient, condition for putting the rabbit into the hat. But whether that rabbit turns out to be perceived as a scrawny, burr-encrusted hare or an adorable bunny will be decided by a president's own political eyes and ears. Those eyes and ears may be the president's own political fifth sense, or the eyes and ears of immediate staff; most of the time the president will rely a little on both.

The most critical requirement of the policy process (and the result the media pays the least attention to) is that it produce *a policy that can be implemented.* Promising the end of the drug scourge or a generation of fully literate schoolchildren, is, like promising a chicken in every pot, risky business. At some point the bill comes due in politics just as it does in household finance. Hence the importance of a coordinating process that allows all existing federal agencies to register a vote of confidence in a proposed policy. Federal agencies, parties to the "iron triangle" of bureaucracy, interest groups, and members of Congress, can give a president an early warning of the possibility that a policy that sounds good from a podium has not a ghost of a chance of being carried out. This kind of assessment can be especially urgent when national security issues are at stake. But the most important reason for "interagency policy coordination" is to obtain consensus in support of a policy, thus reducing the possibility that the policy will be defeated through passive sabotage by the bureaucracy. This, no doubt, is what Harry S. Truman had discovered when he remarked, on the election of President-elect Eisenhower, "He'll sit here and he'll say, 'Do this! Do that!' And nothing will happen! Poor Ike."[5]

Given the arduous process of obtaining bureaucratic consensus—a process that can involve months of meetings notorious for the amount of posturing and agonized word-smithing that takes place in them—it's a wonder that presidents seriously try to introduce *new* policy. (*Old* policy lives off of inertia.) But try, they do—finding irresistible the urge to attach their names to anything of importance that the government does.

Undoubtedly it was just this urge which lay behind the White House decision, announced midway into President Clinton's first term, that there would be a Clinton space policy just as there had been Kennedy, Nixon, Carter, Reagan, and Bush space policies. Being somewhat less facetious, we must remember that the purpose of "policy" is to establish general guidelines by which individual issues can be resolved throughout the government, lest the president (or any organizational leadership) stumble into a morass of endless ad hoc, personal judgments, thus laying himself open to the charge of favoritism and "arbitrary and capricious" rule. And often there *are* genuine political or ideological principles involved.

In an era when very little can be done by a government without marshaling significant organizational resources, the willing support of lesser officials up and down the ranks is a likely prerequisite of any successful policy. Hence the necessity for an effective policy-maker to be, first and foremost, an informed and skilled negotiator—someone who can distinguish between posturing and a real issue, and someone who is a capable of identifying alternative solutions to a problem.[6] Both attributes are well served by the study of history: for the first, history helps us to know the roots of a problem, and thus better appreciate what realities will need to be accommodated; for the second, history educates the imagination, thus giving range to our sense of the possible. The biweekly negotiations surrounding the development of the national space policy offered numerous examples of this simple truth.

THE ISSUES

A January 20, 1993, article in the Washington *Post* previewing Clinton administration objectives reported that the new administration's space policy objectives were to (1) increase joint ventures with Europe, Japan, and Russia, (2) maintain the Space Shuttle fleet and continue with the Space Station Program (an important vehicle for cooperative activities with the Russian Federation), (3) develop new, less costly launch systems, (4) increase Earth-oriented environmental space research, (5) explore the outer planets with automated probes and robots, and (6) modify the Reagan/Bush initiative directing NASA to conduct a "Space Exploration Initiative" which would send humans to the Moon and Mars. Viewed against the backdrop of U.S. space policy during the preceding four decades, the Clinton policy objectives have not varied substantially from those of predecessors, with the exception of shifting human space exploration into a lower gear.

Every president since John F. Kennedy has endorsed these pursuits as objectives for U.S. activities in outer space: (a) space science (e.g., astronomy, space physics), (b) space applications (e.g., communications and weather satellites), and (c) international cooperation in space as a tool of U.S. diplomacy and foreign policy. Every president since Lyndon B. Johnson, who allowed the NASA budget to drift downward after the Apollo program buildup during the early 1960s, has sought the magic key to continuing an impressive U.S. presence in space at minimum federal expense.

NASA Administrator George Low (Act.) persuaded President Richard Nixon in 1971 that the Space Shuttle, promising both low-cost and routine access to space, would be that magic key. When that hope evaporated along with the exhaust from the Shuttle's complex main engines, Nixon's successors seized upon "commercialization" and "privatization"—or, coaxing into being a private industrial space sector as a way of minimizing space activities' drain on the U.S. treasury.[7] Finally, every president since Dwight D. Eisenhower has maintained that the U.S. commitment to "peaceful purposes" in outer space as a signatory to the 1967 United Nations Outer Space Treaty[8] does not preclude "defense and intelligence-related activities in pursuit of national security and other goals."[9]

The continuity represented by these objectives does not mean that the periodic redefinition of U.S. space policy by successive occupants of the White House has been free of issues or controversy. What constitutes an "issue" may vary among the various federal departments and agencies, not to mention the many interest groups with a stake in U.S. space policy. But, from my own historical perspective, the following four issues—issues which surfaced repeatedly during our White House meetings—are likely to prove the most persistent:

1. how much fiscal and political support the U.S. government should give to those among us, both within and without the federal bureaucracy, who believe that human space travel and settlement beyond Earth's orbit is our "destiny;"
2. how to square the policy of "commercializing" and "privatizing" space goods and services (which can also serve as a subsidy to the U.S. aerospace industry) with the current U.S. commitment to achieve free trade, as reflected in our support of the General Agreement on Tariffs and Trade (GATT) and the North American Free Trade Alliance (NAFTA);[10]
3. whether, and how, to restrict access to remote sensing data; and
4. which of the federal bureaucracies (if any) with a mission interest in space activities should be allowed to review, and possibly obstruct, a programmatic or policy initiative proposed by one or more of the others. The four bureaucracies typically tangling over this issue are the National Aeronautics and Space Administration, the Departments of Defense and State, and the Central Intelligence Agency.

At the risk of appearing to be a historical determinist, I believe these issues proved persistent because of the depth of their roots in American experience and opinion.

The first issue is only superficially about human exploration of space. Underneath it is about the American landscape, and whether this frontier, with its flora and fauna, should be abandoned for a frontier sustained only by sophisticated technology, of which Americans, for over a century, have had an ambivalent view at best. It is also about what the American people, in their increasingly varied array, value the most. Our current values are still informed by religious traditions that have grappled for millennia with the character of human experience—in individuals and in communities. While not rejecting "exploration" out of hand, these religious traditions have yet to conquer the moral frontiers of the human soul and human society. The most urgent issues troubling us revolve less around what we *can* do than around what we *should* do.

The second issue also has a long pedigree and is not likely to go away any time soon. The invisible hand of the marketplace or the visible hand of government—which holds the key to prosperity? And prosperity for whom? GATT, NAFTA—these arise out of a vision of a global economy, and the associated view that an industry that has to compete in a global economy will prove stronger in the long run. But, can much of the U.S. aerospace industry remain viable without federal subsidies, however indirect? "Buy America" policies serve not only patriotism but labor's concern for jobs and industry's interest in predictable markets.

The third issue is as fundamental as any space policy issue is ever likely to be. The principle of unfettered public access to publicly acquired information has enjoyed bipartisan political support in the United States for decades, and has been reaffirmed in various post–World War II statutes and Executive Orders enunciating U.S. information policy. For Americans information has been "a public good," and the concept of a "free market of ideas" has long been interwoven in our political rhetoric and jurisprudence. But for others around the globe, publicly acquired information may be a commodity, its commercial value closely protected. For Third World countries in particular, information about their resources collected by sensors on satellites can be, and have been, perceived as another twentieth-century variant of nineteenth-century Western colonialism.

Finally, the fourth issue contains more substance than may be immediately apparent. Our political and governmental system was designed to frustrate the accretion of power. The federal bureaucracy has developed, over the past half-century, around this elementary design principle. While the heads of federal departments and agencies may be subordinates of the White House, they also have their "patrons" in the Congress, whose members are able to serve their constituents through their influence over the bureaucracy, an influence that is "purchased" with appropriations. A federal department's freedom of action is critical to its survival, and the latitude that is being protected is as likely to be the latitude to respond to the Congress as it is the freedom to respond to the president. These multiple tensions may be a bit more elaborate than what James Madison had in mind when he wrote the Tenth Federalist, but they result from essentially the same design.

So, can having this historical perspective on the recurring issues in U.S. space policy help in making policy? It certainly can, for it lets us know where the center of gravity is likely to be in each issue. The further one party wants to stray from that center of gravity, the greater will be the burden on that party to convince the others that a departure is warranted and will benefit more than a minority, both now and in the future. This knowledge is also helpful in another respect, in that it reminds us that a "better" decision may not be the cleanest or simplest resolution of an issue. Some ambiguity may be necessary in order to "move on", or to allow a little flexibility for the decision-maker who will be trying to make the policy fit a particular set of circumstances at a given time and place.

POLICY AND HISTORY

The natural inclination of professional historians (like professional psychiatrists, lawyers, clergymen, etc.) is to frame the question thus: "how can my discipline (e.g., history) enlighten policy?" That, of course, is the starting point of *Thinking in Time*. The truth is, however, that experience in policy making can offer as much to the continuing education of a historian as the knowledge of history can enlighten the policy-maker. The experience of policy making quickly challenges historians' concerns over academic questions, questions that are academic not only because their answers have no practical impact on anyone or anything, but academic in the sense that they are important primarily only to members of university history faculties.

One such question may be the deadest horse in the stable, namely, the question of "objectivity" in the work of historians employed outside of the academy. We can thank the postmodernist critique (i.e., politics shapes consciousness, language, thought, etc.) for attempting to deconstruct the notion that the intellect can engender a wholly autonomous interpretation of materially real "facts." Some postmodernists go too far and would have us believe that the identity of the winning hitter on the winning team of the 1996 World Series is a political construct. But the postmodernist critique does serve to remind us that social science can never reproduce what occurs in the physical and natural sciences well enough to borrow the latter's claim to purely detached observation or "objectivity."

If, however, historians can never achieve true "objectivity" in their investigations, does not their insistence on empirical data, or upon first-person accounts of events when empirical data is inadequate, make their work sufficiently analogous to science to qualify as a social science? Perhaps; but I would argue that the issue of whether historians can perform as if they were scientists has much more to do with a young profession's desire for legitimacy in the universities of Germany and the new American university of the late-nineteenth century than it does with what historians actually *do*, individually or as a group.

What most historians actually do is essentially the same as what lawyers preparing for trial do. Few, if any, historians wander *tabula rasa* into a forest of facts. Rather, they wander into the forest with a question in mind, and they're looking for the facts that will answer their question. If they are very capable and resolve to advance the most plausible argument to answer their question, they will also look for counterfactual evidence so that they will be able to recognize weaknesses in their argument before their critics do. Lawyers preparing for court do the same thing. They must collect facts, and not only the facts that will support the briefs they are preparing, but the facts that may be used against their clients by their opponents in the courtroom. Through their knowledge of legal precedents they will be able to argue their cases on the strength of the law governing the issues before the court. For its part, the court is as determined to know the truth as are the historian's peers, for the court will be making law by giving legal significance to certain facts, in much the same way that historians will be recording history by interpreting (giving significance to) the facts they use in their arguments. The respective venues in which historians and trial lawyers ply their trade are dissimilar, but the process in which they are engaged is the same: Both struggle with the burden of proof to achieve an enduring judgment on actions of men and women.

Viewed in this way, the work of historians is fully compatible with the work of those who must make policy decisions, because both history and law are, at the very least, about "past politics." Both historians and decision-makers have a great interest in knowing the "facts"—the one, the facts behind a historical judgment, and the other, the facts behind a proposed policy. One of the more important of these facts for both is the likely reception of the historical interpretation, or the proposed policy, among each professional's constituents (who, in the case of historians, will be their peers, students, and reading audience should they publish).

If there are incompatibilities between what historians do and what decision-makers do, they arise from the training, common experiences, and proclivities of academically trained and usually academically employed historians. A historian seeking a tenured faculty position must publish books advancing interpretations that are attractive to professional peers.

This process promotes verboseness, the book being the most prized "unit" of communication. The process also places a premium on an interpretation of history exciting to historians as the thing most worth communicating about. The policy-maker, however, must make dozens of potentially significant decisions each week. If the essential information needed to make those decisions cannot be captured on one easily read piece of paper, that information will not be used; or what could be worse, only parts of it may be used to inform the decision about to be made.

Secondly, the information prepared by historians for decision-makers must be tailored to their needs. A one-page sheet outlining the argument of most urgent concern on a contemporary social policy issue at the last meeting of the American Historical Association might be useless to the person faced with having to resolve that issue. Being "tailored to their needs" means not only information framed around the right question but information that is neutrally presented. At this point the historian is like a law clerk: policy-makers, like judges, want to know what is important for them to know *in order to make rulings that will be upheld,* and a good historian, like a good law clerk, can make that judgment accurately time after time. If there is to be a bias, the bias belongs to the policy-maker; that's why he or she was appointed or elected.

This essay opens by noting that over a decade has passed since the publication of a major work on the connections between history and policy in the public sphere. It will close by commenting on the establishment, about a century ago, of history and political science as legitimate disciplines in the American university. English historian Sir John Seeley's aphorism, "history is past politics, and politics present history"[11] captured what was axiomatic among that first generation of professional American scholars. A century of diverging paths—paths to social history, business history, labor history, economic history, history of science, history of technology and, most recently, history deconstructed to accommodate identity group politics—has enabled countless budding historians and struggling history departments to find niches from which to proclaim their expertise. But this long and sometimes quarrelsome process has done little to educate three generations about the way things do work, and can work, in the public world. Arthur Meier Schlesinger, Jr. stands out as one of the few historians who could hear, and enjoyed replaying, the melodies in the noise of politics. For the rest, much of the field was surrendered to political scientists and journalists—one thinks of Hannah Arendt, whose account of the Eichmann trial appeared first in the pages of the *New Yorker* magazine.[12]

If recent politics in the United States lacks depth—and many thoughtful people pointed to the presidential campaigns of 1996 as proof of this sad conclusion—it is because an informed sense of the greater historical possibilities of politics has been replaced by empty slogans and sound bites. And if much of current historical writing holds little interest to policy decision-makers, perhaps it is because current historical writing has too little to say of compelling value to those who do the very hard work of finding politically viable solutions to the large public questions of our day, day in and day out. Historians could do worse than to devote some of their time and energies to politics—local, state, or federal—and rediscover the gravelly strata that shape policy and, in so doing, shape the contours of our public life.

NOTES

1. The author is indebted to Alan Ladwig, Roger D. Launius, June Edwards, Page Putnam Miller, J. Samuel Walker, and William Z. Slany for the observations and insights which they generously shared with me during the preparation of this chapter.
2. Richard E. Neustadt and Ernest R. May, *Thinking in Time: The Uses of History for Decision-Makers* (New York: The Free Press, 1986).
3. In the interest of full disclosure, the author was a member of this group, a committee of the Society for History in the Federal Government.
4. Draft bill circulated with letter dated May 13, 1988, to heads of federal history programs from David K. Allison, president of the Society for History in the Federal Government; copy is in the possession of the author.
5. Quoted in Joseph R. Conlin, ed., *The Morrow Book of Quotations in American History* (New York: William Morrow & Co., Inc., 1984).
6. One of the best guides to effective negotiation, its lessons applicable to virtually any situation, is Roger Fisher and William Ury, *Getting to Yes: Negotiating Agreement Without Giving In* (New York, N. Y.: Penguin Books, 1991).
7. Throughout its history NASA has spent around $9 out of every $10 procuring goods and services from the private sector, so the margin for shifting yet more activity into the private sector has been pretty slim. Furthermore, the high visibility of NASA's activities has fostered a public and media perception that the *civil* space program consumes far more tax dollars than it ever has. Even at the height of the Apollo program buildup, the 1965 NASA budget was considerably less than 5 percent of net outlays for the federal government for that year. (1960 was the last year the federal government saw a budget surplus.) Another instructive comparison is between the U.S. budget for NASA's space activities and space activities conducted by the Department of Defense (DoD). While NASA's space budget exceeded DoD's between 1961 and 1981, in 1982 DoD's space budget surpassed NASA's and remained larger than NASA's space budget through 1995—in 1988, the year of the largest discrepancy, the DoD space budget was over twice as large as NASA's space budget.
8. The treaty's full name is the "Treaty on Principles Governing the Activities of

States in the Exploration and Use of Outer Space, Including the Moon and Other Celestial Bodies," in effect as of January 27, 1967. The treaty prohibits placing into orbit around the Earth nuclear weapons or any other weapons of mass destruction, as well as "the establishment of military bases, installations, and fortifications, the testing of any type of weapons and the conduct of military maneuvers on celestial bodies."

9. Presidential Decision Directive/National Space Policy-8 (PDD/NSTC-8; September 19, 1996), Introduction, Sect. (3).

10. The September 19, 1996 National Space Policy directive contains, among its provisions, the following three declarations: "The fundamental goal of U.S. Commercial space policy is to support and enhance U.S. economic competitiveness in space activities. . . . U.S. Government agencies shall purchase commercially available [i.e., currently offered commercially] space goods and services to the fullest extent feasible. . . . The United States will pursue its commercial space objectives without the use of direct Federal subsidies. . . . Free and fair trade in commercial space launch services is a goal of the United States. In support of this goal, the United States will implement, at the expiration of current space launch agreements, a strategy for transitioning from negotiated trade in launch services towards a trade environment characterized by the free and open interaction of market economies." In addition, Presidential Decision Directive/National Science and Technology Council-4 (PDD/NSTC-4), "National Space Transportation Policy," also issued by the Clinton administration, declares: "For the foreseeable future, United States Government payloads will be launched on space launch vehicles manufactured in the United States, unless exempted by the President or his designated representative."

11. From *The Growth of British Policy* (1895), quoted in *The Oxford Dictionary of Quotations,* 3rd. ed. (New York: Oxford University Press, 1980), 419.

12. Hannah Arendt, "A Reporter at Large: Eichmann in Jerusalem-1," *New Yorker* 38 (February 16, 1963): 40ff.

PART III
THE PRACTICE OF PUBLIC HISTORY

INTRODUCTION

The essays that follow focus on the institutional contexts in which public historians work. Just as the position which you hold affects your roles and responsibilities, so does the institution in which you work. As the authors of the following essays demonstrate, with each kind of institution come different resources, needs, and priorities.

Because of the different institutional contexts from which they write, the authors of the essays in this section have very different perspectives, in every case reflecting the factors that determine how they go about their work. For example, in her essay on urban history museums and historical societies, Barbara Franco devotes more time to historiographical issues than do any of the others, a reflection of the significant scholarly tradition within which such institutions are situated. For others, historiography has far less significance, but they face other challenges. In writing about parks, which are usually government owned and operated, Bruce Noble appropriately addresses the legislative context and requirements which he and his colleagues must address. George McDaniel, on the other hand, discusses issues such as viewsheds, which are of particular concern to the historic houses and buildings of which he writes. While all have to be concerned about paying the bills, it should come as no surprise that Robert Patterson, in writing about local institutions, pays particular attention to how to get the most mileage out of limited resources. Fund raising is not an issue, however, for Elizabeth Adkins, who focuses instead on the necessity for corporate historians and archivists to respond to the unique corporate cultures within which they work, whose needs and priorities will probably be very different from those of colleagues in history.

Without reviewing every essay, the point is simply that in this section you will find eleven very different points of view, each reflecting and responding to special circumstances that impact the practice of public history. What all the authors in this section will agree on is that *where* you work is as important as any job description in determining *what* you do.

GEORGE W. McDANIEL is director of Drayton Hall, a historic site of the National Trust for Historic Preservation in Charleston, S.C., and was formerly director of museums and education at the Atlanta History Center. He holds a B.A. in history from the University of the South, an M.A.T. in history from Brown University, and a Ph.D. in history from Duke University. Committed to heritage education, he has served on education committees at the state and national levels. His efforts to protect the environmental context of historic sites led him to serve as chairman of the Ashley River Historic District Preservation Coalition. Currently co-chair of the S.C. Governor's Mansion Foundation, he also serves on the steering committee of the International Museum of African American History. He is the author of Hearth and Home: Preserving a People's Culture *(1982) and of numerous articles or reviews in* History News, Public History News, the Journal of American History, and Winterthur Portfolio. *In recent years he has served as faculty for the American Association for State and Local History's workshops on historic house museum management and has presented at numerous conferences on museums, history, education, and historic preservation.*

AT HISTORIC HOUSES AND BUILDINGS: CONNECTING PAST, PRESENT, AND FUTURE

George W. McDaniel

As I reflect on the public's relationship to history, it appears that we live in a bifurcated culture. On the one hand, the increasing number of history programs on television and of accesses to historical resources on the Internet illustrate a growing interest in the subject. Historic preservation is entering the American mainstream, no longer the province of the elite, and heritage tourism is outpacing other sectors of the multibillion dollar tourism industry. Yet, on the other hand, we are witnessing increasingly the destruction of historical resources as rural landscapes are being bulldozed for subdivisions, small towns dry up or are overwhelmed by suburban sprawl, inner cities decay from neglect, and modest historical neighborhoods are gentrified to a style they never knew. Families are increasingly transient, and time once spent in passing down stories from generation to generation is increasingly devoted to television or to video and computer games. It seems increasingly difficult for the public to connect to history. Perhaps these two trends, seemingly in opposite directions, are related. As we Americans lose our history, up close and personal, we are pushed all the more to look elsewhere for it.

Amidst such circumstances, the maxim of the environmental movement has relevance for us public historians—"Think globally. Act locally"—because what is happening to historical resources in cities, communities, or campuses is connected to larger patterns. And as public historians, I believe we are called not just to think about history but to act. We are called to strive to connect people with their history and to help them thereby achieve a sense of belonging to a larger community, of belonging to those who came before and to those who will come after.

My belief is that historic house museums can play a central role in supporting this effort and can both educate the public about history and inspire them to become engaged in the study and preservation of history. If they set their sights high, house museums can communicate an authentic sense of place about their region and help people develop a sense of connectedness to others and strengthen the sense of worth and responsibility that goes with that.

Historic house museums can do these things because they bring history to people in both tangible and abstract ways and thereby meet a deeply felt human need. A story I heard illustrates what I mean.

It seems that a young girl felt very lonely one night as she went to bed, and she came to her mother for comfort. The conversation turned to religion, and the mother tried to explain to her daughter that she was not alone, that God's love was with her. The girl then began asking pointed questions about the subject—questions rather difficult to answer honestly and satisfactorily as only a child's questions can be. The mother again tried to explain who God was and to assure the child that a loving God was close by. She tried one way and then another. Finally, in exasperation, the girl exclaimed, "But Mama, right now I want something with skin on."

Don't we all? Then, it seems, we could see. We could believe all the more readily and surely. Belief in abstractions, of course, is necessary to guide and inspire our work, but finally we need something tangible. In the case of history, many people have loved the subject, the story of the past; historic houses and buildings make it tangible. They put "skin" on the abstraction of time past.

Perhaps a historic house or building has evoked such a response in you. Maybe that is a principal reason for why you are interested in public history. As you think about that interest, it may be helpful to learn more about some of the work necessary to keep the "skin" on a historic house museum, to preserve its history, and to tell the story that it embodies, a story that is at once deeply local yet with global connections.

A TOUCH OF REALITY

What is it like working with a historic house or building museum? There is no one answer. Personally, I enjoy working somewhere that joins past and future, buildings and landscapes, people and their creations, the academic and the public, the intellectual and emotional, all in a small place. There is always something more that can be done, something more to be learned, and one can see more readily the results of those efforts. And since there is often less of a bureaucracy to move at a historic house museum, new ideas can sometimes grow to fruition with less hassle.

Some might say it is impossible to express the range of things that those of us who work in historic house museums do. Borrowing a page from historian Thomas Schlereth and taking a "material culture" approach might help. Since you cannot visit my office, let me invite you to look at one day's contents of my mailbox as "artifacts" and use them as an illustrative sample. They are as follows:

> Memos from two staff members, one about a personnel issue and another about research; a fax from CompuServe about an Internet opportunity and another from the historic site, Stagville, about an upcoming publication of my previous research; e-mail from three colleagues at the National Trust for Historic Preservation about finances, membership, and congressional politics respectively; a thank-you letter from a friend of Drayton Hall; a kind note from a donor; an application from an intern; an advertisement from a temporary employment business; a program notice from the Historic Charleston Foundation; reports from the Charleston Soil and Water Conservation District and the Charleston Convention and Visitors Bureau; an application from a credit card company in partnership with the Organization of American Historians; and magazines from the South Carolina Department of Natural Resources and the National Audubon Society.

What my In box illustrates is the many areas of interests and responsibilities of a house museum director. And this list, by the way, is simply my mail for one day and does not include my telephone calls or the stacks of correspondence received by the thirteen other members of my staff.

While larger house museums like Monticello or Mount Vernon may claim the spotlight, we should remember that the more typical ones possess much fewer resources with which to meet their responsibilities. There is no directory of historic house museums, but studies suggest that, of the approximate total of 6,000, about three-fourths have annual, operating cash budgets under $50,000, and less than 10 percent have cash budgets over $300,000. Roughly one-half are private, the others government run. According to one study, median full-time staff numbers about four; part-time staff, three. Another survey sketched an even more sparse situation, finding that 65 percent had no full-time staff. Studies do not show the median number of volunteers, but no doubt it is considerable, their service being fundamental to museum survival. In many towns and small cities, the historic house museum is the only history museum—sometimes the only museum at all—and is often headquarters for the local historical society or preservation organization.

Responding to the wide range of functions and responsibilities with such minimal resources taxes the physical facilities, staff, and financial resources of almost all house museums close to their limits. Thus, we learn that it is one thing to turn a building into a house museum; it is another to be its responsible steward and to keep its doors open.[1]

Working amidst these circumstances, public historians may sometimes see their employment in a house museum as more akin to working in a circus. Ask any historian so employed, and many circus analogies may be suggested, but let's take one—the tightrope-walking juggler. In house museums, you have to keep many balls in motion and maintain balance at the same time, all the while moving towards a destination, without a lot of support below. You continually feel your way, learning from experience, gaining new skills, and trying to make it appear effortless. That is the challenge and the pleasure of the job.

As you move up the administrative ladder, the wider and more diverse become your responsibilities. That is why beginning work with a house museum, in which you have to perform many tasks, provides excellent training for public historians who may later move on to careers in larger organizations. On the other hand, some historians choose to make their entire careers in house museums, because they believe house museums enable them to ask large questions of small places, to think "globally" in "local" spaces, and to see more clearly the differences they can personally make.

ISSUES IN THE FIELD

Discussion of the full range of issues facing historic house museums would fill this book. I have therefore selected a sample which I have found to be central to operating a house museum.[2] I have tried to deal with them in a manner illustrative of any house museum operation. To add a measure of realism, I have drawn from my own experience and from what I have learned from others.

Strategic Planning

Though often put off because of the tyranny of the immediate, strategic planning can be very constructive for historic house museums of any size. Its purpose is simple: to chart the future and to establish a framework for decision making. It is developed through a sequential process, which usually includes: identifying and assessing the current character of the institution—its history, operations, policies, and goals; identifying the museum's shortcomings and obstacles; envisioning what the museum would best be like in the future; and identifying the goals and strategies to achieve that vision. This process may be guided by a staff or board member or with the help of consultants. Time, always a precious commodity, should be set aside to focus on the endeavor, and a schedule developed, which has been informed by reality and patience. Functionally, this process should involve everyone in the museum, together with a commitment to respect their input and to revise the plan periodically.

That plan should guide everything the museum does—from mission statement to research and interpretation to marketing and resource development to the number of admissions and the character of the gift shop. For example, since preservation of the historic fabric is central to the mission statements of most house museums, neither board nor staff should seek to balance budgets at the expense of the house by bringing in large crowds day in and day out or by sponsoring potentially damaging programs within the house. Instead, admissions and programs should be consistent with what the site can actually handle, and alternative strategies developed.

Since a complete description of strategic planning is beyond the scope of this chapter, I would like to elaborate on two tools, usually developed or revised in strategic planning, which I have found helpful to my work in historic house museums. These are a mission statement and a statement of ethics or values.

Strategic Planning: The Mission Statement

The mission statement expresses the *raison d'être* of an institution. Because that statement should guide the plans, policies, operations, and products of a house museum, it can reveal a lot. When you apply for a job at a historic house museum, you might see if a mission statement exists, review it, and assess how your talents and interests fit into that statement. Ask the director and staff how they feel about it, and ask if there is a process for review and revision. Answers to those questions can tell much about the institution and its respect for staff involvement and for personal and organizational growth.

The development of such a statement is a skill unto itself. Some museums hire outside consultants to help develop one. Others work within themselves. Whichever, a statement should be developed with input and review by all the staff, board members, and others associated with the institution. Over the years, it should be reviewed and revised accordingly. Mission statements should be true, simply stated, and easy to remember. One can always tell when a mission statement has been drafted by a committee whose members do not have a unified view, because the statement

As a product of their mission to promote tolerance and historical perspective, the Lower East Side Tenement Museum in New York offers community-based programs. Shown here are staff and graduates of the museum's English as a Second Language Program. Students learn English by studying the history of immigration and of the tenement museum. To graduate, they must give a house tour. *Courtesy of the Lower East Side Tenement Museum.*

consists of compromised wording and is too long, clumsily phrased, and difficult to repeat.

While historic house museums have a range of mission statements, most pertain to collecting and preserving history and to educating the public. Some missions include a call to action. For example, Drayton Hall's seeks not only to "educate the public" but to "inspire them to embrace historic preservation." Others have a broader social mission. For instance, the Lower East Tenement Museum in New York seeks to present and interpret history in order, among other things, to "promote tolerance and historical perspective." To do so, it engages in an innovative range of programs in literacy, community development, gay and lesbian history, and other community-based issues rarely dealt with by house museums. Regardless of the contents of the mission statement, its purpose is to give cohesion to the institution.

Strategic Planning: Ethics and Values

In the museum world, ethics usually have a specific meaning associated with policies regarding collecting, deaccessioning, and governance. The Code of Ethics produced by the American Association of Museums clearly states those important items.[3] However, in this discussion, I would like to address something different in terms of ethics: how do we work with people? If public history is grounded in the belief that people have inherent worth, how do we practice what we preach with those around us?

Like the mission statement, this statement of ethics or values should be produced by staff and board members, agreed upon by them, and reviewed periodically. At some house museums, templates may be available from parent or sister organizations, but I believe each museum should develop its own set of values tailored to fit its character and reality. The statement should seek to be inclusive. Examples of values that it might cite include commitments to the following: the preservation and conservation of historical resources according to the highest professional standards; a fundamental respect for other people—visitors, the public, each other, and those who lived, worked, and died at the site; inclusiveness in programming, staffing, and interpretation; management and administration with integrity and fiscal responsibility; education and a site interpretation based on fact, developed from scholarly research and a free exchange of ideas; and the acceptance of responsibility for stewardship and education in the wider community and for coalition building locally and nationally.

As seen by those examples, statements of ethics or values affect all operations and relationships within a museum and beyond it. There are financial implications, because the institution's values should inform development of the budget. For example, if a value is to foster research and education, then investment in the intellectual growth among staff through staff development is not an extraneous nicety; instead, it is a clear commitment by the institution. Everyone should participate in this process, in some reasonable manner, because when hard decisions have to be made—for budget cuts, for example—they should not be made in isolation from those values, but rather guided by them.

I say this to be realistic. When museums go through the bitter process of cost reductions, staff downsizing, or salary cuts or freezes, jealousies, cliques, and intrigues often arise, and outwardly ethical people may do unethical things. As anyone in the profession knows, hard times will come to any historic house museum, and development of a mutually agreed-upon statement of values or ethics, in advance of that situation, can provide a set of guidelines to see the institution through. They can help keep communication honest and bring people together to figure out solutions, instead of being splintered by distrust. For public historians in museums, adherence to such values in hard times marks the moment when the "rubber hits the road."

Adherence to values also helps build a climate that encourages support from outside the institution. In his recently acclaimed book, *The Loyalty Effect: The Hidden Force Behind Growth, Profits, and Lasting Value,* business writer Frederick Reichheld shows that it is from long-term customers that companies obtain the most profit. Translating that into the museum world, the staff time and hard costs of securing a new membership, for example, may equal or surpass the income during the first year. In the next year and subsequent ones, if the member continues to renew, the cost percentage decreases in comparison to income. Compounding the benefit is that the member may not just renew but respond to year-end appeals, capital campaigns, or planned giving programs. The maxim is true: "People give to people." By creating a work environment that avoids constant upheaval and retains good staff, the museum is able to build relationships with its members and major donors, develop a corporate memory, and create a base of support with "lasting value."[4]

Another critical advantage to a supportive working environment of this type, cited by Reichheld and relevant to house museums, is that staff and board are more motivated because they are less fearful of failure. When we create an environment in which failure is scolded, people have less confidence and experiment less. They do not "push the envelope," though it is that exercise which invigorates a museum. Further, as Reichheld explains, staff may learn that success is the only message rewarded and devise ways to put the right "spin" on their work. Political acumen becomes more important in gaining a job promotion or salary raise than skills in museum work. By creating such a work culture, the director or supervisor is not fully informed, even misled, and makes decisions based on partial truths. The staff in turn supports such decisions half-heartedly, if at all. Mistrust and demoralization become more entrenched. If not remedied, politics becomes the coin of the realm in place of museum skills.[5]

In most house museums, such pitfalls are ever present and plague even the best of efforts. But the hope is that by creating a work culture based on ethical treatment of one another, we can set our sights on the high ground and facilitate better communications among ourselves. Again and again at historic house museums, I hear the complaint about communications. It seems there are so many demands on our time that it is hard to hear—to really hear—the concerns, professional or private, of colleagues. However, not only do we have to have the time, but we have to have the *willingness* to be open. We have all encountered historians, museum directors, or others who proclaim in public or to professional audiences how much they care about people and their rights, yet who in private belittle and humiliate their staff or students. A question we must ask ourselves is therefore, if we as public historians *claim* to care about people, do we really care unless we strive to carry out that ethic among those with whom we work?

Basic Research

Respect for research and investment in it should be interwoven into all operations of the museum, from interpretation to marketing. This may seem obvious to historians, but sometimes board members, volunteers, or others at historic house museums are not trained in history and want answers immediately, without appreciating the investment of time, talent, and funding necessary for research of professional quality. Yet research is critical because it is the process that gathers, for example, the necessary information about the house museum's history, from which the interpretive ideas and story lines are developed for tours. Thus, research produces value.

The obstacles to research are many. Money, always in short supply, is often needed elsewhere, usually in areas where the results are more visible. In addition, research may threaten established thinking. In many places, local legend or cursory research has led to accepted "facts." In such cases, staff need to be skilled not only in research but in human relations, because ways need to be found to research those interpretations and correct them as necessary, in a manner that does not humiliate and alienate tradition-bearers, many of whom may be respected figures in the museum or community and have much to offer and to value. The sad thing is that sometimes professional staff also internalize these "facts" or set of beliefs, so that they over time become the defenders of orthodoxy.

For house museums, one of the basic research documents is the historic structures report. Produced by a team of historians, architectural historians, curators, and others, it is the product of their review and analysis of the documentary, artifactual, and structural evidence and should form the basis for future conservation and interpretation of the historic buildings. Every decade or so, it should be updated and revised. Other important research documents include collections inventories and assessments, furnishings plans, historic landscapes reports, and archaeological surveys, in addition to the collection of primary sources.

Often neglected by house museums, archaeological surveys are highly recommended for the area around the house, and preferably for the entire site. No shovel should be put in the ground to plant a tree or dig a ditch until such a survey has been completed. To proceed otherwise is to risk destroying precious evidence that can tell the story of life outside the main house. This evidence is often fragile and shallow in the ground and consists not just of artifacts but of different soil layers and features, whose interpretation lies in their relationships to one another. Once sundered by a new walkway, water line, garden, or other feature, the site cannot be put back together. Upon completion, an archaeological survey can show on a grid the location of sites and offer critical information about historical outbuildings, walkways, fences, gardens, and other natural and human-made places, all essential to educating visitors about the entire site and to locating future facilities.

Archaeological surveys can be done by the conventional method of spade and trowel, though a range of new tools can cover a wider area more quickly and inexpensively, permit more precise excavation, and limit the extent of digging. Among the new methods are ground-penetrating radar, resistivity, magnetometry, and aerial photography, while radio-controlled "FlowMoles" from oil drilling technology can dig tunnels for underground conduits through sterile sub-soil at a safe distance beneath archaeological sites. This kind of respect for archaeological research should not be thought of as an "extra" when and if there is money, but rather as a central element in our holistic thinking about a site.[6]

Ongoing Research

But research does not end with basic documentation. Ongoing research is essential to the development of interpretive programs and virtually every activity undertaken at your museum. Unfortunately, obstacles to good research are legion. Time is demanded elsewhere; staff is small;

Methods of archaeological research are illustrated at Cliveden, a historic house museum in Germantown, Pennsylvania. First, a ground-penetrating radar survey was conducted to locate anomalies possibly related to the 1777 Battle of Germantown at Cliveden. Next, one of the anomalies was excavated and documented. The results have expanded the interpretation of the entire site. *Courtesy of Cliveden.*

funding, unavailable; or the skills and experience to write research grant proposals, not present. At one historic house museum after another, staff complain of the demands on their time, pulling them away from research. It may not be one big demand but many interruptions, and at the end of the day or week, no reading or no writing has been done.

Another problem is the lack of funding. Basic research—i.e., the investigation and study intended to acquire new or expand existing knowledge without regard to immediate or specific applications—is the hardest to support, yet pays dividends in the long run. Program research—i.e., the investigation and study for programmatic purposes with application to specific exhibits or projects—is easier to support since it leads to a product. Usually it is programmatic research that corporations, individual donors, or public sector agencies, such as humanities councils, will fund.

The point is that no solutions to research obstacles can be found without an institutional commitment to it, clearly stated in the planning documents or mission statement. If the commitments to research and open communications are there, then research will not be seen as something extra but instead as integral to museum operations. For example, in developing a tour or exhibit comparing the lifestyles of the children of the homeowners with those of the servants' children, the board and staff should not think exclusively in terms of programmatic research. Instead, they should think more holistically and seek to produce multiplier effects from this one project. Among the additional products might be: a fresh and enlivened tour featuring new perspectives; new school programs on site; new educational materials for teachers to use; a new series of public programs; new merchandise for the gift shop; a revised Web site; or engaging approaches to donors to build capital reserves and endowments, which in turn support basic research.

Thinking about research in this way may represent to some museums a new and more holistic way of thinking about museum operations. It brings board and staff into the process, so that research, in this case, becomes seen not just as something that only historians or curators do but rather as a process that enhances the work of the entire museum.

Interpretation

The interpretation of historic house museums, i.e., the methods by which the history of the site is communicated, has changed significantly in recent years and has become one of the most challenging areas in which to work. The lid has been lifted. The days of the "This is a Philadelphia Chippendale chair, and this is a New York Hepplewhite table" tour are pretty much over. More and more, house museums are striving to develop site interpretations that appeal to a range of senses in addition to the intellect, that are rich and multilayered in content, and that embody the central themes of the site. These themes are not just site specific but are connected to the larger context of history.

One of the specific characteristics of house museums is that usually it is a tour guide who does the interpretation, and thus the museum staff must be sure that the stories conveyed are of consistent quality in both content and style. To do so, staff should perceive and treat tour guides as professionals, whether they be volunteer or paid, and expect from them performance according to professional standards. Consistently having good guides is never an accident, but is instead the result of careful hiring, training, and evaluating and of continually communicating back and forth.

Thanks to the infusion of years of work from historians, educators, and other professionals and to funding from humanities councils, corporations, individuals, and others, many historic houses and buildings are now being researched and interpreted from multiple perspectives. We have opportunities now to learn more about the different people who made up the household—adult male and female homeowners, their sons and daughters, and the servants, cooks, gardeners, and other workers. We can learn about different stages in their lives—about childbirth, infancy, childhood, youth, middle age, and growing old; about sickness, dying, and funerals. Increasingly, interpretation at historic house museums is extending beyond the walls of the building to include the landscape and the people who shaped it, used it, and saw it from different perspectives. Guides are now more likely to share with visitors in their tours what they know and what they do not know, to discuss the research that is underway, to compare past interpretations with present ones, and to discuss questions for future research.[7]

To give coherence to these multiple perspectives, museums are developing thematic tours, organized more or less around a story line, into which the voices of different persons are interwoven. In addition, some museums are developing specialized tours, focusing on a particular topic or set of perspectives. At Monticello, for example, there are, in addition to the house tours, tours that focus on the landscape and gardens of Thomas Jefferson or on African American life. They may take the same route to the same places but interpret those places and landscapes through a different lens. For most visitors, such initiatives in interpretation are refreshing.

New technology offers exciting possibilities to interpret the multilayered past of a historic house or building. Some museums, for example, are documenting oral histories from people who grew up at the site,

Historic house museums are expanding both the topics and methods of interpretation, as illustrated at Monticello, where specialized tours supplement the
standard house tour and interpret African American history and culture. *Courtesy
of Monticello, Home of Thomas Jefferson.*

worked there, or helped preserve it or convert into a house museum.
From that material, audiotours or videotours can be produced, so visitors
can see and hear from someone who was part of the site's history, long
after that person has gone. Thanks to CD-ROMs, the viewer can explore
a menu of questions at greater depth. Borrowing from medical technology, architectural conservators, as at Drayton Hall, are using small endo-
scopes to probe behind walls and record details of historical materials
and construction methods not visible to the public. This technology
could later be used in public programming to allow historic houses and
buildings to be "deconstructed," if you will, via CD-ROM or through
more innovative technologies still to be developed.

   In the face of so many interpretive possibilities, how can historic house
museums respond when they typically have very limited facilities, funding, and staff? Preferably, answers should proceed from the basic vision
of the museum, as enunciated in its strategic plan, mission statement, and
goals and strategies. Innovative, low-cost tactics can perhaps then be developed, especially through partnerships, which meet the objectives
within the capabilities of the museums.

To do so, museums can learn from historian David McCullough, who has reminded us that opportunities await if we are resourceful. I would like to outline three tactics for being "resourceful" and to use a research and interpretive project in archaeology and oral history at Drayton Hall as a case study. All of these tactics involve partnerships within and without the organization. The institutional goals were to research and preserve African American historical resources and to expand the interpretation of the historical plantation. To do so, the strategy was to excavate the site of an African American tenant house and to conduct oral history interviews with a former resident.

The first tactic in terms of being "resourceful" is to look for resources *within* your house museum. In this case, we used volunteers and staff of Drayton Hall for documentary and photographic research and for transcriptions of oral interviews. Further, we used our own limited collection of documents and funds, not to mention the principal resources—the archaeological site, which was on our property, and the oral informant, who was on staff.

The second tactic is to look for resources *in the wider system* of which your museum is a part, such as a national, state, or municipal public sector agency; a private, statewide preservation or historical organization; or a university system. In this case, Drayton Hall is a historic site of the National Trust for Historic Preservation, so we turned to the archaeologists of the Trust, who conducted the excavation at a more affordable rate and with greater efficiency than could a new contractual crew. If not funding or staffing, perhaps your larger organization could provide services or equipment for your use. The point is to network within the wider organization.

The third tactic is to look *outside your organization* to individuals and institutions not related to you at all. In this case, we hired a teacher in our community during the summer to assist in our research, especially in our oral history interviews in the local African American community. We also hired an intern from a nearby college for the summer to research and produce drawings of the tenant house we were to excavate, based on oral history interviews with the former resident. These drawings included elevations of the exterior, furnishings plans of the rooms, and sketches of the homestead layout of house, yards, outbuildings, gardens, and fields.

Pressing the idea of partnerships further, we turned to Coastal Carolina University and allied with a member of its faculty, historian Charles Joyner. He brought with him videographers from the university's Media Center to videotape with professional quality the excavations and oral history interviews with the former resident, Richmond Bowens, who had been born there in 1908, the grandson of freed slaves. At the end of the excavation, the facilities of the Media Center were made available at no charge. There, Joyner and the technicians from the Media Center contributed their substantial expertise to my meager experience, and together we edited the hours of raw footage into a twenty-eight-minute videotape of television quality.

Together, these "resourceful" tactics produced comprehensive documentation of a tenant house site combining oral history with artifactual, photographic, and documentary evidence. The research corrected errors in documentary evidence and provided invaluable sketches of African American history. The artifacts unearthed and now enlivened by oral histories about them will be used in future exhibits to add insights into the story of African American life, not available beforehand. The site itself will be featured in self-guided trails, thereby extending the interpretation to a home and family beyond the plantation's "big house." In addition to being used on site, the videotape has been selected for broadcast on the History Channel, thus taking this story to hundreds of thousands of people across the nation.

Finally, these tactics made production of this videotape affordable. Ours was a twenty-eight-minute production, which could have cost from $100,000 to $280,000. Because of these partnerships, the total direct expenses were about $5000.

Thus, through partnerships or otherwise, house museums can create interpretive products that build bridges between the history in their own backyards and the nation at large. The thing or place to be interpreted could be below ground or above ground—a house, church, school, farm, neighborhood, or main street. By allying with others, historic house museums can find that the budget need not be the obstacle preventing them from reaching their goals.

Landscapes

While much attention has conventionally focused on the historic houses themselves and on the exhibits and period rooms within them, house museum professionals are giving closer scrutiny to the context of their structures. By context, I mean the landscape around the house that the museum owns and manages as well as the landscape around and beyond the site itself. Staff are realizing that this context of both types of landscape profoundly shapes the visitor's cognitive and affective experience. They are seeking to marshal the educational potential of landscapes to reinforce their mission and to inspire "informed imagination"—that is, the mental process that allows visitors to go from time present to time past, to form images in their mind's eye of the people, events, and places of the past—what they looked like and sounded like, and how it might have felt to be there. It is this context of landscapes, both on site and off, that substantially generates the power of place unique to every house museum.

Museum professionals also recognize that if visitors are allowed simply to imagine historical landscapes using only the limited information they bring with them, they may not learn much. Worse, visitors may simply have the stereotypes they bring with them reinforced, and their visit, while pleasurable, will not have produced a more educated understanding of time past. For example, at many antebellum Southern plantations, the tendency of many visitors is to imagine a romantic "Tara" from *Gone with the Wind* and neglect the concurrent reality of human bondage as lived out by real people in the nearby fields. At Civil War sites or "Indian forts" in the west, visitors may focus on personalities and strategies and forget the carnage that took place in those beautiful open spaces. It is therefore the responsibility of the staff at a site to *inform* the visitor's imagination by giving it both the framework of interpretive ideas and the content of specific facts.

Whenever I tour historic house museums, I can usually tell that the tour is in trouble when it begins by the front door or even inside the house, with the guide saying, "This house was built in such and such year by such and such family," with little or no regard to context. As historian Tom Woods and cultural geographer Pierce Lewis have emphasized, the landscapes around historic houses can be read like a book, if only we take the time to help visitors decipher their stories. The task may be difficult, because landscapes, unlike books, were not designed to be read by the casual reader and often require skills on the part of the observer or assistance from other sources to discern their multilayered meanings. What do we see today as we walk about the site and look beyond its boundaries? What do those things—whether natural or man-made, recent or historical—tell us about the place and its setting today? What might we have observed, heard, or even smelled 50, 100, or 1,000 years ago? What might we have seen if we could go farther back into geological times, and how would those things explain the topography, soil types, or waterways which shaped subsequent developments in agriculture, industry, human settlements, building types, and building materials? As historian William Cronon in *Changes in the Land* has urged us, we need to "locate a nature which is within rather than without history" and tell how our specific sites reflect the larger story of the interactions between nature and humans.[8]

Another major benefit of using this context of landscapes is that they give visitors time and space to relax, to contemplate, to have fun, and to appreciate what their senses take in. Inside house museums, visitors are

A variety of strategies are used to secure viewsheds of historic sites from development-ments intrusive to visitors' experience. At Drayton Hall, innovative technology was used to disguise a telephone tower as a pine tree. At Mount Vernon, easements, governmental regulations, and land acquisitions prevent commercial complexes from scarring the viewshed across the Potomac River. *Courtesy of Drayton Hall and the Mount Vernon Ladies Association.*

normally conducted on tours from one room to another, often with little time to stop and think. When viewing exhibits, other visitors may be standing near them, pressing them by body language to move along. Compounding the situation is the noise bleed from videotapes and other audible exhibits. All of this risks an "information overload." Visitors need to be able to withdraw from the crowds and to reflect on the information they have received and on what it means. Within a museum setting, the landscape offers respite for visitors to contemplate and to appreciate both cognitive learning *and* affective feelings.

As a result, historic house museums are devoting their time, talents, and funds not only to managing their own landscape but to securing the future of their environs, especially their viewsheds. Mount Vernon, Monticello, and Drayton Hall are just a few of those sites which have been engaged in efforts to secure their environs from intrusive modern developments. Not long ago, commercial centers, high rise buildings, or condominiums were proposed directly opposite them. Allying themselves with environmental conservation organizations, governmental planning departments, political leaders, and others, they rallied support from a myriad of sources and stopped or diminished those developments. Nonetheless, the threats to the historic and scenic environs of those and many other sites across the nation remain very real. In striving to safeguard their viewsheds for posterity, public historians at house museums are not looking backward but instead are looking to the future and trying to secure there a place for people to learn directly about the past, a place for "informed imagination" to take root.

Engaging the Public

Just as public historians at historic house museums have been striving to preserve the context of their sites, they have also been trying to inspire and enable visitors to become engaged in the study and preservation of history when they return to their own communities. Too often, visitors leave with the impression that the history presented at that site is a neatly wrapped package, and their visit does not prompt them to look anew at the historical resources that warrant preservation in their own family or town. They may leave without understanding that their history might be reflected not just in a "big house" but in vernacular buildings, workplaces, landscapes, main streets, or waterways and may be found in everyday artifacts, oral histories, written materials, or photographs.

I would argue that a principal, though often overlooked, role for historic house museums is to educate the public about the range of places

that deserve preservation. To date, the levels of achievement in this regard are very uneven, because the vast majority of historical buildings
used as museums are still houses, and houses of the affluent white families at that. Most are located east of the Mississippi River and were saved
because they were associated with a famous person or event or because
they represented the best in architectural style or aesthetic accomplishment, according to the established tastes of the period when the house
was preserved.[9]

I am not denigrating those efforts. In the face of an aggressive culture primed to destroy the past in the name of progress, these places
served as rallying points to galvanize a fledgling preservation movement. The beauty or historical significance of those places may have
been readily apparent, but even then preserving them always required
vision and hard work. More often than not, it took a fight. Tragically,
thousands of places in recent decades have been lost to "progress,"
whether it assumed the form of new highways and interstates, strip centers, fast food restaurants, or parking lots. The comparatively few places
that have been preserved and opened as museums are with us today,
thanks in large measure to women who led the campaigns. The carica-
ture of these "little old ladies in tennis shoes" or of "blue-haired ladies"
does them no justice, and theirs is a story that warrants more research
and interpretation at the places they helped save and in the larger field
of public history. Without them, many of us would not have the jobs we
enjoy today.

In recent years the types of historic places open to the public have
been expanding beyond the homes of the wealthy. For example, the Far-
ish Street Historic District Neighborhood Foundation, in collaboration
with the National Trust for Historic Preservation and with support from
the Mississippi Department of Archives and History, is preserving the
Scott-Ford Houses in Jackson, Mississippi. Built in the 1890s, they were
the homes of a former slave and her daughter, who was a prominent
midwife in the city. In New York City, the Lower East Side Tenement Museum has partially restored and opened for tours a mid-nineteenth-century tenement building, the first to be designated a National Historic
Landmark. In Pittsburgh, the Historical Society of Western Pennsylvania
uses the Kins House, the home of an immigrant family, to educate the
public about the region's industrial and ethnic history through the
everyday lives of this working class family.[10] Even at sites conventionally
seen as exclusive domains of affluent white families, the rooms, workplaces, and landscapes are being re-interpreted through the perspectives of servants, cooks, gardeners, laborers, and so forth, not to mention

The types of historic "buildings" preserved and open to the public are becoming increasingly diverse and may no longer include buildings per se. An illustration is the Medicine Wheel Historic Landmark in the Bighorn Mountains in Wyoming. Possibly constructed between 1200 CE and 1700 CE, it consists of a circle of boulders with twenty-eight rock spokes radiating from a central cairn. To Native Americans, the Wheel represents religious architecture and is still used as a spiritual site. *Courtesy of the National Park Service.*

people of different ages and stages of health. Living quarters and houses of workers are also being presented, as at the reconstructed slave quarters of Carter's Grove in Williamsburg. Churches, bridges, airports, public housing units, ranches, and other types of places will no doubt be considered as future historic sites. In Native American culture, for example, it is not the four walls of a building that are seen to be historically significant, but rather the landscape or the vista, in which the spirit of the place resides. As we look at recent developments for future trends, we see that not only are specific buildings or places being saved, but so too are whole historic environments, such as the Illinois and Michigan Canal, a federally designated Heritage Corridor, consisting of interconnected buildings, landscapes, and routes of transportation over hundreds of miles in length. Such places are not owned and operated by one entity but are managed through partnerships of public and private organizations.

CONCLUSION

As I conclude, what comes to mind is my hope that as the field of possibilities expands and as different types of places are preserved and opened to the public, they will touch more people and engage them in learning about history and in doing something about the preservation of our heritage. It is also my hope that by engendering a stronger appreciation for history, these historic places, whether house museums or otherwise, will develop among us a stronger sense of community with those who came before us, those who are with us now, and those who will come after.

NOTES

1. Sherry Butcher-Younghans, *Historic House Museums: A Practical Handbook for Their Care, Preservation, and Management* (New York: Oxford University Press, 1993), 6; Peggy Coats, "Survey of Historic House Museums," *History News* 45 (January/February 1990): 26–28; Gerald George, "Historic Property Museums: What Are They Preserving?" *Preservation Forum* 3 (Summer 1989): 5; Gerald George, "Historic-Property Museums in the United States" (Unpublished report to the National Trust for Historic Preservation, 1989, in the possession of the Department of Historic Sites, National Trust for Historic Preservation, and of the author), 1–18.
2. I want to underscore that my discussion deals with a *sample* of issues basic to all house museums; space does not permit review of staff and volunteer training, marketing, conservation of buildings and collections, education programs, the Americans with Disabilities Act and museum accessibility, and other important issues.
3. Contact the AAM for a copy of its Code of Ethics (see "Resources" section of this volume).
4. Frederick F. Reichheld, *The Loyalty Effect: The Hidden Force Behind Growth, Profits, and Lasting Value* (Boston: Bain & Company, Inc., Harvard Business School Press, 1996), 91–105.
5. Ibid., pp. 187–92.
6. Neville Agnew, "Preservation of Archaeological Sites: A Holistic Perspective," *The Getty Conservation Institute Newsletter* 12 (1997): 4–8; George Neil, "Problem Solving Just a 'Boring Job' for Power Company," *Interiors,* Spring 1993, 4.
7. Butcher-Younghans, *Historic House Museums,* 183–212. Also, for cogent critiques of the state of interpretation at historic sites, see Philip Burnham, *How the Other Half Lived: A People's Guide to American Historic Sites* (Boston: Faber and Faber, 1995), and Mike Wallace, *Mickey Mouse History and Other Essays on American Memory* (Philadelphia: Temple University Press, 1996).
8. Quoted in Thomas A. Woods, "Nature Within History: Using Environmental History to Interpret Historic Sites," *History News* 52 (Summer 1997): 5–8;

Nora J. Mitchell and Katharine T. Lacy, "Reading Stories Written on the Land," *History News* 52 (Summer 1997): 25–27.

9. George, "Historic Property Museums," 3–5.

10. Lauren Uhl, "The Kins House: Museum of the American Immigrant Experience," *History News* 51 (Spring 1996): 6–9.

WILLIAM S. PRETZER is curator of political history at the Henry Ford, where he has curated exhibits on Noah Webster, Thomas A. Edison, and American industrial history. He received his B.A. from Stanford University and his M.A. and Ph.D. from Northern Illinois University. Before coming to the Henry Ford, he worked at the Winterthur Museum and the National Museum of American History, Smithsonian Institution. His publications include Working at Inventing: Thomas A. Edison and the Menlo Park Experience *(1989); chapters in* American Artisans: Crafting Social Identity, 1750–1850 *(1995),* Time and Work in Preindustrial America *(1991), and other volumes; and articles in periodicals such as* History News *and* Labor History. *He serves as exhibit review editor for* Technology and Culture.

AT HISTORIC SITES AND OUTDOOR MUSEUMS: A HIGH-PERFORMANCE ACT

William S. Pretzer[1]

I have in my office a reproduction of a drawing done by the famed African American inventor Lewis Latimer. It is a self-portrait of the engineer/inventor walking on the edge of a ruler representing his new employer, the electrical engineering firm of E. W. Hammer. On one side of the ruler is a rolling landscape labeled "The wide, wide world" and on the other side is a bed of feathers entitled "General Electric Co./Feathers." Latimer is traversing the ruler toward an "uncertain future," using a mechanical pencil holder like a tightrope walker's balance. Drawn at the age of sixty-five, the image is Latimer's self-reflection on the balancing act he performed by working in a consulting firm rather than as an independent consultant or in a corporate environment, or between risk and security. It may also represent his sense of the tenuous nature of an African American of his generation pursuing a career in a technical field.

What appeals to me most about this image is Latimer's ability to produce a visualization that employs the tools of his trade to represent his social circumstances; he drew a creative, symbolic expression with a personal and social perspective. Confident in his skills, Latimer concen-

Lewis Latimer's "My Situation as It Looked to Me in 1912" reflected the African American inventor's view of his career as an opportunity to balance between risk and security. *Courtesy of the Queens Borough Public Library, Latimer-Norman Family Collection.*

trated on the context in which he worked, his relationship with employer and client. Significantly, Latimer focuses our attention on his precarious balance; his instability is further emphasized in the caption he provided: "Which way will he fall?"

I often feel that the work of a public historian is, at its most productive levels, a high-wire act, balancing risk and comfort. Daily work combines aspects of politics, performance art, and education. The doing of history in an institutional context for public interaction involves playing one of several different character roles depending on the immediate circumstances. Doing history publicly means acting as politician, diplomat and translator, performer, curriculum developer and teacher, and, always, knowledge worker.

This may be another way of saying that it matters less where one's "job" as historian is than how one employs historical knowledge and history's "habits of mind." In some organizations, the historian's position is placed administratively within a research center, differentiated from the curatorial, educational, or public presentation staff. In others, the work of the historian is integrated with the work of the curator or the educator. In smaller sites, it is not uncommon for the educator, presenter, curator, and historian to be found in one person. It would be unreasonable to say that such things as organizational structure or bureaucratic process do not matter, but I think they matter less than the person's approach to working as a public historian.

What is crucial is that the historian get as close to the audiences as possible, that you find the place where people are asking questions and help them develop skills and access resources to address those questions. It goes without saying that one has to be a good historian, capable of thorough research, persuasive analysis, imaginative interpretation, and engaging presentation in a variety of modes and media. However, it would be a shame if historians, because of either personal predilection or commitment to "disinterested scholarship," ultimately serve as mere researchers and technical advisors of historical fact and interpretation. As new conceptions of learning and public discourse evolve, it is essential that public historians adopt the role of institutional teacher/leader. That is, we can lead and model the intellectual and cultural processes that help our own institutions become "learning organizations" and participate in creating public experiences that promote historical "meaning making."

Historians have the opportunity to serve as educational leaders, helping redefine the learning process and visitor experience in ways more far-reaching than merely historical understanding. It is this approach that leads me to think of museum presentations as less like a scholar's monograph than a teacher's lesson plan, an activity that is predicated on active participation and where linking pedagogy and content is crucial to learning. I liken the exhibition development process to improvisational choreography, establishing a rhythm of social interactions for physical, emotional, and cognitive development. The dynamics of museum professionalism evolve and individual organizational charts continue to change in response to the public environment. The keys to the historians' contributions are, in my mind, a desire to continually learn, flexibility in the workplace, a commitment to collaboration and teamwork, a focused attention on the audience, and an infectious passion for the processes of historical discovery and dialogue that inspires others.

Working in a large organization with multiple sites in one place, as I do, offers a number of opportunities. Each site offers challenges in preservation and conservation, historical understanding, interpretation and reinterpretation, and presentation and programs. If working at a single-focus historic site allows the mastery of deep knowledge and intimate community relationships, working at an outdoor museum encourages and demands the development of usable local knowledge appropriate to the work at hand. It relies on a willingness to begin each new project as a novice learner, starting anew each time a specific site is considered. Reconstructing the development of several specific sites in Greenfield Village will serve here as a set of case studies in doing history in an outdoor museum.

THE HISTORIAN AS POLITICIAN

Making the best and highest use of an existing resource is an inherently political process. This means listening carefully to your constituents and creating an interpretation meaningful to them. Thomas A. Edison's Menlo Park laboratory, reconstructed under the direction of Henry Ford himself in Greenfield Village in 1929, is a case in point. By the mid-1980s, the lab had been visited by over 50 million people. It showed the evidence of two generations of physical wear-and-tear. There was no small irony in the fact that deteriorating air quality caused by automobiles and industry, largely associated with Ford, threatened the copper gutters, brass instruments, and other metal artifacts. Restoration and conservation were in order. So, too, was a new understanding of the historical record and meaning of Edison and his work during the Menlo Park years.

Several histories overlapped at this site, and the first requirement was to separate the experience of Menlo Park as created by Henry Ford (1929–47) and recreated by his successors (1947–87) from the Menlo Park of Thomas Edison (1876–82). It was up to the historian to convince everyone that even if Henry Ford had not saved Menlo Park, what Edison did there was worth presenting. Additionally, while Ford's pioneering preservation work was eminently worth honoring, the major "lesson" of Menlo Park focused attention on Edison's invention and creativity, not historic preservation. In other words, Edison, not Ford, was the protagonist; Menlo Park, New Jersey, not Greenfield Village, Dearborn, Michigan, was the site; the 1870s not the 1930s was the time period; and invention not preservation was the plot.

Much conspired to make this a hard sell. The site as constituted by Ford was itself considered a landmark. It was known as one of the early efforts at historic preservation and reconstruction. What could be changed without suffering public and staff recriminations? For some, to change anything Ford put in place was desecration. Veteran staff reminded the team that Edison himself had complimented Ford on the accuracy of the installation.

Some of the best, and best known, stories related to Ford's preservation work, not Edison's invention. The seven railroad carloads of red New Jersey soil that Ford transported to Michigan epitomized his fetish for accuracy. The display cases with 1920s trash dug up along with the initial historical archaeological materials and the tree stump to which the infamous bear was tied in 1880 spoke to the romance of Ford's reconstruction. The endless framed photos showing Edison from childhood to old age and Edison and Ford together lined the walls of the lab and provided endless opportunities to reflect on their relationship, which, of course, flourished only after Ford became successful in his forties and Edison's best days were far behind him. And then there was the chair in which the elderly Edison had sat during the 1929 Golden Jubilee of Light and which Ford, in a pique of hero worship, had nailed to the floor. An appearance on the 1970s television show, "Ripley's Believe It or Not," had made the chair a national conversation piece, almost as well known as Archie Bunker's chair in the Smithsonian. Peeling off the layers and meanings of this institutional history required the skills of a cultural historian.

Public reinterpretation was necessary. And the two distinct generations of the public showed the way. Everyone who spent time at the site could tell stories of the elderly people who visited and were overcome with emotion, remembering the first time they saw a lightbulb or heard a phonograph. They were of a generation, soon to be gone, whose history Edison's work immutably altered, who personally and viscerally felt Edison's impact, and whom being in "the presence of the real" visibly moved. We needed to honor and capitalize on that experience.

At the other end of the spectrum were their grandchildren or great-grandchildren who stood impassively as museum staff tried to impress them with the fact that this is the place where "the phonograph" was invented. Finally, a few discussions with school groups indicated the depth of our misconceptions. Young people did not know what a phonograph was, and if they did, they did not care that it was invented here. Could we communicate effectively the power and impact of what Thomas Edison originally had wrought?

As it turned out, the key to reinterpretation was to act politically. Audience research indicated that many people wanted to know why this place

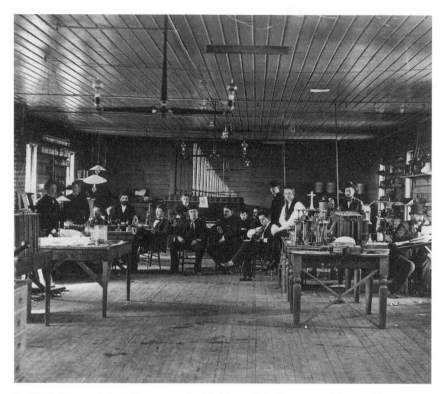

In 1880, Thomas A. Edison posed with his staff in the second floor of his Menlo Park, New Jersey, laboratory—the birthplace of modern sound and light technology. *Courtesy of the Henry Ford Museum & Greenfield Village, Dearborn, Michigan.*

was important (and not just to Ford) and how Edison achieved his successes. Somehow, what had been neglected in the institutional consciousness and was nearly unknown in the public consciousness were the world-changing process and products of Edison's inventions. To recognize and promote the fact that this was the birthplace of modern sound and light communications was the peculiar role of the technological historian.

That is, our job was to understand the issues that interested people, research those issues, and develop an experience or interaction with environments, artifacts, and people that addressed those issues. We had to create a strategy and delivery system (a "program" or "experience"), obtain the necessary resources, and motivate people to participate by demonstrating how the program responded to their interests. We focused attention on a single point in time, created greater public access to more parts of the complex, gave attention to the people and process

The reconstructed interior of Thomas A. Edison's laboratory in Greenfield Village interprets for the public the interaction of resources, skills, and creative process that were the foundation of Edison's inventiveness. *Courtesy of the Henry Ford Museum & Greenfield Village, Dearborn, Michigan.*

rather than the "genius," and explicitly commented on the impact of Edison's work on modern life.

Students in the Henry Ford Academy of Manufacturing Arts and Sciences, a public high school academy sponsored by the museum and the Ford Motor Company and located at Henry Ford Museum and Greenfield Village, use this laboratory extensively. Students and teachers are enveloped by the historical context and site presentations, making for an extraordinary learning environment. Casual visitors and formal students can make the best and highest use of the resource, the inspirational and intensive learning power of the place.

In the best sense, politicians and historians provide leadership by putting on the public (or institutional) agenda the problems that are brought to their attention by their constituents. They then define the problem in a specific way, suggesting it as an opportunity for learning and

Beginning in 1997, students at the Henry Ford Academy of Manufacturing Arts and Sciences, a public high school located at Henry Ford Museum & Greenfield Village, began using the Menlo Park laboratory and other museum sites as part of their daily school activities. *Courtesy of the Henry Ford Museum & Greenfield Village, Dearborn, Michigan.*

developing the resources and process for capitalizing on the opportunity. Along the way, the politician relies on building a coalition of supporters who can commit to the end goals and contribute to the process.

THE HISTORIAN AS DIPLOMAT, PART I

Sometimes you are lucky enough to get to establish a new historic site. In such cases, it is a bit like establishing diplomatic relations with a new country, and the work is both professional and public. Such was the case in 1983–85 as staff from Henry Ford Museum and Greenfield Village participated in relocating the Firestone Farm from its original location in Columbiana County, Ohio, to Dearborn, Michigan. The talents of an agricultural historian/curator, domestic life curator, building conservator, historical archaeologist, and farm manager were at the heart of this enterprise.

The first issue, of course, is why would your institution want these structures? In fact, precisely which remaining farm structures would a new host institution want? These are not concerns about historical fact or accuracy; they are issues of historical meaning and importance. They are neither obvious nor readily answered. The historian is best served by listening carefully and engaging other perspectives. The historian must recognize the genuine limits and opportunities of the contemporary context: fiscal responsibility, stakeholder interests, communication and learning processes, organizational strategy, and institutional mission. These decisions are collaborative, and the role of the historian is to help frame the discourse. This is when the historian has to act like a diplomat, helping colleagues from other occupational cultures see the benefits of collaboration and historical "habits of mind."

No small part of this work as diplomat is to represent the people of the past to the people of the present. To the extent that "the past is a foreign country," then diplomacy is needed. In the case of the Firestones, the diplomacy came most eloquently in the definition of their choice of housing. What can we learn from a house about family relationships, material meanings, and life's works? In the process of dismantling the Firestone house for relocation, the staff uncovered evidence of structural rearrangement of rooms and several layers of wall coverings. They also recovered a handwritten note left like a time capsule behind the lathe and plaster, dating the renovation to 1882.

When combined with data on the family and the local economy in the early 1880s, this curatorial information provided the bedrock for an interpretive focus and thus a public presentation. The work resulted in a sixty-plus page edition of the institutional magazine aimed at friends and supporters of the museum with articles by staff on the history of the farm and family, the process of dismantling and reconstructing the buildings, and the research that went into creating the fully furnished house and program of daily activities that presenters were to make available to the visiting public. More prominently, it resulted in what is one of the most visited farms in the world, a twelve-acre working historic farm with a carefully crafted, historically authentic presentation program.

Certainly, dealing with a single family, site, or building allows prodigious and deep research into both internal and external issues. The historian can continually develop programs by paying attention to seasonal and life cycle changes within the social unit or to changes in the larger community that placed the site in a different historical context. It is of course true that one of the strengths of outdoor museums and sites is that they can engage all the senses more easily than can exhibits within a museum. Burning wood, drying herbs, the swelter of summer, and the shiver of a snowy winter day are authentic experiences (as long as you do not consider the goose-down jacket or quick retreat into the air-conditioned restaurant). Their value, and it is not inconsequential, is as inspiration to historical imagination.

Visitors pitch in and help staff with farm chores at the Firestone Farm in Green-field Village. *Courtesy of the Henry Ford Museum & Greenfield Village, Dearborn, Michigan.*

Here, visitors to this foreign land explore the diurnal and seasonal cycles of farm life and the life cycles of plants and animal life. People explore this land for many of the same reasons they travel to foreign countries. The architecture, modes of production and consumption, transportation systems, social rituals, material culture, language, and food are different and intriguing. They want to experience this because it broadens their perspective on their own world and sensitizes them to their own environments. Traveling challenges them to overcome personal limitations and provides them with contrasting memories to their own daily experiences with which they can construct meanings for their own lives. Traveling provides a heightened—and broadened—sense of self. Besides, it's fun.

Diplomats help by ensuring a convenient journey to a safe yet foreign context. They often provide previsit materials that explain communication patterns in language and custom and point out the standard highlights as well as the exotica. They communicate the wants and needs of the travelers to the "locals," and vice versa, in hopes of encouraging mutually satisfactory interactions. They represent the need of each culture to maintain its integrity while "entertaining" the other, often negotiating new relationships in response to changing circumstances and opportunities. The historian does much the same in preparing the way for people in the present to meet and converse with the past.

THE HISTORIAN AS DIPLOMAT, PART II

It is true that places like Old World Wisconsin or Greenfield Village, neither of which were historic places but are modern amalgamations of times and places, are quite unlike the Sloss Furnaces National Historic Landmark in Birmingham, Alabama, or Colonial Williamsburg. What it is like to work in those other places, I can only conjecture. What is perennial and continually demands rethinking are the evolving uses to which one wants to put historical or financial resources. What changes, more fundamentally than historical scholarship, are the wants, needs, and resources of the public, our audiences. Producing usable public platforms or narrative opportunities for historical discourse requires sensitivity to primary sources, historical "habits of mind," and the uses to which various audiences might want to put historical meaning. Providing a sense of contextualization is essential to the historian's role in the collaborative process. Just as diplomats have to recognize the impact of culture on contemporary situations, public historians, more explicitly than academic historians, have to exploit and dramatize the dynamic between the historical and the contemporary.

A case in point: When considering how to best employ the machine shop within the Edison Menlo Park laboratory complex, it was necessary to recognize a couple of different contexts. What was the meaning of the machine shop to Edison at Menlo Park? What was the meaning of a machine shop in Greenfield Village? To demonstrate the meaning and role of metalworking within Edison's invention process; the importance of having skilled labor directly on site; and the actual work that went on there. It was also necessary to consider that another industrial era machine shop, this one fully operational and staffed, existed within Greenfield Village, about 250 feet from the Menlo Park shop.

Was there a need to interpret the machinery of the Menlo shop or to commit resources to making this shop operational also? What level of interpretive burden for the Menlo Park site did the machine shop carry? How about for Greenfield Village as a whole? For the planning team, the machine shop's mission was more important for carrying integral elements of the Edison story than for the nature of machine shops in general or for the overall Greenfield Village experience. Thus, the interpretation focuses on the persona of John Kruesi, the foreman and Edison's trusted master mechanic; the importance of ready access to innovative machinists so that Edison's team could quickly fabricate, test, evaluate, and improve devices; and the iconic role of the machine shop as the site for the construction and testing of the first Edison electric dynamos.

Similarly, when dealing with the mission of Sloss Furnaces, one could reasonably discuss a similar set of questions. What are the histories within the Sloss Furnaces? Which are most important to tell? What are the opportunities for capitalizing on those histories? Here, however, the mission statement for an entire site has to be integrated and yet be distinctive from other opportunities potential visitors have within the community. The "history" presented at Sloss Furnaces would be heavily influenced by the types of visitors the site managers think they can attract and the financial implications of drawing those visitors. Except that we do it for multiple sites instead of for just one, the staff at outdoor museums make very similar calculations.

One suggested way of dealing with this is to use the idea of a "core competency" that would help define the services or products that the organization could offer at economically attractive rates. In the case of Sloss Furnaces, the story might be "the birth, life and death of an industrial enterprise and the people (entrepreneurs, mangers, and workers) who participated." However, the core competency need not merely present engagingly that historical story with its myriad plots, events, characters, and actions. Rather, the institution's core competency could be seen in one of three ways:

1. Tell that history with a special focus on the fact that few competing organizations can deal with the history of African American workers in as much detail.
2. Tell that story as it relates to and symbolizes the history of the city of Birmingham, thus effectively making Sloss into the city museum.
3. Use the story as a theme that would focus the site's programs on in-

Nearly a century after its heyday, Sloss Furnaces National Historic Landmark is still a prominent part of the Birmingham, Alabama, skyline. *Courtesy of Sloss Furnaces National Historic Landmark.*

teractions of history, technology, and art. Sloss was a place where people engaged in science, technology, labor-management interactions,
ethnic and racial relationships, familial and domestic activities, and
cultural expression. The events and activities at the site need not be
confined to the historical issues; they could run the gamut from science and technology to music and art.

Recognizing economic considerations is crucial in establishing mission statements as well as institutional goals and objectives. Facing reductions in public funding, Sloss managers have rightly looked for
means of increasing earned revenue and creating a niche in the local
market for educational and leisure audiences. Playing to one's traditional strengths and resources, however, is not the same as being strait-
jacketed by history. Of course, the consulting historian has the luxury of
saying things that can be either insightful or foolish; the staff is best
served by responding creatively to stakeholders and audiences. In this
instance, the historian's role was to identify the most compelling story
lines and translate those into contemporary activities that attract audiences. The historian should be of immense help in focusing institutional
resources on events and activities that reinforce rather than dilute institutional vision.

THE HISTORIAN AS PERFORMANCE ARTIST

One of my favorite sayings is Louis Pasteur's "chance favors the prepared mind." Some years ago I had the occasion to experience how this
would help me understand the process of museum historian as learner
and performer. I was scheduled to speak at a conference of museum staff,
many part-time or volunteer, on the importance of audience needs and
the "sharing of authority" in exhibit preparation. At the lunch break, I
wandered into a local bookstore. As I passed the poetry section (not normally the focus of my attention), the cover of a small book caught my eye.
It was a black-and-white image from about 1920 of Coney Island spectac-
ularly lit at night. A book of poems by Lawrence Ferlinghetti, the "Beat"
poet, it was entitled *A Coney Island of the Mind*. The title sounded a lot like
a museum I would enjoy visiting.

Picking up the book, I was astonished to find one section entitled "Pictures of the Gone World." Again, the resonance with a history museum
perspective was uncanny. And there, fifteen minutes before speaking, I
found a new introduction for my talk. I felt it might be a bit extreme for
some in the audience, but I decided to risk it:

'Truth is not the secret of a few'
yet
you would maybe think so
the way some
librarians
and cultural ambassadors and
especially museum directors
act
you'd think they had a corner
on it
the way they
walk around shaking
their high heads and
looking as if they never
went to the bath
room or anything
But I wouldn't blame them
if I were you
They say the Spiritual is best conceived
in abstract terms
and then too
walking around in museums always makes me
want to
'sit down'
I always feel so
constipated in those
high altitudes[2]

by Lawerence Ferlinghetti, from A CONEY ISLAND OF THE MIND.
Copyright ©1958 by Lawerence Ferlinghetti. Reprinted with permission
of New Directions Publishing Corp.

In the ensuing conversation, we discussed perceptions, biases, and fears that lead people to distrust scholarship or prevent them from visiting museums. We talked about the changing role of professionalism and the difficult relationship between experts and lay people within American society. We debated the relationship between historical scholarship and local experience, or rather, the memory of local experience. We discussed ways of communicating better within our communities. We laughed about Ferlinghetti's image of cultural ambassadors and museum directors, but ruefully acknowledged the insight therein.

Introducing Ferlinghetti's passage was cathartic and provided a memorable way of expressing an idea and sparking a conversation. Of course, it was essential that the conference participants encouraged a playful sense of improvisation and theatricality. It reminded me of some good participatory learning I had seen in outdoor museums and sites. Still, I felt a bit like a performer about to try a new act. Or a traveler setting out to explore unfamiliar terrain.

THE HISTORIAN AS TEACHER

The historian working for the public needs to provide access as well as accuracy, value as well as verisimilitude. Think of yourself as a teacher, a teacher who facilitates others' growth and provokes others to form coherent, disciplined interpretations, not merely as the font of knowledge. The mantra among advocates of constructivist learning is that a teacher is the "guide on the side, not the sage on the stage." It is worth remembering that the best teachers and the best tour guides are masters of their subject matter, sure-footed trailblazers, and consummate leaders.

Considering a renovation of a single site within a multisite "history park" should be the occasion for reconsidering interpretive experiences as well as story lines. A team established to develop the reinstallation of the Noah Webster House in Greenfield Village took advantage of just such an occasion to experiment with techniques. The team revolved around a project manager with extensive knowledge of the building's history and audiences within Greenfield Village and a furnishings curator with deep knowledge of the social history of family life and the material culture of the era. The first knew from experience that visitors commonly confused Noah with Daniel and that few knew why either was worth remembering; the second recognized that a furnishings plan dedicated to social history bore little resemblance to one established by decorative arts categories. The project historian, also drawn from the ranks of the curatorial staff, believed that Webster's meaning could be explored through attention to his impact on education, literacy, and print culture. But these topics were difficult to convey through period settings: Could a presentation be negotiated that explicitly addressed these elements? As it turned out, the team used these diverse interests as rationales for including different interpretive techniques within a single structure, something that was not common within Greenfield Village.

The result was a sequence of experiences that moves the visitor from the immediate house and family life, to the context of intellectual biography, to the impact on children in schools. The visitor enters the building to a series of "period rooms" furnished as if the Websters were living there in 1830, two years after completing his monumental *American Dictionary of the*

English Language. The surprises come in that the house is interpreted with the Websters as an elderly couple who shut off unused rooms, slept on different floors, entertained only their young grandchildren, and lived with an emotionally impaired granddaughter who was cared for by a live-in, free African American woman. After seeing the living room, parlor, and several bedrooms on two floors and ascending the stairs to view the library and round table at which Webster finished his famous *Dictionary,* it seemed anticlimatic to show yet another period bedroom.

The solution was to shift abruptly from historic house to a frankly modern museum display, "Noah Webster, Educator to the Republic." As prologue, a centrally placed case displays several versions of Webster's dictionary including a first, 1828 edition; various nineteenth-century versions; a common paperback edition published by Merriam-Webster in the 1970s; and a computer floppy disk from the late 1980s. Three other cases display important works by Webster published before he built the house in 1823, during the years (1823–43) he occupied the New Haven home, and after his 1843 death.

Descending the stairs into a twentieth-century addition to the original structure, visitors can sit though a nine-minute multiscreen video that begins, "There was a time when children didn't have to go to school. Noah Webster wanted to change that." Narrated by a ten-year-old boy and often employing the voices of his fifth-grade classmates, the video uses "colorized" period graphics and modern photographs to explore Webster's goal of nation building through standardized language, cultural cohesion, shared moral standards, and universal education. Of course, since its intended audience is ten to eighteen years of age, the video does not include any of these "highfalutin" words.

Here the historian's role was to encourage new topics and methods of public presentation and interaction. The subject matter and the method of presentation were, as always, inextricably intertwined. The innovation, such as it was, was to mix interpretive techniques within a single historic site in a sequence that moves visitors from the personal to the political, from an adult to a child's perspective. The "lesson plan," if you will, was designed out of a knowledge of the learning process and the desire for curriculum and pedagogy to reinforce one another.

THE HISTORIAN AS KNOWLEDGE WORKER

One of the obvious defining and uniting characteristics of most public historians is the institutional context of their employment. Public historians are knowledge workers, bringing broad intellectual and social capabilities, not technical, manual, or administrative skills to an institution.

Their institutional future often rides on their intellectual dexterity and on their ability to embody history's "habits of mind" in their daily work lives as well as their work products. It makes a huge difference (if only rhetorically and psychologically) if the institution is publicly supported or market oriented. An organization that earns most of its revenue is more immediately concerned with visitors' satisfaction than with scholarly approbation. The nature of the audiences—demographic, geographic, and psychographic—is critical. Institutions that rely on the travel market or represent nonlocal stories often have difficulty cementing local relationships and being responsive to community needs. And, of course, the institutional mission and the historical subject matter and context are fundamental to the terms of employment.

One of the mantras of the organization where I work is "Mission, Market, and Money." Does our work contribute to fulfilling our mission? Do our programs attract the audiences we want? Are they fiscally responsible? Are we making the best and highest use of our resources: historical, financial, and intellectual? Personally, I have added a fourth M: "Morale." Is the work my colleagues and I do socially valuable, mutually inspiring, and personally fulfilling?

One way of observing trends in the work of the public historian at a historic site or outdoor museum is to look at job descriptions and job performance evaluation forms over time. My first job description in the early 1980s indicated that I should independently initiate, develop, and participate in research programs. Those projects involved a systematic research attack on a problem area of considerable scope and would result in publications of a scholarly nature in addition to developing museum exhibit plans within my area of specialization. It noted that I worked with substantial freedom within my own area of primary interest and should be considered a substantial contributor to my field of scholarship.

Annually I developed a plan with my supervisor that outlined what I was to accomplish during the next year. Actual activities were articulated, the critical ones identified and asterisked, and standards of quality, quantity, and timeliness listed. My supervisor and I agreed on when it would be *organizationally* disastrous (as opposed to merely inconvenient or embarrassing) if I failed to fulfill my responsibilities. Critical items generally included finishing a script on time, working within the approved budget, providing information to the marketing department in a timely fashion, producing written curricular materials on time and within budget, and teaching the interpreters what and how to present the information to visitors. I was judged primarily on how well I communicated the findings of my research to various internal and external audiences. Research, write, and teach—it all sounded pretty familiar.

By the mid-1980s, evaluations took on a different form. My supervisor and I each wrote paragraphs evaluating the quality and quantity of my work as well as my attendance, dependability, and attitude. We further assessed my potential to grow in the position I was in as well as my potential for promotion. Finally, we discussed the things I had done to improve my performance during the year (additional education, training, conferences, etc.) and what I needed to improve during the next year. The evaluation itself said nothing about specific projects or products, although an annual list of projects and goals was used to assess whether or not I had been as productive as expected.

By the early 1990s this expository evaluation had been replaced by a combination of numerical ratings as well as written responses. The key change, however, was in the areas and the qualities to be assessed. Now, there were ten specific things to be assessed:

1. Commitment to the institution's mission and goals
2. Timely progress on projects
3. Quality of work
4. Effective and flexible team play
5. Flexibility in assignments
6. Problem-solving initiative
7. Demonstrated knowledge in field of responsibility
8. Effective communication with others
9. Effective supervision of others when necessary
10. Attendance

The same ten criteria, albeit with different emphases, were used for chefs, conservators, or curators.

Increasingly, evaluation criteria focus more on process than product and emphasize the quality of one's work relationships more than the quality of one's scholarship. (In fact, the concept of independent scholarship or self-directed study is not a part of the organizational culture in the institution where I work. Scholarship is my avocation, something I pursue for personal satisfaction on personal time.) Increasingly, it seems, the historian's work will be gauged as interpersonal processes (teamwork, communication, organization) and leadership and staff development (demonstrating an institutional perspective, providing opportunity for others) as well as job performance (quality and quantity of work, knowledge and skills, problem solving). Equally telling perhaps are the personal qualities associated with success: "works well under pressure of deadlines and heavy workloads, works productively, demonstrates positive attitude, customer focused."

EPILOGUE

Over the past few years, the professional literature in both academic and public history has included useful discussions about the relationship between memory and history, personal meaning and scholarship.[3] Creating a dialogue between the two pairs, connecting the personal and social experience, seems to provide high public value. Scholarship provides a counterbalance to personal self-absorption; history helps situate memory. Memory contributes to contextualizing historical discourse. Personal and public meanings interrelate. I see no need to reify memory or deify scholarship.

In thinking about this essay, I have primarily used the past to guide me. However, in order to be most helpful, I probably should be writing more about what working as a public historian is likely to mean in the future. Comfortable with history's "habits of mind," I have difficulty playing futurist. As a mathematician would observe, the line that divided Lewis Latimer's wide world from his comfort zone was also a series of points that connected his sense of risk and security . Walking along that line, his own actions created a series of points that he termed a "ragged edge" that was his life's work. I like to balance on a line (much like Latimer) that both divides and connects the personal life of the mind and the social actions of the public servant. And I occasionally remind myself that, in some small way, my work contributes to our understanding of who we are and want to be by helping each of us, as diverse as we are, understand what our ancestors have been and done.

NOTES

1. Rather than produce multiple notes, it seems best to suggest a list of readings that have informed my outlook: Paul Gagnon and the Bradley Commission on History in Schools, eds., *Historical Literacy: The Case for History in American Education* (Boston: Houghton Mifflin Co., 1989); John H. Falk and Lynn D. Dierking, eds., *Public Institutions for Personal Learning: Establishing a Research Agenda* (Washington, DC: American Association of Museums, 1995); David Glassberg, "Public History and the Study of Memory," *The Public Historian* 18 (Spring 1996): 7–23 and the "Roundtable: Responses to David Glassberg's "Public History and the Study of Memory,' " *The Public Historian* 19 (Spring 1997): 30–72; David Lowenthal, *The Past Is a Foreign Country* (Cambridge and New York: Cambridge University Press, 1985); Peter Novick, *That Noble Dream: The "Objectivity Question" and the American Historical Profession* (Cambridge and New York: Cambridge University Press, 1986); David Perkins, *Smart Schools: Better Thinking and Learning for Every Child* (New York: The Free Press, 1995); Neil Postman, *The End of Education* (New York: Alfred A. Knopf,

1995); and Lisa C. Roberts, *From Knowledge to Narrative: Educators and the Changing Museum* (Washington, DC: Smithsonian Institution Press, 1997).

2. Lawrence Ferlinghetti, *A Coney Island of the Mind* (New York: New Directions Books, 1958).

3. See, for example, Glassberg, "Public History and the Study of Memory" and the roundtable of responses published in *The Public Historian.*

BRUCE J. NOBLE, JR. is the superintendent of the Klondike Gold Rush National Historical Park in Skogway, AK. He earned both a B.A. in American studies and an M.A. in history at the University of Wyoming. He began his career as a survey historian for the Wyoming State Historic Preservation Office and then worked in the National Park Service's National Register of Historic Places programs for eight years before becoming the chief of interpretation and cultural resources management at the Harpers Ferry National Historical Park. Mr. Noble has published articles in such publications as Annals of Wyoming, Colorado Heritage, *and* CRM *on historical topics ranging from mining to settlement in the American West, from national parks to historic preservation.*

AT HISTORICAL PARKS: BALANCING A MULTITUDE OF INTERESTS

Bruce J. Noble, Jr.[1]

In a tribute to the individuals working in the nationwide network of state historic preservation programs, Alabama State Historic Preservation Officer Larry Oaks wrote that he was "impressed with the dedication of these individuals who . . . manage to obey the dictates of governor and secretary, to respond to the many voices of the preservation community and, somehow, to use law, moral suasion, and gambler's bluff to preserve a nation's heritage."[2] I have always liked this statement because it aptly captures the spirit of the work conducted by many public historians and cultural resources managers who strive to preserve and protect historic places. What Mr. Oaks clearly conveys is the very realistic manner in which these places are preserved through a combination of legal mandates, creativity, and a conviction that it needs to be done. The work, in other words, is both art and science. In the pages that follow, I will attempt to define the "science" behind the management of historical parks, but hopefully I will succeed in revealing at least a glimmer of the "art" that goes into the work as well.

WHAT IS A PARK?

I should explain at the outset that I will use the terms *park* and *historical park* more or less interchangeably. Because the world includes many kinds of parks, let me try to clarify what I mean when using the word. A park can consist of a single building that might, for example, have been the home of an important historical figure. Parks in this category would include the Clara Barton National Historic Site just outside Washington, D.C., and the Eugene O'Neill National Historic Site in California. In general, however, my use of the term *park* will refer to a legislatively defined area that consists of a multiplicity of significant cultural resources. In most cases, a park will not include just a single resource but a series of resources such as the portions of the town of Skagway, Alaska, included in Klondike Goldrush National Historical Park, an industrial operation like that found in Lowell National Historical Park in Massachusetts, or a military battlefield like Little Bighorn Battlefield National Monument in Montana.

Although I will raise many points that apply in general to all parks, the primary emphasis will be placed on historical parks. More specifically, much of what I say will speak most directly to *national* historical parks, since that is where the bulk of my own park experience has occurred. However, I believe that most of the essay will relate generally to all parks, and, when this is not the case, I will try to distinguish between issues of relevance to national parks in general, national historical parks in particular, and other, nonfederal park areas.

In closing this discussion, my focus on historical parks should not suggest that "natural" parks lack cultural resources. A "natural" park like Yellowstone certainly contains a multitude of cultural resources. Nor should my emphasis on cultural resources in historical parks suggest that these parks have no natural resources. Many historical parks will include important natural resources. Indeed, to separate parks into categories like "natural," "cultural," and "historical" is rather arbitrary. In the vast majority of cases, parks will exhibit a combination of natural and cultural resource types. This fact should be kept in mind during the course of the following discussion of historical parks.

THE LEGISLATIVE CONTEXT

I began this chapter by noting the level of personal commitment that often accompanies the management of historical parks, but I do not mean to suggest that such places operate on pure emotion. Indeed, there is an extensive legislative framework that acts to define historical park management at the federal level. State historic sites also have legislative mandates to consider. A complete survey of laws impacting historic site management would fall outside the scope of this essay,[3] but some discussion of major federal laws will provide a sense of the legislative structure within which historical parks operate.

Among numerous possibilities, I will limit my discussion to five laws that help to define federal park management responsibilities. The earliest was the Antiquities Act of 1906, which originally sought to prevent the excavation and removal of archaeological treasures to locations outside the United States. To achieve this goal, the law gave the president broad authority to set aside "national monuments" as federally protected areas. Over ninety years later, it remains an important source of presidential authority in this area, as witnessed by President Clinton's use of this law to establish the Grand Staircase-Escalante National Monument in southern Utah.

In 1916, Congress created the National Park Service, thus providing further recognition that the federal government had an affirmative role in protecting the nation's cultural resources. The 1916 act also resulted in the classic dual mandate: to preserve and protect fragile resources, while making them available to the visiting public. Managers of cultural sites throughout the country will attest to the fact that this dilemma is not unique to the National Park Service.

Although many of the earliest national parks can be loosely classified as "wilderness areas," a number of historic sites came into the national park system during the Franklin D. Roosevelt administration. Many of these sites were national battlefields that had previously been under military jurisdiction. In addition, Congress enacted the Historic Sites Act of 1935 to authorize the identification of "nationally" significant historic sites that might warrant eventual inclusion in the national park system. This act provided the foundation of the National Historic Landmarks program which is still administered by the National Park Service.

The Museum Act of 1955 augmented the public benefits derived from museums operated by the National Park Service. Among other things, this law authorized national park museums to receive donations for the purpose of acquiring museum objects, to exchange objects with other qualified museums, to accept objects on loan, and to make loans. The 1996 amendments to this act enable the National Park Service to transfer and convey museum objects that no longer meet the museum needs of the organization.

The National Historic Preservation Act of 1966 supplemented the Historic Sites Act by creating a National Register of Historic Places that would include properties significant at the national, state, *and* local levels. This act expanded public understanding of the meaning of the word *historic* by acknowledging that each community had historic places worthy of recognition, even if those places had not influenced the national course of events.

In addition to this general legislative context, Congress enacts legislation

authorizing specific parks. Although the basic criterion of national significance has been called into question with the creation of so-called "pork
barrel parks," the fact remains that Congress has the power to determine
what qualifies as nationally significant, and the laws that create parks have
great impact in determining their course of operation. Any park's "organic
act" should receive periodic review to determine whether the park continues to function within its legislative limits. Even private historical parks
must reassess whether their course remains true to the mission or vision of
their founders. Deviation from that course may require formal revision of
a park's "charter." Whether a park has been created by a law, a charter, or
through articles of incorporation, its founding documents should serve as
a touchstone for ongoing park management.

RESEARCH

It would seem self-evident that the management of historical sites
should be based on solid research. Yet, achieving this objective with public money can often be elusive. Former National Park Service Director
George Hartzog alluded to the difficulties of obtaining research funding
during a conference held in Corpus Christi, Texas, in 1996. Mr. Hartzog
remembered going to visit Ohio Congressman Mike Kirwan in 1964 to
discuss a possible increase in scientific research funding for the National
Park Service. At that time, when Congressman Kirwan served as chairman
of the Interior Appropriations Subcommittee, the National Park Service
had a research budget of only $12,000. After listening to the director's re-
quest for more research money, Kirwan replied, "Research? That is the
job of the NIH [National Institute of Health], not the National Park Service!" Realizing that he had hit a dead end, Hartzog cleverly asked for
funding for "Resource Studies" instead. This tactic proved to be more
fruitful and the sought-after budget increase went forward.

The congressman's response to Director Hartzog's request for research money may come as a surprise. Yet, the situation Mr. Hartzog encountered in the 1960s remains in evidence today. The National Park
Service is a nationwide organization with many stories to tell, numerous
historic buildings to repair, and huge ecosystems to nurture and restore.
In other words, there are many critical interests that compete with research for funding support. When forced to choose between the need to
stabilize a historic structure and the desire to conduct further research,
it can become difficult to justify the urgency of research. In this organizational environment, research often ends up looking like a luxury.

Nevertheless, research remains a critical component of historical park
management. Without research, it is impossible to present historical pro-

grams to the public or to prioritize the historic buildings that require preservation work. In recognition of this fact, more money has begun to flow into research over the years. Unlike the early 1960s, the National Park Service now devotes much more than $12,000 to research, but funding still lags behind the voluminous catalog of research needs.

This situation has required creative solutions. Although it may seem paradoxical, the National Park Service conducts considerable historical and archaeological research under the guise of construction projects. When funding is available for any major construction activity, particularly those involving historic buildings, planning money can and should be set aside to fund historical and archaeological research prior to launching the project. If funding has been secured for an entirely new facility such as a visitors' center, archaeological work should be done at the construction site before the groundbreaking occurs.

The net result of such research, however, is that documentation will be produced in a manner very specific to a particular construction or restoration site. The need for broadly defined research remains unresolved in such cases. This is the place where links with the academic community can be essential. Parks throughout the nation offer fertile terrain for countless books and dissertations, and park managers should try to supplement scarce research funds through collaborative projects with neighboring academic institutions.

INTERPRETATION

The National Park Service has written lengthy guidelines to explain the process of interpretation (known as NPS-6, *Interpretation & Visitor Services*), and, in fact, entire books have been written on the subject.[4] The National Park Service has also formulated a detailed Interpretive Development Program and certification process that forms the foundation of a training program that has been delivered to over 2,000 interpreters nationwide. Once thought of simply as a rote public presentation, interpretation is a dynamic field that has acquired greater sophistication as park personnel pursue the skillful revelation of meanings.

For the purposes of this essay, interpretation will be defined as a process that facilitates a connection between the interests of the visitor and the meanings of one or more resources. In an interpretive context, tangible and intangible factors collide to create meaning. For example, a tangible resource, such as a historic building, will acquire meaning through its connection with intangibles such as the families that once lived there, their source of employment, their ethnicity, their socioeconomic status, and a host of other potential factors. By creating greater understanding about the basis of a resource's significance, interpretation seeks to impart to the visitor a greater sense of care and stewardship for the resource.

Within the National Park Service, interpretation is organized around a series of themes. These themes are generally outlined in a park's "Long Range Interpretive Plan." The themes that a particular park emphasizes may derive from its authorizing legislation or from other prominent areas of history relevant to a park's mission. This thematic structure then becomes the basis of a park's selection of interpretive programs and also provides a foundation for determining whether a proposed special program is relevant for a given park. Relevant themes may not, however, always be "historical" in nature. Interpretation can also revolve around archaeology, architecture, natural resources, or really any subject appropriate to a given park area.[5] Consequently, the interpretive message can assume a wide variety of shapes and forms even when confined within a park arena.

Given this variety, it follows naturally that the National Park Service utilizes numerous channels to deliver that message. These channels in-

National Park Service ranger leading a tour at Harpers Ferry National Historical Park. *Courtesy of the National Park Service.*

clude, but are not necessarily limited to, demonstrations, educational programs delivered by uniformed rangers, museum exhibits, Web pages, roadside signs or "waysides," films, and living history. No one method of interpretation is inherently superior to another. Instead, all work together in an effort to create historical meaning for the visitor.

All types of interpretation do not work equally well in all settings. Take, for example, living history. Popular at many historical sites, living history programs utilize people who dress in period clothing and seek to stimulate visitors to think creatively about the habits and activities of bygone days. This interpretive approach is immensely popular with visitors who like to give free reign to their imaginations as they contemplate the everyday living habits and customs of those from whom they have descended. However, effective living history programs require a significant monetary investment in appropriate clothing and accoutrements, along with a commitment to rigorous staff training. Thus, each park has to decide about its capabilities for delivering this kind of program. The same sort of decisions have to be made about other types of interpretive activities.

Certain interpretive possibilities actually extend beyond park boundaries thanks to the growing influence of new technology. Just as living history programs may not work equally well in all places, not all parks nec-

At the Harpers Ferry National Historical Park, an interpreter in a living history exhibit demonstrates machinery that operated in the U.S. Armory during the nineteenth century. *Courtesy of the National Park Service.*

essarily have the chance to utilize all facets of emerging technology. However, it is increasingly evident that technology is affecting the history profession just as it affects the world at large. The proliferation of CD-ROMs, World Wide Web sites, and the History Channel has changed the ways we learn about our nation's past. Rather than deplore the demise of "traditional" ways of learning history, public historians need to embrace the new technologies and channel them in the right direction.

Technology can alter the very essence of the term "park visitor." The World Wide Web has created the concept of "virtual visitors" who, due to disability, advanced age, or lack of geographic proximity, might never visit a given park were it not for their computers and modems. Some fear that virtual visitation could replace actual visitation, but such fears are unfounded. What Web sites have done, in many cases, is to produce better prepared park visitors. Having seen a park's Web site and developed some familiarity with its resources before getting in their cars, Web-savvy visitors arrive ready and eager to take advantage of a park's many educational opportunities.

CULTURAL RESOURCES MANAGEMENT

Research and interpretation are only part of the responsibilities involved in managing the diverse resources of a historic park. At the federal level, cultural resources management also assumes a prominent role. As with interpretation, cultural resources management is the subject of a hefty National Park Service guideline (known as NPS-28, *Cultural Resources Management*) and entire books have also been written on this subject.[6] As these publications explain, cultural resources management refers to a wide range of historic preservation functions that revolve around identifying resources that are eligible for listing in the National Register of Historic Places, documenting their significance, and protecting them from impacts that may intrude upon their historic character. While the availability of ample background literature minimizes the need for lengthy discussion of this topic,[7] a few words of clarification should be offered in light of some previous comments.

Parks are often created as a result of some legislative purpose. In the case of national parks, this purpose has to do with the park's national significance. However, Section 110 of the National Historic Preservation Act essentially says that park managers, at least at the federal level, need to recognize that their responsibilities encompass all properties eligible for listing in the National Register, not just those of national significance. This suggests possible tension between the National Historic Preservation Act and the legislative rationale for which a park was created.

Consider a hypothetical case—a federal park which exists due to its national significance as a nineteenth-century whaling town. Despite a legislative mandate which suggests that the significance of this town concludes in 1899, it is not appropriate to demolish every 1920s bungalow within the park's boundaries. The National Register eligibility of those bungalows should be evaluated, and, if found to be eligible, they should receive the same preservation considerations as the "nationally" significant resources for which the park was established. In the eyes of the National Historic Preservation Act, all historic properties are created equal. This legislative reality applies not only to parks but to all historic properties that federal agencies manage.

More specifically, Section 106 of the National Historic Preservation Act requires federal agencies to consider the impacts of their projects or activities on properties that may be listed in or eligible for the National Register. The state historic preservation officer and, in some cases, the Advisory Council on Historic Preservation must review and comment on such projects before they can be initiated. The process is so thoroughly defined in law and regulation that it may, with some justification, strike fear into the hearts of even the most hardened federal bureaucrats. While some state parks may have a state level counterpart to Section 106 that they must comply with, other states and private parks no doubt take some comfort in the fact that Section 106 only applies to federal agencies.

Whether or not Section 106 anxiety is really justified, there can be no doubts about the value of the process. To return to our hypothetical case—the situation will inevitably arise where pressure from various sources will compel park managers in the nineteenth-century whaling town to contemplate demolishing the 1920s bungalows, even though they have been determined eligible for the National Register at the locally significant level. Contrary to common views of the process, Section 106 does not require the preservation of those bungalows. What it does do is require the federal park to consult with the state historic preservation officer and the Advisory Council while confronting this essential question: "Do we really want to tear down these historic properties?" Whatever the decision, the Section 106 compliance process will have provided the opportunity to consider the various alternatives and determine the appropriate course of action. The decision, in other words, will not be hasty, but instead will be based on rational consideration of a variety of different perspectives on the subject. The ability to resolve such serious matters by consulting with parties outside the park can not be underestimated.

New technology can play a role in this aspect of park management as well. Geographic Information Systems, more commonly known simply as

GIS, enable users to create thematically layered computerized maps. Once a park's resources have been incorporated into a GIS system, an almost unlimited range of maps can be created with great ease. For example, a map might be developed that shows all properties constructed before 1900 that are listed in the National Register and in poor condition. This would enable a park to use a series of maps to develop a schedule of maintenance priorities. Countless other mapping possibilities also exist. While some initial expense is involved in purchasing GIS software and hardware, the technology has much to offer park managers and will undoubtedly become increasingly common in the coming years.

RELATIONSHIP BETWEEN INTERPRETATION AND CULTURAL RESOURCES MANAGEMENT

Interpreters and cultural resources managers clearly have much in common. After all, cultural resources professionals strive to preserve the very resources that interpreters present to the public. For their part, interpreters endeavor to use education as a tool to impart a resource preservation ethic to the visiting public. But while the two groups of professionals often work in tandem, both must also struggle in pursuit of the public visibility necessary for greater professional recognition and funding.

On the one hand, cultural resources management activities often suffer from the fact that they frequently occur out of public view. Visitors do not see the historical report that influences an interpretive program, the architectural drawings that facilitate the restoration of a historic building, or the curator's work in planning a museum exhibit. But although unseen, these activities have a profound impact on the way that the visiting public perceives parks.

On the other hand, interpretation occurs very much in the limelight. Still, it is easy to overlook the extensive research and preparation that takes place prior to delivering an interpretive program. Because this preparation time is unseen, interpretation is sometimes inappropriately stigmatized as a mere "hobby" conducted by people who happen to have a knack for public speaking. Thus, interpretation does not always receive the professional credibility that it deserves.

Consider, for example, the role that archaeology plays in both cultural resources management and interpretation. All parks are likely to possess archaeological resources—historic and prehistoric—and archaeological survey work is a necessary component of most park planning activities. Planting trees, digging fence post holes, building roads and new facilities, and other ground-disturbing activities should be planned and undertaken in such a way as to minimally impact archaeological sites. This type

An archaeological excavation in progress at Harpers Ferry National Historical Park. *Courtesy of the National Park Service.*

of preservation through avoidance can only occur, however, when archaeological sites have been located in advance as part of the cultural resources management of the park.

Archaeology can play an equally valuable role in expanding or enhancing park interpretation. Although historians are becoming more adept at studying nonelite peoples, the historical record is often slanted in the direction of people who had sufficient income to purchase real estate, file lawsuits, write wills, and the like. Archaeology can nicely complement the written evidence available to historians. Both prehistoric sites and historic archaeological sites that produce objects like housewares, weapons, tools, discarded food products, and liquor bottles can offer invaluable insight regarding the daily lives, work, diet, and recreational habits of people who may not readily appear in the historical record.

Often, however, archaeology gets little credit for either role—its critical role in cultural resources management does not garner much public recognition, and its interpretive potential is too often underutilized and unappreciated. The ideal situation is to have adequate funding to support a program of archaeological research which aims to proactively identify, document, preserve, *and* interpret sites and resources, but that is often not financially possible. The park manager must set priorities. While an ambitious archaeological program can significantly expand a park's interpretive horizons, a more modest program will at least spare managers the embarrassment of inadvertently harming important cultural resources. At the very minimum, parks should at least have ready access to archaeological expertise through contracts or cooperative arrangements with other agencies.

In the final analysis, it is important for managers to ascribe proper value to essential activities that may take place partially out of the public eye. Both cultural resources management and interpretation are striving for greater professional recognition and increased professionalization, and both also need appropriate financial support. Savvy managers support both professionalization and adequate funding because they understand that the collective value of these two programs transcend the fractional portion of these activities seen by the visiting public.

MUSEUM AND RESEARCH COLLECTIONS

Historical parks are also more than just old buildings and open areas with archaeological potential. One of the delights of working in a historical park is to witness the many people who voluntarily come forward with offers to loan or donate items of great financial or sentimental value to park museum collections. This tendency is impressive because of the sense of public service which motivates people to loan or donate these objects rather than to attempt to profit from their sale. But in some cases, altruism may be less significant than a desire to clean out an attic or a garage. In such situations, parks need to have collection management plans in place that explain why certain things can and cannot be integrated into the collection. Whatever motivates the donor, many parks have very significant museum collections that grow ever larger.

Many years ago, professional curation of park museum collections was almost an afterthought. With park collections growing and their value increasingly recognized, museum curation now ranks in the forefront of park cultural resources management programs. The increasing number of park museums that receive accreditation from the American Association of Museums testifies to the value of their collections.[8] Few would contest the fact that park museums are now included among the nation's leading material culture repositories.[9]

The rising status of park museum collections is a critical step toward broader recognition of parks as major research centers. In some respects, however, the ability of parks to fulfill their potential as research destinations is hindered by the stunted development of park archival and library collections. The lack of progress in this area is partially because these two programs lack integration, since their overall management is divided between two different branches of the National Park Service. In addition, funding limitations dictate that most parks lack staff specifically trained in library and archival fields. These staffing constraints undoubtedly account both for the lack of organization in many park libraries and the fact that park archival records are sometimes treated as museum objects to be catalogued and hidden from public view in locked drawers. While such actions make good sense from a preservation standpoint, only through hiring additional staff will there be any assurance that these materials can be made readily available to researchers.

Despite these circumstances, both the general public and professional researchers increasingly turn to parks for a wide variety of source materials, and parks are employing new technologies to facilitate communication. This has led to a need for operational adjustments. With the increasing use of e-mail, the public has come to expect immediate answers to questions. This places an additional burden on staff members who already respond to a heavy volume of research questions arriving through the mail and by phone. My personal hope is that this concern will prove to be only transitional in nature. I can readily foresee the day when the Internet and the World Wide Web will serve as the vehicles for delivering a wide range of information and materials to researchers and the general public. This would provide a self-service smorgasbord of historical documents, photographs, museum inventories, and other data to the researcher, while requiring little or no direct involvement from the park staff. This is the reality toward which we move as parks begin to claim their rightful place among the major centers of material culture studies in this country.

ENTREPRENEURIAL PARTNERSHIPS

Partnerships represent something new and something old. Parks have always relied on partnerships with cooperating associations, friends groups, volunteers, and private donors. In their more recent iteration, partnerships are now being espoused in response to a decline in legislative appropriations. This funding crisis is severe and has resulted in a variety of reactions. In perhaps the most extreme case, Canadian national parks have been threatened with closure if they cannot, by an established deadline, demonstrate a capacity to generate all their own operating expenses. Fortunately, the situation has not become quite so severe in the United States, but the Canadian example does demonstrate that the trend toward "entrepreneurial thinking" is a fact that many parks are now facing.

Corporate partnerships represent one important opportunity. Corporations often recognize that parks raise the quality of life in a given area, and they may be willing to donate generously to support this outcome. What must be avoided is any form of corporate sponsorship that threatens to compromise the integrity of a park and its resources. The search for corporate partners can be a delicate subject, but the goal is achievable. Museums have long track records of successfully working with corporations, and parks need to learn to emulate the success of their museum colleagues.

National parks have long benefitted from close relationships with their cooperating associations. Cooperating associations are established as not-for-profit organizations authorized to operate sales outlets within park boundaries. These stores primarily sell books, but may also sell other items associated with the park's overall educational objectives. Any profits they earn are donated back to the host park. In the case of parks with very high visitation, such relationships can result in significant financial rewards for the host park. Even in less visited parks, the partnerships that exist between parks and their cooperating associations have generally been extremely beneficial.

Parks can also benefit from working with the booming heritage tourism business. More and more, tour group companies utilize their own staff to interpret a park's history. This is not an entirely new phenomenon—parks like Gettysburg have supported "licensed battlefield guide" programs for decades. These guides are not park employees, but the program works well because aspiring battlefield guides must meet park standards if they want to receive a license. Every park may not need a program like Gettysburg's, but all should recognize the need to monitor and evaluate nonpark tour guides as heritage tourism grows. Even in an age of staff limitations, parks should retain quality control over all programs that interpret their resources to the public.

Partnerships with volunteers, especially living history groups, have also become increasingly valuable in these days of funding limitations. As previously mentioned, the clothing and other apparel living history practitioners utilize can be quite costly and well beyond the means of many historical parks. Volunteer living history groups offer opportunities to expand park interpretation into this area. The park benefits from the color and pageantry these groups provide, and the volunteers benefit from the opportunity to display publicly both their historical knowledge and their expertise in accurately re-creating the appearance of the era they represent. However, as with tour groups, parks must remain firmly in control of their interpretive message. Parks should not invite living history groups into their midst merely to excite the public with booming musket volleys but rather to support established park programs and historical themes. Volunteer training is an essential means for achieving this objective.

It is important to emphasize the need to exercise caution before rushing headlong into any relationship with a partner that seemingly offers unlimited potential for bringing money into a park. Proposals must be carefully evaluated in terms of what they offer and how they support the objectives of the park. As with any relationship, parks must be selective about the types of partnerships into which they enter. At the same time, budget considerations compel parks to be open-minded toward partners who offer legitimate means of supplementing the financial resources necessary to advance a park's preservation goals and educational agenda.

CONCLUSION

A park is not just a museum, or a resource preservation laboratory, or a place to conduct historical research, or a venue for presenting interpretive programs. Parks represent an amalgamation of all these things and more. Therein lie the challenge and the excitement of parks both as places to work and as places to visit.

Parks have reached something of an evolutionary crossroads. All sorts of recreational attractions compete for the public's attention while the growing onslaught of mass media has diminished the ability to distinguish clearly between real history and glitzy re-creations of the past. With public money on the decline, parks have been thrust into a competitive arena that demands a considerable measure of entrepreneurial skill. The advantage that parks bring to this dynamic quest for "market share" is the authenticity they offer as the actual sites of genuinely important historical events. Fortunately, this advantage is not lost on the public. Cultivating and retaining this public respect for authenticity hold the key for ensuring that parks remain at the center of the nation's cultural landscape into the twenty-first century and beyond.

NOTES

1. The author wishes to thank the following individuals for their comments on an initial draft of this chapter: Donald W. Campbell, Ann Hitchcock, David Larsen, Barry Mackintosh, and Corky Mayo.
2. From the preface to Virginia E. DeMarce, comp., *Compendium of Policy Resolutions, 1969–1990* (Washington, DC: National Conference of State Historic Preservation Officers, 1991).

3. General summaries of laws and legal issues related to the national parks can be found in the following sources: David J. Simon, ed., *Our Common Lands: Defending the National Parks* (Washington, DC: Island Press, 1988); Michael A. Mantell, ed., *Managing National Park System Resources: A Handbook on Legal Duties, Opportunities, and Tools* (Washington, DC: The Conservation Foundation, 1990); and Edmund B. Rogers, comp., *History of Legislation Relating to the National Park System Through the 82nd Congress* (Washington, DC: U.S. Department of the Interior, 1958).

4. All numerical installments in the NPS guideline series, such as NPS-6, are slated to be reissued as "Director's Orders" beginning in late 1998 or 1999. Perhaps the best known books on interpretation are William T. Alderson and Shirley Payne Low, *Interpretation of Historic Sites,* 2nd ed. (Walnut Creek, CA: AltaMira Press, 1996), and Freeman Tilden, *Interpreting Our Heritage,* Revised ed. (Chapel Hill, NC: University of North Carolina Press, 1967).

5. For information about archaeological interpretation, see John H. Jameson, Jr., ed., *Presenting Archeology to the Public: Digging for Truths* (Walnut Creek, CA: AltaMira Press, 1997).

6. Ronald W. Johnson and Michael G. Schene, eds., *Cultural Resources Management* (Malabar, FL: Robert E. Krieger Publishing Co., 1987).

7. General sources regarding cultural resources management practices include Johnson and Schene, eds., *Cultural Resources Management;* Robert E. Stipe and Antoinette J. Lee, eds., *The America Mosaic: Preserving a Nation's Heritage* (Washington, DC: U.S. Committee, International Council on Monuments and Sites, 1987); and Michael G. Schene, guest ed., "The National Park Service and Historic Preservation," *The Public Historian* 9 (Spring 1987).

8. For information on the museum accreditation process, contact AAM (see "Resources" section in this volume).

9. For information on the evolution of park museums, see Ralph H. Lewis, *Museum Curatorship in the National Park Service, 1904–1982* (Washington, DC: Department of the Interior, National Park Service, Curatorial Services Division, 1993).

ROBERT B. PATTERSON, JR. is director of the Great Smoky Mountain Heritage Center in Townsend, Tennessee. He earned a B.A. in history and library science and an M.A. in historical administration at Florida State University. He previously served as the director of Great Explorations: The Hands On Museum and the Clarksville-Montgomery County Museum. Mr. Patterson served on the board of the Clarksville Area Chamber of Commerce and the River District Commission, as chair of Main Street Clarksville, as president of the Mid-Cumberland Arts League and the Tennessee Association of Museums, on the board of the Florida Association of Museums, and on the advisory board for the Museum Assessment Program.

IN LOCAL HISTORICAL AGENCIES, MUSEUMS, AND SOCIETIES

Robert B. Patterson, Jr.

I moved to Clarksville, Tennessee, in 1983 to begin the operation of the Clarksville-Montgomery County Historical Museum. Founded in 1784, Clarksville was a small to mid-size community with a population of only 45,000 in a county of 70,000 but with ambitious plans for a new museum. The city's 1898 post office—the second most photographed building in the state of Tennessee—had been turned over to the museum's board of trustees in 1982, but the city had committed only $100,000 in capital dollars to fund the renovation of this historic building. The museum board managed to locate an architect and a contractor who were willing to work for a pittance in order to give the community its first museum, but we still had no collections, no furniture, no policies, and, most of all, no staff. My office furniture consisted of one eight-foot folding table and seven chairs. I did not even have a trash can.

In its two hundred years, Clarksville had never had a museum, and there seemed to be little public engagement in its colorful past. Yes, there were two chapters of the Daughters of the American Revolution, a chapter of the Sons of Confederate Veterans, a historical society, and a county historian, but the interest in history was fragmented and kept in the possession of only a handful of the community's residents. Trying to stimulate broader support for the museum proved an exciting but also strenuous task. Within the first week, I had to make the first of many public speeches. While I had done some public speaking in my previous positions, I was not prepared for the level of public presentations that was required in Clarksville. During the year, I became a regular radio personality, talked an average of four times per week to morning, noon, and evening civic clubs, and was taped for television several times. At the same time, we moved forward with a membership drive and the museum's first fund-raiser. Needless to say, this schedule was demanding and nerve wracking. But it was necessary in order to find sufficient financial support to open the museum the following year as part of the celebration of the city's 200th birthday.

The evolution of the museum since that time has been both exhilarating and exhausting. In the early 1990s, the board of trustees decided that our mission as a history institution was too limited. Our exhibits, programs, and activities were not as enticing or varied as in other communities—Clarksville did not have any famous stars, well-known athletes, or politicians but was the typical small town U.S.A. Therefore, we decided to broaden our mission to become more involved in arts and sciences with our anchor remaining history. This allowed us to produce more programs using resources from travelling exhibitions as well as those designed in-house. With this change came enormous new challenges. For example, I was the only staff person in 1983, but we now have thirteen— nine full-time and four part-time. As the museum grew, my own responsibilities changed significantly. The job description for the position when I arrived in 1983 bears little resemblance to the director's current responsibilities. Initially, I was not only the administrator but also the curator, meeting donors of objects or listening to oral history stories. But I have not researched a history project of any kind in eight years. That's no longer my job. Now I am strictly an administrator performing three key functions: dealing with board and personnel issues, trouble shooting, and raising money by the bucketsful.

In sum, my own experience demonstrates that there is no "one size fits all" when it comes to local history museums and historical societies. They vary in size and complexity, from one institution to another and over time, from small one-person operations to complex institutions with sizeable staffs and diverse missions.[1] But, in the following pages, I will try to lay out what I believe are the critical issues common to us all.

THE CONTEXT

Every museum is different. The patrons, as they enter the institution, seem to take on the character that is projected. Some museums have an air of sophistication, and the patrons view precious collections with reverence. But others, such as children's museums, explode with contagious energy, excitement, and, of course, deafening sounds. So what about the Clarksville-Montgomery County Museum? Where does our visitation come from, our interest, our excitement? It comes from our region and the special character of our local economy, which centers on a number of large industrial plants, many of which are foreign owned, and the Fort Campbell Military Base, the largest single economic factor in the region. One consequence is that our population is very transient—the military population turns over approximately every three to four years, and the industrial employees are scarcely more stable. This is both good and bad. The downside is that, with such a large transient population, we have to resell the institution every two or three years to a similar but new audience. On the positive side, Clarksville's residents, like those of many other communities, are eager to visit an institution or a locale that explains the community's history and its life in relation to them. This is where our museum comes into the picture—we are a local museum, a community-oriented museum.

But we are not alone. Museums are only a small part of the growing nonprofit community, and we face serious competition from other nonprofits for funding. With less government funding available, we are all competing for the corporate dollar, and the competition is keen. Museums compete not only with other museums but with children's hospitals, United Way agencies, libraries, archives, and a variety of other worthwhile organizations. But how can we compete with the care-giving agencies? They affect all of us. We all have friends or family members who died of cancer or have been affected by some other disease or tragic event, and that influences our giving. Giving to United Way agencies is institutionalized in most businesses. In order for us to compete, we have to find a way to be more visible and to use our financial support to the best advantage for marketing and long-lasting benefits. We must make sure we are on the cutting edge of current events that affect our community. Multiculturalism, hands-on activities, community partnerships, and aspects of education that are considered weak in our schools are of utmost importance. Paying attention to the concerns of the community we live in is essential to our success.

We also need to recognize that we are competing with for-profit operations such as theme parks, movie theaters, miniature golf courses, and other leisure time activities. We cannot advertise like theme parks nor do we have ready television access. However, we can be a successful partner in the same community if we learn from for-profits and then use those concepts on a smaller scale to find our niche.

Unfortunately, too many local history museums are stuck in the past and are not engaged with the communities in which they are located. Too often, they are little more than amateur operations addressing antiquarian interests with dull and dusty exhibits. It is essential that local museums be more professional in their operations and programs and address contemporary audiences and interests.

For example, local museums need to follow the example of for-profits and embrace new technology and active learning techniques. The days of people wanting simply to see the garments of some historical icon are coming to a close; the public wants instead to become involved with that historical figure. Developing video performances, theatrical endeavors, or hands-on events that allow the patron to participate are expensive but, in the long run, extremely profitable. It does mean a significant shift in the way history museums look at artifacts and their audience. It even affects personnel development. Exhibit technicians need to be able to wire sound, lighting, or other electronic devices that can excite the audience through push buttons, electronic eyes, or computer programs. The staff needs to have someone available who can program computers so children can take a trip on the Oregon Trail and determine if they would have made it with the supplies and skills of the nineteenth century. In order to strengthen history's importance in the educational process, it is our responsibility as history museum staff members to make it enticing and enjoyable. That means no longer displaying every object—fifteen different typewriters, thirty women's dresses, and dozens of military insignias—in a conglomeration of nonrelated cases with little or no narrative or interpretation. Exhibit design must be more engaging and dramatic, and we can learn much from department stores, theme parks, and other businesses. But the learning is not just one way—for-profits are beginning to learn from us. Numerous corporations have developed their own museums to showcase their development and success, and in many cases the key is the educational component, which they have learned from us.

WORKING IN A LOCAL MUSEUM
OR HISTORICAL SOCIETY

Working as the director or administrator of a small- or medium-sized museum or historical society can be extremely rewarding but at the same time very frustrating. Sometimes, when the pressure mounts and the responsibilities multiply, I think my best option may be cloning. Indeed, as a director, you have to be willing to wear a variety of hats—not only administrator, financial officer, and personnel director but also public speaker, marketer, educator, historian, janitor, and maintenance man.

But that is what makes the life in a small museum so wonderful—each day you have new challenges and new opportunities.

One of a director's principal roles is being the senior cheerleader for the institution. This means being willing and able to speak in public or in the media on a regular basis. Civic clubs, historical societies, special events, radio, and newspapers are all looking for stories, programs, or activities, and the museum director should take advantage of those needs. Indeed it is imperative that the director be as visible as possible—attending social events, working with other nonprofit organizations, and joining other worthy causes. Such activity not only demonstrates the director's broad interest in the community but also provides opportunities for the director to connect with business leaders and supporters of other organizations who have not previously been involved with the museum. The director's participation in social events can be particularly important to a museum's future. Parties are one of the best ways for the director to "get the word out" about the institution. They provide a nonthreatening environment where you can discuss your institution openly and create enthusiasm. The downside to all this is that the director often does not have a private life—time away from the museum is consumed by other museum-related activities. In sum, being the administrator of a local history museum is the furthest thing from being bored. There is more to do than there is time to do it in, and you will soon find that you relish the idea of even more challenges.

Visibility and accessibility are also important within the museum. Whatever happens, the director has to be prepared to step forward and address it. When, for example, problems arise with major donors of objects, funding sources, schools, or individuals, it is the director's responsibility to telephone the injured parties and find ways to make amends, no matter who is at fault. This is not taught in the hallowed halls of a university but comes from real-life experiences. A director must learn to "take it on the chin" and smile while being hit.

But the director is not always alone—even the smallest of institutions may have an additional staff or two. Sometimes, however, the level of professionalism is low. At my first museum job, I was the only staff member with a professional degree in museum management. We had in positions of authority a psychologist, a businessman, a retired department store manager, and a variety of other individuals who had degrees in physical education, history, and science—or no degree at all—and little or no experience. We have come a long way since those days. Thanks to the work of organizations such as the American Association of Museums, the American Association for State and Local History, and our regional and state organizations, we now recognize the necessity of specialized training and experience, and more and more of the staff in local museums are taking advantage of workshops, programs, conferences, and other activities offered across the country. But that does not mean that everyone has to have a history or museum degree. For example, putting a historian in charge of marketing is probably not a good idea. Nor is interest in history a requirement for exhibit design; more important is enjoying the challenge of creating an engaging exhibition with three-and two-dimensional objects. And, of course, the best educators may have degrees in education or related fields.

The biggest staff problem for the small- or medium-sized museum is that there are few if any opportunities for career advancement. Typically, the only way to move forward is to move to another institution of larger size. While most staff are loyal to the institution, they understandably want to own their own homes, drive acceptable vehicles, and have some of the luxuries of life. While our profession has come a long way from the days of paying poverty wages, we are still not competitive with other professions and businesses. In fact, schoolteachers and administrators in a school system typically make more money than most of a small museum's staff and, in some cases, even the director. This is where maintaining quality becomes problematic. Young professionals can not be counted on to stay; they see their positions as career stepping-stones. That means a lot of turnover, and the director ends up spending a lot of time looking for new employees to replace the more experienced ones moving on to larger institutions or more demanding positions. Even more discouraging is the loss of good professionals to the corporate world. Benefits, higher salaries, and better working environments have drawn many high-quality professionals from our field.

But there are ways to slow the process of staff turnover. First of all, as the administrator it is your responsibility to educate the board of trustees on the level of staff salary and benefits necessary in order for your institution to remain competitive with other museums. Board members who have backgrounds in business will know the competitive nature of hiring and maintaining a strong staff. But as a director you must also be prepared to set standards and insist on the best qualified staff. In many cases, we are our own worst enemies—we willingly fill key positions with people who will work for extremely low wages. We end up with key components of our institutions in the hands of undereducated or incompetent staff. This is changing, and none too soon.

REACHING OUT INTO THE COMMUNITY

The real strength of local museums and historical societies lies in the educational and programming opportunities they provide to their communities. Here is where we can and do excel. We can bring history to life. The opportunities are endless. Museums have a wealth of resources and can even take programs beyond their institutions to day care centers, schools, colleges and universities, and hospitals. Walking tours, programs in parks, or activities or tours in businesses such as newspaper and manufacturing plants can also offer historical insight. The only problem is that too often when we develop these wonderful exhibitions and educational programs, the community never hears about them. Board members tell their friends, the museum gets a small article in the newspaper, and we all wonder why no one turns out. In short, most of our local museums are poorly marketed. We just do not take advantage of the opportunities and networks that we have. For example, museum educators usually have good connections into the schools. Those schools usually have a mail service, and for the nominal cost of printing, the museum can have a flyer inserted in the schools' mail system that will be handed to each student. This exposure can yield tremendous success. This targets school-age students and not adults—most museums have found more success focusing on children, who then bring parents, and not the reverse.

What this gets down to is marketing. For a small museum to survive, the director can no longer be just a historian or curator. Developing public relations and marketing skills is a necessity. The director must understand what is involved in marketing an institution—who, where, and why to do advertising and what exhibits will entice visitors, school groups, and, most importantly, financial donors. Unfortunately, marketing is often the one component in a museum's overall operation that is lacking in sophistication. Of course, museums are not alone—many corporations and businesses themselves experience problems in getting the word out. We watch small businesses come and go in the malls and downtowns and wonder why they were not successful. In many cases they did not know the market or how to approach it properly. Museums face the same situations. We expect people to enter our facilities because we are symbols of learning, cultural meccas. But marketers can tell you that there are more and more competitors for the public's limited time for leisure activities. We must find avenues and resources through which we can convince the public to come to our institutions. And that means marketing.

Look for new advertising opportunities. Deals with newspapers, radio, and television stations are not impossible. In fact, the local media is often eager to work with nonprofits. In some cases, they may split the cost with you; or they may give you some ads if you purchase others. You might even sign them up as sponsors, which means an even better deal on advertising. Here again, we need to follow the example of the for-profit sector, which uses a variety of advertising messages to entice the public. Consider, for example, discounts on admission in partnership with fast food restaurants or other businesses.

We also need to think about the different audiences out there and how we might reach them better. What about baby boomers, whose interest in their families and communities ties in with the museum's genealogical research resources and its local history exhibits? Or consider how to attract senior citizens, whose increasing mobility makes them likely new audiences for your institution. We need to be developing strong marketing plans for those audiences.

In other words, in order for a museum to reach out and engage the community in which it is located, the community has to know it is there and that it has exhibits and programs of interest. That will not happen unless the museum markets itself. Museums must allocate funds for marketing and hire staff who can explore the opportunities available to them. The museum of today and in the future must become more business oriented in order to survive.

FUNDING AND FUND-RAISING

The days of large subsidies from the city, county, or state are gone for most of us. Museums and historical societies nationwide are experiencing funding crises. The director of a museum like mine must find other sources of funds, taking full advantage of memberships, memorial gifts, travelling exhibits, programs, major fund-raising campaigns, slick brochures, rental opportunities, and a myriad of other possibilities to expand its financial base.

In recent years, the first targets in government retrenchment have often been cultural agencies and institutions, because they are not seen as necessary for the community's growth and longevity. This is beginning to change. In many cases, corporations are now looking at the quality of life and not just the tax ramifications when they consider moving their offices or industry into a community. They examine the school system, cultural amenities, and medical facilities available for their employees and their families. The issue is no longer just road systems, tax infrastructure, and the price of land. A museum can play a key role in a community's marketing strategy. In Clarksville, it is not unusual for our local economic development council to entertain a group of dignitaries from around the world at our institution. They use it because of the ambiance of the facility. The corporations in turn send their families to the museum to get a sense of what the community is like and whether they would enjoy it. The museum can use that to demonstrate to the local government that cultural activities are not fluff but are critical to the future of the community. When we make a case for continued funding to our local, county, or state governments, we should not only emphasize the importance of preserving history but also argue for broader impact and worth.

But no museum or historical society can depend entirely on government funding; we must all raise private dollars. The possibilities are endless—annual and deferred giving, capital and other fund-raising campaigns, memberships, earned income through admission and sales, and special fund-raising events. But the key in every case will be the museum's governing board or board of trustees. If you look at successful institutions across the country, you will find that their boards are made up of individuals who not only are recognized citizens of the community but have the business experience and economic clout necessary to put the institution on sound financial footing. Too often, however, small history museums have boards made up of concerned citizens who are not business oriented and are unable to raise significant sums of money for the institution. Often professors, teachers, members of a prominent family, or retired citizens who have time to devote to the museum, they are very dedicated individuals who care about the institution because they care about the community. But while most of them have a lot of time and talent, too few have the economic means or clout needed. More specifically, they have the institution at heart but are unable to approach prominent citizens or large corporations to invest in the institution. And, of course, this has a domino effect on staff development, exhibit construction, marketing, and other activities—indeed, the institution's future. I am not saying that you should not have educators or retired citizens on your board; however, it is crucial that your board be more astute to the financial needs of the institution. We have to run museums like a business; and in doing so, this means that we cannot operate at a loss.

Assuming you have board members who are willing and able to fund-raise, you need to make sure that they are well versed in the museum and its work. A board retreat can be a useful vehicle for focusing on the long- and short-range goals of the institution and its needs, be they financial or otherwise. It is the administrator's responsibility to educate board members on how a museum works, and the retreat offers an opportunity to discuss all issues of the institution openly and in order of priority. If boards follow long-range plans, they have a tendency to be stronger and more successful.

It is also critical that board members making fund-raising calls understand the giving potential of the individual or corporation being approached. We have all heard horror stories of improperly trained board members asking for $3,000 when they could have received ten times that if they had known to ask. This is another reason why it is important to have professional business people on your board—they are better prepared to make that sort of assessment. Board and staff also need to understand how to make presentations. Corporate executives, for example, are continually pursued by nonprofit organizations, and in order to get the attention of a CEO, you need to have a presentation packet as well as a presenter who is effective. In all honesty, most times it is trial and error. However, if the small museum can recruit a corporate executive or other professional with experience in this area to help, you can avert some of these mistakes. The old adage that you have only one opportunity to make a first impression is very true, particularly when raising funds.

And where does the corporate support typically come from? Occasionally from their foundations but typically it is from their marketing and advertising budgets in the form of sponsorship of an exhibit, event, or activity. That means the company will expect to receive a return for their investment in your institution. This is where the museum walks a very fine line. In order to sell a corporation on an exhibit or program, the museum in return must promote the corporation. One rule of thumb is that a corporate sponsor's name should never be larger than the museum's name in any kind of advertisement. Even on those terms, you may find yourself in a quandary about the identity of the institution versus the identity of the sponsor. And the larger the gift, the higher the demands of the sponsor. You may be asked to allow food or drinks in a gallery that had always been off limits before or to set up private parties, special tours, and other benefits. While such concessions may violate your concept of the sanctity of your museum, they are necessary for survival. In order to keep our doors open and our profession alive, we have to learn how to compromise without sacrificing the original ideals of the profession and its public trust.

While we tend to think mainly in terms of corporate gifts and sponsorship, do not forget the importance of individual gifts. Indeed, the largest gifts in a campaign usually come from individuals rather than corporations or foundations. In some cases, the payoff may not be immediate but in the long term through bequests and endowments. There are a variety of planned giving opportunities available that can begin even with young children, not just senior citizens. Many institutions have received large pieces of property in wills that were established twenty to forty years prior.

Of course, there are many other ways to raise funds—admissions, memberships, museum store sales, and sales of publications. All have been proven successful, and most museums use all or some combination of them to raise monies. However, there are other opportunities available

For its annual fund-raiser "Flying High," the Clarksville-Montgomery County Museum depends on the work of dedicated volunteers to raise funds crucial to the museum's financial stability. *Courtesy of the Clarksville-Montgomery County Museum.*

to museums which are being more and more touted as crucial to the stability of the institution—fund-raisers and special events. At my museum, we have held an annual dinner/auction for fourteen years and it has developed from a small $7,000 net profit to this year's expected $80,000—a sizeable chunk of money for a small museum. Successful fund-raisers depend on active and dedicated volunteers. But volunteer-run does not mean simple—a large once-a-year blockbuster fund-raiser can be so sophisticated that there is an after-action report in order to improve the success for the future. In Clarksville, volunteers have pulled, pushed, and tweaked the event until it is a machine that operates itself. They know when to begin writing letters and soliciting for auction items, how to determine committees and committee chair people, how to garner the publicity necessary, and how to find locations and caterers, as well a host of other necessary components that make an event like this successful. Again, the key to success is the corps of volunteers and their relationship with the director and the staff. It is imperative that the director develop a relationship not of intimidation but of support for volunteers who wish to develop an event. Consider working with the individuals on a close basis until you become comfortable with their style of operation. Then hand over control of the event. They will appreciate the vote of confidence and thrive on the satisfaction that you entrust them with a key component in the success of the museum's operations. The key is to stay in contact with them but not to interfere unless it is necessary.

Special events are as varied and diverse as the museums in our society. They can include trips abroad, tours of local hot spots, or one-day events at the institution in which the community can participate. Again, just as with fund-raisers, the key is making sure people become involved. And even if these events do not raise large dollars for the institution, they are identifiers for the institution. You'll soon find that patrons enjoy themselves so much that they look forward to particular events each year and expect you to continue them year after year. Of course, the danger is that they may not like it when you change these events or upgrade them in order to draw a more diverse audience. Both special events and annual fund-raisers can offer the museum flexibility in the marketing and promotion of the institution because these events are typically outside of the general day-to-day operation of the institution.

CONCLUSION

Working in a community museum or historical society presents more challenges and headaches than you might expect, but it's worth it. Our profession is one of only a handful where we receive immediate gratification for our endeavors. When an exhibit is installed, the audience, be they children, adults, or otherwise, either love it or hate it. Children many times become awestruck, and in turn, parents become excited. We hear words like "awesome," "I can't believe this is in our community," or "I wish you would do more research about this subject because it's so interesting and I would love to know more." That is what makes the museum profession so addictive, so exciting, and so rewarding.

NOTES

1. For background on establishing and running a small museum, see Gerald George and Cindy Sherrell-Leo, *Starting Right: A Basic Guide to Museum Planning* (Nashville, TN: American Association for State and Local History, 1986), and Barry Lord and Gail Dexter Lord, *Manual of Museum Management* (London: The Stationery Office, 1997).

BARBARA FRANCO is president of the Historical Society of Washington, D.C. She earned a B.A. in history at Bryn Mawr and an M.A. in the Cooperstown Graduate Program. She previously served as assistant director for museums at the Minnesota Historical Society and on the staffs of the Museum of Our National Heritage and the Munson-Williams-Proctor Institute. Her professional activities include service on the boards of the American Association for State and Local History and the National Council on Public History and in various capacities for the Midwest Museums Conference, the Minnesota Association of Museums, and the Organization of American Historians. Ms. Franco has published a number of books and catalogues, including Ideas and Images: Developing Interpretive Exhibits *(1992) and* Folk Roots, New Roots: Folklore in American Life *(1988), as well as numerous articles in* Antiques, History News, *the* Journal of American History, Museum News, Perspectives, *and other publications. She has curated over a dozen exhibits with special interest in nineteenth-century social history and fraternal organizations.*

IN URBAN HISTORY MUSEUMS AND HISTORICAL SOCIETIES

Barbara Franco

Public history in an urban historical society or museum presents particular opportunities and special challenges that are as complex as the urban communities that these institutions represent. Working in urban history institutions often means balancing multiple roles. Urban museums enjoy the advantage of being part of a community at the same time that they are challenged to retain scholarly objectivity to study and interpret a city's past in relation to its present and future. Institutions and their staffs can develop close personal ties to the individuals, families, and neighborhoods who have been the primary players in a city's history, and they may have access to authentic stories and collections that are based in individual experience. But the details of personal and local stories can obscure the larger context for these events.

Cities are often contested spaces in which competing ideas and interests struggle, and the story of most cities cannot be told without addressing substantial conflicts and continuous change. The dynamic nature of cities means that their historical societies must keep current with new issues and developments, while maintaining and preserving continuity through collections and information about earlier periods. Neighborhood and community projects generate energy and enthusiasm, but urban historical societies often find it difficult to respond to multiple requests from diverse constituencies, while attempting to balance limited resources of money and time.

THE FOUNDING OF URBAN
HISTORY INSTITUTIONS

The issues that face public historians in urban institutions have changed over time in response to shifting audiences and issues as well as modifications in how urban history is defined and practiced by historians. What defines a historical society or museum as "urban"? Many major museums are located in cities, and museums of all kinds have been part of the urban landscape since the nineteenth century. For history museums, their urban identity springs from their subject matter as well as their location. Urban history is a fairly recent addition as an area of historical specialization. The development of interest in urban history can be traced in the founding dates and purposes of historical societies during the last two hundred years. The earliest historical societies—Massachusetts Historical Society (1791), New-York Historical Society (1804), and the Historical Society of Pennsylvania (1824)—did not have "city" in their names but nonetheless were urban institutions concerned with collecting the history and accomplishments of local residents as well as national events. The Chicago Historical Society (1856) and the Brooklyn Historical Society (1863) were among the earliest institutions to address the city as their subject and include a city in their name. The Chicago Historical Society and other nineteenth-century urban institutions followed the model of earlier historical societies and collected national history as well as the local history of the city.

Whereas earlier historical societies rarely referenced the city as their specific subject, turn-of-the-century historical societies were more likely to be organized around the idea of the emerging city. The late nineteenth century saw the enormous growth of cities as they became centers of transportation, entertainment, business, and shopping. The Bostonian Society was founded in Boston, Massachusetts, in 1881, and the Valentine Museum was founded in Richmond, Virginia, in 1892. Both institutions defined their purpose and collecting more specifically toward preserving the history of the local residents of their city. The Historical Society of Washington, D.C., was founded in 1894 as the Columbia Historical Society and stated as its mission "the collection, preservation, and diffusion of knowledge respecting the history and topography of the District of Columbia and national history and biography." The subject of the city came first, but national history and biography were not far behind in the interests of founding members.

By the turn of the century, cities had become a valid subject of study for a number of scholarly disciplines and reform movements. The Columbian Exposition held in Chicago in 1893 marked the beginning of a new interest in city planning, the city beautiful movement, and other reform efforts to improve the physical appearance of urban environments. During the Progressive Era (1890–1920), history and social relevance became linked. As history came to be regarded as a tool for uplifting society through public education, historical societies came to be seen

The Historic Annapolis Foundation was a pioneer in preserving the city's architectural heritage through historic districts and preservation projects. A system of historic markers is part of its interpretation efforts. *Courtesy of the Historic Annapolis Foundation.*

The William Paca House and Garden is one of the preservation projects of the Historic Annapolis Foundation. *Courtesy of the Historic Annapolis Foundation.*

as institutions of public education that could further this effort. Many city historical societies were outgrowths of the Progressive Era. The enormous growth of nineteenth-century cities, the impact of immigration, architectural innovations of skyscrapers, new modes of transportation—all created sweeping changes that spurred an interest in preserving the history of cities undergoing rapid change.

By the 1920s, the idea of city and the need to preserve its history was well established and is reflected in the large number of city institutions founded during this period. The Museum of the City of New York (1923) and the Detroit Historical Museum (1926) were part of a new generation of urban museums that grew out of settlement house efforts to educate and Americanize immigrants. In other cases, city museums were a way for the founding families and other elites to preserve their stories in the face of the radical changes that were occurring as the eth-

The Historic Annapolis Foundation also conducts interpretive activities at its historic properties. *Courtesy of the Historic Annapolis Foundation.*

nic identity of cities shifted due to massive immigration. From the 1920s to the 1960s, a "melting pot" concept of cultural history and broad themes of national consensus celebrating technological and industrial progress dominated the historical interpretations found in urban history institutions.

The 1950s saw the beginnings of historical organizations devoted to preserving city architecture threatened by postwar urban renewal. Some earlier historical societies expanded their focus and became involved in the historic preservation movement during this time. New historical organizations were founded around issues of historic preservation in response to endangered historic buildings in neighborhoods threatened by redevelopment. Based on the model of early preservation societies like the Philadelphia Society for the Preservation of Landmarks (1931), the Historic Charleston Foundation (1947), Historic Annapolis (1952), and the Providence Preservation Society (1956) were all founded to preserve and interpret the history of the built environment of cities. New research and scholarship in architectural history and architectural preservation were incorporated into the efforts of these organizations. In their zeal to preserve early and endangered buildings from demolition, these historical organizations concentrated on the history of architecture and the built environment while the history of the more recent social and political environments in the community went unexamined. Issues of city planning and urban sociology remained outside the purview of most historical societies and museums.

The 1980s saw the creation of new programs using urban archaeology collections that resulted from the historic preservation legislation of the 1960s. Alexandria, Virginia, began an extensive archaeology program in 1977 with Alexandria Archaeology, run by the city. The Center for Urban Archaeology at the Baltimore City Life Museums was founded in 1986. Because of the space requirements for archaeology collections, most existing historical societies have not been able to take over the responsibility for these collections, many of which result from state and federal highway projects or other federally funded building projects. Vast collections of urban archaeology exist as important documentation for everyday life in many cities, but without facilities for storage, curation, and interpretation, they remain inaccessible for public viewing or scholarly research.

THE ROLE OF URBAN HISTORIOGRAPHY

The types of institutions that deal with urban history also reflect different periods of urban historiography. The earliest historical societies were based on the athenaeum model of eighteenth-century literary and scientific societies and were unconcerned about collecting broadly among disciplines and across jurisdictions. Their membership consisted of men

A mannequin shows an "Archaeologist at Work" in exhibits at Alexandria Archaeology. *Courtesy of Alexandria Archaeology, Office of Historic Alexandria.*

of the educated and professional class who amassed libraries of books, maps, documents, and pamphlets that served as memorials to other great men and as monuments to a national sense of destiny and progress.

The emergence of new scholarly disciplines in the late 1800s prompted many historical societies to become more specialized scholarly organizations and to include professional academicians as well as amateur scholars. Following the more scientific methodologies of natural history museums, historical societies began more systematic collecting in defined fields of research. Many once-antiquarian historical societies began to professionalize with a paid librarian or scholar on staff and began publishing research in the form of journals and proceedings as their contribution to ongoing scholarship.

The 1960s initiated a period of rapid growth for history museums due to government support and increased awareness of history through public celebration of the Bicentennial of American Independence in 1976. An oversupply of academically trained historians and too few university positions brought an influx of new talent into the museum field in the 1970s. Schooled in the new social history, this generation brought a fresh wave of professionalization to historical societies and museums.

The 1960s were also a time when the historical profession became increasingly specialized. As sharp distinctions developed between academic and public history, historical societies often found themselves juggling conflicting traditions of antiquarians and academics, popular interpretations and new research. Despite increased staff professionalization, city historical societies remained outside the lively discussions taking place among scholars who were developing a new historiography for urban studies.

Urban historians in the 1960s believed that studying the history of cities could contribute to the solution of contemporary problems, and they sought to ally themselves with their colleagues in associated disciplines who were dealing with the problems and issues of city life. Interdisciplinary collaboration and conferences helped define and direct a body of scholarly work that came to be called "the new urban history." The creation of the *Journal of Urban History* in 1974, new university courses on the subject of urban history, and the increased use of historical research in transportation studies and city planning showed the success of these efforts. Architectural historians and preservation organizations have continued to work together effectively as advocates for preserving the historical fabric of city landscapes.

A new historiography of cities, developed since the 1960s, raises questions for public historians currently working in urban historical societies. Some historians now challenge the validity of urban history as a subject of investigation, arguing that metropolitan areas have become regional centers that encompass large suburban and interurban areas beyond city lines. Urban history raises questions about place and its meaning. What makes a city a distinctive place? Is every city's history distinct, or should urban historical societies be engaged in comparative studies of city life? With new waves of immigration, and the importance of new global economies, is urban history truly local, regional, national, or global in nature? People have personal histories that are tied to the geography of a city, but how does one separate the need for individual memory from the responsibility for broader analysis of experiences? How does individual experience fit into and relate to larger issues of urban development and ultimately back to a national narrative? Do cities have a composite identity or are they the sum of individual neighborhoods? Increasingly, many urban institutions are turning their energies to studies of neighborhoods and specific communities within the city.

COLLECTING, PRESERVING, AND INTERPRETING

Defining the work of a public historian in the setting of an urban museum or historical society begins with the mission statement of the particular institution. Mission statements for historical societies of almost every period and all kinds have traditionally outlined a trilogy of collecting, preserving, and interpreting the past for purposes of educating and uplifting public audiences. While these traditional responsibilities continue to shape the work of urban historical societies, new responsibilities have emerged for organizations that document and interpret the unfolding history of cities at the end of the twentieth century.

The work of every museum or historical society begins with its collections, which may combine written and visual sources, ranging from traditional library collections of books and manuscripts to the wide range of three-dimensional artifacts that form museum collections. For many historical societies that collect the full range of historical evidence, this dual function of library and museum remains a source of internal conflict about how collections are to be used for research or for public exhibitions. Methodologies of cataloging and arrangement differ between museums and libraries. Should photographs be treated as a research collection organized for easy access to the information they contain, or are they works of art that need to be cataloged as museum objects? Merging library and museum collections practices has often been problematic for some urban institutions where rivalry for scarce funds can pit one department of the institution against the other. In some communities, these dual functions have been divided among different organizations, with a historical society, library, or archive collecting the written records and another institution collecting the material evidence of the past as a museum of primarily three-dimensional collections. Because the early historical societies began their collecting as athenaeum-style organizations in the nineteenth century, many older institutions began collecting according to library and archival practices. Greater emphasis on public programming and exhibitions in recent years has moved collections management from pure research library practices to include a more comprehensive view of collections as information. New technology and computerization of collections records are making it possible for museum and library collections to become more integrated than ever before.

The subject areas in which urban historical societies collected have also changed over time. The oldest organizations collected historical materials that documented national history and viewed themselves as local outlets for telling the larger national story. The New-York Historical Society and the Chicago Historical Society both collected national history as well as the story of the local city. Before urban history was considered a *bona fide* historical topic, the history of a local city was not thought to be as important as the grand narratives of American history that chronicled colonial and early settlement, the American Revolution, national politics, and the Civil War. Major national events were regarded as the chief components of American history. Materials about prominent local individuals and events were saved for antiquarian and nostalgic reasons or as memorials to successful individuals and their accomplishments. Collections of maps, books, and manuscripts, portraits, and sculpture usually reflected national stories, while historic houses and decorative arts portrayed the local stories of prominent families. Only recently, urban historical societies have begun to redefine their collecting to encompass the subject of the urban experience in a broader way that includes urban history themes of immigration, ethnicity, working-class families, as well as the chronicles of the elite. As urban historical societies now look to cover more diverse topics such as the social institutions that make up city life, their existing collections of furniture and portraits of prominent families are sometimes inadequate to tell the more complex stories of city life. The history of churches, educational institutions, clubs and organizations, and local businesses remained undocumented in the traditional collecting categories of many historical societies. From the late nineteenth century on, city life is more likely to be captured in the more accessible visual record provided by photography and in the proliferation of ephemera and advertising materials that illustrate everyday life in cities.

Issues of collecting also affect the traditional mission of most histor-

ical societies to preserve the past. Does the responsibility of preservation apply only to existing collections that have already been collected
or does it also entail responsibility for preserving the stories of city life
that may have been previously overlooked? While many older historical
societies have large collections that may already be straining existing
storage and exhibit capacity, those collections may now be irrelevant to
new city dwellers and current audiences. The transient nature of city
populations means that the first families of many cities no longer remain in the community as supporters and members. Instead, new populations with their own history now clamor for recognition but may find
little to connect their stories to the collections that currently exist in the
static historical society or museum. A central issue for city museums is
how to continue to preserve existing collections and still find the resources to continue collecting to record the city's history and include
previously neglected stories as well as new stories that reflect changing
populations.

Urban historical societies usually include the interpretation of a city's
history as one of their basic responsibilities, but the nature of that interpretation has changed over time. Urban historiography is still fairly
recent and evolving. For many city institutions prior to the 1960s, the history of the city was only significant as it intersected with national events.
Nineteenth-century urban historical societies adopted a Progressive Era
attitude at the turn of the century, advocating growth, expansion, and
local boosterism. Since the 1960s urban scholarship has stressed themes
of race, class, and the social institutions of civic culture. Many institutions are attempting to meet these new interpretive challenges by creating advisory groups from the community who can serve as community
ambassadors to help collect the historical evidence of specific ethnic
groups that helped shape a city's history, but who may not yet view the
dominant culture historical society as a repository for their past. In many
cities, culturally and racially specific historical societies have emerged as
energetic rivals to the older institutions and are moving forward in preserving and interpreting the individual stories of particular groups
within a city's history.

New narratives of city history have emerged since the founding of those
older organizations that date back to the nineteenth century. Public history has the responsibility for telling a story that has no end. As the chapters of a city's history continue to unfold, public historians working in city
museums are faced with the daunting task of rewriting the early chapters
to fit the constantly changing ending in the latest chapters. Local businesses, for example, have often been neglected in city museum collections
as familiar and unremarkable. But changes in corporate structures in re-

Advertising materials from the Woodward & Lothrop Department Store were donated to the Historical Society's collections when the department store closed in 1995. As businesses close, urban historical societies become the repositories for important local business collections. *Courtesy of the Historical Society of Washington, D.C.*

cent years have meant that local corporations and businesses, once taken for granted as part of a city's landscape, have disappeared along with their historical archives and important records of city life. The departure of local family-owned and operated department stores, once the mainstay of urban downtowns, leave important legacies that need to be documented and preserved. The archives of small family businesses are particularly vulnerable when these enterprises are acquired by larger companies.

The modes and methods of interpretation that historical societies use to present history also continue to change. Many city historical societies and museums began as membership organizations that presented programs for their members. Members were usually likeminded individuals who shared a common socioeconomic background and a common perspective of the past. Today, historical societies and museums may still be membership organizations, but increasingly their work is directed outward to educational programs for schools, public programs and exhibitions, and journals and magazines written for more popular audiences. Interpretation and public programs increasingly reflect a variety of perspectives. Rather than viewing themselves as elite or scholarly experts who take responsibility for telling the community's history, historical societies increasingly see themselves as facilitators who are helping various communities within the city tell their stories.

Passersby stop to study "Remembering U Street," a sidewalk exhibit sponsored by the Historical Society of Washington, D.C., in collaboration with neighborhood organizations to depict the history of the area as a center of African American business, entertainment, and social life from 1900 to 1950. *Courtesy of the Historical Society of Washington, D.C.*

GOVERNANCE AND THE WORKPLACE

The organizational structures and the facilities of urban historical organizations have also changed over the years along with their collections and interpretations. Most urban historical societies are private institutions that may or may not receive municipal funding. A quick survey of city historical societies reveals that few urban history institutions were founded as agencies of local government and only a small number currently exist within municipal departments. The Atwater Kent Museum in Philadelphia is unusual as one of the few historical societies founded as a city institution in 1939. With cutbacks in municipal budgets, its public funding is being withdrawn. The most typical arrangement is some combination of public and private partnership. A number of urban historical societies and museums remain private nonprofit institutions, but receive a portion of their operating funds from municipal support, often through park authorities because of the location of their facility within public park lands. Many historical societies began as membership organizations that were exclusive because they were limited to people of particular social standing or scholarly status. Membership remains an important function of many historical societies and a major source of financial support, but most institutions actively seek to broaden their membership for financial and programmatic success.

The facilities for urban historical societies present an interesting evolution from institutions that began without permanent homes, to a recent trend toward larger and more public history centers in a number of cities. The Historical Society of Washington, D.C., began as an organization that held meetings in restaurants and clubs before acquiring a physical site in 1956. Other historical societies with more resources built turn-of-the-century beaux arts structures that echoed their athenaeum, clublike identities. As the preservation movement became more active, many historical societies sought space in historic houses or in buildings acquired as part of a preservation project. Most recently, city museums have followed a pattern of building new history centers with expanded gallery space and public areas as a way to broaden their audience and appeal. The Historical Society of Western Pennsylvania, for example, began in 1879, and for many years occupied a classical revival building that served as a meeting space and library for members rather than a facility for broad public visitation. In 1995, the society opened the Senator John Heinz Pittsburgh Regional History Center in a renovated warehouse adjacent to the city's downtown convention center and other attractions. The Atlanta Historical Society opened a new Atlanta History Center in 1993, providing separate facilities for its research library and its expanded museum program. All of this reflects a significant change in focus from libraries and research faculties to history institutions with more public access to popular exhibitions and public programming. Similarly, scholarly journals are being replaced or augmented by more popular magazine publications in many institutions.

As the work of historical societies has changed, so has the workplace. Urban history organizations may be smaller than statewide or national institutions, but they often provide a full array of services comparable to the larger institutions. The work of urban historical societies, depending on the particular mission statement, may combine the roles of library, museum presentations as a historic house or interpretive exhibitions, educational programming for schools and adults, and publications. As small or mid-size organizations, urban historical societies demand staff who can perform multiple functions. It is rare in a city museum setting to have highly specialized jobs. Most staff members are asked to combine a number of skills and duties. As historians, the skills of a generalist come into use more than expertise in a narrow area of scholarly specialization. The work of various staff members often intersects with one another and with volunteers and consultants who help augment the small staffs of most institutions. The staff of a typical historical society might include positions of a librarian, a curator of collections and exhibitions, an editor to manage the publications, and an educational director to manage public programs and school groups. In addition to the program staff to perform traditional responsibilities, historical societies now also require the skills of fund-raising, public relations and marketing, membership coordination, financial and facilities management, volunteer coordination, and store management.

CHANGING AUDIENCES AND ROLES

The external focus of these newer staff positions parallels the changing audiences for urban history institutions. As historical societies have become more professionalized and more focused on broader public participation, the audiences for their services have also changed. The earlier athenaeum-style historical societies served their members and knew what would interest them, and their members knew what to expect. Because of the transient nature of city populations, urban historical societies are challenged to reconnect themselves with a constantly changing local audience. Balancing the needs of older, more established communities within a city with the demands of newer residents can be a challenge. For many urban institutions, their constituents no longer live within the city but now reside in the surrounding suburban communities. Finding ways for suburban residents to reestablish their connection to urban history is a particular challenge for urban institutions. The traditional audience for history museums is older adults, so the aging population suggests that there is a large potential audience for the programs and exhibits that urban historical societies present.

Cities have become major destinations in a growing worldwide industry known as heritage tourism. Historical institutions, working with neighborhood and civic groups, can play an essential role in the economic development of their cities as heritage tourism destinations that provide authentic and educational experiences for a sophisticated audience of travelers who find local heritage an important part of travel.

In response to many of these changes, a number of city historical institutions have made major changes. The Historical Society of Western Pennsylvania, originally named to represent a regional mission, built the new Pittsburgh Regional History Center after an almost ten-year effort to redefine itself as a more diverse institution that is preserving the history of the city's ethnic communities and industries as well as its elite and well-to-do. The Atlanta Historical Society opened its Atlanta History Center in 1993 with "Metropolitan Frontiers: Atlanta, 1835–2000," a permanent ex-

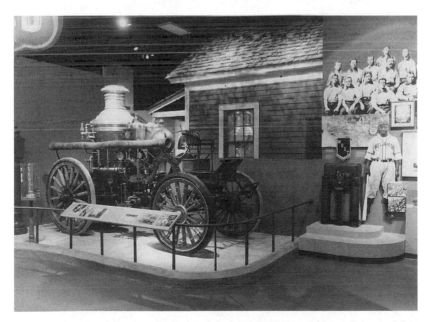

The Atlanta History Center's inaugural exhibit, "Metropolitan Frontiers," included the story of the city's racial diversity. *Courtesy of the Atlanta History Center.*

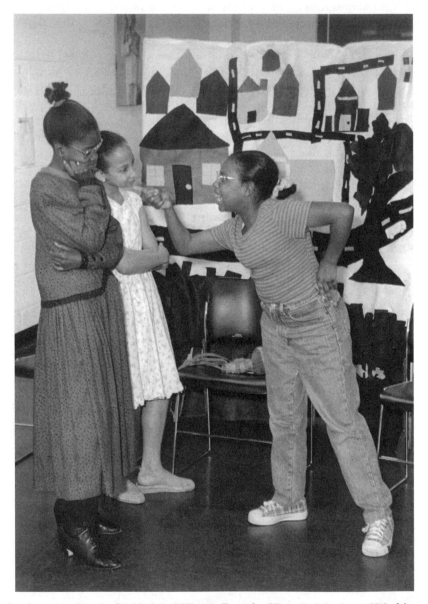

As state coordinator for National History Day, the Historical Society of Washington, D.C., encourages students to use local neighborhood history in their National History Day projects. *Courtesy of the Historical Society of Washington, D.C.*

hibition on the city and changing exhibits dealing with many aspects of the city's past.

Within an environment of shifting historiography and changes in the cities themselves, urban historical societies are being asked to fulfill new responsibilities to their communities. Historical societies are often looked to as stabilizing forces and neutral institutions of civic culture. Historical societies are asked to serve as part of the community at the same time that they must step back from the community as objective commentators about the history and past of the city. Their identity in the community has moved beyond civic boosterism to become advocates and even agents of change.

Increasingly, historical societies are being asked to provide services and to respond to community needs. Historical societies are involved in using history to strengthen community identity. They find themselves involved in social services—working with young people, helping to provide educational opportunities for struggling school systems—and as activists and advocates for the economic survival of their cities. Rather than institutions that stand aloof from the community, historical societies are entering into partnerships with other civic institutions to be more effective. The Historical Society of Washington, D.C., and the Humanities Council of Washington, D.C., are cosponsoring a coalition of local historical and community organizations as the D.C. Heritage Tourism Coalition, in order to use the historic resources of the city to develop heritage tourism as a tool for economic development in the city's neighborhoods.

THE FUTURE

What does the future hold for urban historical societies? Just as historical societies have changed and evolved in the past, the future indicates continued change and adaptation to new issues and challenges. Historical societies are faced with new responsibilities as they seek to adapt to the information age. They must forge a new relationship with the communities that they serve as the role of expert and expertise shifts and people seek access to information in order to find meaning rather than completed historical products. Authenticity of real things and real experiences is an important asset that historical societies bring to their role in educating public audiences. The challenge of determining what to collect for the future that is distinctive about a particular city in an era of mass consumption and mass media will be a significant one. Equally challenging will be finding new ways to relate existing collections to the changing identity of cities and changing audiences.

Every city has a local story and also plays a role in national and international stories. Urban history will probably become more important as urban life becomes the experience of many more people worldwide. More people than ever before are living in urban areas and an ever-increasing number of residents are taking an interest in the tangible history that is around them in old buildings, local institutions, and the layout of the city itself.

While turn-of-the-century societies taught progress and subsequent generations of historical societies have helped educate the public about historic preservation and ethnic and racial diversity, cities are now being studied as places of community. Cities embody stories of people of diverse backgrounds living together in neighborhoods where African Americans, Eastern European Jews, and Anglo Americans coexisted in parallel communities. Urban history also includes conflict and contestation in desegregation efforts, gentrification of neighborhoods, and economic competition between longtime residents and recent immigrants. Community has been the topic of a number of exhibitions at the Chicago Historical Society, the Historical Society of Pennsylvania, and the Brooklyn Historical Society to name a few. These exhibitions and new collecting initiatives examine neighborhood structures and institutions as building blocks of civic culture, and historical societies find themselves playing a role as forums for discussions about social issues. The Lower East Side Tenement Museum, founded in 1988, has a mission to "promote tolerance and historic perspective through the presentation and interpretation of the variety of immigrant and migrant experiences on Manhattan's Lower East Side, a gateway to America." The museum's 1995–96 Annual Report describes the museum's plans to "produce both scholarship and public programming on a wide range of historic issues with the conscious goal of stimulating thoughtful exchange among people of diverse backgrounds on contemporary issues."

Just as memory is essential for individuals to maintain a healthy sense of reality, continuity, and context, history provides a city and its residents with an identity that enables it to withstand and manage the stresses and changes of modern society. Urban historical societies that will succeed in the next century will serve their residents in new ways. The changing nature of cities suggests that urban historical societies must also continue to change.

CHARLES F. BRYAN, JR. is president and CEO of the Virginia Historical Society. A graduate of the Virginia Military Academy, Dr. Bryan holds an M.A. in history from the University of Georgia and a Ph.D. in history from the University of Tennessee. He previously served as executive director of the St. Louis Mercantile Library Association, executive director of the East Tennessee Historical Society, and assistant editor of the Andrew Jackson Papers. He has served as chair of the American Association for State and Local History and on the board at the Smithsonian's National Museum of American History. Dr. Bryan has also taught in the history departments of the University of Missouri-St. Louis and the University of Tennessee and in the public history program at Arizona State University. His publications include Eye of the Storm, a Civil War Odyssey *(2001) and* Images from the Storm *(2002).*

IN STATE HISTORICAL AGENCIES, MUSEUMS, AND SOCIETIES: A CONSTANT STATE OF CHANGE

Charles F. Bryan, Jr.

At a meeting of the American Association for State and Local History in 1954, William E. Rachal, a senior staff member at the Virginia Historical Society (VHS), delivered a paper that reflected the thinking of many American historical societies at that time. In describing its mission and how it allocated its resources, Rachal noted that his institution's main function "was to serve at the top level." He frankly admitted that the Virginia Historical Society did not welcome people other than scholars. Referring to young people who might come into the society, Rachal asserted: "We don't throw them out; we try to be as nice to them as we can, but we are not encouraging them to come down there. We would rather have one university professor stay fifteen days in our library than one junior high school pupil stay fifteen minutes."[1]

FROM HISTORY FOR THE FEW
TO HISTORY FOR THE MANY

Had Rachal discussed his board of trustees or the makeup of his society's membership, he would have described a group of people no less exclusive than the scholars who patronized his library. The board of trustees was all white, all male, and mostly from old Richmond families, some of whom were descendants of members of the original governing body in 1831. Several prided themselves in being referred to as "gentleman scholars." They oversaw a modest endowment that provided majority support for the Society's $75,000 annual operating budget. Federal grants were unheard of. The two secretaries who pounded away on Royal manual typewriters were the only women on the ten-person staff. The custodian was the only African American with any connection to the institution. Membership was by invitation only, and for all practical purposes it was restricted to worthy people whose Virginia lineage was long and respectable. Membership benefits were limited to infrequent lectures and receipt of the quarterly magazine that featured articles mainly on colo-

Museum Gallery circa 1950 at the Lee House, which served as headquarters of the Virginia Historical Society from 1893 to 1959. Like most historical societies and museums, exhibits at the VHS were mainly displays of objects with little or no interpretation. *Courtesy of the Virginia Historical Society.*

nial history and occasional pieces on the Civil War and genealogy.[2]

Headquartered in a nineteenth-century house in downtown Richmond that had been home to Robert E. Lee's family during the Civil War, the Virginia Historical Society was said to more closely resemble the city's elite and stuffy Commonwealth Club than a public institution. Confederate flags hanging in one room served as reminders of the institution's Civil War heritage when the society's board of trustees invested the institution's entire $8,000 endowment in Confederate war bonds. Lack of public signage was not a problem for the barely one thousand people a year who visited the society, the majority of whom came to use the library. As one trustee was reported to have said: "Well, if they don't know where we are in the first place, they really have no business coming in here."[3]

Scholars did know where it was. They came from throughout the United States to mine the rich collection of colonial manuscripts, Civil War papers, and rare books, all of which were housed in overcrowded and unairconditioned stacks and were served up in a small library reading room. Specialists occasionally examined early Virginia silver and textiles that were neatly wrapped in newspapers and rested in stacked cardboard boxes in the basement. Soot-covered portraits by Peale, Sully, and Stuart hung next to always-open windows during the hot, humid Richmond summer days.

Over four decades later, visitors to the Virginia Historical Society encounter a vastly different institution, one that would have been difficult to imagine in 1954. The headquarters building, located four miles west of the downtown, is nearly eight times larger than the old Lee House and has state-of-the-art climate control and security systems. Some 20,000 square feet of gallery space, housing the Museum of Virginia History, is a big draw for the nearly 60,000 people who visit the VHS annually, including thousands of schoolchildren. Many visitors have come to see a bold, new exhibition that looks at Reconstruction very differently from the interpretation that prevailed in Virginia textbooks well into the twentieth century. Scholars using the spacious library reading room are adjusting to using computer terminals rather than card catalogs to gain access to the collections. One researcher had scanned the card catalog from his office in England earlier in the year. It is not at all unusual to see an African American researcher sitting at a table using a laptop computer to help trace her family history.

Historical Society members and the general public alike attend regular programs of lectures, seminars, and gallery talks on a variety of subjects from colonial silver to the civil rights movement in Virginia. Secondary school teachers from throughout Virginia attend frequent workshops or have VHS staff members come to their schools for regular

The grand opening of the "new" Virginia Historical Society in 1992 marked a clear change in direction and mission for the 161-year-old institution. The attendance for the opening day festivities exceeded the annual visitation of a few years before. *Courtesy of the Virginia Historical Society.*

The 1992 addition to the Virginia Historical Society which houses the library, exhibition galleries, and lecture hall. Since its completion, the VHS has added another 40,000-square-foot wing. *Courtesy of the Virginia Historical Society.*

programs. Traveling exhibits, including ones on the civil rights movement and women's history, go from town to town from one end of the state to the other.

While the public face of the Virginia Historical Society provides ample evidence of how much the institution has changed since the 1950s, behind the scenes there are other less visible but no less profound examples of a major transformation. A board of trustees that had long since gone to a rotating system is geographically, gender, and racially diverse. Several of the state's key corporate executives sit on the board. The seventy-person staff has women heading two of the society's largest departments, one of which is development and public relations. An African American woman is head of another department. The institution's sophisticated conservation laboratory is staffed by women. Every department and most offices have fully networked computer terminals that store, handle, and transfer amounts of information that were the stuff of science fiction in the 1950s. The director oversees a $3 million annual budget that is supported in large part by the Society's $25 million endowment but also by a sizable state appropriation and significant earned income, including a bustling museum shop.

The physical and programmatic manifestations of change at the Virginia Historical Society have been profound, but issues relating to management have been transformed no less so. In the 1950s, the director, a scholar of Virginia history and a librarian, spent a good part of his workweek cataloging rare books. He often worked in the library reading room, assisting scholars with their research. His fund-raising responsibilities were limited mainly to occasionally asking a wealthy patron to assist in the purchase of a rare book or manuscript collection. Institutional management was not terribly complicated. It resembled that of a college academic department where long-range planning, complex financial decisions, and staff policy issues simply were not major considerations. Like his colleagues in academe, the director spent most of his time within the confines of his place of work. With the institution having a low community profile, there was little demand for the director to spend time developing a network beyond the historical society's small circle of friends and supporters.[4]

In the 1990s, the director of the Virginia Historical Society holds a Ph.D. in history, but unlike his predecessor forty years earlier, he can devote very little of his working hours to scholarship and curatorial duties. Rather than practicing the craft of history, he now practices the crafts of fund-raising, budget management, lobbying, public relations, and personnel supervision. He has put together a "senior management team" to help him carry out his duties. No longer does running a state historical society resemble an academic department. In its stead is an organization more closely resembling a small business. The upgrading of professional standards, the development of regular educational programs and exhibits, and the corresponding increase in public visibility have come at a price, requiring skillful management practices and regular infusions of money in sums unheard of in the 1950s. In the 1990s alone, the Virginia Historical Society has raised nearly $40 million for capital and programmatic expansions.[5]

Long gone are the days when the only public to be satisfied were white, male scholars and members from upper crust Richmond. Located in a city with a majority black population and mostly African American elected officials, the Historical Society now deals with a variety of issues, from exhibit content to lobbying city hall, that were virtually nonexistent when Jim Crow was alive and well.

WINDS OF CHANGE

The significant institutional transformation of the Virginia Historical Society is a story that can be repeated in one form or another at virtually every other state historical society in America. While varying in degree from institution to institution, our state museums and societies, which are the oldest historical institutions in the country, have experienced more change in the 1980s and 1990s than all of their previous histories combined. The mission and institutional culture of the Virginia Historical Society, for example, remained virtually the same during its first one-hundred and fifty years. Yet in the 1980s, the South's oldest historical society began to redefine itself. Like most other historical institutions in the country, it moved from an elitist philosophy to a more democratic one in which the doors have swung open to a much wider audience. Indeed, with the emphasis on educational outreach, traveling exhibits, and electronic access, historical societies now carry their messages directly to the people.[6]

State historical agencies are a diverse group of institutions. While they each have the collection and interpretation of their respective state's history as central to their mission, they go about it differently. They vary in size, in the ways they are funded and governed, and in the functions they perform. On one end of the spectrum are the dozen or so large central agencies such as the State Historical Society of Wisconsin and the Minnesota Historical Society. Almost fully funded by public dollars and staffed in some cases by hundreds of employees, each serves as the state historical library and archives, the state history museum, the state historic preservation office, the overseer of numerous historic sites, and the providers of extensive field service programs. On the other end of the spectrum are small, private institutions like the Tennessee and South Carolina historical societies, which receive little public funding, have small but rich collections, and are often overshadowed by larger, publicly funded history museums, libraries and archives, and historic preservation offices that operate as separate state agencies. The small to medium size, private historical society coexisting with separate state agencies model predominates on the East coast, while the large centralized public institutions are the prototype for the Midwest. In between, however, are many exceptions. Scores of other state historical institutions differ in size, funding, governance, and function. The staff, budget, and collections of the private Virginia Historical Society, for example, exceed those of several publicly funded historical agencies in other states. Regardless of their size and type, however, all state historical institutions have experienced a shift in paradigm that has greatly affected the way they operate and fulfill their missions.

Ironically, while historical agencies preserve and interpret the past, they are profoundly affected by the present. As a result, they have changed significantly in the last few decades. Why? Four major factors have been the chief determinants: fundamental changes in the nature of

American society, the infusion of large sums of money for capital projects and public programs sparked by the American Revolutionary Bicentennial, the shift from curatorial/collections based missions to education based missions, and finally the rise of professional standards and business practices. Each factor is worth examining on its own merit.

HISTORICAL SOCIETIES IN A
RAPIDLY CHANGING SOCIETY

Until the mid-twentieth century, the majority of American society was segregated by gender, race, ethnic background, and even class. With rare exception, state historical societies, both privately and publicly supported, tended to concentrate their collections and interpretation on a history that was viewed as having been shaped mostly by white males who were "movers and shakers." The voices from the past of women, African Americans, Native Americans, or newly arrived ethnic groups remained, to a large extent, unheard, whether in the museum galleries of historical societies or in the textbooks used in schools. State history museums in the East, for example, built their collections around the decorative arts and portraits of prominent merchant families. Historical institutions in the South concentrated on the colonial planter elite and often the icons of the "Lost Cause." Western historical societies collected the materials of the state's pioneers and founding fathers, along with large quantities of Native American artifacts, often acquired under questionable circumstances by today's standards.

As the civil rights and women's movements and the rise of a vast middle class in the last decades of the century dramatically changed American society, academic historians embraced a "new social history" by looking at the past "from the bottom up." By the late 1960s many scholars had lost interest in elites and shifted their attention to the lives of those they had ignored. A decade or so later, state historical societies and museums followed suit. In part they drew their inspiration from the academic world. But they also responded to the fact that more members of minority groups and women were serving as elected officials and on institutional boards, thus controlling purse strings and setting policy. More women and some racial and ethnic minorities began working in historical institutions in professional positions and in management jobs. Historical institutions started publishing articles, mounting exhibits, and producing programs in which elites were not necessarily treated with reverence. They shifted from a concern with governors, presidents, generals, and "captains of industry," to a focus on the "common folk" and their unpretentious but important activities. In 1992, the staid Maryland Historical Society (MHS), long noted for only exhibiting the decorative arts, allowed an outside curator, contemporary artist Fred Wilson, to mount "Mining the Museum," a highly controversial exhibit that showed the many elements of Maryland history the MHS had ignored in the past. When the South Dakota State Historical Society opened its new Native American gallery in 1994, funded by actor Kevin Costner, the museum interpreted the story of the Sioux Indians in a way that would not have been considered in decades past.[7]

Collections policies even began to reflect this shift in emphasis. State historical agencies now pay more attention to collecting the materials of the non-elites. Southern institutions, for example, scramble for their state's African American collections, particularly items relating to slavery. Closely following the laws of supply and demand, African American materials often command higher prices on the dealer's market than those that had belonged to white elites. Ephemera from immigrant groups, the minutes of early women's clubs, and records of labor unions are considered important additions to collections now, often resulting in front-page articles in institutional newsletters.

Institutional collecting has not been without controversy, however, especially as it relates to whose history is being "saved" and interpreted. State historical societies, which have long run into competition from local historical societies for collections, have occasionally found themselves coming up against newly formed black history museums and ethnic cultural centers that resented the perceived hegemony of the big institution in the state capital.

No better example of this can be found than the controversy leading up to the passage of the Native American Grave Protection and Repatriation Act (NAGPRA) in 1990. Indian tribes had long questioned the right of museums, including many state historical societies, to claim title to the artifacts, and in some cases the human remains, of their ancestors. Native American groups argued with considerable force that most of these artifacts, many of which are sacred religious objects, were acquired under highly questionable circumstances, including the robbing of burial grounds. Despite the protests of many museum professionals that these objects were being preserved in a museum environment better than they would be elsewhere, Congress enacted NAGPRA. Since then, state historical societies and other museums, mostly from the Midwest, Plains, and Western states have returned tens of thousands of objects to their respective tribes. While the issue of returning human remains was never seriously debated, many museum professionals question the return of the objects, arguing that they can no longer be studied by scholars, viewed by the public, and run the risk of being lost forever because of lack of care and conservation. Nevertheless, the issues surrounding NAGPRA demonstrated that, with fundamental changes in society beginning in the 1960s, historical agencies had to become more sensitive than ever to people whose history had been ignored or neglected in the past. The ground rules of collecting and interpreting the past had changed fundamentally.[8]

THE BICENTENNIAL SPIRIT

In the early 1980s, Alan Rogers, professor of history at the University of Nottingham and a specialist in British local history, visited the newly opened Tennessee State Museum in Nashville. He later admitted that he was stunned by the vastness of its galleries. The sophistication of the exhibits exceeded anything he had seen in his native England. What surprised Rogers most was the reality that this multimillion dollar edifice had been constructed in Tennessee of all places. Had he traveled to some other states, he would have been no less impressed. Beginning in the late 1970s and lasting well into the 1990s, the country's state historical institutions experienced an amazing growth spurt that has totaled more than a billion and a half dollars in construction projects alone.

There is little doubt as to the origin of this phenomenon—the American Revolution Bicentennial in 1976, following on the heels of the publication of Alex Haley's *Roots* a year earlier. The American people, jaded by a lost war in Vietnam and left cynical in the aftermath of Watergate, turned to their past for inspiration and celebration. Haley's best-selling saga of several generations of his family lineage, followed by a top-rated television "docudrama" based on the book, inspired many Americans to examine their own roots. And from remote rural counties to major metropolitan centers, Americans celebrated a grand two-hundredth birthday party by participating in a host of activities from patriotic parades to concerts to historic reenactments. People of all ages, colors, ethnic backgrounds, and geographic corners of the country became participants in the process. History, once the province of the classroom and musty old museums, had gone public in a big way.[10]

Local and state historical societies played a key role in planning the Bicentennial. Every state and virtually every county in the country had its own Bicentennial committee composed of business people, "civic volunteers," educators, political appointees and elected officials, and, in most instances, historians and museum professionals. The bringing together of these people had a profound effect on historical institutions for years to come, particularly in seeing that large sums of money were poured into heritage related projects. Through the American Revolution Bicentennial Commission, Congress distributed millions of dollars to the states to support projects of all kinds. It is no coincidence that the number of museums in America has nearly doubled since 1976. Many a county history museum can trace its origins to the impetus, including funding, created during the Bicentennial celebration.[11]

Bicentennial momentum had an effect on the state level as well. Tennessee serves as a good example of how the "spirit of '76" led to the construction of the large state history museum that Professor Rogers visited in the early 1980s. Although citizens of the Volunteer State had long prided themselves on their history, only a relatively small amount of public money was ever appropriated to historical institutions. The largest historical attraction in the state was the privately owned and operated Hermitage, the home of Andrew Jackson. In the early 1970s, a small historical commission served as the state historic preservation office. An underfunded state library and archives occupied an overcrowded building in downtown Nashville. The Tennessee State Museum, created in 1937, quietly existed in the basement of Nashville's old War Memorial Building. The small staff, few of whom were professionals, served as little more than caretakers of exhibits on the Civil War and World War I that had changed little since their installation more than three decades earlier.[12]

In the early 1970s, however, key members of the Tennessee General Assembly and civic leaders in Nashville began to argue for a greatly expanded state history museum, asserting that the people of Tennessee deserved such an institution and that it would become a major draw for tourism in an economically troubled downtown Nashville. Using the growing momentum of the Bicentennial to help support their arguments, museum backers secured in 1971 a $15 million appropriation to place a new state museum in the proposed James K. Polk building, a massive structure in downtown Nashville designed to house state offices and a performing arts center. For the next several years, large sums of money flowed into the state museum project from the General Assembly on an unprecedented scale for any previous historical project. The new museum director, Ellsworth Brown, was given a hefty budget to hire a large professional staff, buy collections, and design and build nearly 60,000 square feet of exhibits. One former curator recalled those heady days when money seemed to be no object. He traveled from one end of the state to the other buying early paintings, silver, firearms, uniforms, quilts, and even an entire grist mill to fill the vast new galleries. Five years after the Bicentennial celebration, phase one of the museum opened with great fanfare and well-grounded boasts that Tennessee's history museum could stand up to almost any other in size and quality.[13]

As if citizen pride were at stake, several other states in every region of the country jumped on the bandwagon to build large history museums or history centers in the two decades following the Bicentennial. South Carolina cited the Tennessee example to develop its even bigger state museum in Columbia. West of the Mississippi River, the Kansas State Historical Society led the way in the early 1980s with a large multiphased history center on the outskirts of Topeka. Moving spirits in several other states managed to persuade their legislatures to appropriate generous sums of money for history centers that would have been unthinkable a generation earlier. Perhaps the most stunning example was the opening of the massive Minnesota History Center in 1992. A 450,000 square foot complex housing a museum, research library and archives, two shops, a dining facility, classrooms, and generous amounts of collections storage space, the price tag for the project was $70 million, 80 percent of which came from state funds.

The pace of building projects began to slow down in the 1990s, but, as of this writing, the state-funded Kentucky Historical Society is halfway through the construction of a large history center in downtown Frankfort. Georgia, now one of only seven states not to have a state history museum, is planning a new state history center by the turn of the century. And using only private funds, the Virginia Historical Society has nearly tripled the size of its building since the early 1990s, greatly expanding its museum galleries space, library, meeting space, and collections storage. With greatly expanded facilities, state agencies now need programs and services to fill their spaces and to bring in revenue.

THE RISE OF THE "PARALLEL SCHOOL"

In the late 1980s, the controversial chairman of the National Endowment for the Humanities, Lynne V. Cheney, used her bully pulpit to proclaim the virtues of America's museums, historical societies, and libraries. To her, such institutions are "parallel schools." Citing the inadequacies of American schools, she argued forcefully that cultural institutions play a vital role in filling the educational gap that exists in the country.

Although Cheney was never fully embraced by the historical and museum communities because of her staunchly conservative political views, the NEH chairman had struck a responsive chord with her "parallel school" argument. Indeed, just as the country experienced the building of large new state history centers, historical institutions of all kinds began a major shift in philosophy and mission.

Until the late 1970s, most historical institutions revolved around their archive and publication departments, staffed by scholars, many of whom held Ph.D.s. Any educational programs that were offered came from these departments. But with the spirit of the Bicentennial still holding forth long after 1976, historical institutions began developing education departments independent of curatorial offices in response to public demand and, maybe just as important, the availability of large sums of grant money that required broad-based public participation. Most institutions assumed, for one reason or another, that the archivist/curator/scholar was incapable of or unwilling to serve a broad general audience, and that the institution's message had to be communicated by a corps of "educators," many of whom were not trained as scholars.[14]

The growth of the educational function has been greeted with approval by the public and by those who run and govern historical institutions. Indeed, the president of the Virginia Historical Society in the mid-1990s, a retired Fortune 500 corporate executive, contended, with the full endorsement of his fellow trustees, that education was the institution's primary function. A decade earlier, the Society's president had argued that scholarship was the institution's sole purpose and that it should not deviate from that path.

Embracing education as central to mission has had a dramatic effect on state historical institutions. Along with the major building expansion efforts, educational programs have led to significant increases in visitation and public visibility. While state historical societies and museums may complain about "flat" visitation figures in the 1990s, with rare exception their numbers are far higher than a decade or two earlier. The Virginia Historical Society, for example, went from a little more than 5,000 visitors in 1987 to more than twelve times that number ten years later. With the opening of its new history center, the Minnesota Historical Society's annual visitation soared from less than 100,000 to more than 400,000. Without the expanded building and public programs that occurred at these institutions, visitation probably would not be significantly higher today than it was a decade ago.

Expanded educational programs could not happen without large sums of money. Publicly funded institutions effectively used the education trump card to persuade governors and legislators to support a host of new "public outreach" programs and services. For private institutions, the National Endowment for the Humanities, state humanities councils, the Institute of Museum Services, and other public funding sources made available millions of dollars for exhibits, conferences, workshops, and even endowment and operating support for institutions that clearly demonstrated widespread public outreach. And in the 1980s, many corporate and private foundations, directors of which had listened to a steady drumbeat of news about the problems of American schools, shifted much of their giving emphasis to education. In response to the availability of this largesse, cultural organizations of all kinds, including historical agencies, increasingly described themselves as educational institutions.

The move to an education based mission, ironically, has led usually to increased administrative staffs, particularly those handling public relations and fund-raising. While curatorial departments have tended to remain about the same in size, other more public and administrative divisions have grown. In the early 1990s, one large historical institution revised its organizational chart to show the curatorial staff under one of five boxes marked "Historical Resources," along with "External Affairs," "Public Services," "Capital Programs," and "Administrative and Automation Services."[15]

FROM AN ACADEMIC MODEL
TO A BUSINESS MODEL

When business consultant Ben Helms arrived at the Virginia Historical Society in 1993 to help the staff and board develop a new long-range plan, he was struck by the complexity of the organization. He later admitted that when he first took the assignment, he had mental images of a building, a few staff people, and a collection of objects. "What I had discovered instead," he noted, "was an intricate operation that required all of the management skills of any business client I had ever served." He went on to observe that the complexity of the operation was exacerbated by the variety of its "customers" who had their own unique demands— museum visitors, library researchers, schoolchildren, shop customers, volunteers, trustees, financial supporters, and donors of collections.[16]

With the increase in the size and scope of historical agencies in the last two decades, not only do historical agencies have larger staffs and buildings, but the requirements for increased professionalism and business acumen have also risen accordingly. The resources required to maintain programs and capital outlays have increased at a corresponding rate. And for the most part, the financial agencies responsible for giving funds have insisted that historical agencies be well-run operations. To qualify for National Endowment for the Humanities grants, a requesting institution must demonstrate that its personnel are professionally qualified, that the program is based on solid humanities scholarship, and that the organization is fully accountable financially. With the implementation of general operating support grants in 1978, the Institute of Museum Services required successful applicants to demonstrate institutional excellence in all aspects of their operation, from care of collections to governance. By raising the bar, NEH, IMS, and other granting agencies had an enormous effect on increasing the professional standards of historical institutions around the country. Although varying in degree from one state to another, state governments require all of their agencies to uphold high professional standards and to run financially responsible institutions. And whether a private or public institution, adherence to labor law, liability issues, changes in the tax code, or environmental law are often as important issues as collections policies or questions of interpretation.

The results of raising the bar are significant. Across the country, collections at historical agencies are stronger than they were in the past, new scholarly resources have been acquired, sophisticated conservation measures have been adopted, and collections are better housed. And in the last several years, most state agencies have taken advantage of the new electronic technologies, improving bibliographic tools and enhancing public access. These institutions also have taken on broader educational responsibilities. The cost has not been small. Indeed, it has been enormous. In the words of a management study of nonprofit institutions commissioned by the Andrew W. Mellon Foundation, many nonprofit institutions have evolved from "income spenders to fund seekers."[17]

Staring at such large expenditures of funds, historical agency directors today are forced to devote a good deal of their time to finding the resources to keep budgets balanced. The director of yesterday usually did not have this concern on a day-to-day basis. Small staffs were paid small salaries, and modest budgets were met by membership subscriptions, sale of publications, and often the generous unsolicited gift of a trustee or two. Many large historical societies had endowments that enabled them to balance the relatively modest budgets of the time. Public agencies spent what little they were appropriated by the state legislature. "Money was always a problem, but the pressure to raise money year after year simply was not there," recalled Ed Alexander, who retired from a long and distinguished career in the historical agency field in the 1970s.[18]

Today, boards and professional staff are concerned with balancing their budgets by raising sums of money that would have been unthinkable in the past. It is not an easy job, mainly because there are so many organizations doing it. The proliferation of museums and historical societies, not to mention a host of nonprofit social service and health organizations, has meant that the relatively small pie of funds available for historical agencies is being sliced more thinly. While many publicly supported state agencies experienced significant increases in their budgets in the 1970s and 1980s, most have been forced to take deep cuts in recent years. As a result, many have created their own private foundations charged with raising money to sustain programs and services. They now stand in line for grants from corporations and foundations, just like their colleagues from private institutions.

Build up your membership base. Sell relevant and popular books, objects, and other materials in your museum shop. Project a much more visible and public image to the public. Establish good relations with the local press. Raise money. Do fun and exciting things. Shed the dull and boring image. Hire or train staff members in the skills of marketing. Mount a blockbuster exhibit. Create an attractive and responsive Web page. All are concerns that have become as important to any director as collections management, conservation, effective historical interpretation, or research and publications. Almost without exception, every state historical institution in the country, whether private or public, has had to adapt to the new way of doing business and fulfilling its mission.[19]

As a result, directors of these institutions must be qualified and willing to spend much of their working day performing the tasks of virtually running a business, developing strategies for increasing revenue and holding down expenditures. Employment ads for historical agency directors in professional journals inevitably list extensive fund-raising experience and "management skills" as essential qualifications for the job. Rare is the ad that asks for "solid record of scholarship." At the same time, the strongest boards of trustees often are judged now by the number of corporate executives and community leaders they have, rather than by the number of scholars who serve. At times, board meetings can revolve more around business and fund-raising issues than curatorial matters. Unfortunately, the complexities of institutional management in the 1990s have forced the collecting, preservation, and interpretation of history to share equal, and sometimes less than equal, billing with business and financial concerns. As one veteran state historical society director was heard to lament recently: "If it weren't for budget and personnel, this would be a fun job."[20]

WHERE DO WE GO FROM HERE?

At the close of the twentieth century, state historical agencies continue to experience the forces of change that were set in motion in the 1960s and 1970s. Increased public access has led to increased public expectations and, not surprisingly, sometimes to controversy. Exhibits, which in the past were more object based than interpretive, have begun to discuss alternative historical interpretations of often sensitive topics. "America's Reconstruction," an NEH-funded exhibition, caused one visitor to accuse the Virginia Historical Society of "bigotry toward southerners." There was no little irony that this revisionist interpretation of a controversial topic was first exhibited in a building originally built as a memorial to the fallen heroes of the Confederacy. For the most part, however, state historical agencies have shied away from controversial topics, no doubt because of funding from both private and public sources.[21]

Far more important an issue in the 1990s is technology. While state historical institutions devoted huge resources and time to major building projects and the expansion of educational programs in the 1970s and 1980s, the new cause célèbre is information technology. Millions of dollars are being raised and spent so that historical agencies can fully automate their collections, digitize their graphic images, install interactive computer programs in exhibits, and develop sophisticated Web sites. While "curator of education" became the newly created position in the 1970s, "data manager" and computer programmer are now the hot jobs. The full effects of entering the information superhighway are only beginning to be understood, with historical agency staff debating the consequences of virtual exhibits and virtual visits to the library.[22]

The pressures to embrace technology and to pay for it are enormous, but they are not replacing old pressures and the other demands being placed on state historical societies. Many an institution that spent millions of dollars to build museum galleries and introduce educational programs in the 1970s is looking at a host of deferred curatorial issues such as overcrowded collections storage areas, uncatalogued manuscript collections, and thousands of objects in dire need of conservation. Some institutions that served as models for innovative educational programs and exhibitions must now figure out how to raise large sums of money to replace a roof or install a new climate control system.

The job will not be easy. As of this writing, many state historical institutions reflect the retrenchment characteristics that have trickled down from Washington. The once relatively flush humanities and arts endowments have seen their budgets slashed drastically since the early 1990s. Many state legislatures that earlier poured millions of dollars into history projects now are very parsimonious in their appropriations for history. Cutbacks in staff and programs often have been severe.

The South Dakota State Historical Society, for example, opened its new history center in Pierre in 1994. Yet within two years, its state funds were cut severely, forcing the layoff of several staff members and a reduction in services. At one point the governor threatened to shut down the museum if private monies could not be raised to support the institution. Despite opening with a flourish in 1981, the Tennessee State Museum saw its funding cut in the late 1980s to such an extent that the final phase of its permanent exhibit was never installed.

In 1995, the Wyoming State Historical Society, a small state agency since its inception in the 1940s, was removed from the state government altogether and forced to fend for itself on private funds. The private New-

York Historical Society found itself in such dire economic circumstances that it began to sell off parts of its collection and radically reconstitute its programs, including turning administration of its research library over to New York University. The private Historical Society of Pennsylvania in Philadelphia launched major educational initiatives and an ambitious museum program in the 1980s. Yet within the next decade, it eliminated its education department, shut down its museum, and announced its intentions to focus its mission on becoming a special collections library only.[23]

Ironically, while many institutions are struggling to adequately fulfill their missions, the whole question of state history has come under scrutiny by those who practice and administer it. An entire session at the 1997 annual meeting of the American Association for State and Local History (AASLH), for example, was devoted to the subject of "State History: Does it Matter?" One speaker argued that the increased emphasis on the new social history and its examination of everyday life had reduced states "to mere collections of local places" and "arbitrary constructs whose only meaningful history is political." Another raised the question "Can state history help us understand how diverse interests can be reconciled, or is it simply outmoded?" He went on to argue that state boundaries are in reality artificial and that state identities have been greatly weakened by large numbers of "new" people moving into them.[24]

That the subject of the legitimacy of state history would be questioned at an AASLH meeting further demonstrates just how much the profession and the world in which it operates have changed since the founding of the Association in 1940. The session elicited a lively discussion among panel and audience, but in the end the majority in the room came down strongly on the side of state history's validity. Sandra Clark, director of the Michigan Historical Center, observed that, even though the new social history may have changed the paradigm of studying the past, "history is still about finding common links and bonds." With the shift in the balance of power away from the federal government in the 1990s, she noted that "states are where the important decisions that affect us all are being made." Therefore, state history cannot be ignored. A member of the audience argued that although state history may be harder to do than when it was little more than an accounting of the political, economic, and military highlights of the past, state histories provide excellent case studies for understanding the richness and complexity of the American experience, both past and present.[25]

Indeed, today, as a group, our state historical societies and museums are better armed than ever to inform Americans of their past. They have gone from serving the few to reaching the many. They have embraced education as central to their missions. They have invested more than a billion dollars in building facilities to carry out their missions. And more often than not, they set the standards for professionalism and scholarship for other historical institutions in their states to follow.

Their role in American society is essential, especially today. Historian David McCullough has observed that we live in an era of momentous change, of major transitions in every aspect of life that create great pressures and tensions. "But history shows that times of change are the times when we are most likely to learn," he argues. Our nation and its states were founded on change. "We should embrace the possibilities of these exciting times and hold to a steady course," he notes, "because we have a sense of navigation, a sense of what we've been through in times past and who we are." As America prepares to enter the twenty-first century, its state historical societies and museums are better prepared than ever to navigate people through a "sense of times past."[26]

NOTES

1. Walter Muir Whitehill, *Independent Historical Societies* (Boston: Boston Athenaeum, 1962), 147–48.
2. Oral interview with Howson W. Cole, June 11, 1997. Mr. Cole joined the staff of the Virginia Historical Society in 1953.
3. Virginius C. Hall, "The Virginia Historical Society, An Anniversary Narrative of its First Century and a Half," *Virginia Magazine of History and Biography* 90 (January 1982): 67–88; oral interview with Stuart G. Christian, Jr., May 3, 1997. Mr. Christian served as a trustee of the Virginia Historical Society for more than a decade, including one term as president.
4. Cole interview.
5. Charles F. Bryan, Jr., "Creating a Center For Virginia History: The Virginia Historical Society and the Fifth Century Campaign," *History News* 47 (January/February 1992): 16–19.
6. Wilcomb E. Washburn, "Education and the New Elite: American Museums in the 1980s and 1990s," *Museum News* 75 (March/April 1996): 60–61.
7. Michael Kammen, *Mystic Chords of Memory: The Transformation of Tradition in American Culture* (New York: Knopf, 1991), 572; Washburn, "Education" *Museum News*, 62.
8. Raymond H. Thompson, "Dealing with the Past, and Looking to the Future: Museums and Native Americans," *Museum News* 70 (January/February 1991):36–40; Candace Floyd, "The Repatriation Blues: Museum Professionals and Native Americans Wrestle with Questions of Ownership and Disposition of Tribal Materials," *History News* 40 (April 1985): 6–12.
9. Gerald George, "Alan Rogers and English Local History," *History News* 37 (January 1982): 26–27.
10. Kammen, *Mystic Chords*, 618–54.

11. Ibid., 636–38.
12. Interview with Dr. James C. Kelly, July 18, 1997. Dr. Kelly served as executive director of the Tennessee American Revolution Bicentennial Commission, 1974–77, and as chief of research, 1977–80 and then chief curator, 1980–89, at the Tennessee State Museum. He serves as assistant director for museum programs at the Virginia Historical Society.
13. Ibid.
14. Washburn, "Education," *Museum News,* 61.
15. Ibid.
16. Ben Helms, "The Consultant's Perspective [on long-range planning]," *History News* 49 (July/August 1994): 17.
17. Jed Bergman, *Managing Change in the Nonprofit Sector* (San Francisco: Jossey-Bass, 1996), 203.
18. Charles F. Bryan, Jr., "Marketing History: How Far Have We Come, How Far Do We Go?" *History News* 44 (July/August 1989): 13.
19. Ibid., 13. One major exception has been the country's oldest historical institution, the Massachusetts Historical Society, which has steadfastly limited itself to scholars and maintained a low public profile.
20. Interview with Dr. Mark V. Wetherington, director, Filson Club Historical Society, Louisville, Kentucky, April 24, 1997; interview with Ann Toplovich, executive director, Tennessee Historical Society, April 24, 1997; interview with Dr. James Klotter, director, Kentucky Historical Society, April 27, 1997.
21. Barbara Franco, "The History Museum Curator of the 21st Century," *History News* 51 (Summer 1996): 6–10.
22. Robert Cheatham, "Cultural Organizations and the 21st Century Computer Age," *History News* 51 (Summer 1996): 17–21.
23. Kevin M. Guthrie, *The New-York Historical Society: Lessons From One Nonprofit's Long Struggle for Survival* (San Francisco: Jossey-Bass, 1996), xv-xvii; Gary B. Nash, "Eviscerating a National Treasure," *Perspectives* (October 1997): 29–30; Susan Stitt, "The [Historical Society of Pennsylvania's] Viewpoint," ibid.
24. Notes taken at session entitled "State History: Does it Matter?" at annual meeting of the American Association for State and Local History, Denver, Colorado, October 4, 1997.
25. Ibid.
26. David McCullough, *Why History?* (New York: Simon and Schuster, 1995), 18–19.

LONNIE G. BUNCH III is president of the Chicago Historical Society. He holds both a B.A. and an M.A. in history from American University and has done doctoral work in Afro-American and U.S. history there as well. Prior to his current position, he was associate director for curatorial affairs at the National Museum of American History, Smithsonian Institution, and curator of history/program manager at the California Afro-American Museum. Mr. Bunch taught as an adjunct professor of museum studies at George Washington University, the University of Massachusetts-Dartmouth, and American University. He has served on the council of the American Association for State and Local History (AASLH), the board of the American Association of Museums, the executive board of the Museum Management Institute, and the editorial boards of The Public Historian, The Magazine of California History, *and the* Journal of California History. *He frequently appears on the programs of such national organizations as the American Association of Museums, AASLH, and the Organization of American Historians and of regional, state, and local organizations across the country. His publications include* The American Presidency: A Glorious Burden *(2000),* Visions Toward Tomorrow: The Afro-American Community in East Bay *(1989),* Black Angelenos: The Afro-American in Los Angeles, 1850–1950 *(1988), and numerous exhibition catalogues; articles in* History News, Museum News, *and* The Public Historian; *and essays in volumes such as* Exhibiting Controversy *(1996), and* Black California: Recent Scholarship *(1997). He has curated over a dozen exhibits, including "The Smithsonian's America" (1994).*

IN MUSEUMS AT THE NATIONAL LEVEL: FIGHTING THE GOOD FIGHT

Lonnie G. Bunch III

Working in a national museum poses unique challenges to public historians.[1] While the National Museum of American History (NMAH) is perhaps the most well-known museum with a national focus, other public and private cultural institutions such as the U.S. Holocaust Memorial Museum, the Hagley Museum and Library, and the Henry Ford Museum and Greenfield Village also have agendas that transcend local, state, or regional experiences. Such institutions play critical roles in preserving and interpreting the shared intellectual and cultural life of the nation. But with that responsibility comes public scrutiny, and in the 1990s such museums have too often found themselves the focus of unfavorable public attention and media coverage, the subject of governmental review and funding uncertainties, and the lightning rod in a politically charged inquiry into the role of museums in American society.

In the 1980s and early 1990s, a standard topic of conversation at any gathering of museum professionals was the lament that we wished the public would "pay more attention" to the exhibitions, collections, programs, and publications of our institutions. After all, museums had recognized the importance of education and outreach, embraced new technologies, explored a myriad of exhibition topics, and experimented with a multiplicity of presentation modes, all geared to garner attention, visitors, and support. We now know, however, that our grandmothers were correct when they warned us to "be careful what you wish for." The cultural wars and the debates over school curricula and history textbooks have expanded and shifted from the academy to the mu-

The exhibit "Sitting for Justice: The Greensboro Sit-In of 1960" opened at the National Museum of American History in December 1994. *Photo by Richard Strauss, Smithsonian Institution.*

seum field, heightened by the rhetoric and results of congressional elections. Exhibitions like the National Air and Space Museum's original examination of the *Enola Gay* and the end of World War II—replaced with a scaled-back version after public and political protests—have been criticized as examples of the arrogance, elitism, political correctness, and the "way-out-of-the-mainstream" nature of history museums and their staff. National newspapers have published calls for the dismissal of curators and directors who dared to challenge the primacy of popular memory or the cultural vision of political leaders. It seems that any museum endeavor—from a living history program at Colonial Williamsburg that depicted an eighteenth-century slave auction to NMAH's acquisition of the lunch counter from the Greensboro sit-in—becomes either a casualty of or fodder for the contested nature of contemporary cultural interpretation.

These culture wars have left many public historians uncertain, concerned, distracted, angry, and fearful about the future. They wonder whether this is a momentary storm or the dawning of an ice age of conservative change and control. We could, as songwriter Don McLean has suggested, simply "sing dirges in the dark," or hum as our mantra the Ruby and the Romantics' hit, "Our day will come, if we just wait awhile." Or we could, as colleagues have suggested, "wait out the storm" or "retreat a little in order to struggle later" or "be a bit more timid"—all legitimate responses in a time of uncertainty. Yet anyone who survived childhood in the late 1950s and early 1960s remembers the fallacy of "duck and cover." In the event of a nuclear attack, children were to lay their heads on their desktops or seek protection under the cover of tables and desks. It was as if averting one's eyes from the blast would somehow ensure survival. Obviously that technique was ineffective then and it is ineffective now. Rather than "duck and cover," public historians would be better served if they look and learn.

At stake are the direction, role, and importance of museums in American life. Critics of the museum community have legitimate questions which we as public historians must be prepared to answer. What are the appropriate uses of public funds? Who has the authority to interpret history and culture to the public, and what are the limits of that authority? Should museums such as NMAH be simply places of confirmation, validation, and tradition? Are museums truly out of the American mainstream and is that necessarily bad? To what extent is academic freedom a concept that is germane, appropriate, or applicable to museums? How do cultural institutions balance public expectation with scholarly inquiry? What is the role of the public in public history? Who has the right to shape museum interpretations or presentations—university scholars, funding sources, trustees, politicians, or anyone at all? What is to be the role of cultural institutions in the twenty-first century?

Curators, directors, educators, collections managers, and trustees all must participate fully, thoughtfully, candidly, and aggressively in this struggle to define or redefine the place of museums. Museums have, to borrow from W. E. B. DuBois, at least "two warring ideals in one dark body."[2] It is essential that the museum profession articulate that museums are places of commemoration and reverence, sacred spaces that allow the public to revel in tradition and celebratory episodes. It also must be clear that museums are much more—that they also contextualize, inspire, challenge, prod, and stimulate. We must find ways to wrestle with and service both of our "warring ideals." We must struggle to ensure that museums never return to a time where significant intellectual inquiry, the examination of difficult yet fundamental issues, is ignored. We must not allow our museums to become places where scholars and curators fail to wrestle with certain questions, not because of the lack of evidence, expertise, or collections but because of the lack of institutional resolve.

While these problems are not new and also apply to other kinds of museums and cultural organizations, their resolution becomes more difficult at the national level. The higher visibility of the exhibitions and programs at national museums simply increases the stakes and heightens the debate. Given the previous skirmishes of the culture wars and regardless of the intentions of the museum's curators, any NMAH exhibition will almost certainly be viewed and discussed within the context of larger questions about the meaning of the past and the appropriate roles and responsibilities of museums as interpreters of history. But the solution is not to pull back from exhibition plans—inaction also constitutes a response. If NMAH and other national museums do not produce exhibitions that treat important but controversial topics in the American past, then their silence will stand as institutional policy, affecting the museum community at large and the national discussion alike. In other words, working at a national museum is frontline duty, at the heart of debates about the future of history and museums.

SEIZING THE INITIATIVE

We cannot allow our critics to dictate the terms of debate. We as a profession must seize the initiative, frame the questions, and articulate clearly and forcefully a position (or series of positions) that allows museums to define themselves and craft a strategy to survive the culture wars. We need a more systematic and holistic response. Much of what passes for discourse is often the profession reacting to criticism that museums are dominated by loony left-wingers bent on thrashing cherished American myths and ideals. I have yet to see the profession effectively debunk these criticisms in a thoughtful manner that recognizes the public's right to question. While a great deal has been said about the *Enola Gay* exhibition,[3] little has been written that defends the difficult exhibition and scholarly decisions made or that underscores the fact that much of what American history museums do is as main street as Peoria and as celebratory as the Fourth of July.

Indeed there is a paucity of critical literature in history or museology that explores essential debates and issues and makes accessible a body of considered thought and research. A filmmaker or a novelist has access to an array of journals, monographs, and books that delineate debates about structure, content, methodology, and product. That is not the case for history museum professionals, who often follow the advice of an early twentieth-century Boston ward boss, Martin Lomasney: "Never write when you can speak, never speak when you can nod."[4] A sign of the maturation of any profession is a commitment to developing a corpus of published knowledge. In a time of change, that literature is also a bulwark against those who seek to define you and represent you without your participation. Thus it is important that, as history museums struggle with the many questions of the day, the profession address many of these questions by putting pen to paper or finger to keyboard.

Part of the difficulty that the history museum profession faces in charting an effective course is related to a discomfort with candid introspection and debate. It is difficult to offer definitions to a broader public until we as professionals are willing to engage in critical dialogue that transcends "show and tell" sessions at annual conferences. While such sessions provide important functions, their contributions would be greater if they emulated some of the trappings of academic bodies like the Organization of American Historians, which structures presentations to ensure that effective analysis and critical debate of an issue or topic are present in the form of a session commentator. Rather than simply present information, we must use our conferences as one of the ways the profession debates, analyzes, and evaluates its goals, its products, its political situation, and its vision. As my grandmother used to say, "We're family, it is O.K. to fight, as long as your squabbles stay inside the house."

Nor can we simply sit back and wait for the next round of criticism—we need to be proactive. In a press conference prior to a championship fight in 1941, Joe Louis, remarking on the purported speed of his opponent, said "He can run, but he can't hide."[5] Clearly, museums cannot hide either from the punches being thrown in the political arena. In a time of politics, museums must be even more politic and political. Since there are no constitutional guarantees of a vibrant, diverse, and academically free museum community, it is essential that museums do a better job of using the media and lobbying and utilizing the political system. To accomplish this, the profession, though peopled with gifted generalists who believe that they can accomplish any task, must recognize the limits of its expertise. Contrary to public opinion, not all historians are effective lobbyists, nor are all educators skilled in developing an effective media strategy. It is suicidal not to reach outside the walls of our institutions for expertise in these murky times.

Fortunately there are many appropriate models within the profession to emulate. National museums should look to the experiences of state and local museums, which have to face probing and problematic lawmakers yearly and know that to be successful they must learn to demonstrate and articulate why they are worthy of public dollars. We must also learn how to address the idiosyncrasies, needs, and criticisms of politicians, and how to identify and develop potential allies. Developing an array of allies—politicians, academicians, journalists, media experts, and corporate executives—is essential if museums are to respond effectively to their critics. State and local museums have survived because they understand the sentiment espoused by labor leader A. Philip Randolph: "At the banquet table of life, there are no reserved seats. You get what you can take and you keep what you can hold. You can't take anything without power, and power comes from organization."[6] Ultimately, being politic and political is, for all museums, the cost of doing business in an age of uncertainty.

STRATEGIES TO SURVIVE

While the larger public and political battles are being fought, we still have our work to do in our individual institutions. How do we move forward in a time of uncertainty?

Most museum directors would echo the poetic sentiments of Langston Hughes when he wrote "I wish the rent / was heaven sent."[7] But the support of museums is a more earthly function, and directors and administrators are often criticized when the realities of fiscal, political, and institutional concerns outweigh curatorial prerogatives. This legitimate friction between an institutional and a curatorial vision, problematic in the best of times, can be destructive in a time of crisis, unless institutions work to alleviate that tension. Negotiating these different visions requires a fluid and candid collaboration, a waltz in which each partner occasionally leads.

Curators must realize the validity and be supportive of the need to explore and evaluate exhibition ideas and research agendas through an institutional prism. And directors must underscore the importance of a clear and courageous curatorial vision, embracing and supporting curatorial exhibition efforts so that curators do not feel like characters in the World War II-era movie *They Were Expendable*. Directors should recognize that overcoming the contested nature of historical interpretation is more complex than calling for balance and multiple points of view. Rather than expect a single exhibition to present and develop, like a book, an array of interpretations, curators and directors should work collaboratively to ensure that the totality of an institution's products—exhibitions, public programs, educational initiatives, and publications—reflects and conveys a multiplicity of perspectives. Ultimately, we must negotiate the tensions between curatorial and institutional prerogatives because "a house divided against itself cannot stand,"[8] nor can it fend off its critics.

But the greatest danger to museums is not from conflicting curatorial and institutional agendas or even threats to funding sources or pressures exerted by government officials. More troubling is the potential of the profession (wittingly or unwittingly) to self-censor exhibitions and public presentations, to smooth the rough edges of history in order not to offend in this contentious atmosphere. As a senior curator who has faced the fire of unwanted media attention recently remarked, "I am disappointed. I always thought that doing good work, solid history that is imaginatively presented was enough. Now I realize that at this moment it is not good enough." No curator or director is immune to these pressures. After all, jobs, reputations, psyches, and families are all affected.

Crafting public expressions based on curatorial or scholarly research in museums always involves some sort of compromise: Are there significant artifacts to tell the story? Is this an issue that does not translate well to the exhibition medium? Or is the ability to convey certain issues limited by considerations of design or budget? Museum directors and administrators must support their research and curatorial staffs so that such compromises are made only because of scholarly or museum concerns, not in spite of them. The profession must, as essayist bell hooks has argued, do all that it can "not to accept an atmosphere where repression [real or perceived] leads to self censorship."[9]

Consider, for example, the problem of interpreting contemporary history. In light of all the critical outcry that has accompanied many of the profession's attempts to present the recent past, it would not be surprising that some public historians might feel that they are better off when they chronicle the more distant past. Clearly, exploring contemporary history in exhibitions is a dark, bloody, and contested ground that is not for the faint of heart. After all, presenting the history of the living means treading on dreams and wrestling with recollections, both cherished and painful. But it also means exploring difficult or controversial subjects such as Vietnam, Hiroshima, civil rights, urban de-industrialization, and changing notions of family. These topics are full of complexity, emotion, and unresolved, often unarticulated, feelings.

But despite the potential costs, museums should periodically examine and contextualize contemporary history, especially if the institution is able to acknowledge and attempt to negotiate the tricky terrain between academic history and popular memory. A museum can begin to negotiate that chasm by crafting a dialogue early in the exhibition process with diverse representatives of the groups whose history it hopes to chart. These discussions will not address all issues, but they will allow the institution to articulate a vision with clarity and candor, delineate the exhibit process, and initiate a discourse that may limit later criticism.

While some institutions, for legitimate and compelling reasons, may opt not to explore controversy or issues of contemporary history, I hope that directors will not reject out of hand any exhibition whose subject, title, or main label seems controversial. Instead, I hope they will make their decisions only after candid discussions with curators and careful analysis of the scholarship, the mode of presentation, the support of and communication with external scholars and community members, and the risk to the museum. Ultimately, museums must either have the vision to support and nurture exhibition ideas developed by their scholars or have the courage to walk away forthrightly, cleanly, and completely from an exhibition that is deemed inappropriate.

Although there may be debate within an institution about the appropriateness of certain interpretations or issues, there should be no debate about its commitment to public education. Now more than ever, museums are needed to shape, contextualize, and help lead a measured discourse. Though I am less certain of the ultimate contribution museums can make to public education—is there enough research to claim that all museums can be moral educators or change agents?—I would argue that museums must strive to help Americans reach what Brazilian educator Paulo Freire called "critical consciousness."[10] The goal is not to educate visitors to a singular point of view but to create an informed public—people who can analyze, criticize, understand, and manipulate history and culture to inform their lives and aid them in addressing the issues, problems, and normal dilemmas of life. Museums cannot, however, be effective and valuable educational institutions unless they are free not only to teach, support, validate, and celebrate but also to challenge, question, illuminate, and confront.

DECONSTRUCTING THE MUSEUM

At an American University panel discussion in November 1994 on the controversy surrounding the National Air and Space Museum's planned *Enola Gay* exhibition, one of the speakers, a congressman from Massachusetts, professed to being "amazed and shocked" when he learned that the exhibition would not simply commemorate the achievements of veterans of the Second World War. In a *Washington Post* interview, First Lady Hillary Rodham Clinton addressed the setbacks suffered by the Clinton administration by acknowledging that much of the problem was "our failure to explain to people what was at stake in simple terms."[11] These seemingly disparate comments are really quite instructive for the museum profession. The congressman's statement undergirds the fact that there is a great chasm between what museum professionals see as their roles and how the general public sees and understands museums. Mrs. Clinton, meanwhile, offers a simple but instructive way to reduce this chasm.

Now more than ever, we need to deconstruct museums and the museum profession. We must explain in simple terms to people, to corporations, to trustees, and to government officials what museums do, what we are, what we collect, how we arrive at the decisions that we make, and how cultural institutions at the end of the twentieth century are different from the cultural institutions of the 1940s. The public needs to know, and it is the profession's obligation to inform, that museums can be "temples" and "cathedrals" and wonderfully comfortable "nation's attics." But they are also places of scholarship and interpretation, places where celebration can often coexist with controversy. We need, for example, to explain to the public why history museums explore social history that includes difficult and not easily answered questions of race, class, and gender. It is not enough to say that we "know best." While museums cannot expect to change their audience into experts on or patrons of history by being more forthcoming, museums can teach visitors more about points of view, the scholarly underpinnings of museum work, and the inherent fluidity of museum interpretation. As the clothing store advertisement extols, "an educated consumer is our best customer."

FINAL THOUGHTS

The 1980s and 1990s have been a period of wondrous change and significant achievement for the American museum community. Exhibitions as diverse as "A More Perfect Union: Japanese Americans and the U.S. Constitution" and "Mining the Museum" have stimulated and challenged both the public and the history museum professionals to broaden our no-

This photo of students at the Raphael Weill Public School in San Francisco appears in "A More Perfect Union: Japanese Americans and the U.S. Constitution," an exhibition at the National Museum of American History. Taken by Dorothea Lange in April 1942, the photo shows young Japanese Americans pledging allegiance to the United States flag. *Courtesy of the National Archives.*

tions of what an exhibition can accomplish.[12] An array of new museums such as the Holocaust Museum in Washington, D.C., has helped public historians explore new ideas and forms and develop alternative modes of presentation. Rejuvenated older institutions like the Valentine Museum have stretched the exhibition and interpretive parameters of our museums. Well-crafted exhibitions, public programs, educational initiatives, and collections have grappled with difficult yet essential questions of race, gender, mythology, multiculturalism, urban culture, and religion.

While there have been missteps, and there is still much more to explore, there is no reason for the profession to apologize for what it has achieved and how it has changed in the last twenty years. History museums are better cultural and educational entities because institutions and individuals fought to become more scholarly, inclusive, and relevant. If we retreat from, and fail to build upon, these recent changes, it is highly possible that some of the very work that we now celebrate as essential to the profession will disappear in this age of "duck and cover."

In this photo from "A More Perfect Union: Japanese Americans and the U.S. Constitution," an exhibition at the National Museum of American History, an American soldier delivers an evacuation notice to the home of a Japanese American at Terminal Island, Los Angeles, 1942. Japanese Americans were urged by their social and political organizations to cooperate with the evacuation as a demonstration of their patriotism and because no effective alternative course was available. *Courtesy of the National Japanese American Historical Society.*

Building upon their prior achievements, museums must continue to explore subjects that, shaped by sound scholarship, are challenging and important to visitors; to craft exhibitions and build collections that reflect and find meaning in America's diversity; and to remain a place for informed reflection. Even in a time of uncertainty, museums must have the courage of their convictions and their scholarship and, in the words of abolitionist William Lloyd Garrison, "stand against [the] wind and tide" of unwanted change and challenge.[13] We must be willing to fight the good fight.

NOTES

1. Portions of this chapter were published earlier in Lonnie G. Bunch, "Museums in an Age of Uncertainty: Fighting the Good Fight," *Museum News* (March/April, 1995): 32–62.
2. W. E. B. DuBois, *The Souls of Black Folk* (New York: The Modern Library, 1996), 5.
3. See, for example, "History and the Public: What Can We Handle? A Round Table about History after the *Enola Gay* Controversy," *Journal of American History* 82 (December 1995): 1029–1144.
4. Quoted in the *Washington Post,* January 17, 1994.
5. Quoted in Stephen Donadio, Joan Smith, Susan Mesner, and Rebecca Davison, eds., *The New York Public Library Book of Twentieth-Century American Quotations* (New York: Warner Books, Inc., 1992), 427.
6. Quoted in Paula F. Pfeffer, *A. Philip Randolph, Pioneer of the Civil Rights Movement* (Baton Rouge: Louisiana State University Press, 1990), 103.
7. Langston Hughes, "Little Lyric (of Great Importance)," *The Collected Poems of Langston Hughes,* Arnold Rampersand and David Roessel, eds. (New York: Alfred A. Knopf, 1994), 226.
8. Abraham Lincoln, speech, June 16, 1858, quoted in Peter J. Parish, ed., *Abraham Lincoln: Speeches and Letters* (Rutland, VT: Charles E. Tuttle, 1993), 80.
9. bell hooks, *Outlaw Culture: Resisting Representations* (New York: Routledge, 1994).
10. See Paolo Freire, *Pedagogy of the Oppressed,* translated by Myra Bergman Ramos (New York: Herder and Herder, 1970).
11. Quoted in the *Washington Post,* November 17, 1993.
12. "A More Perfect Union: Japanese Americans and the U.S. Constitution" opened at the National Museum of American History in 1987. "Mining the Museum" was a temporary exhibition at the Maryland Historical Society in 1991.
13. *The Liberator,* September 10, 1836, quoted in Walter M. Merrill, *Against Wind and Tide: A Biography of William Lloyd Garrison* (Cambridge, MA: Harvard University Press, 1963), v.

JESSE H. STILLER is historian for the Office of the Comptroller of the Currency. He received his B.A. in history at the City College of New York and his Ph.D. in history at the City University of New York Graduate School. He previously served as command historian for the U.S. Air Defense Artillery Center and Fort Bliss and as staff historian for the U.S. Army Communications-Electronics Command at Fort Monmouth. He also serves as professorial lecturer in international affairs at George Washington University and previously taught at the University of Texas-El Paso and Baruch College, City University of New York. Dr. Stiller has presented papers at meetings of such organizations as the Organization of American Historians and the Society for Historians of American Foreign Relations, and his publications include Essays in the History of the National Banking System *(1995),* The Comptroller and Bank Supervision *(1995),* George S. Messersmith, Diplomat of Democracy *(1987),* War and Depression, 1917–1933 *(1986), and contributions to* Diplomatic History, The Public Historian, *the* Foreign Service Journal, *and other periodicals and compilations.*

IN FEDERAL HISTORY PROGRAMS: ENSURING THE FUTURE[1]

Jesse H. Stiller

When U.S. Army Corps of Engineers historian Martin Reuss surveyed the field of federal history in 1986, the world was a different place.[2] New history programs were being created, old ones were expanding, and there was reason for optimism that federal agencies still without historians would soon have them. Informal talks between key congressmen and leaders of the federal historical community pointed to the possibility of legislation mandating a historical office at every cabinet-level department.[3] Between 1984 and 1985, a single year, one U.S. Army command alone hired sixteen additional historians.[4] With 214 historians then on the rolls, the Air Force history program initially opted not to be included in the 1984 *Directory of Federal Historical Programs and Activities* (published by the Society for History in the Federal Government), on the assumption that such disclosure would invite closer scrutiny from congressional

357

budget-cutters. No such negative publicity materialized; the Air Force added another twelve historians the following year.[5]

By the time Reuss wrote, the hiring surge had peaked, but the future still seemed bright for historians interested in federal employment. Thus, Reuss concluded his essay with sensible advice on completing the necessary application paperwork and in deciding upon a duty station, noting that with historical offices scattered throughout the country, especially in Defense Department establishments, "the chances of finding employment are improved if one is willing to settle for a less attractive geographical location."[6]

Today, physical mobility and duty stations off the beaten track are the least of the problems confronting competitors for federal history jobs. From its high water mark in the mid-1980s, the Air Force program has lost almost half of its positions; enlisted technicians now perform documents collection and other routine historical work once carried out by Ph.D. historians.[7] For fiscal year 1997, the Army's Center of Military History absorbed a 30 percent reduction in its personnel allowance. At this writing, plans were going forward to relocate the Center from Washington to the Army War College in Pennsylvania, which would diminish if not eliminate its role in front line support of senior Army policy makers.[8]

Civilian agencies of the federal government have scarcely fared better. At the Department of Agriculture (DOA), a historical office in operation since 1916 was disbanded, and its employees reclassified into other job series and then scattered to the winds among various DOA offices. Programs at the Environmental Protection Agency, the General Accounting Office, the Federal Bureau of Investigation, and the Internal Revenue Service—all relative newcomers to the federal historical community—have either been abolished outright or materially reduced.[9]

The impact of this disastrous downward spiral is not limited to historians seeking federal employment. Directly or indirectly, all historians have felt or will feel the effects. During the late 1970s and early 1980s, the surge in federal history programs somewhat mitigated the collapsing academic job market. That was a relief to most graduate school professors, who were thus spared the awkward necessity of confronting the irrationalities of a system which each year produced hundreds of new Ph.D.s trained for nonexistent or marginal academic jobs. But despite the discouraging realities of the academic marketplace, few historians-in-training were encouraged to pursue nonacademic options or to think of such work as a fitting environment for their talents. Outside of a few second-tier institutions where public history was taken seriously, like Carnegie-Mellon, New York University, and the University of California at Santa Barbara, the message most graduate students heard was that nonacademic employment was somehow disreputable and that, having bottomed out, the academic market was sure to improve for those with the patience to wait it out. Many who persisted in looking elsewhere found themselves written off as wayward souls who had permanently left the fold.

Not all senior historians thought of government work—when they thought about it at all—solely in terms of a paycheck for their least able or dedicated protegees. Some were able to transcend the supply side assumption that historians were entitled to employment as a condition of their Ph.D.s and to think in terms of the value that historians might add to the nonacademic workplace. Writing in 1980, Michael Kammen saw real benefits accruing to the government that hired disfranchised historians. He imagined that the public sector would become home for ever larger numbers of historians, who would "not only help to counteract the job crisis for new Ph.D.s but help to demonstrate the imperative of a historical perspective as well."[10] Without addressing the question of how exactly they would bring this perspective to bear, Kammen predicted that the historians and their specialized skills would quickly prove their worth. It was only a matter of time, he thought, before all federal agencies would recognize this and bring them on board.

That day may yet come, but it seems more and more like a forlorn hope. Meanwhile, with graduate programs churning out new Ph.D.s at the fastest rate in a decade, the loss of alternative career opportunities for historians would seem to be cause for greater alarm in the profession than ever.[11]

THE DECLINE OF FEDERAL HISTORY

On the surface, the reasons for federal history's fall from grace are obvious. Neither government workers nor professional scholars enjoy much standing in the public's esteem these days; government historians are twice cursed. The contemporary paradox of professional history's decline in the face of an apparently insatiable appetite for history on the part of the general public has elicited many explanations, not all of which blame the professors for alienating their audience. But most do, citing their weak writing, disdain for narrative, liberal bias, elitism, and penchant for carving history into ever-narrower and more esoteric subspecialties.[12] A number of incidents have dramatized the estrangement between historians and the people: the controversy over national history standards, the dismissal of the House of Representatives historian, and the *Enola Gay* exhibit at the National Air and Space Museum have all involved in one way or another allegations that professional historians are increasingly out of step with mainstream America.

The federal government has been damned in similarly categorical terms. Federal historians have shared in the pain of government downsizing, which, by the start of Bill Clinton's second term of office in 1997, had already claimed more than 250,000 federal positions. All occupational groups have been affected by these pressures, but those viewed as peripheral or optional have been more vulnerable than most.

Therein lies the problem. Kammen's 1980 prediction that historians would in short order become as indispensable as economists and lawyers to the agencies that hired them has clearly not come to pass. The question is why not. Only two explanations are possible. Either we have overrated the value of the perspective we add to the "real world" outside of academe or we have not effectively provided it.

Although discomfiting, the first possibility should not be rejected out of hand. The social utility of history has never been an unquestioned truth.[13] In fact, those dismissive of history's relevance and predictive power seem to have had somewhat the better of the argument of late. The end of the Cold War, the dismantling of the welfare state, and the economic expansion that began in 1993 lend plausibility to the proposition, increasingly voiced,[13] that all bets are off in terms of the lessons of the past—that we are at a millennial turning point in which the old paradigms of U.S. diplomatic, political, and economic behavior have ceased to have meaning; that history, with its emphasis on continuity, is not only irrelevant but dangerously misleading in an age which has embraced new modes of thought and behavior.

This line of argument is hardly unique to our age; it is, however, essentially unanswerable because it depends upon the logic of history to refute it. But most government officials are practical people who, I would venture to guess, would never embrace it in the first place. Even if they secretly believed it, few executives in the Defense or State Department are likely to announce that war and disorder have been banished from international relations, considering what such an admission would do to their bureaucratic interests. Nor, I can say from personal experience, would many bank regulators stake their reputations on the proposition that the economic cycle has been permanently tamed simply because, by historical standards, it is overdue for a turn. The point is that most policy makers would presumably agree with Arthur M. Schlesinger, Jr.'s formulation, that "public decision in rational politics necessarily implies a guess about the future derived from the experience of the past."[15] And who better to help sort and organize the experience of the past than historians? It follows that the need for systematic application of perspective should support many more historians than presently inhabit the federal service, just as Kammen had argued in 1980.

It stands to reason, then, that historians are a dwindling breed in the federal government because those already on the scene—and especially those recently removed from it—have not been particularly effective in providing what their agencies or offices need from them most. That is not to say that federal historians do not do many worthwhile things. Reuss's 1986 inventory included eleven categories of activity:

1. Publishing agency histories
2. Responding to inquiries
3. Conducting oral histories
4. Writing reports
5. Supporting public affairs activities
6. Administering contract history
7. Administering museums
8. Editing documents
9. Developing cultural interpretations
10. Cultural resources management
11. Preserving historical materials[16]

A 1989 study by David F. Trask, then chief historian of the U.S. Army, found a similar range of activities, as did a survey two years later by Roger Trask, then chief historian of the General Accounting Office (GAO).[17]

What is interesting about these surveys is what they all discovered federal historians were generally *not* doing. Few historians apparently participate in the policy-making process as advisers, despite the fact that, as Roger Trask wrote,

> This activity constitutes one of the strongest arguments for the existence of federal historical offices. The writing of institutional history and the conduct of oral history interviews are legitimate, important functions of these programs. Indeed, if agency decision-makers extract from institutional and oral histories lessons or ideas for use in making current policy decisions, these historians perform the role of policy research. But too few top agency managers call on their historians for research to be utilized in the policy-making process, and too few agency historians are willing to do policy research or even to offer such services to their agencies. But how better to demonstrate the value of federal history programs, or to strengthen the rationale for their existence?[18]

How indeed. Assembling collections of documents or compiling exhaustive institutional histories might fill a leisurely academic career, but it will not satisfactorily answer the question all federal historians continue to confront: "Why do we need a historian?" Productive scholarship alone will not dispel the assumption that a history program is like nice office furniture: good for morale but basically a frill; justifiable when resources

are plentiful and the public is feeling relatively indulgent toward its government, but a potential public relations liability in a more constrained
environment. At such times, the history office which merely produces history—even good history—is sure to come out the loser most of the time
in competing for agency resources.

Trask's division of responsibility for this failure between superiors who
do not ask for historical perspective and historians who do not offer to
provide it is, I think, overly generous to the historians. The idea that professionals—especially professionals whose organizational value is a matter of controversy—should sit back and wait for a superior to come knock-
ing before they respond flies in the face of everything we know about
surviving and thriving in a competitive world—a world that rewards those
who take risks, volunteer for new challenges, and demonstrate adapt-
ability and sensitivity to the bottom line.

On the other hand, it may be unreasonable to expect historians to do
what they may never have thought of doing and, in fact, have never been
trained to do. Applied policy history—history as practiced by a professional who contributes *to* policy as opposed to one who is merely a student *of* policy—requires specialized skills traditionally taught in the classroom, along with some untraditional ones as well.

APPLIED POLICY HISTORY

What skills and knowledge are we talking about? First, policy history requires what almost any historian of modern America would have been assumed to possess twenty years ago, namely a thorough grounding in the
history of policy. In his influential 1993 article, "The Stunted Career of
Policy History," Hugh Davis Graham notes the irony of the 1970s and
1980s: declining academic interest in political history at the very time that
the subject—i.e., the American government—was rapidly expanding.[19]
Yet, the rising preeminence of what Graham refers to as "bottom up" history is hardly incompatible with a policy orientation.[20] No social historian
can deny or ignore the impact of government policies—for better or
worse—on welfare, the environment, organized (and unorganized) labor, health care, and a host of other issues. The social historian who is
unfamiliar with those policies is a poorly trained historian, indeed. Today, the safety net may be fraying at the edges, but social policy, broadly
defined, continues to absorb the bulk of government's resources—and
to call for the insight historians can provide to help policy makers spend
those resources wisely and humanely. For those of an activist nature interested in influencing the debate on social issues and not simply studying them, policy history can provide an immensely satisfying outlet.[21]

Second, policy historians must take a multidisciplinary approach to history, both intellectually and functionally. Historians are generally broad-minded in recognizing the complexities of causation, but curiously parochial in the way we process historical information. We tend to discount the insights which nonhistorical specialists—attorneys, political scientists, sociologists, and economists—bring to historical issues. We do not speak their language or read their journals or consult with them to enrich our work, at least not much. Certainly, as a quick count of the titles in any history publisher's catalogue will attest, it is uncommon for historians to collaborate with nonhistorians on writing projects, whereas such partnerships are routine in the social sciences.

But although the federal bureaucracy in its middle reaches does not much differ from the university campus in terms of the compartmentalization of disciplines, at the senior levels of government these functional divisions break down. Historians who proffer policy advice—regardless of where they themselves are situated in the bureaucracy—must be synthesizers who draw on the specialized expertise of other practitioners, decipher their jargon, weigh and integrate their findings into a comprehensible whole, and develop recommendations.[22]

Although one occasionally turns up an anthropologist or political scientist actually practicing his or her disciplinary specialty in the federal service, lawyers and economists wield disproportionate influence in the substantive debate. Their work, therefore, must be reckoned with by anyone else seeking to participate in it. For the traditionally trained historian, it is certainly possible to acquire the rudiments of law and economics through self-study. Historians are agile learners. Though lawyers and economists like to maintain a certain aura of impenetrability about their fields, a working knowledge of their technique can be grasped with a good textbook at one's side. Historians who had the good fortune in graduate school to substitute quantitative methods for a foreign language will be at an advantage in unravelling the economists' work. One gets the sense, however, that for many of the most influential economists themselves, their hearts are in the narrative and not the numbers. This suggests that while the ability to penetrate and evaluate the statistical back matter helps, it is not essential to digest the meaning of most economic input.

But on-the-job training is no substitute for systematic learning in a structured setting, where problems and ideas can be discussed collegially. In short, formal graduate work in interdisciplinary public history would seem to be the best route for the acquisition of the skills that the role of policy historian demands.

What should such a course of study include? Intensive, applied course work in law and economics, quantitative methods, and policy analysis should certainly be required. But policy study in history should be long on practical training: on role playing, case studies, and internships. It should help students understand the power and the limitations of history as a guide to decision making. It should examine the power and pitfalls of analogy as a policy-making tool. It should focus on the history of applied history—how it has been applied and misapplied in the past.

Formal training for a career as a practicing policy historian should also address ethical and temperamental issues. Indeed, the right combination of personal traits may be as important to one's success in this milieu as one's technical skills and academic preparation. Policy history is relatively high-pressure, high-visibility work. Not all historians are cut out for it. The hours can be long. If twelve hours of contact time or a standard 9 to 5 regimen is all you think you can endure, look elsewhere. Policy work requires an energetic, activist frame of mind and an ego that finds gratification in influence, even though that influence is likely to go unheralded outside one's office. It requires good face-to-face skills and an ability to think on one's feet. It helps to have a taste for bureaucratic combat, for when the stakes are high, everyone who affects the outcome is fair game, like it or not.

Using history as an aid to policy requires an uncommon assertiveness about evidence. Many historians are uncomfortable drawing flat conclusions about the past—and even more uncomfortable venturing guesses about the future—from evidence that seems ambiguous. In our age of intellectual hubris, history's honesty in confronting the limitations of evidence seems refreshing next to the unconscionable huckstering that so often passes for learning from other social scientists. We know, as one historian recently explained, "that our knowledge is incomplete,"[23] and so are reluctant to come flat out and say what we think it means.

Outside of academe, however, this kind of studied equivocation is hard to sustain. Decision makers rarely deal in absolutes; they operate in a framework of compromise and small differences between the best choice and lesser ones. They operate in a world of conflict, where almost everyone is assumed to have an ulterior motive. They have to choose among conflicting recommendations of staff experts. I once produced a fairly lengthy paper whose title was phrased in the form of a question to reflect the divergent opinions about the institution I was describing, something like "The Influence of the Department of State on U.S. Foreign Policy: Professionalism or Conservatism?" I vividly remember the decision maker I was then working for asking me which of the two I thought it was, and his impatience when I suggested that it was a little of both. That was certainly an honest answer, but not an especially useful one. The better answer, for his purposes, was that, on balance, it was more of one than the other—an answer that was just as well founded on the facts, but a little more venturesome.

Risk is something that the policy historian has to be prepared to take—not only in articulating one's opinions but in first forming them on the basis of research limited by the press of deadline. We have to learn to trust in our historical instincts when the sources and the time to consult them are not available to the extent that we would like, and overcome the fussy urge to examine everything before coming to a conclusion. We have to sharpen our powers of summary and synthesis to a greater degree than the academic audience requires, because our decision-making clients cannot and will not read more than they must.

Working at the side of senior policy makers in government or the private sector can be exhilarating. Observing the exercise of authority at close quarters offers an unparalleled education in a process that cannot be fully understood just by reading about it. In short, experience as a policy historian makes you a better historian. One will never write about policy the same way after having contributed to it.

Proximity can also be a liability. Perspective—that intellectual detachment which historians are looked to to provide—can be hard to sustain under the pressure of time and charismatic—or at least sympathetic—leadership. It is natural to develop an identification with the source of one's income and power, and this can lead to potentially compromising situations.

In most cases—the best cases—history comes to bear early in the process of formulating policy, while options and their impact are still being weighed. Sometimes, however, the rational, bottom-up approach to policy making yields to external urgencies—a crisis of some sort that requires an agency position to be cobbled together more hastily than anyone would prefer. In such cases it is not uncommon for historical precedent to be mustered *post facto,* to justify a policy already decided upon. Where the evidence supports that policy, it does not seem to matter whether it is adduced earlier or later in the process. The difficulty arises when the historian's judgment leads to some other conclusion—one at odds with the position taken. Bureaucratic pressures to mold history to the occasion—to turn the historian into an advocate—must be resisted in the interests of the historian's as well as the organization's credibility. Truth, as best the historian can reconstruct it, can never be sacrificed to expediency or superficiality. We must strive, as Seymour Mandelbaum put it, to achieve "integration, but not subservience"—that is, to enter into a dialogue with the policy maker to help him or her understand that history's true value lies in the independent and fair-minded judgments it generates.[24]

GRADUATE PROGRAMS IN POLICY HISTORY

For now, the graduate programs that offer specializations in the policy aspects of public history are low in number, but high in quality. Only six of the sixteen Ph.D.-granting institutions listed in the National Council on Public History's *Guide to Graduate Programs in Public History* (1996) provide a public policy track for their students. None of these—indeed, none of the sixteen—rank among the most prestigious history graduate programs in the land. Yet they are doing yeoman's work in preparing their students to make important contributions to government, society, and to professional history.

At Bowling Green State University, for example, doctoral students in policy history are required to complete a course in quantitative methods and an eight-week internship. They take seven or eight colloquia in subjects ranging from national security policy to civil rights policy to gender and public policy. They can take advantage of course work options in economics, statistics, law, political science, and sociology. During a week-long seminar in Washington in 1996, Bowling Green students met with federal historians and government policy analysts, as well as with representatives from corporations like AT&T to bring students into contact with possible employers outside academe.

Carnegie Mellon University offers a close coupling of public and policy history. Its doctoral program in history and policy encompasses cross-disciplinary studies, an active internship program, and a novel contract history component, which acquaints students with the challenges of sponsored research.

Case Western Reserve's program emphasis on social policy history has attracted candidates with law degrees and master's degrees in fields like nursing. Because most of the program's doctoral students are already working professionals seeking to broaden their knowledge base, Case Western does not emphasize internships but does encourage cross-disciplinary training in the university's professional schools.

As these programs show, opportunities do exist to acquire the kind of formal training in policy history that the government workplace needs to make use of. The problem is that, as yet, few do. According to the university's listings in 1996, not one of the eighteen Ph.D. graduates of Case Western's social policy program have found their way into government at any level. Instead, they are employed, predictably, in social service agencies and, less predictably, in academe. As a pool of qualified candidates with policy history backgrounds grows, the challenge will increasingly become one of moving them into positions where they can bring their expertise to bear most fruitfully. Linkages with the federal government of the sort being pioneered by Bowling Green should get some feet through the door. Once policy historians have had the opportunity to prove their worth and the federal government begins to rebuild its depleted workforce, as it surely will, others will follow.

THE FUTURE

Does this portend a sustainable reversal in the decade-long decline in the fortunes of federal history? What judgment will we pronounce when we revisit the subject ten years from now? Indeed, how many of us will still be available to perform the task—or will it fall to some academic outsider to write the postmortem for federal history?

Having argued for greater forthrightness in the way we extrapolate from the past, it would hardly do to take refuge in equivocation about the future. Let us then seek an answer in history, which suggests, first, that the American people will have exactly as much government as they need to deal with the problems before them. Peace and prosperity have always argued for little government, and they still do today. Major new challenges or the reappearance of old ones will inevitably call for an organized response. As they always have in the past, people will look to the government when the problems are too big for them to handle themselves.

The effectiveness of government's response to the next crisis will depend in part on the resources— human, technical, material, and intellectual—available to those responsible for formulating it. At the end of the day, agency heads and subheads are managers who will use whatever is available to them that serves to get the job done. Most are open to different ideological or methodological approaches. Prove to them that history—or anything else—works, that it will make their life easier, and they will embrace it. The silver lining to federal history's current difficulties is that we have hardly begun to add the value we have to offer. We must make certain that when the next opportunity arises to make our case and prove our worth, we get it right. We owe our profession and our country no less. "What lies before us in policy history," Robert Kelley wrote in 1988, "is not simply an interesting challenge. It is a duty and an obligation."[25]

NOTES

1. The views expressed herein are those of the author and do not necessarily represent the opinions of the Office of the Comptroller of the Currency or the United States Government.

2. Martin Reuss, "Public History in the Federal Government," in Barbara J. Howe and Emory L. Kemp, eds., *Public History: An Introduction* (Malabar, FL: Robert E. Krieger Publishing Co., 1986).

3. Dennis Roth, "The First Decade of the Society for History in the Federal Government," unpublished manuscript, 1989, available at http://shfg.org./history.htm.

4. Fact Sheet, Historical Office, Headquarters TRADOC, 11 April 1983, Subject: Establishment of Historian Positions in Army Service Schools.

5. Larry Benson to the author, April 11, 1997.

6. Reuss, "Public History in the Federal Government," in *Public History: An Introduction,* (Malabar, FL: Robert E. Krieger Publishing Co., 1986), 306–8.

7. Conversation with Larry Benson, Office of Air Force History, April 7, 1997.

8. Conversation with John Sherwood, U.S. Army Center of Military History, April 7, 1997.

9. Gerald K. Haines, "The Future of Federal Government History Programs," unpublished paper delivered at the Society for History in the Federal Government annual conference, April 1995.

10. Michael Kammen, quoted in Theodore S. Hamerow, *Reflections on History and Historians* (Madison, WI: University of Wisconsin Press, 1987), 9.

11. Robert B. Townsend, "Studies Report Mixed News for History Job Seekers," *Perspectives* 35 (March 1997): 7.

12. For contemporary critiques, see James M. McPherson, "What's the Matter with History," *Princeton Alumni Weekly,* January 22, 1997, 14–21; Simon Schama, "Clio Has a Problem," *New York Times Magazine,* September 8, 1991, 30–34; Patricia Nelson Limerick, "Dancing with Professors: The Trouble with Academic Prose," *The New York Times Book Review,* October 31, 1993, 3–4.

13. Hamerow, *Reflections on History,* 227–30; Stephen Vaughn, "History: Is It Relevant?" in Vaughn, ed., *The Vital Past: Writings on the Uses of History* (Athens, GA: University of Georgia Press, 1985), 1–5.

14. Francis Fukuyama, *The End of History and the Last Man* (New York: Free Press, 1992); L. William Seidman, radio interview, "Marketplace," May 21,1997.

15. Arthur M. Schlesinger, Jr., "The Inscrutability of History," in Vaughn, ed., *The Vital Past,* 311.

16. Reuss, "Public History," 305.

17. David F. Trask, "Does Official History Have a Future?" *The Public Historian* 11 (Spring 1989): 47–52; Roger R. Trask, "Small Federal History Offices in the Nation's Capital," *The Public Historian* 13 (Winter 1991): 47–60.

18. Ibid., 53.

19. Hugh Davis Graham, "The Stunted Career of Policy History: A Critique and Agenda," *The Public Historian* 15 (Spring 1993): 26–30.

20. See, for example, the work of Edward Berkowitz, most recently his biography of Wilbur Cohen, *Mr. Social Security: The Life of Wilbur J. Cohen* (Lawrence, KS: University Press of Kansas, 1996). Berkowitz, who served as a staffer on a White House commission on welfare policy during the late 1970s, describes himself as a political historian who "hide[s] behind the label of policy history." Berkowitz, "History and Public Policy: A Personal Perspective," paper

delivered at 1995 annual meeting of the Organization of American Historians, Washington, DC. He is, more precisely, a historian specializing in the politics of social issues.

21. Case Western Reserve University has made a specialty of social policy history. Since the program began in 1984, it has turned out eighteen Ph.D.s, whose dissertation topics ranged from health care reform to the criminal justice system to birth control, mostly with a focus on the Cleveland area. Conversation with David Hammack, July 23, 1997.

22. David B. Mock, "Introduction," in Mock, ed., *History and Public Policy* (Malabar, FL: Robert E. Krieger Publishing Co., 1991), 4. This book offers a useful collection of essays on the theoretical and practical aspects of policy history.

23. Michael Cassity, "History and the Public Purpose," *Journal of American History* 81 (December 1994): 975.

24. Seymour Mandelbaum, "The Past in Service to the Future," in Mock, ed., *History and Public Policy,* 51.

25. Robert Kelley, "The Idea of Policy History," *The Public Historian* 10 (Winter 1988): 39

ELIZABETH W. ADKINS is director of Global Information Management for the Ford Motor Company in Dearborn, Michigan. A Certified Archivist (CA), she holds a B.A. in history from Harpur College, State University of New York at Binghamton, and an M.A. in history from Carnegie Mellon University. Ms. Adkins previously served as archives manager at Kraft Foods, Inc. and archivist for Laird Norton Company. Her many activities within the archival community include serving as the president of the Academy of Certified Archivists, as treasurer of the Society of American Archivists, as chair of the Business Archives Section of the Society of American Archivists, on the steering committee of the Section on Business and Labour Archives of the International Council on Archives, and as a member of the advisory committee for the Records of American Business Project, an NEH-funded effort to improve documentation of twentieth-century U.S. business. She serves as an instructor in SAA's Business Archives Workshops and in 2002 was elected a fellow of the Society of American Archivists. Her publications include "The Development of Business Archives in the United States" in The American Archivist *(1997) and book reviews in* The American Archivist.

IN BUSINESSES AND CORPORATIONS: SERVING AS THE CORPORATE MEMORY

Elizabeth W. Adkins

Working as an archivist or historian in a corporation can provide both satisfaction and frustration. When I took my first job as a corporate archivist in 1981, I recognized one benefit immediately: Archives programs are self-funded by the parent organization, and there is no need to apply for grants to keep going. On the other hand, corporate archives programs are at a disadvantage because they generally do not contribute directly to the bottom line; therefore they are constantly in danger of being cut back or even shut down. Over the years, I have experienced many of the rewards and roadblocks that come with managing an archives in a business setting. What follows are my reflections on some of the lessons I have learned.

HISTORICAL CONTEXT

The first widely recognized, professionally run corporate archives program in the United States was that of the Firestone Tire and Rubber Company, established in 1943. A small number of corporate archives were established by the 1960s, but most companies did not perceive the value of investing in and preserving their past. Some of these attitudes changed in the 1970s, when more than twenty major corporations established archives programs.[1] But corporate archivists received a harsh reality check in the 1980s and 1990s, when mergers, reorganizations, downsizing, and reengineering resulted in the closure of a number of highly regarded corporate archives programs. These closings have driven home the point that in order for public historians to survive in corporate America, it is necessary to understand the needs and wants of their employers.

UNDERSTANDING HOW TO
SERVE YOUR INSTITUTION

As a corporate archivist or historian, your primary loyalty and responsibility are to your employer. Your company's history may be of interest to scholars, but that may not necessarily be the major focus of your work and your efforts. Instead, you have to understand how your company's history will help the institution overall. Can it be used to a marketing advantage? Does the company have a corporate culture based on its history that is important to maintain and communicate? Is the company's current success built on an understanding of its past technical or other accomplishments? Is there an anniversary coming up which will result in a good deal of publicity? Can a thorough historical record of the company's trademarks help protect them against infringement? Are there ways in which an archives or history program can support legal and corporate secretary functions? Can a current strategic initiative benefit from a study of the strategies of the past?[2]

Understanding the present or potential uses of a company's archives will provide a keystone to all of the decisions you make about your program. For example, in archival appraisal, records that employees are likely to use frequently should receive the highest attention for arrangement, description, and preservation efforts. Records that might be used by people outside the company—e.g., genealogists interested in researching family members who worked for your company—generally get much less attention.

While scholarly researchers are an important user group for many public repositories, the research requirements of scholars are a low priority for many corporate archives. It is true that some companies may

Corporate archives may include more than just records. Here a retiree identifies photos in the Phillips Corporate Archives. *Courtesy of Phillips Petroleum Company.*

Advertising materials can be used for the development of contemporary consumer promotions. The materials shown here were part of a nationwide nostalgia promotion created by Coca-Cola in the 1970s. Today, a wide variety of licensed goods can be found in retail outlets in the United States, Europe, and the Pacific. *Courtesy of the Coca-Cola Company.*

find it advantageous to open their historical resources to outside researchers but for the most part only if there is a business benefit in doing so. Generally, the degree of a company's commitment to and investment in a history program is directly related to the perceived benefits in public relations, legal, financial, or marketing areas. For example, consumer products companies such as Coca-Cola, Procter and Gamble, and Kraft Foods have made extensive use of their archives to understand and capitalize on the essence of their brands in marketing efforts. Disney's archives has been a tremendous public relations tool for reaching out to the many Disney collectors who have helped keep Mickey Mouse an American icon long after he stopped appearing in feature-length cartoons. Both Disney and Coca-Cola have established licensing programs that generate substantial revenues from marketing items (such as Christmas ornaments, toys, and collector's plates) that portray historical images from their archives. Insurance companies such as CIGNA and Aetna have used their archives to settle claims relating to policies purchased many decades earlier. Pharmaceutical companies such as Eli Lilly rely on their archives to comply with legal and regulatory requirements, while multinational companies of all sorts use archives and records management techniques to comply with international quality standards such as ISO 9000.[3]

ACCESS

When providing service to company employees, you should be prepared for the probability of having to restrict access to your company's
historical resources. For those who have been trained in an academic setting, this poses a dilemma. Historians and archivists generally value programs that provide free and equal access to as many records as possible.
In fact, the Society of American Archivists' code of ethics requires equal
access to all researchers, regardless of their motives in doing the research. However, in a corporate setting, it is unwise to follow such a
course of action.

Unlike many historical societies and libraries that are supported with
public funds, for-profit corporations have no obligation to provide public access to their records. They are perfectly within their rights to deny
anyone outside their companies the right to see internal documents. Of
course, one could argue that if a company is willing to provide access to
its records, its accomplishments and contributions will be more widely
recognized and admired. Conversely, by denying access to its archives, a
company's executives may provoke researchers into the suspicion that
they are trying to hide something. Nevertheless, it is your responsibility
as a corporate archivist to weigh all access requests carefully, because *you
must understand a researcher's motivation for gaining access to your collections.*

Let us look at how two seemingly similar access requests can produce
widely varying results. In the first case, the producers of a documentary
request access to your founder's correspondence files in order to better
understand the importance of your company in the establishment of an
industry. As the outcome of the request appears to be positive for your
company, you will most likely approve it. In the second instance, an author requests permission to access the same files as part of her research
for a book. However, in this case you learn that the author is planning an
exposé on what she perceives to be questionable early business practices
by the company's founder. The publicity from such a book could bring
unfavorable attention to your company and might raise questions about
the wisdom of maintaining files with apparently damaging information.
Therefore, you should discuss the request and its possible consequences
with your management, as well as with the public relations and legal
staffs, in order to come to a mutual decision regarding the proper course
of action. Often, the decision can and should be made to deny the author's request.

While the archivist or public historian may be fully aware of the
importance of the company's history to the public, it is more important

to address corporate needs first. Otherwise, there is a danger that the information will never be preserved or shared with *any* interested audiences, internal or external.

HISTORICAL ACCURACY

One of the benefits a company gains from employing an archivist or historian is a public perception of corporate integrity due to the pursuit of historical accuracy. Yet almost every corporate archivist has a story to tell about when business needs and historical accuracy came into conflict. Let us consider a hypothetical scenario wherein a brand manager has a brilliant idea to create a new brand that would use the company founder's image on the product label, thereby conveying a sense of longevity and trust. Assuming that the marketing staff can get legal approval for use of the image, you may find yourself negotiating with the brand manager regarding the appropriate portrayal of your founder. For example, it may help position the product if your founder is portrayed wearing a Stetson hat, but you know for a fact that he never did so. If you choose to advocate for a change in the label, you should work with the brand manager on alternate ways to incorporate the product positioning message.

A more common problem comes when a company is preparing text for a press release, training video, or anniversary publicity. Your company's complex history may be reduced to "sound bites" or bullet points that are manageable but don't quite capture a completely accurate picture. In your attempt to correct the wording, you may destroy the snappy, concise phrasing that the marketing or PR staff had worked so hard to create. At such times, it is necessary to call upon all of your writing skills to incorporate both brevity and accuracy.

There are no right or wrong answers in these cases. It is your job to fight for historical accuracy. However, you need to do so in a way that does not alienate your internal users. It is a certainty that *if the archives or history department ever becomes difficult to use, the value it brings to the company will begin to decline.*

PLANNING/PRIORITIZING/BUDGETING

Typical graduate history programs do not prepare their students for the reality of working in a corporate setting. Training in research, writing, oral history, exhibits, and records processing provides an important professional groundwork, but the successful corporate historian or archivist must learn how to plan his or her own program. I for one never learned about strategic planning, goal setting, or budget planning during my undergraduate or graduate schooling. Instead, I learned almost all of it on the job or through company-sponsored training programs. That is a sobering thought, since I now consider my planning skills to be a key factor in my success.

You may believe that one of the reasons you decided to pursue public history was because you disliked finance and business management classes. The truth is, however, that all historians and archivists, regardless of where they work, need to become proficient managers of their time and their money. Corporate archivists have had to deal with this reality for quite some time and are actually at an advantage when compared to their colleagues in public repositories. We are now better prepared to compete for scarce resources based on our planning and budgeting skills, just when the harsh reality of reengineering and downsizing are extending beyond the business world into government and universities.

I learned about the value of strategic planning in the early 1990s, after Philip Morris Companies acquired Kraft Foods (my former employer) and merged it with General Foods Corporation, another Philip Morris subsidiary. The company went through a substantial reorganization that had a direct impact on Kraft's archival program. With the encouragement of my management, I decided to go through a strategic planning process. I prepared a benchmarking survey with other corporate archives to discover how our procedures and policies compared with other top programs. I conducted phone interviews with major internal archives clients to find out what they did or did not like about the level of service they were receiving from us. My staff and I then performed a SWOT (Strengths/Weaknesses/Opportunities/Threats) analysis that identified major areas in our program that needed to be addressed, revised, or strengthened.

From this analysis, my staff and I prepared a mission statement and planning document that guided our efforts for the next three years. The first draft of this strategic plan took us more than a year to research and prepare. But it was well worth the effort, since my management responded positively to it. As a supplement to the plan, my staff and I prepared a couple of cost-benefit analyses to justify increased funding for two particularly worrisome shortcomings in our program. All of this work—based, significantly, on standard business planning models—paid off, and funds were allocated at a time when budgets were shrinking corporate-wide.

For many years, I have been responsible for preparing an annual budget of operating expenses. I track the expenses monthly and am responsible for keeping within that budget. All of this requires much more number-crunching than I ever thought I would have to do as a historian. However, my ability to plan and live within a budget has resulted in strong performance reviews as well as a great deal of autonomy in making spending decisions for my program.

COMMUNICATING

I remember struggling in college to meet the minimum length requirements for essay tests and term papers. I became skilled at the long way to say things, and I often managed to prepare thirty-page term papers. When I first started as a corporate archivist in 1981, I had to work hard to overcome years of training in academic writing techniques.

Brevity and clarity, not length and density, are key virtues in a corporate environment. It is important to make your point quickly and support it persuasively. Whenever possible, letters and memos should be kept to one page. Corporate managers and executives are swamped with paperwork, and your point will be ignored if you cannot express it concisely. Excellent writing skills are a necessity when marshaling support for your program.

Oral communication is also important. Speak clearly and concisely. Good eye contact and body language that conveys a sense of confidence will increase the chance that your message will be well received. And do not forget that listening skills are an essential part of good communication. Wait to hear what a person has to say, then repeat the salient points before you try to respond.

When speaking or writing to your management about problems, be sure to present the issues clearly and always include possible solutions. Managers at all levels of business are now handling more workload than ever, and they probably would not welcome having more problems dumped on them. By providing a coherent analysis of the situation and suggesting solutions, you create a good starting point for further discussion. Your management may or may not agree with your ideas, but they will certainly appreciate your foresight and preparedness.

Pay attention to the buzzwords of your company. At Kraft, the people who bought our products were our "consumers"; at Ford they are our "customers." At Kraft we spoke about "strategic competitive advantages" and "brand equity." At Ford there is such an overwhelming array of acronyms for programs, departments, and buildings that a page on the company's Intranet is devoted to "Ford Speak."[4] While it is tempting to dismiss corporate vernacular as cultural gimmickry, it is essential to your credibility that you take it very seriously. The more you speak and write in terms that are commonly accepted and used in your company, the more likely it is that your points and arguments will be accepted.

When talking to someone who is not an archivist, especially a corporate manager, try to avoid using the buzzwords of your profession. For example, when I talk about the origin of files in the archives, I avoid referring to the "provenance" of the records. And although we have explained to our direct management that "accessioning" means accepting records into the archives, it is not a term that we can easily use with the uninitiated.

OUTREACH

Every corporate archivist or historian must be a salesperson for the profession. If you enjoy the pleasure of retreating from the world with your historical "treasures" to do research or processing, then working for a corporation is not for you. Few individuals anywhere understand what archivists or historians do; business people are no different. Furthermore, the reorganizations and downsizings that are so common today result in frequent management changes. Therefore, the process of educat-

At the World of Coca-Cola, a public museum developed and operated by the company, nearly 1,200 artifacts from the company's archival collections are used to tell the 111-year history of Coca-Cola. Opened in 1990, the museum has an annual attendance of 1 million visitors. *Courtesy of the Coca-Cola Company.*

Corporate archives are a rich source of visual imagery and historical data that can be used in a variety of outreach efforts, including historical booklets and pamphlets, employee newsletters, and catalogs. *Courtesy of the Coca-Cola Company.*

ing your management and your clients about the value of your work is never-ending.

Outreach includes many elements—among them, exhibits, brochures, and articles in the company newsletter—but it starts with the archivist/historian presenting himself or herself professionally to colleagues. You must be tireless in your efforts to introduce yourself to others and explain your department and services to potential customers. Every activity report or staff meeting provides an opportunity to express the value of your services. Every phone contact or research request is an opportunity to shine—and do not be shy about asking your clients to tell your management if they are particularly happy with your services.

One of the most effective outreach tools is a presentation about your program. I still remember being terrified at my first corporate presentation. But I made it through without a major disaster and have since learned to welcome presentations as opportunities for self-improvement. Professional conferences can be a wonderful training ground for corporate presentations, and many employers offer presentation skills training programs. You can also study others who do well in front of an audience and try to emulate them.

Not all outreach is formal or planned, however. You can gain a great deal from informal daily contacts with your fellow employees. Every public historian must interact successfully with a number of constituencies, including records managers, librarians, consultants, public relations staff, attorneys, and marketing staff. A big part of your job is to ensure that you get out from behind your desk to meet these people and spend enough time with them so that you understand their needs and wants. They should also understand who you are, what you do, and why it is important for them to cooperate with your efforts. There is much to be gained from informal contacts in the halls, at lunch, or after work.

BUSINESS DRESS

An important corollary to presenting yourself well in a corporate setting is dressing appropriately. In recent years, the advent of "business casual" clothing has relaxed the standards seen in many companies. However, when in doubt, dress conservatively. Suits and ties are appropriate for men, and dresses or suits are best for women. Investing in a good wardrobe will help to promote your importance and that of your department. Your fellow employees, as well as managers and executives, will take you more seriously if you present yourself professionally. Pay attention to how others dress, especially those who are perceived as leaders, and emulate them. This strategy may offend your sense of individuality and freedom of expression, but it will help to advance your career and your program.

LEARNING MORE

If you are interested in learning more about business archives, a good place to start is the Business Archives Section of the Society of American Archivists (SAA).[5] This special interest group includes individuals who work in corporate archives as well as archivists who work for repositories which collect business records. The Section meets once per year at the SAA annual meeting and often sponsors special workshops, seminars, and tours in conjunction with the annual meeting. The Section also issues two newsletters per year, packed with news items about business archives programs and developments. About once per year, SAA offers a three-day workshop called "Business Archives: The Basics and Beyond," which presents an overview of the fundamentals involved in managing a business archives and stresses practical solutions to issues faced in a corporate environment. Emphasis is placed on garnering management support for the establishment of an archival program and on marketing archival assets and services to company employees. The workshop incorporates lectures, discussion, case studies, and tours of corporate archives and is designed to encourage participation by attendees, with mutual sharing of information. You should also consider subscribing to the Business Archives listserve, which provides a forum for the discussion of current issues and future international developments.[6]

Key publications include *The Records of American Business*, edited by James M. O'Toole, a collection of essays written by business archives leaders that represents the most current research and writings in the field. While slightly dated, *Corporate Archives and History: Making the Past Work*, edited by Arnita A. Jones and Philip L. Cantelon, includes some classic business archives articles, including "Present Value of Corporate History," by George David Smith and Laurence E. Steadman. For practical advice on how to be a better advocate for your program, see *Advocating Archives: An Introduction to Public Relations for Archivists*, edited by Elsie Freeman Finch. Finally, *A Selected and Annotated Bibliography on Business Archives and Records Management*, compiled and edited by Karen M. Benedict, provides a list of articles and books on the topic of business archives, with brief descriptions for each entry.[7]

CONCLUSION

Individuals who are trained in traditional scholarly history programs might find the corporate world to be not to their taste, but I have found that working in corporations has sharpened some essential skills that can be applied in any environment. It is just a matter of time before other types of archives have to deal with the same constraints and demands with which corporate archives are coping now. Several trends bear me out: steady decreases in government funding for the arts and humanities are forcing not-for-profit organizations to find other ways of keeping their programs going; cries for a balanced U.S. budget are forcing the "reinvention" of government; and declining enrollment in colleges and universities is placing a myriad of budget pressures on academia. Therefore, the lessons that corporate archivists have learned by working in a financially restrictive and rapidly changing environment could be a model for the rest of the archives and public history fields.

Practicing public history in a corporate environment is generally rewarding and always challenging. Since most corporate history programs are small, the archivist/historian wears many hats and continually adds skills. This opportunity to learn and grow is almost limitless. You have the chance to make a substantial difference in the success of your program—more so than you would in a historical society or large government archives. That success, however, is based on your ability to understand and work within the key parameters of your company: its business needs and its culture.

NOTES

1. No one can state unequivocally the reasons for the unprecedented growth in corporate archives in the 1970s. I believe that the two most important factors were the U.S. Bicentennial and the economy. The Bicentennial raised general public awareness of history in general, and companies probably started to see some substantial public relations benefits in emphasizing their heritage. The 1970s were also a generally prosperous decade, despite some problems with inflation. Companies could afford to take the luxury of investing in history programs that may have been viewed in harder times as nice, but not necessary.

2. In 1981, George David Smith and Laurence E. Steadman wrote a seminal essay titled "Present Value of Corporate History" for the *Harvard Business Review* 59 (November/December 1981): 164–73. Their article is an excellent overview of the potential benefits that a company can realize from history. To this day their persuasive, well-targeted arguments are recommended reading for any historian or archivist interested in working with corporate management. This essay is reprinted in Arnita A. Jones and Philip L. Cantelon, eds., *Corporate Archives and History: Making the Past Work* (Malabar, FL: Krieger Publishing Company, 1993).

3. ISO 9000 is a series of quality system standards developed by international organizations and industries and published by the International Organization for Standardization (ISO). A major component of ISO 9000 is careful record keeping to document quality processes. ISO certification is an increasingly important credential for companies which want to conduct business on a global basis with other ISO-certified companies.

4. The "Ford Speak" site on Ford's Intranet currently includes more than 8,000 acronyms and terms. Examples of some of the more commonly used abbreviations include:

ACD	Automotive Components Division
BE	Body Engineering
CS	Customer Satisfaction
LMD	Lincoln-Mercury Division
MVGP	Mission, Values and Guiding Principles
PM	Either Participative Management or Preventive Maintenance (depending on how it is used)
TER	Travel Expense Report
WCT	World Class Timing
WHQ	World Headquarters

5. For additional information on SAA, see the "Resources" section of this volume.

6. To subscribe to the Business Archives listserve, send an e-mail note to majordomo@gla.ac.uk and leave the subject line blank. In the body of the text type the following: subscribe busarch [your e-mail address].

7. James M. O'Toole, ed., *The Records of American Business* (Chicago, IL: Society of American Archivists, 1997); Jones and Cantelon, eds., *Corporate Archives*

and History; Elsie Freeman Finch, ed., *Advocating Archives: An Introduction to Public Relations for Archivists* (Metuchen, NJ: Society of American Archivists and the Scarecrow Press, Inc., 1994); and Karen M. Benedict, comp. and ed., *A Selected and Annotated Bibliography on Business Archives and Records Management* (Chicago, IL: Society of American Archivists, 1992).

PHILIP L. CANTELON is president and chief executive officer of History Associates Incorporated. A graduate of Dartmouth College, he earned a master's degree in history from the University of Michigan and a Ph.D. at Indiana University. Prior to establishing his consulting business, Dr. Cantelon served as a visiting lecturer at Yale University, taught at Williams College, and was a Fulbright professor of American civilization in Japan. His numerous professional activities include serving as president of the Society for History in the Federal Government, as executive director and a member of the board of directors of the National Council on Public History, on the board of editors of The Public Historian, *as chairman of the Montgomery County (Maryland) Historic Preservation Commission, and on the Organization of American Historians' Committee on Research and Access to Historical Documentation. His publications include* Never Stand Still: A History of CNF Transportation Inc., 1929–2000 *(1999),* The Roadway Story *(1996),* The History of MCI, 1968–1988: The Early Years *(1993),* Corporate Archives and History: Making the Past Work *(1993),* The American Atom *(1984, 1991), and* Crisis Contained: The Department of Energy at Three Mile Island *(1980).*

AS A BUSINESS: HIRED, NOT BOUGHT

Philip L. Cantelon

"You do what? I've never heard of someone who makes a business of history." I don't know how many times I've heard this response when I explained what I do for a living. "I really like history," they continue, "but I didn't know you could make a living at it unless you taught."

This all-too-familiar exchange underlines several aspects of being a professional historian. First, the prevailing wisdom is that historians only teach. Second, historians outside the academy have done a poor job explaining and marketing the value and use of their skills. And third, all this is changing. As historians once again face the specter of a shrinking academic job market, undergraduate and graduate departments alike are reexamining career opportunities for their students. In the future, going into the "history business" may be a good bet for those individuals with the flexibility, the personality, and the inclination to bring professional history to those who can profit from it.

During the continuing job crisis for historians in the 1970s and 1980s, the *Radical History Review*, in a burst of delicious irony, issued fiery red T-shirts and yellow matchbooks bearing the slogan: "EARN BIG MONEY! BECOME A HISTORIAN." The glut of historians coming out of graduate schools at that time ran smack into declining enrollments in history courses and shrinking history departments. Newly minted Ph.D. historians entered a professional world that lacked the college and university teaching jobs for which they were trained. Radical historians were quick to seize on this contradiction, though the solution of subscribing to the *Radical History Review* probably did little to solve either the unemployment or underemployment problems faced by historians.

A more realistic response was to look for employment elsewhere. Some historians urged retraining for the business world; others suggested educating a "new" type of historian in public or applied history; still others voted with their feet and pocketbooks and abandoned the profession altogether. A smaller number of historians took a somewhat different road, going into the "history business" as individual consultants, in partnerships, or by forming small companies. I took this less traveled path, forming History Associates in the summer of 1980. Over the next quarter of a century, the work of many of these professional practitioners altered the landscape of the history profession.

The mother of us all was Darlene Roth, who began a historical consulting company named The History Group, Inc. in Atlanta in 1975. Others may have started before Dr. Roth, but none publicized and proselytized the advantages of hiring historians as she did. The nation's Bicentennial had awakened interest in our past, and The History Group and several other collections of historians took advantage of the historic preservation, oral history, and research opportunities offered by local, state, and federal government agencies. By the spring of 1981, the National Coordinating Committee for the Promotion of History, under the leadership of Page Putnam Miller, published the first *Directory of Historical Consultants,* which listed thirty separate groups identifying themselves as offering professional historical services.

To be sure, the barriers to entering the history business in 1980 were relatively low: usually an advanced degree in history, stationery, business cards, telephone, a mailing address, and, with luck, a client were sufficient. Many of those listed in the 1981 *Directory* also held a full- or part-time academic appointment to cushion the uncertainties associated with obtaining a steady stream of clients.

In the years since then, some of those individuals and companies who called themselves historical consultants disappeared from the scene. New arrivals have taken their place. Historical services companies have reorganized; others have expanded. Of the thirty companies or partnerships listed in the 1981 *Directory,* only five or six are still operating. To be certain, an up-to-date edition of *Directory of Historical Consultants* would produce an informative picture of the travels and travails of practicing historians and the changing nature of public history. Such a directory should also include the historical consulting firms operating in Europe and Australia.

ENTREPRENEURSHIP TO ENTERPRISE

Do you like to take risks? Do you have a thick skin? Can you rebound from defeat? Can you survive periods of no work? Are you intellectually flexible? Are you patient? Do you enjoy working with others? If you've answered "yes" to all the above, you can be a politician. If you answered "yes" *and* can write clearly and believe there's a lot of teaching to be done outside a classroom to noncaptive students who actually want to learn from what you do, then the history business may be for you. Working for clients can be stressful; at other times it can be exhilarating. In my experience, it has always been educational. And after twenty years as a professional, largely nonacademic, historian, I still find my work exciting, frustrating, stimulating, and rewarding. Pretty normal for any job, I suspect. Best of all, I realize that in spite of my traditional historical training, which concentrated on scholarship and teaching, there really is life after the academy.

Surprisingly, or perhaps not so surprisingly, the life of a practicing historian is not all that different professionally from a teaching historian, though the clients are generally more demanding. Both kinds of historians are occupied with research, teaching, writing and publication, management meetings, professional committees, fellow employees, and organizational budgets. However, there is one major difference: practicing historians keep longer office hours.

Historians who contract their services enter the first phase of history for hire. They have begun thinking of history in entrepreneurial terms. Most historians hate to hustle. A cold sales call is anathema. Simply put, historians don't like to sell themselves. Nonetheless, considering history in entrepreneurial terms—such as asking how a specific organization can use the past and then selling its management on how it might profit from that use—is the first step to creating a history business. Once the habit of entrepreneurial thinking—making the unusual connection, creating a great idea, and selling it to others—is institutionalized, once you have turned the idea into a first-rate useable product, once you have built a

track record of experience and excellence, you are more than a historical entrepreneur. You have built a historical enterprise.

The process of going from entrepreneurship to enterprise may sound
easy but, of course, it rarely happens the way we plan it. At least in my case
it didn't. In 1980, I was doing some research at the National Archives
when I could not help but overhear a deep, booming Texas drawl in the
next room demanding that the archivist do some research for him. No,
the archivist explained, he didn't have time to do research for those who
needed information held in federal records. I seized the opportunity, offered my card and historical research services, fully expecting to be able
to get to such a project in several weeks when my current assignment had
wound down. "Meet me at my hotel in the morning with a contract," he
thundered, identifying himself as the head of the Texas General Land
Office. "I need this material right away." A contract? I'd never written
one. Moreover, since I was already fully engaged, who would do the work?
Necessity proved to be the mother of completion. By morning I had a
draft contract, a researcher, and a realization that someone would pay for
historical work. The rest, one could say, is History Associates Incorporated (HAI).

SETTING UP A PROFESSIONAL OPERATION

In founding History Associates, we were committed to doing more
than just getting some business and getting by. We wanted to establish a
company where professional historians could operate professionally. By
that, we meant that each staff member would earn a salary; receive a benefits package that included paid vacation, sick leave, health insurance,
and professional leave; and be hired for his or her skills rather than on a
project basis. The company would provide office space and equipment.
Further, we encouraged the staff to take an active role in professional organizations, such as the Society for History in the Federal Government,
the Society of American Archivists, and the National Council on Public
History. In short, we were trying to create a scholarly and professional environment not unlike a history department.

History Associates incorporated mainly for financial, legal, and tax reasons. That meant that each of the founders invested the same amount of
money into the corporation and received an equal number of shares in
return. The initial cash investment was used to establish an office, purchase stationery and equipment, hire an attorney and bookkeeper, and
generally get the operation running. Next came attracting new business,
hiring professional and support personnel, and then worrying how to
match invoices and cash flow with the payroll requirements. Meeting a

payroll month after month is no small achievement, which is why adequate capitalization of any business is so critical.

As a business, history is much like any other commercial operation, filled with risks and uncertainty and punctuated by good times and bad. Some have compared running a history consulting business to an academic department. There are some similarities, but a business, I believe, is more exacting and complex. Our customers are more experienced, more demanding than most students. Tenure decisions are all too immediate in the business world, where employees are constantly evaluated and there are few, if any, long-term contracts. It is difficult to hide a nonproducer in business; the bottom line cannot absorb a drone for long.

WHO HIRES HISTORIANS?

The General Land Office in Texas provided HAI with a good start, but one client cannot sustain a business for long. Fortunately, we found that there is a considerable need for the professional historical services offered by a firm like HAI. Government agencies of all types and at all levels, corporations, not-for-profits, law firms, clubs, museums, families, and individuals need, commission, and use historical studies. These same groups often seek archives and records management work, cultural resources management assistance, litigation research help, writing and editing services, or some combination of several of these areas. The spread of possible customers is breathtaking, limited only by our imagination and our potential clients' pocketbooks. Some historical services companies cover a wide range of businesses; others have carved out specific niches or fields of expertise. One way is not necessarily better than the other; they only differ. But a good rule of thumb is to stick with the kind of historical skills and services you know best.

Without pretending to be all-inclusive, I'd like to explain in greater detail some of the business areas in which practicing professional historians have made an impact, if not necessarily BIG MONEY. All of these fields have evolved in recent years and continue to change to meet the increasing sophistication of client needs and technologies. The first is in the area of writing histories, both monographic and celebratory studies; the second is historic preservation and cultural resources management; a third is archives and records management; a fourth is litigation research and expert witness testimony; and a fifth is historical interpretation and communications, including publications, film, and museums.

Writing historical monographs would appear to be the traditional stuff of the training of generations of historians. And indeed it should be. But because a historian is commissioned to do a history of, say, a corporation or government agency, many in the profession dismiss it as "court history," even before reading it. "How can your book be good history," I once was asked by such a nonreader, "if the client paid for it?" I was more than a little steamed. If I were a bad historian, it probably would be bad history. But at the very least, I'd like to have someone who read the book to say so, not someone who would ignore the evidence, the basic element of historical inquiry.

The question is one of those "when did you stop beating your wife" queries. It presupposes that professionally trained historians skew their products to collect their salaries or fees. It presupposes that the dash for the cash is more important than professional competence. It presupposes that clients want to spend money for inaccurate history. And the question presupposes that all parties to the work are morally, ethically, and professionally bankrupt. While there may be such historians available to be bought on a moment's notice, I don't know any who had much impact at all on the continued development and growth of historical studies written by professional historians either in or outside the academy. Puff pieces, as most practicing historians will admit, are better handled by people who specialize in public relations and advertising. Being hired, I would emphasize, does not mean being bought.

Scholarly historical monographs, commissioned by federal agencies, corporations, or nonprofit organizations, comprise a substantial percentage of the business of several historical services companies and individual practitioners. Most of these studies receive rigorous peer review and are often published by university or trade presses. However, only *The Public Historian* will review privately published works and scholarly studies produced for government agencies. If there is a major professional failing in regard to these works, it is that our largest professional journals, the *Journal of American History* and the *American Historical Review*, do not, as a matter of policy, review much "gray literature," much to the detriment of the entire profession. If those organizations seek to represent the entirety of the historical profession, such out-of-date policies will not survive into the twenty-first century.

Traditionally, government agencies have been large consumers of professional history. Some—the Atomic Energy Commission and the Nuclear Regulatory Commission, for instance—have earned reputations as agencies that have produced excellent, award-winning histories written by scholars employed by the agencies. The Office of the Secretary of Defense, the National Aeronautics and Space Administration, the U.S. Army Corps of Engineers, the Office of Air Force History, the National Science Foundation, the National Park Service, the Department of the Navy, the National Institutes of Health, the Department of Energy, and other agencies in the defense and intelligence communities put numerous requests for historical studies out to bid annually. Unfortunately, not all agencies require this work to be done by professional historians. Nonetheless, federal studies remain a large part of the total nonacademic work done by professional historians throughout the country.

While the federal history pot is relatively large, it is not always easy for individuals or small companies to land large contracts. Government accounting requirements for larger, multiyear contracts necessitate more extensive bookkeeping, legal, and insurance costs than most history companies can afford. Moreover, small business "set asides," those contracts specifically reserved for small companies or individuals, under which many historical projects fall, are being cut in numbers as contracting offices try to hold down their costs by consolidating smaller projects into larger service contracts containing tasks that no small company could handle on its own. Therefore, teaming with other kinds of companies that offer technology or other types of service support appears to be where federal opportunities are heading.

Public and private corporations are also major customers for historians. In 1981, George David Smith and Laurence E. Steadman published "Present Value of Corporate History" in the *Harvard Business Review*. That article remains the basic text for those writing the histories of corporations and the many uses to which those histories might be put, including strategic planning, policy formulation, management and employee orientation and development, marketing, and legal support. Anyone considering approaching a corporation should read this article first.[1]

A corporation may consider several uses or applications for its history, ranging from the celebratory to the cerebral, from an anniversary history to a thorough scholarly study of the company's development and corporate culture. Not-for-profit organizations have similar motivations. The need for a history can be dictated by a major change in senior management, a transition from one generation of managers to another, a merger or acquisition, a desire for new employees to understand the principles and development of the company, or any one of a number of other reasons to better understand current conditions or to commemorate them. Whatever the purpose for a history, it is incumbent upon any historian to produce the highest quality research, analysis, and writing possible for every commissioned study.

A second major aspect of historical consulting concerns what has become known as cultural resources management. Most of this work stems from federal, state, and local legislation relating to historic preservation, including National Register of Historic Places nominations, historic property evaluations, architectural histories, and Section 106 reviews for historic sites. Historical contractors also obtain work doing specific sections of Environmental Impact Statements required on certain projects involving federal funds. The National Park Service, the U.S. Department of Agriculture, the Forest Service, the Bureau of Reclamation, and the U.S. Army Corps of Engineers offer frequent contracting opportunities for administrative histories and other historical studies. In addition, historical societies and nonprofits at all levels have a continuing need to research and interpret the historical properties in their stewardship and should not to be overlooked when casting a consultant's net.

Archives and records management is a third growing area of expertise offered by several historical consulting companies. Many corporate executives and some government officials consider historical records a critical informational element to their organization's operation. With the explosion of information that accumulates in any office, businesses and governments need to manage and control both paper and electronic records as never before. As a result, information resource management has become crucial to organizations of all shapes and sizes. This growth in the number of records in various formats has opened a number of doors for consulting historians, archivists, and records managers.

The requirements for entering the information resource management business, however, tend to be higher than an advanced degree in history. Though historians without specialized training or field experience may find work in an archival setting, most organizations have grown more sophisticated in their requirements for archives and records management experience, expecting their consultants to have advanced degrees in archives management and pass additional exams for certification by the Society of American Archivists or the Association of Records Managers and Administrators. Thorough training in electronic records and digitization is essential for anyone planning to work in this area in the next decade.

A fourth growth area for consulting historians is litigation research. Attorneys on both sides of many disputes need a wide variety of historical evidence to help them shape strategy long before an issue reaches the courtroom. To date, much of this work has concentrated on environmental and water rights issues, health matters, and personal military service records. History Associates has worked on such high-profile causes as fallout from atmospheric nuclear weapons testing and the movement of Nazi gold in the 1940s to more routine matters such as patent claims.

A fifth area focuses on historical interpretation and communications. Museums will hire historians to assist with developing exhibit concepts and drafting text for exhibits and brochures. Along the same lines, film and television producers will contract with historians to ensure historical accuracy, especially for period costumes and customs, if not always the story line. Because this kind of work is specialized, museum and media work is not an easy area for most historians to crack. Rather, individuals with established reputations and considerable experience in museum work or a specific field are usually tapped for these jobs. Finally, some historians find work in the publishing business as manuscript evaluators, proofreaders, and documentary editors.

LANDING A CONTRACT

There are several ways to go after consulting contracts. The most obvious is to develop a concept and proposal, take it to the potential client, and sell the project on the spot. But, like an iceberg, what appears on the surface represents an enormous body of supporting work. Research, planning, a project outline, details of pertinent experience, proposal writing, costing, and a presentation of some type are necessary to convey to any potential client why you should be selected. Most of all you are selling yourself, your talents, your experience, your personality.

One process, known as "sole source" contracting, allows you to be hired without any competition from other bidders. The advantage is that the customer deals only with you; the downside is the possibility that the potential client likes your ideas and decides to let someone else do the job or to put the information contained in your proposal out for competitive bid, thereby diminishing the value of your original ideas. Such situations can, and have, occurred with both government and private sector officials. Unfortunately, the legal remedies are often more expensive than the value of the work.

Though the process is less personal, the most widespread information about potential historical contracts can be found in *Commerce Business Daily* (*CBD*), a publication available on the Internet which lists the contracting needs of federal agencies.[2] These listings are usually found under Section B, Special Studies and Analyses; Section C, Architect and Engineering Services; Section F, Natural Resources and Conservation Services; Section R, Professional, Administrative and Management Support Services; and Section T, Photographic Mapping, Printing, and Publications Services. The *CBD* listings normally require the potential bidder to request a prepared package detailing the agency's requirements. Most bidder's packages are "Requests for Proposals" or RFPs. The contractor then responds within a specific time frame, submitting a technical proposal that specifies how the individual or company would perform the contract if awarded and a cost proposal detailing what the government will pay for the work.

Competition for government contracts can be severe, especially since many large contractors have moved into areas that they largely disregarded when other areas were more profitable. At the same time, government contracting offices have consolidated historical and records work under larger contracts, effectively squeezing out many small businesses which are not able to team with bigger players. Also, because of the relative low value many government officials place on historical and records management work, often believing that anyone can do history and no one really cares about records, many of these kinds of contracts require no training or special expertise for the tasks to be performed and are set aside for special bid situations.

Who competes for historical business? Large contractors, affectionately known in the Washington, D.C., area as "Beltway Bandits," actively pursue historical and records management contracts awarded by federal agencies. Much of the historical work done for the defense, intelligence, and diplomatic communities goes to retired military officers or former agency employees. Their long experience with an agency or in a particular field makes them especially valuable in areas in which institutional memory is in short supply. Moreover, many of these former federal employees are "double dippers" who draw their retirement or pension income while continuing to work for their old agencies under outside contracts. Having two incomes, in effect, makes them highly competitive from a government procurement perspective.

College and university professors also compete for contracts in both public and private sectors. Because their overhead and administrative costs—telephone, office, utilities, library and Internet fees, health insurance, retirement plans, FICA, unemployment insurance, and the like—are often covered by their full-time employers, they are able to do a project on a part-time basis, while on a sabbatical, or with graduate students at lower rates than either independent scholars or a historical services company.

Journalists and specialized writers are often selected to write histories. Some years ago, Anna Nelson in a classic article, "History Without Historians," bemoaned the fact that many federal agencies preferred nonhistorians for historical jobs.[3] The situation has not greatly changed. For example, the Naval Research Laboratory, which has a historian on staff, recently advertised for a science writer, not a professional historian, to produce its history. The National Institute of Standards and Technology (formerly the National Bureau of Standards) insisted that only a scientist could write its history. In the private sector, some corporations prefer a journalist's treatment to that of a professional historian. This is not to say that these works by nonhistorians are second rate. Some are excellent.

Rather, I believe that, as a profession, historians overall do a fairly poor job of selling their talents.

Others in the hunt for history dollars are independent scholars, partnerships of two or more historians, spouse teams, and incorporated businesses ranging in size from fewer than a handful to over thirty-five historians, archivists, records managers, and other professionals and full-time staff. Some specialize in state and local contracts, others concentrate their work with certain federal agencies, and some focus their business exclusively in the private sector. Some companies view themselves as full-service firms, offering a broad range of skills and experience to clients of every size and type.

IN CONCLUSION

The outlook for young historians working in the history business should only improve. Potential clients in the government and in corporations have become increasingly sophisticated about the uses and value of professional historical, archival, and records management work. Moreover, the generation of historians who pioneered professional history for hire will be retiring over the next decade. The road for the next generation of enthusiastic, innovative, and entrepreneurial historians should be wide open.

NOTES

1. George David Smith and Laurence E. Steadman, "Present Value of Corporate History," *Harvard Business Review* 59 (November/December 1981): 164–73. The article is reprinted in Arnita A. Jones and Philip L. Cantelon, eds., *Corporate Archives and History: Making the Past Work* (Malabar, FL: Krieger Publishing Company, 1993).
2. The Web page for the *Commerce Business Daily* is http://www.cbdweb.com.
3. Anna Nelson, "History without Historians," *AHA Newsletter* 16 (February 1978): 10–11.

JAMES T. SPARROW is assistant professor of history at the University of Chicago. He earned his B.A. at the University of Pennsylvania and his A.M. and Ph.D. at Brown University. Prior to joining the University of Chicago faculty, he was co-director of ECHO: Exploring and Collecting History Online at the Center for History and New Media at George Mason University and taught in the University's Department of History. He was also part of the team of historians working on the September 11 Digital Archive at CHNM and director of the Blackout History Project. Dr. Sparrow has published reviews in the Journal of American History *and* Societá e Storia *and has given papers at numerous meetings and conferences sponsored by the Alfred P. Sloan Foundation, the Gotham Center at the City University of New York, the Organization of American Historians, the Society for the History of Technology, and others.*

ON THE WEB: THE SEPTEMBER 11 DIGITAL ARCHIVE

James T. Sparrow[1]

On September 11, 2002, more than 5,000 people gathered to tell their personal accounts of the tragic day that had rocked their lives exactly a year earlier. Hundreds more shared photographs, urgent messages, and other personal effects they had saved from that fateful day. An audience of more than 100,000 joined them, avidly attending to the minutest details of the witness they bore. As early as lunchtime, the number of those stopping by just to watch video clips presented by other participants approached 10,000. At the end of the day, the total number of objects of all types viewed by visitors ran to well over a million. Once through the entrance, visitors each discovered a space with a view of the past that fit their own circumstances and meandering predilections. As they wandered from exhibit to exhibit, visitors did not so much as brush the shoulders of the more than 700 other people who attempted to join in at the very same instant, in a constant flood of humanity that persisted unabated for over 18 hours. Indeed, they may not have had any inkling of just how large an assembled audience they had joined that night. Yet no visitor could have missed the presence of so many others who were willing to share their small part of history with the public. Indeed, it was precisely this sort of sharing that had drawn them all there in the first place, whether as participants or onlookers.

The place where they crossed paths was no place at all—or rather, it was a virtual space. In the "real" world, their steps fell within the confines of a web server's overloaded circuitry and jammed hard drive, secreted away in a stuffy closet in Fairfax, Virginia. The website they visited—and built in the process, in many cases—was the September 11 Digital Archive, an online archive built by ordinary people who chose to document their small parts of this globe-shaking event by going online and typing or uploading the digital remnants of their personal pasts.

In the months following the anniversary, thousands of visitors would return to the Archive, some on a daily basis to see the new entries as they mounted, others just once or twice to add their voice (or their photographic eye, or witnesses' ear) to the historical record and leave their memories there to rest. As images from digital cameras, forwarded e-mail messages, voicemail narrations, and other digital testaments arrived by wire and mail, the Archive evolved into something wonderfully unanticipated. The team of historians who brought it into being (myself included) are still trying to decide where, exactly, it fits within the spectrum of historical practice. The one thing on which we can agree is that it is clearly and inescapably a work of public history in many senses of the term—some of them very new and still protean. This essay will explore these new valences of practice and meaning, holding up the Archive as a case study of the broader movement to embrace the online environment. The Archive's brief history suggests that the web is indeed a place where meaningful public history can take a new form and perhaps become more democratic as it "gets wired."

PUBLIC HISTORY IN THE DIGITAL AGE

In recent years there has been an explosion of hundreds, if not thousands of websites aiming to democratize public access to the raw materials of the past by placing them online. These range from the humblest personal web page put up by a Civil War enthusiast, to the efforts of local historical societies and museums to develop an online presence, all the way up to the formidable online presence of national museums and historical organizations. It seems that everyone must have a website. The ever-expanding domain of what historian Roy Rosenzweig calls "the history web" is already too massive to catalog or even define.[2] Almost overnight the web has enabled a new and expansive form of public history to emerge—although precisely where and how we should draw boundaries around either the "history" or the "public" we find online may never be determined.

To the skeptical, the great rush to the web may appear to be no more than a techno-mystical way to pour old wine into new bottles. Or worse, it may seem to augur a dystopian nightmare of technological determinism in which the machines decide what history can and should be, forcing the rich complexity of the past and its artifactual legacy into the deracinated cultural shallows of a medium that reduces everything to electrified ones and zeroes. Those inconvenient artifacts and modes of thinking and presentation that fail to translate well into the digital realm may be obscured or destroyed outright.[3] Web-based history may also be especially susceptible to the uncritical "progress talk" that historian Mike Wallace has observed dominating the narratives and modes of exhibition in museums of technology. Just as such museums can reflect the class biases of the engineers and corporate managers who patronize them, so too might the digital medium be prone to a comparably technophilic self-congratulation. And while museums of technology can suffer from the "tyranny of objects, the lure of the authentic," historical websites may likewise privilege digital objects over interpretation and historical relationships. There is a real danger that the magic of the Internet may lead us to reify digital objects, with all their slick production values, even more easily than is the case with "genuine" (physical) artifacts.[4] Finally, there is a fear that the web may threaten the carefully constructed layers of authenticity, context, and documentation that curators, archivists, and other public historians have devoted their careers to establishing and preserving for our precious and fragile historical heritage. This concern is not surprising (or unreasonable) given the "Wild West" atmosphere of the web today and the ease with which digital documents may be altered without a trace. In such a climate, experienced web travelers cannot help wondering, "What am I really looking at, and is it genuine?"

Such concerns have their merits, and we should not allow history to fall prey to the same booster mentality that recently devastated the stock market when the "dot com" bubble burst. But even if we adopt an extremely cautious and pessimistic stance toward the new technology, it is clear that the embrace of the web is not a simple matter of technological determinism. As cultural studies scholar Randy Bass has observed in the context of American studies, changing ideas about both technology and the practice of history have heavily shaped the specific practices we have adopted to take advantage of the web.[5] In general, recent years have seen a growing attention to historical agency, marginal or otherwise over-

looked voices, multiple perspectives, and the broader experiences of ordinary people, all of which have cast a democratic light on recent developments in information technology. The rise of popular history on the
web also dovetails with an evolving interest among curators, documen-
tarists, and other practitioners of public history to more fully involve their
audiences. As public historians have democratized and rethought the nature of their discipline, the siren call of the web has become increasingly
hard to ignore. To those with eyes to see, it is apparent that the web has
already unleashed an enthusiasm and participatory ethos into the public
experience of history that can be harnessed to salutary ends.

The web is built for a high degree of interactivity, which can be brought
into physical exhibit space through the use of terminals or extended out
in time and space through a web presence that persists beyond an exhibit.
Devices promoting popular engagement in historical thinking, such as
quizzes, discussion forums, and opportunities for visitor feedback, are also
relatively easy to set up on a website.[6] Websites provide a degree of flexibility impossible to attain in physical space, allowing for a multiplicity of
views and vantage points. Online exhibits permit contextualization of extraordinary depth, extending well beyond the few hundred words that can
fit on placards and in brochures or catalogues. They can also provide multiple views of artifacts as they were created or unearthed, an effective way
to expose the process of curation and preservation while also increasing
the historian's power to contextualize the raw materials of history. Just as
multiple voices and perspectives enrich a fictional narrative, so too do
multiple media and the diverse vantages they provide amplify the analytical and evocative power of historical accounts.[7]

The web makes possible "the novice in the archive," as Randy Bass has
observed: it has the potential to radically democratize access to historical
materials, thereby decentralizing historical practice as ordinary people
gain access to the record of their own past. When researchers have asked
museum goers and other ordinary Americans about their involvement in
the past, they have discovered that the public's interests differ from what
academics, curators, and other experts anticipated. Many crave a direct
connection to the past, with as little (apparent) mediation as possible.[8]
This popular demand for greater access to the past, unobstructed by layers
of expert control or by the numbing blandishments of textbooks, intersects
powerfully with the decentralizing tendencies of the Internet. To envision
how thoroughly this trend might alter ordinary Americans' understanding
of the past, imagine what would happen if anyone could conduct a full-text,
Google-like search on all government documents under the Freedom of
Information Act (FOIA). When anyone can search, sort, and follow links
between archival materials and digital artifacts, the hierarchical relation-

ships between experts and laypersons are destabilized. The very basis for expert knowledge loses a powerful set of real-world foundations.[9]

Perhaps for this reason, historians have been slow to respond to popular passions for participating in history—especially when they emanate from the Internet. Indeed, some public history sites purposely restrict the open-ended possibilities of their web pages in an attempt to sustain their control over the visitor's experience. They limit links to outside sites and treat their own sites' content as if it were simply another caption that happened to be mounted on a website.[10] Consequently, although there is a proliferation of public history on the web, many "virtual exhibits" are really little more than posters for "real" installations in museums. In such cases, creating a historical website involves no new historical work, but rather becomes simply a chore akin to advertising.

Outside the confines of professional history the situation is somewhat different, with a number of sites devoted to online commemoration and history-making. Flourishing sites devoted to "real-world" communities, like the one devoted to Brainerd, Kansas, or the Rowville-Lysterfield community center in Australia, craft online spaces where local people build their own historical record, contributing family histories, reminiscences, folklore, and personal artifacts such as photos and scanned documents.[11] "Talkback" sites for television broadcasts such as PBS's POV site, "Re: Vietnam, Stories Since the War" feature very active newsgroup-style discussions driven by viewers who, like many Vietnam veterans, are personally invested in both the presentation of history ("getting it right") and recording their place within it.[12] Online communities, including Senior-Net's World War II Living Memorial and the History Channel's Veteran's Forum, host discussion "threads" with thousands of historical recollections and conversations about the past (albeit mixed in with less historical commentary).[13] Some new media art installations also focus on memory in ways that extend the historical record. One such installation, the Collected Visions project at New York University, solicits photographs— both online and during inaugural exhibits—which are annotated by the contributors with explanatory excerpts about their family history.[14] The powerful Atomic Memories virtual exhibit at San Francisco's Exploratorium also began as an installation tied to a web forum, juxtaposing personal memories of how visitors first learned about the bombing of Hiroshima and Nagasaki with reflections on the meaning of nuclear warfare.[15]

The following case study of the September 11 Digital Archive provides a glimpse into the workings of a project that, in a similarly participatory vein, seeks to take full advantage of the flexibility and interactivity of the web. Wedding popular participation to scholarly practice, the Archive aims to bring the public closer to the center of public history, thereby allowing ordinary Americans to literally make their own history.

THE SEPTEMBER 11 DIGITAL ARCHIVE:
911digitalarchive.org

In the late summer of 2001, the Center for History and New Media (CHNM) at George Mason University (GMU) was uniquely positioned to respond to the historical challenge of documenting popular experiences of the disaster about to unfold. Since the early 1990s, it had been a leader in the emerging field of computing and the humanities, producing CD-ROM textbooks, websites, and other projects that sought to move beyond traditional historical practice. In 1998, I joined the center with an experimental pilot, the Blackout History Project, which sought to use the web not simply for historical presentation but to develop a methodology to collect, preserve, and create new, digital types of primary historical materials via the Internet.[16] One of a score of projects funded by the Alfred P. Sloan Foundation between 1997 and 2000 to improve the preservation and documentation of the recent history of science and technology,[17] the Blackout project began from a basic premise. Modern life had "gone digital," leaving traces of the past on hard disks and in other electronic storage media; it was time for history to catch up. Since January of 2001 a second, broader CHNM project named ECHO (Exploring and Collecting History Online) has continued to experiment with new methods in online collecting, producing a series of small projects on the recent history of science and technology. ECHO seeks to learn from its projects, the other collecting projects funded by Sloan, and other early ventures in this new field, distilling their lessons into a set of best practices for online research with historical subjects. After five years of experimentation, we now have a collection of software tools, techniques, and case studies to guide historians in the ways that the web and other new media may be used to extend and enrich the historical record.[18]

As shock gave way to reflection in the days and weeks following the airplane attacks on the World Trade Center and the Pentagon on September 11, 2001, it became clear that ECHO's approach to documenting contemporary history was especially well-suited to the task of capturing a broad canvas of Americans' experiences for the historical record of "9/11" (as it has come to be known). We viewed this challenge with a mixture of hope and trepidation. Here was an event that demanded extraordinary delicacy, considering the sacrosanct wreath of commemoration which most Americans placed around the tragedy and its victims. Like the curators at the National Museum of American History, the Museum of

the City of New York, and the other museums that banded together to respond to 9/11, we faced the dilemma of how to handle the collection of
contemporary historical materials when popular feelings ran so high,
with little emotional or temporal distance to lend perspective. Would our
professional obligation to maintain a critical stance toward historical materials make us appear inappropriately aloof, thus driving away potential
contributors? Or would emotionally gripping stories and artifacts, such
as missing persons' posters, overshadow other important but less dramatic aspects?[19] Despite these worries, we felt a great concern that something valuable would be lost if we didn't act quickly. Memories would
fade, e-mail would be deleted from inboxes, faxes and word-processed di-
ary entries would vanish in the ordinary cycle of hard drive crashes and
software upgrades. The digital substratum that has come to line the foundations of daily life would corrode and slip away due to the relative
fragility of magnetic and other types of electronic storage media.

Turning to historical precedent, we inquired whether an event of comparable magnitude had been preserved in fine-grained detail at the grassroots. Immediately following Pearl Harbor, government-employed social
scientists had rushed out to capture the reactions of ordinary Americans
in quick polls and "man on the street" interviews.[20] Although we lacked
the funding or the staff of these efforts, we enjoyed the advantage of living in a time when millions of Americans self-document their experiences and views by composing weblogs (online diaries), sending e-mail,
joining chat sessions (real-time discussion forums), and otherwise bend-
ing the personal computer to their own devices. We saw an opportunity
to use the web tools and methods we had already developed for ECHO
to allow hundreds, perhaps thousands, to contribute their stories, e-mail,
images, voicemail, chat sessions, pager messages, home movies, digital
artwork, word-processed diaries and letters, and other electronic documents to a permanent historical record. Our web server could accept
scores of thousands of entries and visitors almost as easily as it could accommodate a handful.

The September 11 Digital Archive began, fittingly enough, in an act of
partnership. As with previous collecting efforts, it was through partnership that the most effective outreach was possible. Realizing the need for
a broad foundation of historical expertise based in the two major metro
areas affected by the attacks, the ECHO team and others at CHNM joined
forces with a long-time partner, the American Social History Project
(ASHP) at the City University of New York (CUNY) Graduate Center.[21]
The ASHP had deep roots, both academic and otherwise, in the affected
communities of New York City, as well as considerable expertise in history and new media. Armed with a fresh grant from the Sloan Founda-

tion, which saw both a good cause and a chance to put its vision of online collecting to the test, we got to work in late December of 2001.

Our first challenges were practical and organizational. We had to quickly design a site that would collect the broadest possible range of digital materials from an almost infinitely wide spectrum of contributors, while avoiding the opposing dangers of either censoring or appearing to condone the extreme views that such a charged topic inevitably would attract. A related challenge involved concentrating our limited resources and staff time on the potentially unbounded task of outreach and recruiting, since this was an event that literally the whole world had witnessed in one form or another.

Right away we set up teams to handle critical tasks, including: database and interface programming; web design for look, feel, and accessibility; outreach targeted at specific communities near the crash sites in New York City, Washington, D.C., and Shanksville, Pennsylvania; public relations aimed at local, regional, and national media outlets; editors and vetting reviewers to provide quality control and legal protection for materials displayed on the site; and partnerships with key organizations and institutions. Every few months or so we met in person at CUNY or GMU to firm up those intangible but essential connections that make teamwork possible across multiple sites. In between visits, we collaborated via e-mail, phone, and videoconference.

The first task, building the website, was easier than might otherwise have been the case thanks to our shelf of existing code and templates from ECHO. From our earlier efforts, and from the literature on web usability, we knew that web users' greatest frustrations centered around speed and ease of use, rather than the aesthetics of design, and that these concerns were driven by an overriding desire to locate some specific item or piece of information, rather than browse aimlessly.[22] Within a few weeks we were able to implement an interface in PHP, tied to a back-end MySQL database, that was very quick to respond to users' requests thanks to the efficiency of that particular software configuration. A spare home page featured our logo, some introductory text, and a navigation bar along the left side of the screen that allowed visitors to go directly to what interested them (stories, images, e-mail, etc.). When the visitor clicked on a section or paged through listings of collected objects within sections, they were constantly given clear navigational indicators from the sidebar (which had a consistent and almost rigidly hierarchical appearance on all pages) to help them orient themselves within the site. Throughout the site we took pains to employ the elements of user-centered web design: consistent (if spare) design elements such as font color and size, background color, and logo appearance and placement; careful use of many small tables for layout (rather than larger tables with complex structures); an explicit (sometimes blatant) set of textual signposts; and search engines which allowed the impatient (or the simply curious) to bypass our carefully crafted navigational structure altogether.

In addition to clarity we added simplicity, which served both to assist our visitors and to reinforce the sense of place and permanence provided by the Archive. The domain name, 911digitalarchive.org, was preferable to a longer URL such as chnm.gmu.edu/911 because it was easy to remember and immediately conveyed to our potential contributors who they were dealing with. Instead of the long, complex query strings that often fill the address bar at database-driven sites, making it hard for visitors to bookmark the URL or even decipher it as a navigational clue, we used a configurable feature of our apache web server, "URL rewriting," to transform the appearance of queries into simple, logical directories. So, a visitor looking at the 847th e-mail contributed to the site would see the URL path /email/details/847 that clearly indicated where he or she was, and what he or she was looking at.[23] While this may seem a picayune detail, it is precisely the sort of usability feature that enables visitors to orient themselves. By clarifying the underlying function of the site, the URL provides a definitive and unambiguous declaration that has the added advantage of suggesting that others who contribute will be adding something that will have a lasting location and identity, rather than being absorbed into an arbitrary morass of code that might change from one site revision to the next.

The use of images posed a special dilemma for us, both during the design and once visitors began uploading their own photographs and artwork. Image files can be used to create precise design elements that will not vary from browser to browser. This offers a source of control dearly sought by designers, who often feel vexed by the impossible variety of browsers, operating systems, and hardware platforms on which their sites eventually may appear. Unfortunately, even the smallest and most unobtrusive of images can consume more bandwidth than a full page of simple text. Since visitors generally crave information, there is a corresponding need to minimize the ratio of images to text. However, effective design is nearly impossible without using some carefully selected images. For an event that was experienced by most as an awful vision of fire and destruction forever seared into the mind's eye, it was inadvisable to severely restrict the display of images—especially once contributors began uploading their own images to the Archive!

Our solution was to keep most images off the home page and out of other sections not directly concerned with visual materials. On those pages that did feature images, such as the extremely popular still images section which received more than 2,000 uploads by April of 2003, we allowed visitors to browse through miniatures, or "thumbnails," of contributions, so that when they viewed the full-size version it would be at their discretion and not something that was forced on them by our design. After using the thumbnail-generating software for a while, however, we discovered that under rare circumstances it generated images that would crash certain browsers in subtly maddening ways.[24] This was just one example of the extreme difficulty of controlling the behavior of our site on others' computers. Our visitors might browse the site with extremely high or low screen resolutions, fast or slow processors and graphics cards, millions of colors or just a handful, images enabled or turned off by default, to mention only a few of the variables. Rather than trying to control every last detail of visual display through extensive use of graphics and tables, we opted for a flexible, simple design that would look elegant for most visitors and "degrade gracefully" in sub-optimal conditions.

Before opening the site to visitors and contributors, we also had to prepare a set of basic procedures and protocols. These were needed to ensure the substantive and legal integrity of our collections, protect the privacy and wishes of our contributors without reducing our collections (or the historical record) to their own personal billboard, and allow us to exercise a general level of quality control without enslaving ourselves to our own standards. The lack of authentication on the Internet, and its fundamental statelessness, worked against these goals. How could we know that our contributors were who they claimed to be, and that what they contributed was genuine and belonged to them? A dark specter came to haunt our discussions, personified as an imaginary 13-year-old mischief maker residing in New Jersey and luxuriating in the late-night license afforded by his parents' cable modem hookup. The human subjects protocol required by CUNY's review board prohibited contributions from minors, while fear of violating our most dearly held axioms of professional ethics provided the other specifics of the phantasm.

To address these and related concerns, we adopted some common-sense practices that greatly reduced the chance of problem entries. Our software permitted us to record the unique IP address of our contributors, who were also required to provide a name, e-mail address, and age, before their contributions would be accepted. Immediately upon receiving an entry our software sent an e-mail message to the address provided, thus sending the contributor an official record of his or her entry, while informing us of invented or expired addresses when these messages bounced back to us. Then, before the entry was added to the official Archive collections and displayed publicly on the site, we vetted each entry. Among other things, we checked the contributor's age, tried to establish that the contributed item was not clearly something produced by someone else (e.g., a news agency), and quickly confirmed that it was relevant to September 11 and not wildly inappropriate in its use of language or imagery. After an entry was fully processed, it remained in the collections exactly as it had been entered and was displayed on the website according to the contributor's specifications. In a few cases we did make changes or corrections for individuals who later made the case that their entries should be suppressed or altered in some acceptable manner.

Although these procedures would prove time consuming (particularly when thousands of entries flooded in overnight on the one-year anniversary), they helped us to maintain some basic level of control over the content. The need to exercise this sort of control was especially important given the highly charged climate after 9/11 and the inescapably sensitive nature of the contributions that would come in. In some infrequent cases where we realized that a photo was too professionally composed, or too familiar, to have been produced by the contributor, we withheld it from the public site for legal reasons. We could not conduct a copyright check on each image uploaded (even if such a thing were possible), but rather had to use our judgment as to what was an original. Outside of these limited scenarios where contributions were legally or ethically impermissible, the vetting team made every effort to avoid suppressing an entry unless it was absolutely required, our own personal qualms about the contributor's sensibilities notwithstanding.

Despite the pains we took to craft an effective website and establish quality control procedures, the entire project would have been an exercise in entropy if we had failed to attract contributing visitors. This was no small consideration, as our previous experience with ECHO had shown. With the site in place (although lacking contributions) by January of 2002, we spent three months beta-testing our design and accumulating a critical minimal mass of entries by contacting friends, family, colleagues, and acquaintances. We hoped these contacts would snowball into further entries, although after a hundred or so entries the contacts had been exhausted.

Then, for the six-month anniversary in March, we worked with public relations professionals from CUNY, GMU, and the private sector to develop a basic media plan targeting regional media coverage in the New York and D.C. metro areas. This plan involved considerable planning to get coverage for a press release and to attract interviews with team members. Human interest stories ran in the *Wall Street Journal* (thanks to a little serendipity and our canvassing the financial district of Manhattan with specially made cards) and in the local county inserts for the metro section of the *Washington Post*. Other outlets picked up the story for the computer angle—including *Information Week,* a widely read journal for the information technology industry. A regional distribution network for news radio stations in Virginia also conducted a brief informational interview, thus reaching a broad and active segment of the public we might have missed if we had focused exclusively on Internet audiences.

Due to the high profile and wide circulation of the media outlets in which the Archive was featured, this coverage would have driven traffic to the site no matter what the content. But we needed contributions, not just traffic (although we hoped the former would flow from the latter eventually). Accordingly, we focused our interviews and the wording of our press release very carefully to appeal to the sensibilities of the communities that had been most directly affected by the disaster. Paying due attention to communities close at hand also helped, since both CUNY and GMU had student populations and surrounding neighborhoods with the potential to yield thousands of contributors, located as they were near the two largest crash sites. In the weeks following the six-month commemoration our traffic jumped significantly, and with it the contributions rose by a few hundred. Later in the summer of 2002, when our efforts had resulted in a broader range of partnerships with allied institutions, our exposure in the media yielded a dramatic rise in the number and quality of our contributions. Features that ran on CNN (both the broadcast and the website), in the Associated Press newswire, and on New York City local television, were followed by surges of contributions that immediately ran into the low thousands by the eve of the first anniversary of the attacks.

At the same time that we pursued media coverage, we targeted specific groups and communities in the three crash sites whose contributions we felt were important but potentially hard to attract without special efforts. Chinatown, in New York City, had suffered an enormous blow due to its proximity to the World Trade Center. An outreach team at CUNY worked closely with community leaders there to ensure that Chinese-speakers and others would learn of the site, while also conducting interviews to increase the Archive's relevance for residents of that neighborhood. For similar reasons, we also provided a Spanish-language version of the site to reach the large Latino communities in Washington, D.C. and New York City. Some of our other outreach efforts focused on Arab high school students in the suburbs of Washington; undocumented immigrant workers and unionized American workers whose jobs were located near the crash sites in Washington and New York; residents of the community near the crash site in Somerset County, Pennsylvania; and volunteer medical workers. These outreach efforts were not guaranteed to pro-

duce more contributions directly to our site, but their cumulative effect
was to establish a presence in important communities that were likely to
fall beneath the radar of media coverage and thus remain absent from
the historical record (as has so often been the case with poor, marginal-
ized, or transient communities).

While national media coverage and local community outreach were
critical in prodding contributors to help build the Archive, they were not,
by themselves, sufficient to sustain a momentum of ongoing contribution
after the publicity had faded and the funding for community involvement dried up. The critical factor in getting contributions to sustain
themselves over time was our good fortune in establishing strategic partnerships with institutions whom our potential contributors both trusted
and visited or interacted with in some fashion. Early in the project we had
been animated by the vision of a vast, popular base of "participant historians" who would write their own history. We did eventually attract visitors whose self-documentation approximated this description, but only
by identifying and working with what might best be called "participant-
centered historical institutions." Our efforts to make the Archive visible
and accessible benefited in myriad intangible ways from small exhibits or
other modest collaborations with the Museum of the City of New York
(MCNY), the Columbia Oral History Project, the amateur historians' collective DocumentNY, the Middle East and Middle East American Center
(MEMEAC), the public libraries of Somerset County, Pennsylvania, the
Women in Military Service for America Memorial in Arlington, Virginia,
and select public school systems in the affected communities. These efforts also served to connect the Archive with local communities of interest in concrete and persuasive ways. Slowly these efforts helped to transform what to most people was no more than a name and a URL into an
enterprise whose value they could understand, relate to, and eventually
engage in a highly personal fashion.

If there was one catalyst that could be isolated as the key to transforming the Archive into a large-scale participatory exercise in popular history-
making that now continues to grow of its own momentum, it would have
to be our partnership with the National Museum of American History
and the carefully focused publicity surrounding it. The NMAH's exhibit
on 9/11, "September 11: Bearing Witness to History," opened to wide ac-
claim on the first anniversary of the tragedy—although even before it
opened there was a recognition that this would be a major and highly successful installation.[25] In the spring and summer before the opening we
worked closely with the NMAH to build a website that would allow visitors to the museum, and others arriving only by the Internet, to record
their responses to the exhibit, register their reflections on their lives dur-

ing the year since the attacks, and share their memories of the fateful day, all by adding entries to a specially designed portal to the Archive.[26]

Two important features of the exhibit were designed to encourage visitors to the museum to literally bear witness. In the last room, visitors were invited to reflect on the installation, and on 9/11 generally, by recording their thoughts either in writing, with pencils on index cards, or orally, by telling their story in telephone booths where a voicemail system could record their accounts. The voicemail system, which could also be accessed from outside the museum by dialing a toll-free number, was a particularly promising innovation, since many people who would shy away from recording their experiences on paper or on the web might find the conversational format of a voicemail message less intimidating and more appropriate to the intimate quality of their personal recollections. Voicemail messages held the added advantage that they could be converted on the fly into sound files and sent, as e-mail attachments, to the Archive. Others might prefer the reflective mode encouraged by putting pencil to paper, so we arranged to have the cards scanned in bulk and later imported into the Archive's database.

The direct connection at the exhibit, reinforced by the accessibility of the website and toll-free telephone numbers, proved to be a powerful combination. On September 11, 2002, more than 3,500 new stories came to the Archive through the "Bearing Witness" portal alone. In the first week of the exhibit, the number of first-person narratives in the non-NMAH portion of the Archive also increased dramatically, jumping from around 2,100 to just under 8,000. Stories were not the only things visitors added to the Archive. Visitors uploaded hundreds of images and e-mail messages from their digital cameras and inboxes in the same week. And the contributions continued long after the anniversary. In the four months following the exhibit's opening, both the "Bearing Witness" and the regular Archive story banks received almost 2,000 additional entries apiece, while more than 1,000 voicemail messages and over 4,000 index cards arrived for inclusion in the Archive. (It should be added that old media has played a valuable role, too; thousands of photographs, e-mail messages, and other electronic files have arrived on CD-ROM in the mail, providing the vast bulk of our collections, which now number over 140,000 objects.) Visitors to the September 11 Digital Archive continue to make contributions to this day, long after the most active outreach attempts have concluded.

We are now in the process of securing long-term preservation and archival custody for our collections. In September of 2003 the Library of Congress accessioned the Archive as one of its first major digital acquisitions. In preparation for that day, we worked to inventory and catalog our collections using open standards such as XML to ensure that future researchers will be able to access what our contributors have preserved. In this respect, our web design choices have provided yet another benefit. All objects are assigned a permanent object identifier (reflected in the URL), which allows for stable and precise references, regardless of how those objects will be made available in the future. For similar reasons, the software we have used to store and present these objects is all "open-source," which means that future programmers should stand a decent chance of reproducing our server environment long after specifications for operating system, file structure, and other crucial functionality have evolved into unrecognizable formats. (Open source software is also free or very inexpensive, which allowed us to devote more resources to recruiting contributors. Hopefully it will also allow future archivists to work with our materials without encountering the costly encumbrances of intellectual property law.)[27] Saving these materials for the future thus presents yet another argument for keeping everything as direct and simple as possible—whether we're thinking about middleware code, HTML and web design, electronic file formats for storing contributions (e.g., jpg, pdf, doc), navigational hierarchy, or even the internal documentation and formatting procedures we hide within the code that runs the site.

While long-term archiving and preservation of digital media are tasks that still pose considerable challenges to digital librarians, we are committed to ensuring that the Archive will endure. After all, we have an ethical obligation to our contributors that lies at the core of our guiding vision of the Archive; namely, that their good-faith efforts to help make a truly public history of 9/11 will live on in a permanent and accessible digital historical record.

CONCLUSION

The September 11 Digital Archive has been strikingly dependent on the needs of its visitors and on its ability to foster a sense of community online. In this regard, it resembles efforts by museums in recent decades to reach out more effectively to the audiences and communities they serve. As Andrea Hauenschild has written of the "new museology" that has begun to shape local and community-centered museums around the world, "what produces acceptance of the museum is its usefulness as recognized by the population in question." Indeed, this requirement is even more fundamental on the web, where community is especially tenuous. And unlike the "new" community-centered museums such as the Museum of Chinese in the Americas centered on New York City's Chinatown, our sites, like the Internet in general, have not generally been able to reach hard-to-reach and underserved communities.[28]

The key problematic for online historians is the lack of a sense of place, identity, and authenticity on the web—something all web authors try very consciously to overcome through "branding" to foster a sense of community through shared design. Where are you, exactly, when you are visiting a website? This question, which all but the most naïve web users must ask themselves at one time or another, undercuts the authenticity, authority, and sense of permanence that even the most expertly crafted website must take great pains to establish. Another challenge to authenticity is a byproduct of one of the Internet's great strengths. The web allows us to "explode the narrative," taking advantage of its "convergence of distribution" to enable a "polyvocal" history that captures all voices and perspectives without privileging any one over the other.[29] This gives rise to what might be called the "amateur perplex," in which the enthusiasm and untrained bias of amateurs can foster historical knowledge and a zeal for primary materials, at the same time that it gives free rein to prejudices, distortions, falsehoods, and inaccuracies (if not worse). As the multitude of Civil War sites built by enthusiasts and reenactors attests, the populist energy unleashed by the web can cut both ways.[30]

To be credible, sites must either be tied to trusted real-world institutions or go through the long and demanding process of establishing themselves as trustworthy. Here is an opportunity for museums and other institutions of public history to adopt a special role in the emergence of online history. In *The Presence of the Past*, Rosenzweig and Thelen found that museums were considered by most people to be the most trustworthy of institutional sources for historical information (according to their respondents), holding a special trust due to the immediacy of the past represented by the artifacts they hold.[31] Museums must work to make the most of this advantage, using it as leverage to transmit their high standards of historical practice to online practitioners, whether experts or amateurs. A window of opportunity for exercising this influence remains open to public historians so long as the website continues to evolve and gain definition as a genre of historical writing, presentation, and preservation. It is not clear how long the opportunity will remain open, however, given the extremely short time it takes for technologies and trends to "lock in" on the web.

NOTES

1. The author would like to thank Roy Rosenzweig, Dan Cohen, and Tom Scheinfeldt for their perceptive comments on this essay and for their generosity of spirit and intellect while working on the September 11 Digital Archive, ECHO, and other projects at CHNM. Thanks are also due to Jesse

Ausubel of the Alfred P. Sloan Foundation, who funded both ECHO and
the Archive, and whose vision of online historical research has sustained an
innovative methodology in its fledgling years.

2. Roy Rosenzweig, "The Road to Xanadu: Public and Private Pathways on the
History Web," *Journal of American History* 88 (September 2001): 548–79.

3. Nicholson Baker, *Double Fold: Libraries and the Assault on Paper* (New York: Random House, 2001); and Sven Birkerts, *The Gutenberg Elegies: The Fate of Reading in an Electronic Culture* (Winchester: Faber and Faber, 1994).

4. Mike Wallace, *Mickey Mouse History and Other Essays on American Memory* (Philadelphia: Temple University Press, 1996), ch. 4, esp. 77–79.

5. Randy Bass, "Garden in the Machine: The Impact of American Studies on New Technologies," working paper, www.georgetown.edu/faculty/bassr/garden.html

6. O'Malley and Rosenzweig, "Brave New World or Blind Alley? American History on the World Wide Web," *Journal of American History* 84 (June 1997): 132–55. For an example of how puzzles can be used to increase historical understanding, see History Matters' valuable resource, "Puzzled By the Past," historymatters.gmu.edu/browse/puzzled

7. Roy Rosenzweig, "So, What's Next for Clio: CD-ROM and Historians," *Journal of American History* 81 (March 1995): 1621–40. As Rosenzweig observes, even the personal shallowness of a figure such as Richard Nixon can be reproduced in all its historical specificity, with audio recordings and scanned memoranda providing rich windows into his psyche.

8. Roy Rosenzweig and David Thelen, *The Presence of the Past: Popular Uses of History in American Life* (New York: Columbia University Press, 1998), chs. 1, 4, and *passim*.

9. Bass, "Garden in the Machine."

10. O'Malley and Rosenzweig, "Brave New World or Blind Alley?", 147–48.

11. Brainerd, Kansas: Time, Place and Memory on the Prairie Plains www.rootinaround.com/brainerd, and Rowville-Lysterfield History Project www.rlcnews.org.au

12. www.pbs.org/pov/stories/vietnam/story.html

13. Seniornet's World War II Living Memorial www.seniornet.org/ww2, and HistoryChannel.com's Veteran's Forum www.veteransforum.historychannel.com. As of April 2001, the Veteran's Forum contained nearly 20,000 postings, while SeniorNet's World War II Memories Discussions section held over 6,000 entries. Veterans appear to be especially active online practitioners: e.g., see also the Atomic Veterans History Project www.aracnet.com/~pdxavets and the Drop Zone Virtual Museum Oral History Project www.thedropzone.org/misc/mission.html

14. Collected Visions Gallery www.cvisions.cat.nyu.edu/gallery/index.html

15. Remembering Nagasaki: Atomic Memories www.exploratorium.edu/nagasaki/memories/amemory.html

16. blackout.gmu.edu

17. The Blackout project was part of the first wave of Sloan projects, known as STIM: Science and Technology in the Making sloan.stanford.edu. For a list

of the other Sloan projects, consult the links in the right-hand sidebar of the ECHO Virtual Center echo.gmu.edu/center

18. echo.gmu.edu. Online collecting projects can be found in the Memory Bank echo.gmu.edu/memory. For a précis of best practices, consult the Practical Guide echo.gmu.edu/guide. The guide will be expanded and accompanied by a forthcoming book authored by Roy Rosensweig, the director of CHNM, and Dan Cohen and Tom Scheinfeldt, the other co-directors of ECHO. For an effort that coincided with and shared many of the broad objectives of ECHO, see the History of Recent Science and Technology hrst.mit.edu.

19. James B. Gardner and Sarah M. Henry, "September 11 and the Mourning After: Reflections on Collecting and Interpreting the History of Tragedy," *The Public Historian* 24 (Summer 2002): 37–52.

20. Folklorist Alan Lomax, "assistant in charge" of the Archive of American Folksong in the Library of Congress when Pearl Harbor occurred, instructed ten fieldworkers (by telegram) to interview Americans on their reactions to the event the day after it happened. The tape recordings of those interviews are available in the Library of Congress, as described at memory.loc.gov/ammem/afcphhtml. Pollster Rensis Likert also conducted an opinion survey on the night of 12/7/1943. See Jean Converse, *Survey Research in the United States: Roots and Emergence, 1890–1960* (Berkeley: University of California Press, 1987), 160.

21. Collaborations include History Matters historymatters.gmu.edu, a resource for U.S. history teachers and students, and *Who Built America? From the Centennial Celebration of 1876 to the Great War of 1914*, and *Who Built America? From the Great War of 1914 to the Dawn of the Atomic Age in 1946*, 2 vols. CD-ROM (New York: Worth, 2000).

22. See, e.g., GVU 10th Survey, Group G29, "Problems Using the Web," at www.gvu.gatech.edu/user_surveys/survey-1998-10/graphs/use/q11.htm. Although bandwidth has improved for many web users since the survey was taken in 1998, speed is still a major consideration even for those enjoying fast connections, while clear, direct navigation has become even more prized as the web grows larger and the need to cut through the thicket of information increases apace.

23. I.e., the full URL would be 911digitalarchive.org/email/details/847

24. E.g., the browser would refuse to load images, "hanging" for no apparent reason but still allowing the display of new text.

25. For more information on this exhibit, go to the NMAH website www.americanhistory. si.edu/september11

26. 911digitalarchive.org/smithsonian; linked from americanhistory.si.edu/september11/tellyourstory/index.asp

27. On the challenge that changes in file formats and software pose to future historians, see Roy Rosenzweig, "Can We Save the Present for the Future?", *American Historical Review* 108 (June 2003): 735–62, esp. 741–42, 744–48. For a more general treatment of the pressing need to preserve ideas and other aspects of cultural heritage in open, nonproprietary formats, see Lawrence

Lessig, *The Future of Ideas: The Fate of the Commons in a Connected World* (New York: Random House, 2001).

28. www.moca-nyc.org; Andrea Hauenschild, "Claims and Reality of the New Museology: Case Studies in Canada, the United States and Mexico" (Ph.D. dissertation in Ethnology, Hamburg University, 1988), section 4.1, para. 4–6, available online at museumstudies.si.edu/claims2000.htm

29. Bass, "Garden in the Machine."

30. Rosenzweig, "Road to Xanadu," para. 17, 23, 27.

31. Rosenzweig and Thelen, *The Presence of the Past,* 20–21 (Table 1.3), 105–8, 235 (Table 2), 244–47 (Tables 9–12).

RESOURCES

The following list includes some of the major organizations available to those interested in further exploring various aspects of public history. It is not intended to be a definitive list, and interested individuals should contact the organizations for further information on their programs and publications. Note: Internet addresses frequently change.

Advisory Council on Historic Preservation, Office of Education and Preservation Assistance
Old Post Office
1100 Pennsylvania Avenue NW
Suite 809
Washington, DC 20004
Phone: 202/606-8503
Fax: 202/606-8672
Web site: www.achp.gov
An independent federal agency that serves as the major advisor to the government in the field of historic preservation; provides technical assistance, instructional materials, and training courses regarding Section 106 review, including "Introduction to Federal Projects and Historic Preservation Law."

African American Museums Association
P.O. Box 578
1350 Brush Row Road
Wilberforce, OH 45384
Phone: 937/376-4944
Fax: 937/376-2007
Web site: www.blackmuseums.org
Interdisciplinary organization serving the needs of black museums and cultural institutions and black museum professionals; publishes *Scrip,* a quarterly newsletter which includes employment information, and *AAMA Update,* a quarterly bulletin on museum issues; also publishes *Blacks in Museums,* the AAMA membership directory; sponsors an annual meeting and regional workshops and other functions.

American Association for State and Local History
1717 Church Street
Nashville, TN 37203
Phone: 615/320-3203
Fax: 615/327-9013
E-mail: history@aaslh.org
Web site: www.aaslh.org
Membership organization focusing on the history of North America and including individuals and institutions, from local to national in scope; publishes *History News,* a quarterly magazine, and *Dispatch,* a monthly newsletter which includes employment information; also publishes technical leaflets and technical reports; sponsors an annual meeting and workshops and other professional development opportunities; sponsors a nationwide awards program for excellence in the field of state and local history; makes available audiovisual materials on specialized topics. AASLH's *Directory of Historical Organizations in the United States and Canada* (fifteenth edition, 2001) remains an important reference work for the field of public history. Check your library for this

and other AASLH-sponsored publications, or contact AltaMira Press, 1630 North Main Street, Suite 367, Walnut Creek, CA 94596; 925/938-7243; fax: 925/933-9720; e-mail: explore@altamirapress.com.

American Association of Museums
1575 Eye Street, NW
Suite 400
Washington, DC 20005
Phone: 202/289-1818
Fax: 202/289-6578
Web site: www.aam-us.org
Organization representing the entire scope of museums and professional and nonpaid staff who work for and with museums; publishes *Museum News,* bimonthly magazine, and *Aviso,* monthly newsletter which includes news and employment information; also publishes more than 200 titles on museum subjects; sponsors annual conference, seminars, Standing Professional Committees and Professional Interest Committees, and an annual museum publication design competition; other programs and activities include a Technical Information Service, the AAM Accreditation Commission, the national accrediting body for U.S. museums, and the Museum Assessment Program, offered in cooperation with the Institute of Museum and Library Services. Contact AAM for addresses for the six regional AAM conferences: Mid-Atlantic, New England, Southeast, Midwest, Mountain-Plains, and Western. Also sponsors *The Official Museum Directory,* a comprehensive reference compiled annually and providing profiles and statistics on more than 7,500 museums in the United States, with geographical and special index listings. Check your library for this and other AAM publications or contact the AAM Bookstore, 202/289-9127.

American Historical Association
400 A Street SE
Washington, DC 20003
Phone: 202/544-2422
Fax: 202/544-8307
E-mail: aha@theaha.org
Web site: www.theaha.org
Oldest and largest professional organization for historians, encompassing all geographical, chronological, and topical specializations; publishes the *American Historical Review,* the profession's broadest scholarly journal (published five times a year), and *Perspectives,* a newsletter (published nine times a year) which includes employment information; also publishes occasional pamphlets on historical topics and professional issues; sponsors an annual meeting which includes a job placement service; also sponsors several research grant and fellowship competitions, an awards program, and various special projects and conferences. Students of public history will find particularly useful *Careers for Students of History,* published jointly by the AHA and the National Council on Public History. The AHA's *Guide to History Departments and Organizations* is compiled annually and provides the best current reference on individual historians and the colleges, universities, and organizations in which they work. The AHA's *Directory of Affiliated Societies* provides contacts and other

information on nearly a hundred specialized history organizations, including the American Culture Association, the Conference of Historical Journals, the Historians Film Committee, the Popular Culture Association, the Public Works Historical Society, and the Society for Military History. Check your history department or your library for these and other AHA publications.

American Institute for Conservation of Historic and Artistic Works

1717 K Street NW
Suite 200
Washington, DC 20006
Phone: 202/452-9545
Fax: 202/452-9328
E-mail: info@aic-faic.org
Web site: www.aic-faic.org

National membership organization for conservation professionals; publishes the *Journal of the American Institute for Conservation* (three issues a year) and *AIC News*, a newsletter published six times a year; also publishes membership directory, pamphlets, and other materials on specialized conservation topics; sponsors an annual meeting and occasional courses and seminars; operates the Conservation Services Referral System under the auspices of the Foundation of the AIC.

American Institute of Architects

1735 New York Avenue NW
Washington, DC 20006
Phone: 202/626-7300
Fax: 202/626-7587
E-mail: infocentral@aia.org
Web site: www.aia.org

Professional society of architects, with over three hundred regional, state, and local groups; publishes *ARCHITECTURE* (monthly journal) and *AIArchitect* (monthly newspaper); sponsors Intern Development Program, registration-examination preparation courses, other professional development opportunities, information services, awards, speakers bureau, and placement services; maintains library and archives and sponsors the Octagon Museum.

American Library Association

50 East Huron Street
Chicago, IL 60611
Phone: 312/944-6780
Fax: 312/944-2641
E-mail: membership@ala.org
Web site: www.ala.org

Central organization for the library profession with eleven specialized divisions and seventy chapter and affiliate organizations; publishes monthly *American Libraries* journal and specialized newsletters for various aspects of library work; sponsors annual conference (including job placement service) and midwinter conference. Of special interest to historians are the History Section of the Reference User Services Association and various sections of the Association of College and Research Libraries, an ALA affiliate society.

American Studies Association

1120 19th Street NW
Suite 301
Washington, DC 20036
Phone: 202/467-4783
Fax: 202/467-4786
E-mail: asastaff@theasa.net
Web site: www.theasa.net

Interdisciplinary organization to

promote and encourage the study of American culture; publishes the *American Quarterly,* a quarterly journal, and the *ASA Newsletter* (quarterly); also publishes a membership directory; sponsors an annual convention; provides reduced rates for members for subscriptions to *American Studies International, Canadian Review of American Studies,* and *Prospects.*

Association for Documentary Editing
c/o Anne Cecere
ADE Secretary
The Adams Papers Editorial Project
Massachusetts Historical Society
1154 Boylston Street
Boston, MA 02215
E-mail: acecere@masshist.org
Web site: etext.lib.virginia.edu/ade
    Interdisciplinary organization promoting documentary editing through cooperation and the exchange of ideas among the community of editors; publishes journal/newsletter entitled *Documentary Editing;* sponsors annual conference; maintains placement service.

Association for Information and Image Management International
1100 Wayne Avenue
Suite 1100
Silver Spring, MD 20910
Phone: 301/587-8202
Fax: 301/587-2711
E-mail: aiim@aiim.org
Web site: www.aiim.org
    An international organization bringing together the users and providers of information management technologies and solutions; sponsors annual exposition and conference and over eighty open

industry standards, technical reports, and industry coalitions.

Association for Living Historical Farms and Agricultural Museums
8774 Route 45 NW
North Bloomfield, OH 44450
Phone: 440/685-4410
Fax: 440/685-4410
Web site: www.alhfm.org
    International organization for those working with living historical farms, agricultural museums, and outdoor history and folklike museums; publishes *Bulletin* (quarterly journal including employment notices), *Proceedings* of annual meeting, *Replica Resource List;* sponsors annual meeting; information available on regional organizations, meetings, and newsletters in United States and Canada.

Association for Preservation Technology International
4513 Lincoln Avenue
Suite 213
Lisle, IL 60532
Phone: 630/968-6400
Fax: 888/723-4242
E-mail: information@apti.org
Web site: www.apti.org
    Publishes *The Bulletin: Journal of Preservation Technology* (4 issues per year), *Communiqué* (quarterly newsletter), and other publications on the history of material culture; sponsors annual conference.

Association for the Bibliography of History
c/o Richard Ring
ABH President
Anschutz Library
University of Kansas Libraries

1301 Hoch Auditoria Drive
Lawrence, KS 66045
Phone: 785/864-3425
Fax: 785/864-5705
E-mail: richring@ukans.edu
Web site: www.theaha.org/affiliates/
assn_bibliography_his.htm
Organization to promote and facilitate the bibliography of history and collaboration at the intersection of history, bibliography, and library and information science; publishes biannual *Bulletin* and sponsors annual meeting.

Association of American Cultures
2554 W. 16th Street
419
Yuma, AZ 85364
Phone: 928/783-1757
E-mail: taac@taac.com
Web site: www.taac.com
National arts service organization providing services for people of color in the United States; publishes a biannual newsletter; sponsors a national symposium on cultural diversity every two years and workshops and other programs.

Association of Record Managers and Administrators, Inc.
13725 W. 109th Street
Suite 101
Lenexa, KS 66215
Phone: 913/341-3808
Fax: 913/341-3742
E-mail: hq@arma.org
Web site: www.arma.org
International professional society for information management professionals; publishes *Records Management Quarterly* (journal), a newsletter, and technical publications; sponsors national confer-

ence and chapter meetings and seminars on various aspects of records management; operates a job placement service. The certifying body for ARMA is the Institute of Certified Records Managers.

Costume Society of America
P.O. Box 73
Earleville, MD 21919
Phone: 800/272-9447
Fax: 410/275-8936
E-mail: nationaloffice@costumesocictyamerica.com
Web site: www.costumesocietyamerica.com
Organization focusing on costume and including both specialists and generalists; publishes annual *Dress, The Journal of the Costume Society of America* and *CSA News*, a quarterly newsletter including employment information; also publishes an annual membership directory; sponsors annual national symposium and regional symposia, international study tours, and awards and scholarships.

Federation of State Humanities Councils
1600 Wilson Boulevard
Suite 902
Arlington, VA 22209
Phone: 703/908-9700
Fax: 703/908-9706
E-mail: info@statehumanities.com
Web site: www.statehumanities.com
National organization of the state humanities councils; publishes a newsletter and other publications; sponsors an annual meeting and humanities computer network. Contact for information on how to reach the humanities council in your state.

Heritage Preservation–National Institute for Conservation
1625 K Street NW
Suite 700
Washington, DC 20006
Phone: 202/625-1495
Fax: 202/625-1485
Web site: www.heritagepreservation.org
  Serves as a national forum for conservation in the United States and clearinghouse for information; voting membership is by institution; has published series of titles on conservation issues.

H-Net: Humanities and Social Science On-Line
Department of History
310 Auditorium Building
Michigan State University
East Lansing, MI 48824
Phone: 517/355-9300
Fax: 517/355-8363
E-mail: hbooks@mail.h-net.msu.edu
Web site: www.h-net.msu.edu
  Interdisciplinary organization maintaining an extensive network of more than eighty e-mail lists (see the H-Net Discussion Network Directory); resources include H-Net Reviews, H-Net Announcements Database, H-Net Job Guide, and H-Net Hypertext Links Database.

MAHRO: The Radical Historians' Organization
The Radical History Review
Tamiment Library
New York University
70 Washington Square South
New York, NY 10012
Phone: 212/998-2632
Fax: 212/995-4074
E-mail: rhr@igc.org
Web site: www.chnm.gmu.edu/rhr/
  A collective made up of graduate students, independent scholars, activists, and faculty; publishes journal *The Radical History Review* (three issues a year), including a section on public history.

Museum Education Roundtable
621 Pennsylvania Avenue SE
Washington, DC 20003
Phone: 202/547-8378
Fax: 202/547-8344
E-mail: info@mer-online.org
Web site: www.mer-online.org
  Organization for educators and museum professionals; publishes *The Journal of Museum Education* (three issues per year) and *Network* newsletter (2 issues per year); also publishes *Museum Education Anthology, 1973–1983* and *Patterns in Practice: Selections from the Journal of Museum Education;* and sponsors workshops and other programs.

Museum Studies Reference Library
Smithsonian Institution
P.O. Box 37012
NHB27 MRC154
Washington, DC 20013-7012
Phone: 202/357-2139
Fax: 202/786-2443
E-mail: libmail@si.edu
Web site: www.sil.si.edu
  Branch library of the Smithsonian Institution focusing on museum studies, training, information, and professional service.

National Association for Interpretation
P.O. Box 2246
Fort Collins, CO 80522
Phone: 970/484-8283
Fax: 970/484-8179
E-mail: membership@interpnet.com

Web site: www.interpnet.com

Organization for those involved in discovering and communicating meanings and relationships among people and their natural, historical, and cultural world; publishes *Legacy* (six issues a year) and a membership directory with an Interpretive Consultants and Suppliers Registry; sponsors annual National Interpreters' Workshop and Interpretive Management Institute; sponsors awards and scholarships; operates NAI Job Line, Intern Hotline, and resource library; through regions, publishes newsletters and sponsors workshops, institutes, and other professional activities.

National Association of Government Archives and Records Administrators
c/o Capitol Hill Management Services
48 Howard Street
Albany, NY 12207
Phone: 518/463-8644
Fax: 518/463-8656
Web site: www.nagara.org

Coordinates work of state archivists and records administrators; primarily concerned with strengthening management of state government records, but also interested in improving local government records programs; publishes *Clearinghouse: News and Reports on Government Records* quarterly newsletter; published *State Archives and Records Management Terminology, Measurement, and Reporting Standards;* sponsors annual meeting.

National Center for Preservation Technology and Training
NSU Box 5682
645 College Avenue

Natchitoches, LA 71457
Phone: 318/356-7444
Fax: 318/356-9119
E-mail: ncptt@ncptt.nps.gov
Web site: www.ncptt.nps.gov

Interdisciplinary effort by National Park Service to coordinate and promote research, distribute information, and provide training about preservation skills and technology; publishes *NCPTT Notes* and technical reports; sponsors workshops and other training opportunities in partnership with federal, state, and local agencies and organizations; administers the Preservation Technology and Training Grants program; operates Internet Resources for Heritage Conservation, Historic Preservation, and Archaeology (www.cr.nps. gov/ncptt/irg/).

National Coalition for History
400 A Street SE
Washington, DC 20003
Phone: 202/544-2422
Fax: 202/544-8307
E-mail: rbcraig@historycoalition.org
Web site: www.historycoalition.org

Serves as the lobbying office for the historical and archival professions on federal issues and activities and as a clearinghouse for those interested in promoting all aspects of history. Particularly valuable are the NCC updates published in the newsletters of various sponsoring organizations and available through h-ncc@h-net.msu.edu.

National Conference of State Historic Preservation Officers
Hall of the States
Suite 342
444 North Capitol Street NW
Washington, DC 20001

Phone: 202/624-5465
Fax: 202/624-5419
E-mail: azncshpo@sso.org
Web site: www.sso.org/ncshpo
  Professional association for state
  government officials responsible
  for carrying out the national historic preservation program; can
  provide list of SHPOs to contact for
  state level programs and publications.

**National Council for Preservation Ed-
ucation**
c/o Graduate Program in Historic
  Planning
College of Architecture, Art and Planning
Cornell University
210 West Sibley Hall
Ithaca, NY 14853
Phone: 607/255-7261
Fax: 607/255-1971
E-mail: mat4@cornell.edu
Web site: preservenet.cornell. edu
  Association of preservation educators, including nearly sixty member institutions; publishes *NCPE
  News* (quarterly newsletter) and reports; sponsors an annual meeting
  and cosponsors conferences on
  special topics such as preservation
  law and historical significance;
  sponsors thesis research; offers undergraduate and graduate internships.

National Council on Public History
327 Cavanaugh Hall-IUPUI
425 University Boulevard
Indianapolis, IN 46202-5140
Phone: 317/274-2716
Fax: 317/278-5230
E-mail: ncph@iupui.edu
Web site: www.ncph.org
  Professional organization commit-

ted to broadening public appreciation for and understanding of the
past; publishes *The Public Historian,*
the only journal focusing on the
field (published quarterly) and
Public History News (quarterly, including employment information);
also publishes pamphlets and other
material on training and careers;
sponsors annual conference (including specialized workshops)
and awards. NCPH sponsors the e-
mail discussion group H-Public and
maintains on-line cv/resume bank,
job ads site, consultants directory,
and links to other public history related home pages.

**National Trust for Historic Preserva-
tion**
1785 Massachusetts Avenue NW
Washington, DC 20036
Phone: 202/588-6000
Fax: 202/588-6038
Web site: www.nthp.org
  National organization for the field
  of historic preservation; publishes
  Historic Preservation bimonthly magazine and monthly *Preservation
  News,* in addition to books on
  preservation; sponsors annual conference; sponsors National Main
  Street Center focusing on downtown revitalization; advises on all
  aspects of historic preservation;
  maintains historic properties
  around country. Contact the National Trust for information on
  regional offices in Chicago, Illinois; Boston, Massachusetts;
  Charleston, South Carolina; Denver, Colorado; Fort Worth, Texas;
  and San Francisco, California.

Oral History Association
Dickinson College

P.O. Box 1773
Carlisle, PA 17013
Phone: 717/245-1036
Fax: 717/245-1046
E-mail: oha@dickinson.edu
Web site: www.dickinson.edu/oha
Organization that brings together all persons interested in oral history as a way of collecting human memories; publishes semiannual *Oral History Review* and quarterly *OHA Newsletter* (three issues a year); also publishes annual report and membership directory, *Oral History Evaluation Guidelines,* and pamphlets on such topics as community history and the legal aspects of oral history; sponsors annual meeting with workshops.

Organization of American Historians
112 North Bryan Street
Bloomington, IN 47408
Phone: 812/855-7311
Fax: 812/855-0696
E-mail: oah@oah.org
Web site: www.oah.org
Organization for historians specializing in American or U.S. history; publishes the *Journal of American History,* a quarterly journal focusing on American history, and the *OAH Newsletter,* a quarterly publication which includes employment opportunities; also publishes *CONNECTIONS,* which focuses on international activity and exchanges; sponsors an annual meeting, specialized conferences and projects, awards and prizes, and speakers bureau.

Phi Alpha Theta
University of South Florida
4202 E. Fowler Avenue
SOC107
Tampa, FL 33620-8100

Phone: 800/394-8195
Fax: 813/974-8215
E-mail: phialpha@phialphatheta.org
Web site: www.phialphatheta.org
Honor society in history, with over 700 chapters, for undergraduate and graduate students; publishes *The Historian,* a quarterly journal, and *The Newsletter* (three issues a year); sponsors biennial conference and awards and prizes.

Preservation Action
1054 31st Street NW
Suite 526
Washington, DC 20007
Phone: 202/298-6180
Fax: 202/298-6182
E-mail: mail@preservationaction.org
Web site: www.preservationaction.org
Major lobbying group for historic preservation; publishes *Alert* (quarterly newsletter) and briefings; sponsors annual meeting and lobbying day.

Society for American Archaeology
900 Second Street NE
#12
Washington, DC 20002-3557
Phone: 202/789-8200
Fax: 202/789-0284
E-mail: headquarters@saa.org
Web site: www.saa.org
International organization dedicated to the archaeological heritage of the Americas; publishes *American Antiquity* (quarterly journal), *Archaeology and Public Education* (three issues a year), and *SAA Bulletin* (newsletter published five times a year and including job listings); also publishes *SAA Membership Directory;* sponsors annual meeting (including employment service center) and awards program.

Society for Historical Archaeology
19 Mantua Road
Mount Royal, NJ 08061
Phone: 856/224-0995
Fax: 856/423-3420
E-mail: hq@sha.org
Web site: www.sha.org
> Largest scholarly group concerned with the archaeology of the modern world; publishes *Historical Archaeology* (quarterly journal) and *Newsletter* (quarterly); sponsors annual Conference on Historical and Underwater Archaeology.

Society for History in the Federal Government
Box 14139, Ben Franklin Station
Washington, DC 20044
Web site: www.shfg.org
> Organization to promote study and broader understanding of history of and in the federal government; publishes an electronic bulletin, *Directory of Federal Historical Programs and Activities,* and special publications such as *Federal History Programs: A Guide for Heads of Government Agencies;* sponsors annual meeting and other conferences; serves as network to link historians in federal government around the country. Consult the *Directory of Federal Historical Programs and Activities* for information on history programs in various cabinet agencies such as Agriculture, Defense, Energy, Labor, and State, as well as information on programs in the National Archives, Smithsonian Institution, National Park Service, etc.

Society for Industrial Archaeology
Department of Social Sciences
Michigan Technological University
1400 Townsend Drive
Houghton, MI 49931-1295
Phone: 906/487-2070
Fax: 906/487-2468
E-mail: sia@mtu.edu
Web site: www.sia-web.org
> International organization that promotes the study and preservation of the physical survivals of technological and industrial development and change; publishes *IA, the Journal of the Society for Industrial Archaeology* (semiannual) and quarterly *Newsletter (SIAN);* also publishes a directory of members and other occasional publications; sponsors an annual conference and study tours.

Society for the History of Technology
Department of History of Science
The Johns Hopkins University
3505 N. Charles Street
Baltimore, MD 21218
Phone: 410/516-8349
Fax: 410/516-7502
Web site: www.shot.jhu.edu
> Interdisciplinary organization that encourages the study and teaching of the history of technology and its relations with society and culture; publishes *Technology and Culture* (quarterly journal, which includes frequent museum reviews) and a quarterly newsletter. Technology Museums Special Interest Group publishes *Artifactory* newsletter on museum exhibits related to the history of technology.

Society of American Archivists
527 S. Wells Street
5th Floor
Chicago, IL 60667-3922
Phone: 312/922-0140
Fax: 312/347-1452

E-mail: info@archivists.org

Web site: www.archivists.org

National professional organization for archivists, with sections, standing committees, and roundtables to address particular concerns or areas of interest; publishes the *American Archivist* (journal), *Archival Outlook* (bimonthly newsletter), and *SAA Employment Bulletin* (bimonthly); publishes *Archival Fundamental Series, SAA Membership Directory, Archival Education in the US and Canada,* and other publications; sponsors annual conference and workshops; has placement service.

Society of Architectural Historians

1365 N. Astor Street

Chicago, IL 60610-2144

Phone: 312/573-1365

Fax: 312/573-1141

E-mail: info@sah.org

Web site: www.sah.org

National organization dedicated to the study of the history of the built environment and the preservation of our architectural heritage; publishes quarterly *Journal of the Society of Architectural Historians* and bimonthly *Newsletter;* also publishes reference works and directory of schools offering architectural history programs; sponsors annual conference, tours, awards and fellowships, and SAH-L listserve.

Victorian Society in America

219 South Camac Street

Philadelphia, PA 19107

Phone: 215/545-8340

Fax: 215/545-8379

E-mail: info@victoriansociety.org

Web site: www.victoriansociety.org

Organization dedicated to fostering appreciation and understanding of nineteenth-century America and encouraging the protection and preservation of all things Victorian; publishes *Nineteenth Century* and *The Victorian,* both quarterly; sponsors an annual meeting and annual summer school programs in Newport, Rhode Island and London, England.

INDEX